RECEIVED
21 MAY 2012

Public International Law

For my mother, Carol Ann Boas

Public International Law

Contemporary Principles and Perspectives

Gideon Boas

Associate Professor, Faculty of Law, Monash University, Australia

Edward Elgar

Cheltenham, UK • Northampton, MA, USA

Published by
Edward Elgar Publishing Limited
The Lypiatts
15 Lansdown Road
Cheltenham
Glos GL50 2JA
UK

Edward Elgar Publishing, Inc.
William Pratt House
9 Dewey Court
Northampton
Massachusetts 01060
USA

A catalogue record for this book
is available from the British Library

Library of Congress Control Number: 2011936417

ISBN 978 0 85793 955 5 (cased)

Typeset by Servis Filmsetting Ltd, Stockport, Cheshire
Printed and bound by MPG Books Group, UK

Contents

Preface

Dame Rosalyn Higgins wrote of her invitation to teach the General Course in International Law at the Hague Academy in 1991: 'Can there really be anything new or interesting still to say, or is not all wisdom and scholarship already gathered in the Collected General Courses?'[1] Given her achievements and status as a scholar of international law even then, one might consider it folly to ever endeavour to write comprehensively on the topic of public international law. Of course, Higgins did deliver the Course and publish her highly regarded *Problems and Process* thereafter, and went on not only to publish important works but to preside over the World Court and deliver important opinions and decisions.

The point of course is that, like international law itself, scholarship must continue to be written. As the law progresses or recedes, as challenges to conceptions and practices of international law arise, new ideas and perspectives emerge. These ideas and perspectives need to be developed and explained through a range of academic and practice experiences, as reliance on the same views over time threatens to stifle thought and debate in a profoundly dynamic area of law. This book then is a modest contribution to this ever-evolving scholarship.

The writing of a book is in some ways a profoundly solitary exercise. At the same time, a work of this nature would not be possible without the wisdom and the assistance of others. Pascale Chifflet, whose grasp of structure, clarity of thought and great intellect is perhaps matched only by her modesty, I would like to thank for her meticulous review and advice. Thanks also to Gerry Simpson for reviewing some of this work and bringing to bear on it his perspicacity. I am grateful to Andrew Roe and Sylvester Urban, who provided highly valuable research assistance, as I am to a small hoard of researchers who aided this project in various ways: Irene Argeres, Sayomi Ariyawansa, William Bartley, Julia Kahan, Tyrone Liu, Patricia Saw, Jeremy Shelley, Marika Sosnowski and

[1] Rosalyn Higgins, Problems and Process: International Law and How We Use It (1994), 1.

Christopher Spain. Thanks finally to Tim Williams at Edward Elgar for supporting this project.

Gideon Boas
30 June 2011
Melbourne

Abbreviations

ANZUS	Australia, New Zealand and the United States
CEDAW	Committee on the Elimination of Discrimination against Women
CMILS	Critical Marxist International Law Scholarship
DSB	Dispute Settlement Body
DSU	Dispute Settlement Understanding
ECOSOC	Economic and Social Council
EEZ	Exclusive Economic Zone
EU	European Union
FRY	Federal Republic of Yugoslavia
G8	Group of Eight
GATT	General Agreement on Tariffs and Trade
ICBL	International Campaign to Ban Landmines
ICC	International Criminal Court
ICCPR	International Covenant on Civil and Political Rights
ICERD	International Convention on the Elimination of All Forms of Racial Discrimination
ICISS	Internal Commission on Intervention and State Sovereignty
ICJ	International Court of Justice
ICRC	International Committee of the Red Cross
ICSID	International Centre for Settlement of International Disputes
ICTR	International Criminal Tribunal for Rwanda
ICTY	International Criminal Tribunal for the former Yugoslavia
ILC	International Law Commission
ILO	International Labour Organization
IRA	Irish Republican Army
ITLOS	International Tribunal for the Law of the Sea
LTTE	Liberation Tigers of Tamil Eelam
NATO	North American Treaty Alliance
NGO	Non-governmental organizations
NIOC	National Iranian Oil Company
NNPT	Nuclear Non-Proliferation Treaty
ONUC	United Nations Operation in the Congo
PCA	Permanent Court of Arbitration

PCIJ	Permanent Court of International Justice
PLO	Palestinian Liberation Organization
R2P	Responsibility to Protect doctrine
SC	Security Council
SCSL	Special Court for Sierra Leone
SFRY	Socialist Federal Republic of Yugoslavia
UDHR	Universal Declaration of Human Rights
UN	United Nations
UNCHR	United Nations Commission on Human Rights
UNCLOS	United Nations Convention on the Law of the Sea
UNCRC	United Nations Convention on the Rights of the Child
UNFCCC	United Nations Framework Convention on Climate Change
UNGA	United Nations General Assembly
UNHRC	United Nations Human Rights Council
UNMIK	United Nations Interim Administration Mission in Kosovo
UNTAET	United Nations Transitional Administration in East Timor
UPU	Universal Postal Union
USSR	Union of Soviet Socialist Republics
WHO	World Health Organization
WTO	World Trade Organization

Selected cases

1. International law: history, theory and purpose

1.1 THE APPROACH TO INTERNATIONAL LAW IN THIS BOOK

The focus of this book is upon principles and perspectives in international law. International law is made up of a framework of broadly accepted principles from which rules are developed and applied. The status and precise nature of these principles vary depending upon the views of the states, courts, scholars or practitioners examining them. This does not mean that they necessarily lack certainty or clarity; rather, it reflects the variegated nature of international law, lacking as it does a constitutional or parliamentary framework, and infused as it is with international politics.

This book explains the content and structure of public international law and how it works. It critically examines what the law is, how it has evolved and is applied, and contemporary and future trends. In doing so, it will at times look beyond the legal to consider the political and other extralegal considerations that are an essential aspect of international law. This book does not, however, endeavour to exhaustively describe the entire international legal system. Thus there are no discrete chapters on the Law of the Sea, International Trade Law, Environmental Law, Humanitarian Law, Human Rights or International Criminal Law (although these will each be introduced later in this chapter[1]). Rather, these areas of the practice of international law are examined in the context of the principle of international law under examination. For example, Chapter 5 considers individuals as subjects of international law and the rights and obligations that have accrued through the international human rights and criminal law regimes, in the context of non-state actors. Case studies and contemporary examples are infused in the discussion on a particular topic, and critical analysis and the prospective development of international law are given prominence. In this way, this book will provide

[1] See section 1.5 below.

a solid understanding of the fundamentals of international law, how they are practised and applied, and – where appropriate – what the future holds.

1.2 THE CONCEPT OF INTERNATIONAL LAW

For some, international law is an anarchic system of inter-state relations, used and misused by states and their representatives in a position to exert their power and influence, both over less powerful states and people. For others, it is a promise of peace, justice and a global society that can ameliorate poverty and persecution. Questions about the purpose and nature of international law (and what it is) are many and varied, as are conceptions about what it should be. Like all systems of law, and certainly all social and political systems, international law cannot serve all the interests of all of its stakeholders. It is imperfect to be sure, and acts to entrench and perpetuate certain power paradigms that adversely impact upon those who need it most. At the same time, it is a reflection of the capacity of humanity to work towards a common good, to ameliorate harm and protect the vulnerable.

The following sections of this chapter will examine some of the infrastructural aspects of international law. After considering the place of international law in history, certain different theories will be considered, reflecting the diverse conceptions and perspectives of the system and how it operates. Finally, the question of what is international law will be considered. That international law serves a myriad of functions, forming and regulating an extraordinary range of behaviour outside and between the domestic domain of states, has not silenced questions about whether there even exists a system of international law as such – and if so, what can and should it achieve, and how? These concerns may be more than mere theoretical abstractions and need to be addressed before a consideration of the fundamental aspects of international law can be pursued.

1.3 THE PLACE OF INTERNATIONAL LAW IN HISTORY

In the first lecture delivered to the Academy of International Law at The Hague, Baron Korff asserted that, since ancient times, international relations developed among and between relatively equally civilized peoples, 'and thus always bore the unquestionable mark of cultural and legal equality'.[2] The extent to which this idea reflects reality or has always been a naive or convenient fiction remains the subject of scholarly debate. Writing in 1924, Korff points to nineteenth-century legal scholarship as wrongly conceiving of international law as a product of modern thinking, developed since the Peace of Westphalia in 1648.[3] One thing that legal scholars disagree little on now is that international law is far from a modern construct.[4]

In fact, many modern rules of international law can be traced back through millennia to different civilizations, including the areas of diplomatic immunity, the resort to and conduct of war and even what are now more or less universally accepted human rights principles. Despite the complaint, no doubt merited, that '[n]o area of international law has been so little explored by scholars as the history of the subject',[5] there is enough understood of the lives of ancient and more modern civilizations to glean the nature of their external relations, and the ways in which they regulated these relations with a system of rules. Reason was considered fundamental by Roman philosopher Cicero: 'a veritable law, true reason . . . in conformity with nature, universal, immutable and eternal, the commands of which constitute a call to duty and the prohibitions of which avert evil.'[6] In the seventeenth century, the philosopher and jurist Pufendorf stated that the common rule of actions, or the law of nature, required humans to 'cultivate and maintain towards others a peaceable sociality that is

---

[2] Baron S.A. Korff, 'An Introduction to the History of International Law' (1924) 18 *American Journal of International Law* 246, 259. See also Ernest Nys, 'The Development and Formation of International Law' (1912) 6 *American Journal of International Law* 1.

[3] Korff, above note 2, 247. See section 1.3.2, below.

[4] See, Malcolm Shaw, *International Law* (Cambridge; New York: Cambridge University Press, 2008, 6th edn), 14; D.J. Bederman, *International Law in Antiquity* (Cambridge: Cambridge University Press, 2001), 14. See also Arthur Nussbaum, *A Concise History of the Law of Nations* (New York: MacMillan, 1954, 2nd edn), 1–2, referring to an example of international law existing in a treaty between two Mesopotamian city states dating from 3100 BC.

[5] Stephen C. Neff, 'A Short History of International Law', in Malcolm D. Evans, *International Law* (Oxford: Oxford University Press, 2006, 2nd edn), 31. Georg Schwarzenberger also described the history of international law as 'the Cinderella of the doctrine of international law': Georg Schwarzenberger, 'The Frontiers of International Law' (1952) 6 *Yearbook of World Affairs* 251, cited in Alexandra Kemmerer, 'The Turning Aside: On International Law and its History', in R.M. Bratspies and R.A. Miller (eds), *Progress in International Law* (Leiden; Boston: Martinus Nijhoff Publishers, 2008), 72.

[6] Nys, above note 2, 1.

consistent with the native character and end of humankind in general.'[7] Modern rules of international law can be traced even to classical literature, such as Shakespeare's *Henry V*, in which a demand for war reparations is depicted.[8]

1.3.1 The Ancient Roots of International Law

One of the obvious areas in which international law has persistently emerged as a system of rules and structures is where trade and commerce with the outside world has been required. Greece stands as an example of an ancient civilization which constructed a system of law to regulate trade and travel. This system reflected civilizations that had come before it (for example, the Egyptian and Babylonian civilizations). It developed rules for the creation and enforcement of treaties and contracts, the development of permanent channels of diplomatic exchange, and the protection and granting of extraterritorial privileges to ambassadors.[9] Greece also developed a system to deal with the presence of foreigners on its territories, including such sophisticated processes as rules for the extradition of criminals[10] – an area of international law still giving rise to significant complexity as between international and municipal law.[11]

The Roman Empire is seen as one of the most significant civilizations in the development of international law as we understand it today. Rome developed ambassadorial missions with a system of rights and privileges, and developed procedures for concluding treaties and receiving foreign envoys. Ambassadorial immunities were systematized, as evidenced by Cicero: 'The inviolability of ambassadors is protected by divine and

---

[7] Michael Seidler, 'Pudendorf's Moral and Political Philosophy', *The Stanford Encyclopedia of Philosophy* (Summer 2011 edn), Edward N. Zalta (ed.), forthcoming, available at http://plato.stanford.edu/archives/sum2011/entries/pufendor-moral/

[8] Theodor Meron, *Bloody Constraint: War and Chivalry in Shakespeare* (Oxford; New York: Oxford University Press, 1998), 28

[9] Shaw, above note 4, 16; see also Nussbaum, above note 4, 5–9; Coleman Phillipson, *International Law and Custom of Ancient Greece and Rome, Volume 1* (London: Macmillan & Co. Ltd, 1911, 1st edn), 136–56.

[10] See Korff, above note 2, 250–51. See also Coleman Phillipson, above note 9, Volume 2, 257–63.

[11] Examples of such complexities were well emphasized in the *Pinochet* proceedings: see Andrea Bianci, 'Immunity versus Human Rights: The Pinochet Case', (1999) 10 *European Journal of International Law* 237; J. Craig Barker, Colin Warbrick and Dominic McGoldrick, 'The Future of Former Head of State Immunity after ex parte Pinochet' (1999) 48 *The International and Comparative Law Quarterly* 937.

human laws; their person is sacred and inviolable not only between allies, but also during their sojourn among enemies.'[12] The Romans developed a system of international relations, under which the state was bound by agreements and treaties much like private contracts, revealing a relatively sophisticated system of international law. This system was comprised of two parts: *jus gentium* and *jus inter gentes*. *Jus gentium*, or 'law of nations', originally formed part of Roman civil law applied to special circumstances concerning Rome's dealings with foreigners, distinct from the narrower system of law applicable only to Roman citizens (*jus civile*).[13] However, as the rules of *jus gentium* gradually supplanted the *jus civile* system, *jus gentium* subsequently came to encompass the natural or common law of Rome, considered to be of universal application among nations (what might today be termed customary international law). In contrast, *jus inter gentes,* meaning 'law between the peoples', refers to the body of treaty law, now recognizable in UN conventions and other international agreements that form a major part of public international law.

The distinction between *jus gentium* and *jus inter gentes* can be difficult to grasp given that writers often use 'international law' as a synonym for either term.[14] The original meaning of *jus gentium* is extremely broad, embodying the consensus on legal principles amongst the world's judges, jurists and lawmakers.[15] However, following the rise of the statist territorial order, and as international law continued to grow and develop, legal positivists such as Bentham posited that *jus gentium* was no more than 'the mutual transactions between sovereigns'.[16] In other words, *jus gentium* had been subsumed under international law and *jus inter gentes* interactions. However, this merger with *jus inter gentes* was never entirely complete.[17] Residual connotations of *jus gentium* allow it to capture issues beyond the scope of matters between sovereigns, especially significant to the emergence of human rights law.[18] When considered in the light of

---

[12] Cicero, quoted in Korff, above note 2, 254. See also Korff, above note 2, 253; Meredith B. Colket, Jr, 'The Inviolability of Diplomatic Archives' (1945) 8 *The American Archivist* 26.

[13] See Shaw, above note 4, 17.

[14] Francisco Forrest Martin et al., *International Human Rights and Humanitarian Law: Treaties, Cases and Analysis* (Cambridge; New York: Cambridge University Press, 2006), 1.

[15] Jeremy Waldron, 'Foreign Law and the Modern Ius Gentium' (2005–06) 119 *Harvard Law Review* 129, 132.

[16] Jeremy Bentham, *An Introduction to the Principles of Morals and Legislation* (Oxford: Clarendon Press, 1907), 327.

[17] Waldron, above note 15, 135.

[18] Ibid., 32.

the nature of modern international law, Rome clearly set out a complex system that serves, in many profound ways, as the root of modern public international law.[19]

Another crucial area in the development of the international law of nations throughout the ages has been the rules relating to recourse to and the conduct of war. Often cited as being developed by St Augustine in the Middle Ages, it was the Romans who developed the idea of the just war, thereby providing Rome with a legal justification for its many wars of aggression.[20] The concept of a just war occupied much of the literature on war and the law of nations during the Middle Ages and the Renaissance.[21] In *Henry VI*, the title character declares: 'God will, in justice, ward you as his soldiers.'[22] The concept of a 'just cause' was thus characterized as protective: its presence was considered to absolve one from sin and damnation for causing the loss of innocent life.

Much earlier, in Sumer – one of the early civilizations of the Ancient Near East in what is today south-eastern Iraq – evidence exists that war was regulated, which included the provision of immunity for enemy negotiators.[23] The Code of Hammurabi, dating from 1728 to 1686, BC, provided for the protection of the weak against oppression by the strong, the release of hostages on payment of ransom, and a catalogue of sanctions aimed at repairing the prejudices caused to both victims and society.[24] The Law of Hittites required respect for the inhabitants of an enemy city that had capitulated.[25] In the sixth century BC, Cyrus the Great of Persia prescribed the treatment of enemy soldiers as though they were his own. The Proclamation of Cyrus was divided into three parts: the first two parts explained why Cyrus conquered Babylon, while the third part was recited as a factual account of what he did upon seizing Babylon. This part reveals some extraordinary principles of present-day international humanitarian

---

[19] See Korff, above note 2, 253. See also Phillipson, above note 10, Chapter III. See generally on the Ancient Roman legal system, Nussbaum, above note 4, 10–16.

[20] See Korff, above note 2, 252; Nussbaum, above note 4, 10–11 ('in fact, the invention of the "just war" doctrine constitutes the foremost Roman contribution to the history of international law'); Phillipson, above note 10, Chapter XXII, see particularly 178–9.

[21] Meron, above note 8, 30.

[22] Ibid.

[23] See Christopher Greenwood, 'Historical Development and Legal Basis', in Dieter Fleck (ed.), *The Handbook of Humanitarian Law in Armed Conflicts* (Oxford: Oxford University Press, 1995), [107].

[24] Ibid.

[25] Ibid. The Hittites were an ancient people who established a kingdom centred at Hattusa in north-central Anatolia from the eighteenth century BC.

law and human rights law, including the freedom of thought, conscience and religion, and the protection of civilians and their property.[26]

In the middle ages, St Augustine espoused the popular (but not always or often respected) principle of protecting women, children and the elderly from hostilities.[27] The Code of Chivalry, which originally developed as a moral code of conduct in warfare among knights, had the more general effect of humane treatment for non-combatants in armed conflict.[28] Richard II of England, in the fourteenth century, issued rules for the conduct of war known as the 'Articles of War', which included a prohibition on the taking of booty, robbery and pillage, as well as the 'forcing' of women.[29] And in Japan, *Bushido*, the Japanese medieval code of honour, espoused the principle of humanity in war, which extended to prisoners of war.[30] However, there was general agreement that in war the innocent would always suffer with the guilty. Chivalric authors, therefore, discussed war as akin to a medicine which cures but also produces adverse effects – war was considered a means to establish peace. These chivalric themes are depicted in the literature of the time. In Shakespeare's *Henry VI*, a leader of the rebellion proclaims that his aim is '[n]ot to break peace, or any breach of it, [b]ut to establish here a peace indeed'.[31] Thus, there seem to be inherent limitations to the conduct considered appropriate in warfare.

These examples of a system of international law regulating the conduct of hostilities and the fundamental rights of human beings across ages and cultures is further evidence that a system of international law is an inevitable consequence of any civilization.[32] Where the need arises nations

---

[26] See Hirad Abtahi, 'Reflections on the Ambiguous Universality of Human Rights: Cyrus the Great's Proclamation as a Challenge to the Athenian Democracy's Perceived Monopoly on Human Rights', in Hirad Abtahi and Gideon Boas (eds), *The Dynamics of International Criminal Justice: Essays in Honour of Sir Richard May* (Leiden: Martinus Nijhoff Publishers, 2005), 14–21; Hilaire McCoubrey, *International Humanitarian Law: The Regulation of Armed Conflict* (Aldershot, UK: Dartmouth Publishing, 1990), 6–11.

[27] See Greenwood, above note 23, [109].

[28] See, generally, Gerald Draper, 'The Interaction of Christianity and Chivalry in the Historical Development of the Law of War', (1965) 46 *International Review of the Red Cross* 3. See also Greenwood, above note 23, [109].

[29] See Leslie C. Green, *Essays on the Modern Law of War* (Dobbs Ferry, NY: Transnational Publishers, 1985), 360.

[30] See Greenwood, above note 23, [109]. See also M. Cherif Bassiouni, 'Crimes against Humanity', in Bassiouni (ed.), *International Criminal Law* (The Hague and London: Kluwer Law International, 1999, 2nd edn), 196–7.

[31] Meron, above note 8, 19–20.

[32] Korff, above note 2, 248.

have developed sometimes sophisticated systems of rules that bear the hallmarks of the modern international law system.

1.3.2 The Peace of Westphalia and the Development of Modern International Law

The seventeenth century was an important period in the development of international law. In the early 1600s, the conception of international law was developed by the practitioner and scholar Hugo Grotius, in his famous work *On the Law of War and Peace*.[33] His key contribution to the development of international law was to distinguish the 'law of nations' from natural law, by creating a set of rules applicable solely to states. This was a crucial development because, as Neff notes, 'for the first time in history, there was a clear conception of a systematic body of law applicable specifically to the relationship between nations'.[34]

The modern structure and form of the international system can largely be traced back to the Peace of Westphalia in 1648, bringing about the end of the vicious Thirty Years War – a war that came to involve virtually the entirety of Europe in a struggle for political and military domination.[35] Gerry Simpson describes the Peace of Westphalia (really two treaties adopted at Münster and Osnabrück) as 'the transition from empire to sovereignty'.[36] A key development emerging from Westphalia was a substantial reduction in the role played by religion in the international system, through the decline of the 'presence of two poles of authority: the Pope at the head of the Catholic Church, and the Emperor at the head of the Holy Roman Empire'.[37] This decline opened the door for the begin-

---

[33] Neff, above note 5, 35.

[34] Ibid.

[35] Indeed, the Preamble to the Treaty of Westphalia provides a long and striking list of interlocutors: Treaty of Westphalia, Peace Treaty between the Holy Roman Emperor and the King of France and their respective Allies, reproduced at http://avalon.law.yale.edu/17th_century/westphal.asp (last accessed 20 June 2011). See also Nussbaum, above note 4, 115; S. Beaulac, 'The Westphalian Legal Orthodoxy – Myth or Reality?', 2 *Journal of the History of International Law*, 2000, 148; Leo Gross, 'The Peace of Westphalia', 42(1) *American Journal of International Law* 21; Shaw, above note 4, 26.

[36] Gerry Simpson, 'International Law in Diplomatic History', in James Crawford and Martti Koskenniemi (eds), *The Cambridge Companion to International Law* (Cambridge: Cambridge University Press, 2012). Although Simpson notes that states were later themselves to become (colonial) empires.

[37] Antonio Cassese, *International Law* (Oxford: Oxford University Press, 2005, 2nd edn), 23.

nings of the modern international law system, leading to the rise of the nation state as the key actor in international law and politics. As Cassese notes:

> In short, the Peace of Westphalia testified to the rapid decline of the Church (an institution which had already suffered many blows) and to the de facto disintegration of the Empire. By the same token it recorded the birth of an international system based on a plurality of independent States, recognizing no superior authority over them.[38]

This development of the concept of the nation state increasingly caused states to be seen as 'permanently existing, corporate entities in their own right, separate from the rulers who governed them at any given time'.[39] One of the key concepts to come out of the development of the nation state was that the law of nations only governed inter-state relations, and that rulers were free to 'govern as they please' within their state.[40] This can be seen as the beginnings of the concept of state sovereignty. This exciting development in international law, reflecting a significant evolution in the rights of states within the sphere of international law, has soured increasingly over the past two centuries. The idea of the complete equality of states (no matter how large or small) in international law became lost during the nineteenth century 'under the influence of the diametrically opposed idea of the hegemony of the great Powers'.[41] The same sentiment is reflected in the twentieth-century revolt against massive human rights violations committed by the leadership of states against their own citizens.[42]

Nonetheless, the principle of state sovereignty was and remains the fundamental principle upon which modern international law is based, reflected in the UN Charter,[43] representing the now

---

38 Ibid., 24; Gross, above note 35, 20.

39 Neff, above note 5, 35.

40 Ibid.

41 Ibid., 259.

42 Of the myriad of examples, see William A. Schabas, *Genocide in International Law* (Cambridge: Cambridge University Press, 2000), 1 (referring to the tacit acceptance of the commission of genocide by states under the veil of sovereign equality); see also Gideon Boas, James L. Bischoff and Natalie L. Reid, *Elements of Crimes Under International Law* (Cambridge: Cambridge University Press, 2008), Chapter 2, section 2.1.1 (discussing the failed pre-First World War endeavours to criminalize crimes against humanity, including in the context of the Armenian genocide).

43 United Nations, Charter of the United Nations (24 October 1945) 1 UNTS XVI, Art. 2.

paramount importance of the principle of sovereignty in international law.[44]

1.4 THEORIES OF INTERNATIONAL LAW

1.4.1 The Framework for International Law and the Importance of Norms

Traditionally, international law has been seen as 'a complex of norms regulating the mutual behaviour of states, the specific subjects of international law'.[45] These norms can be distinguished from rules, which may govern other areas of law such as domestic law. By 'norms' is meant 'standards of behaviour defined in terms of rights and obligations'.[46] Rules, in contrast, are the 'specific application of norms to particular situations' that prescribe or proscribe particular acts.[47]

Rosalyn Higgins views international law not as a system of rules, but as a normative system:

> All organized groups and structures require a system of normative conduct – that is to say, conduct which is regarded by each actor, and by the group as a whole, as being obligatory, and for which violation carries a price. Normative systems make possible that degree of order if society is to maximize the common good – and, indeed, even to avoid chaos in the web of bilateral and multilateral relationships that society embraces.[48]

While bearing in mind the importance of these norms and the attraction of viewing international law as a process, it is equally important to note that

---

[44] See Cassese, above note 37, 48 ('It is safe to conclude that sovereign equality constitutes the linchpin of the whole body of international legal standards, the fundamental premise on which all international relations rest.') For a detailed discussion of states and sovereignty, see Chapter 4.

[45] Hans Kelsen, *Pure Theory of Law* (Berkeley, CA: University of California Press, 1967), 320.

[46] Stephen Krasner, 'Structural Causes and Regime Consequences: Regimes as Intervening Variables' in Stephen Krasner (ed.), *International Regimes* (Ithaca, NY: Cornell University Press, 1983), 2.

[47] Andrew P. Cortell and James W. Davis Jr, 'How Do International Institutions Matter? The Domestic Impact of International Rules and Norms' (1996) 40 *International Studies Quarterly* 451, 452.

[48] Rosalyn Higgins, *Problems and Process: International Law and How We Use It* (Oxford: Clarendon Press, 1994), 1.

international law does not exist in an 'intellectual vacuum'.[49] These norms must also be viewed within a theoretical framework (or frameworks). This is because theories, at least in part, underpin the action of states, which in turn leads to the creation of norms, which become international law. International law theory, therefore, essentially relates to understanding, explaining and critiquing the basic propositions of international law. As we shall see, certain theoretical perspectives challenge the legitimacy and threaten the operation of international law; yet others call for reform or the space for different voices in the international legal system.

The role of states in defining and developing international law is well understood. Clearly, it is the contractual behaviour of states that develops the law through treaty. It is also the practice of states, and their belief in that practice, that develops customary international law.[50] Hans Kelsen states:

> International law consists of norms which were created by custom, that is, by acts of the national states or, more correctly formulated, by the state organs authorized by national legal orders to regulate interstate relations. These are the norms of 'general' international law, because they create obligations or rights for all states.[51]

This idea itself raises an interesting question. Why is it that the state as opposed to any other body or actor is given this power? The historical evolution of international law from the Peace of Westphalia, and its little challenged reflection in the sources of law under Article 38(1) of the Statute of the International Court of Justice,[52] provides one answer. Another answer lies in the crucial norm of *pacta sunt servanda* which 'authorizes the states as the subjects of the international community to regulate by treaty their mutual behaviour, that is, the behaviour of their own organs and subjects in relation to the organs and subjects of other states'.[53] Therefore, it is this norm that gives the state the legitimacy to act

---

[49] Iain Scobbie, 'Wicked Heresies or Legitimate Perspectives? Theory and International Law', in Evans, above note 5, 83, 92.

[50] The sources of international law are discussed in Chapter 2. In brief, treaties are bilateral or multilateral agreements between states giving rise to rights and responsibilities as between those contracting states in relation to a particular issue or issues. Customary international law rules are created by the uniform and consistent practice of a significant number of states (the things states say and do in different fora) and their belief that this practice is derived from legal obligation.

[51] Kelsen, above note 45, 323.

[52] United Nations, Statute of the International Court of Justice, 18 April 1946.

[53] Kelsen, above note 45, 323.

on behalf of its subjects as one body. The reason why *pacta sunt servanda* presents only one answer to this question is that it provides but one theoretical framework for an understanding of how international law operates: certainly the predominant post-Westphalian model. Of course, predating this period it was possible to talk about the importance of the development and control of international law by different entities, including protectorates and empires, let alone the extensive political and legal control exercised by the Church. The modern question of the state as the paramount subject of international law, and the relationship of non-state actors with the creation and operation of international law, is a subject giving rise to increasing debate, and will be revisited in other contexts throughout this book.

1.4.2 Different Theoretical Conceptions of International Law

1.4.2.1 Natural and positive law theories

Natural law as a theory of international law held sway for many centuries. Roman jurists viewed natural law as the law derived from the nature of human beings, and as law expressive of the basic ideas of justice.[54] Cicero saw natural law as something immutable.[55] At heart, natural law views law as embodying axiomatic truths. It is because of this universal application that the principles of natural law were equally applicable to either domestic or international law. In the Middle Ages in Europe, natural law diversified into two key schools of thought. The first viewed it as created by God and discoverable by humans. The second, more popular and enduring school of thought was the 'rationalistic' approach, articulated by Thomas Aquinas, holding that natural law could be discovered and applied through human reason and analysis, as opposed to religious revelation. This interpretation viewed all law as already existing, waiting to be discovered. Hugo Grotius further developed this secular interpretation of international law. He focused particularly on the applicability of natural law to an international law framework, seeing natural law as one of the basic elements and sources of international law.[56] He viewed law as governing nations as well as people by universal principle based on morality

---

[54] See, e.g., Philip Allott, 'International Law and the Idea of History', (1999) 1 *Journal of History and International Law* 1.

[55] Alexander Orakhelashvili, 'Natural Law and Justice', in R. Wolfrum (ed.), *Max Planck Encyclopedia of Public International Law* (Heidelberg: Max-Planck-Institut, 2010), [7].

[56] Ibid., [9]. See also Amos S. Hershey, 'International Law since the Peace of Westphalia' (1912) 6 *American Journal of International Law* 30, 31–2.

and divine justice,[57] although his 'eclectic' approach to international law entrenched principles of modern international law – such as legal equality, territorial sovereignty and the independence of states – in the European, and eventually global, political landscape.

While the rise of positive law theory in the sixteenth century clearly led to a substantial decline in support for natural law theory, some scholars contend that natural law still continues to play an important part in the international law system through the principles it provides for, such as natural justice.[58] The development in the twentieth century of the prohibition against crimes against humanity and genocide borrow deeply from the naturalist idea that there are laws of humanity that are immutable and give rise to rights and obligations that transcend the conscious or positive acts of states.[59] Reading Justice Jackson's Opening at Nuremberg, for example, one is struck by the evangelical (in the sense of carrying an almost religious truth) language, reminiscent of naturalist thinking:

> The doctrine was that one could not be regarded as criminal for committing the usual violent acts in the conduct of legitimate warfare. The age of imperialistic expansion during the eighteenth and nineteenth centuries added the foul doctrine . . . that all wars are to be regarded as legitimate wars. The sum of these two doctrines was to give war-making a complete immunity from accountability to law.
>
> This was intolerable for an age that called itself civilized. Plain people with their earthy common sense, revolted at such fictions and legalisms so contrary to ethical principles and demanded checks on war immunities.[60]

The reasoning that scaffolded Jackson's arguments was legally flimsy but morally irresistible, reminding us of Cicero's belief in the immutability of law.

Indeed, certain developments in areas of fundamental human rights and even the use of force based on 'humanitarian intervention' may

---

57 *De Jure Belli ac Pacis Libri Tres* (1625).

58 Orakhelashvili, above note 55, [35].

59 See, e.g., the Martens Clause – which first appeared in the Preamble to the 1899 Hague Convention II and the 1907 Hague Convention IV and is most likely the legal foundation for crimes against humanity – which states that 'populations and belligerents remain under the protection and empire of the principles of international law, as they result from the usages established between civilized nations, from the *laws of humanity* and the requirements of the public conscience'. See Boas et al., above note 42, Chapter 2, section 2.2.1.

60 Opening Speech of Justice Jackson before the Nuremberg Tribunal, in *Trial of the Major War Criminals before the International Military Tribunal, Nuremberg*, Vol. II, 98–102.

signal something of a naturalist view of some norms being deeply rooted in the international legal conscience, not requiring discovery through the usual sources of international law.[61] Although these developments require appraisal from a modern understanding of international law, one is reminded of the words of Pierre Joseph Proudhon from the nineteenth century: 'Whoever invokes humanity wants to cheat.'[62]

Positivist legal theory grew in large part as a reaction to naturalist thought. Originally conceived by the French philosopher Auguste Comte, positivism 'promised to bring the true and final liberation of the human mind from the superstitions and dogmas of the past'.[63] While natural law holds that all law already exists waiting to be discovered, positivist theory views law not as a set of pre-existing or pre-ordained legal rules derived from some mystical source; rather, positivism views international law as discoverable through a scientific, objective or empirical process.[64]

Positivist law was developed in the writings of John Austin, who defined

---

[61] Antonio Cassese appears to call on something like natural law when he suggests that where a rule of international law concerns the 'laws of humanity' or the 'dictates of conscience', it may be unnecessary to look at state practice as the foundation of its legal status (see Cassese, above note 37, 160–1). This seems to suggest that there are some rules that are simply given, justified by virtue purely of their nature and content. Apart from the less controversial references to the prohibition of genocide and crimes against humanity, justification for the NATO bombing of Serbia in the late 1990s as based on 'humanitarian intervention' has a certain natural law (or even 'just war') ring to it. Kartashkin refers to humanitarian interventions 'justified by common interests and humane considerations, such as natural law principles': Vladimir Kartashkin, 'Human Rights and Humanitarian Intervention', in Lori Fisler Damrosch and David J. Scheffer (eds), *Law and Force in the New International Order* (Boulder, CO: Westview, 1991), 202, 203–4. See also Antonio Cassese, 'Ex Injuria Ius Oritur: Are we Moving towards International Legitimation of Forcible Humanitarian Countermeasures in the World Community?' (1999) *European Journal of International Law* 23; cf. Brownlie, who believes 'there is very little evidence to support assertions that a new principle of customary law legitimising humanitarian intervention has crystallised': Ian Brownlie, 'International Law and the Use of Force – Revisited', speech delivered at the Graduate Institute of International Studies, Geneva, 1 February 2010, available at http://www.europaeum.org/files/publications/pamphlets/IanBrownlie.pdf; Higgins, above note 48, 245–8. See also J.B. Scott (ed.), *The Hague Conventions and Declarations of 1899 and 1907* (New York: Oxford University Press, 1915), 101–2.

[62] Quoted by Carl Schmitt and cited in Marttii Koskenniemi, 'What is International Law For?' in Evans, above note 5, 64.

[63] Neff, above note 5, 38.

[64] Ibid.

it as 'set by a sovereign individual or a sovereign body of individuals, to a person or persons in a state of subjection to its author'.[65] Interestingly, while such a conception of law is clearly a rejection of natural law theory, it has deep links to Hugo Grotius' 'law of nations'. Grotius transformed the Romanic *jus gentium*[66] into his idea of a law of nations, which led to it being identified as a body of law distinct from natural law, an idea that Jeremy Bentham would eventually refer to for the first time as 'international law'.[67]

For Neff, '[b]y positivism is meant such a wealth of things that it may be best to avoid using the term altogether'.[68] Indeed, the use of the term legal positivism in international legal scholarship represents a myriad of ideas. Austin's positivism views law as essentially anarchistic – rules set by those individuals or bodies who hold power over others.

The twentieth-century realist, Hans Morgenthau, describes positivism in terms of strict legalism:

> The juridic positivist delimits the subject-matter of his research in a dual way. On the one hand, he proposes to deal exclusively with matters legal, and for this purpose strictly separates the legal sphere from ethics and *mores* as well as psychology and sociology. Hence, his legalism. On the other hand, he restricts his attention within the legal sphere to the legal rules enacted by the state, and excludes all law whose existence cannot be traced to the statute books or the decisions of the courts. Hence his *étatist* monism. This 'positive' law the positivist accepts as it is, without passing judgment upon its ethical value or questioning its practical appropriateness. Hence his agnosticism. The positivist cherishes the belief that the 'positive' law is a logically coherent system which virtually contains, and through a mere process of logical deduction will actually produce, all rules necessary for the decision of all possible cases. Hence, his system worship and dogmatic conceptualism.[69]

---

[65] John Austin, in R. Campbell (ed.), *Lectures on Jurisprudence*, or *The Philosophy of Positive Law*, two volumes (Bristol: Thoemmes Press reprint, 2002), 35. See also John Austin, *The Province of Jurisprudence Determined* (London: John Murray, 1832). See Gerry Simpson's articulation of Austin's conception of international law as anarchic in text accompanying note 201 below. See also Bernard Röling, *International Law in an Expanded World* (Amsterdam: Djambatan, 1960), who viewed international law (like all law) as having 'the inclination to serve primarily the interests of the powerful', at 230.

[66] See section 1.3.1 above for the Roman Law roots of this concept.

[67] Jeremy Bentham, *Principles of Morals and Legislation* (Oxford: Clarendon Press, 1789).

[68] Neff, above note 5, 38.

[69] Hans J. Morgenthau, 'Positivism, Functionalism, and International Law', (1940) 34 *American Journal of International Law* 260, 261.

Traditional positivism denotes a formalism, a search for law objectively, without interference from the extralegal. The attraction of such an approach to law can easily be understood when seen as emerging out of the mysticism and religious trappings of natural law theory. Modern positivism as a search for objective law eschews the teleological development of law (law as it should be), which is interesting when viewed through a humanist lens. Some of the most profound developments in modern international law challenge the firm positivist grip on the discipline. Human rights law and humanitarian law have, in recent years, received platinum teleological treatment before the most exacting and conservative juridical forum of all: criminal courts. The meteoric development of international criminal law in the brief life of the International Criminal Tribunal for the former Yugoslavia, for example, shows how modern international law can be very much a case of law as it should be. This enthusiastic humanism surely paved the way for the doctrine of responsibility to protect, and what Gerry Simpson calls belligerent humanitarianism.[70]

At heart, positivism emerged from the creation of a law of nations, born of a contract (or rather a complex and ever changing web of contracts) between nations consciously dictating their own destiny.[71] In this way international law can be viewed at once as liberating (rescued from the vagaries of dogma and the control of religious institutions)[72] and, at the same time, as a reflection of state power paradigms (out of the frying pan and into thc fire). The latter observation is particularly powerful when considering the contention, advanced by Boyle, that continued investigation of the source of international law is, in short, an attempt to 'develop some conceptual way of differentiating between law and politics'.[73] In the context of modern international law, plagued by challenges to state-centrism, the cold formalism of positivist theory (born of the idea of state as the supreme and self-determiner of the rules of international law) is under something of a challenge. Questions continue to arise regarding how a sov-

---

[70] Gerry Simpson, above note 36.

[71] Ago explains that the development of Grotius' writings in the eighteenth century by scholars such as Emer de Vattel, Christian Wolff George and Frederick de Martens led to the view that '"positive international law" within the body of law in force in international society is that part of law which is laid down by the tacit and expressed consent of different states': Roberto Ago, 'Positive Law and International Law' (1957) 51 *American Journal of International Law* 691, 693.

[72] See, e.g., *SS 'Lotus'* (Judgment No. 9) (1927) PCIJ (Ser. A) No. 10, 14 (describing the rules of law binding upon states as emanating 'from their own free will').

[73] Gerry Simpson, above note 36, 279.

ereign can bind itself to bind itself in the future,[74] and the circularity which legal positivism appears unable to shake in the search for a source which can 'imbue the sovereign's consent with the kind of normative force'[75] required by this doctrine. Considerations of these challenges posed to the positivist theory will re-emerge throughout this book.

1.4.2.2 Relationship between international relations, international law, and different theories of international law

All law has a relationship with politics. Because international law is largely created by the actions of states and their organs, there is an inevitably strong relationship between international relations and international law. Indeed, the international political environment compels states to behave in particular ways, which in turn leads to the variation and creation of international law. Many aspects of international relations and politics have impacted on the theoretical conception of international law. As the voices in the community of the international system grow, as they have dramatically done in the latter half of the twentieth and beginning of the twenty-first centuries, so too theories develop to reflect differing perspectives. In this way one sees the development of theories based on social policy and international relations/politics (such as realism and liberalism, the new haven and socialist schools), of theories developed around counter-culture (critical legal studies), as well as theories developed in response to oppressive aspects of the conservative and exclusive system of international law (feminist theory; lesbian, gay, bisexual and transgender/transsexual theory; Third World theory). While all of these theories merit consideration and reflect important voices in the milieu of international law, only a few will be discussed in this section (and only briefly) to enable an understanding of the international law landscape and to assist in considering, in the final section of this chapter, what is international law.

All forms of law are inevitably subjected to theories that describe, explain and critique them. Such theory may be presented as the origin of a system of law; or to explain, rationalize, justify or challenge it. A unique aspect of international law, however, is the extent to which theory becomes so crucial both in dictating the direction of the law itself, and the set of politics that is intrinsic to it.[76] This is at least in part because the

---

[74] Ibid., 285.

[75] Ibid.

[76] See, Shaw, above note 4, 12: 'Politics is much closer to the heart of the [international] system than is perceived within national legal orders, and power much more in evidence. The interplay of law and politics in world affairs is much more complex and difficult to unravel.' Anne-Marie Slaughter, 'International Law in a

ideology adhered to by a state or group of states influences their approach to international relations and in turn determines their behaviour in the international sphere. This behaviour, or 'state practice', assists in the development of custom, which itself leads to the creation of international law.

1.4.2.2.1 Realism and liberalism Realism and liberalism are two international relations theories used to explain, predict, and justify the actions of states. These are by no means the only international relations theories, but are the dominant ones in contemporary thought.[77]

1.4.2.2.1.1 REALISM The fundamental concept underpinning the realist school of thought is that states are mutually self-interested actors that, in situations where they must choose a particular course of action out of multiple alternatives, will engage in a cost–benefit analysis of each option. To realist legal scholars, states will inevitably make the only 'rational' choice; they will act in a way that best promotes their own interests, to the exclusion of the interests of others. This assumption forms the basis of Rational Choice Theory, which is currently the dominant theoretical paradigm in economic modeling.[78] The predominance of Rational Choice Theory in economic scholarship is, today, possibly the most visible and well-known manifestation of realism.

World of Liberal States', (1995) 6 *European Journal of International Law* 503, 503: 'International Law and international politics cohabit the same conceptual space. Together they comprise the rules and the reality of "the international system", an intellectual construct that lawyers, political scientists, and policymakers use to describe the world they study and seek to manipulate. As a distinguished group of international lawyers and a growing number of political scientists have recognized, it makes little sense to study one without the other.' An interesting example of this relationship can be found in war crimes law: see Gerry Simpson, *Law War and Crime* (2008), 11–12: '[W]ar crimes are political trials. They are political not because they lack a foundation in law or because they are the crude product of political forces but because war crimes law is saturated with conversations about what it means to engage in politics or law, as well as a series of projects that seek to employ these terms in the service of various ideological preferences. War crimes are political trials because concepts of the political remain perpetually in play . . . In the end, war crimes law is a place where politics happens.'

[77] Slaughter, above note 76, 506.

[78] In 1881, F.Y. Edgeworth stated that 'the first principle of Economics is that every agent is actuated only by self-interest': *Mathematical Psychics: An Essay on the Application of Mathematics for the Moral Sciences* (London: C. Kegan Paul & Co., 1881), 6; available at http://socserv.mcmaster.ca/~econ/ugcm/3ll3/edgeworth/mathpsychics.pdf.

This egoistic model, however, generates gloomy predictions regarding the nature of state interactions and for international law in general. In 1513, Niccolò Machiavelli wrote: 'They who lay down the foundations of a State and furnish it with laws must . . . assume that all men are bad, and will always, when they have free field, give loose to their evil inclinations.'[79] Slaughter explains that, for realists, states interact with one another within an uncertain and anarchical system like billiard balls: hard, opaque, unitary actors colliding with one another.[80] In this way, the internal dynamics, political system and ideology of an individual state are irrelevant.[81] All states will act accordingly, leading to a troubling view of international law: 'International norms serve only an instrumental purpose, and are likely to be enforced or enforceable only by a hegemon. The likelihood of positive-sum games in which all states will benefit for cooperation is relatively low.'[82] Thus, from a purely realist perspective, the value of international law to the international community is highly questionable.

1.4.2.2.1.2 LIBERALISM The realist school can be contrasted with liberalism. A key difference between liberalist and realist thought is that while realists focus on relations between states to the exclusion of internal relations, liberalists focus on the relationship between the state and society. Moravcsik refers to three core liberalist assumptions.[83] First, 'the fundamental actors in politics are members of domestic society, understood as individuals and privately constituted groups seeking to promote their independent interests',[84] a clear difference from the statist approach taken under realism. The second core assumption is that 'governments represent some segment of domestic society, whose interests are reflected

---

79 Niccolò Machiavelli, *Discourses on the First Decade of Titus Livius, Book I, Chapter III* (Ninian Hill Thomson trans, 1883), 28; available at http://www2.hn.psu.edu/faculty/jmanis/machiavelli/Machiavelli-Discourses-Titus-Livius.pdf.

80 Slaughter, above note 76, 507 (of the billiard balls metaphor, Slaughter explains that this is the classic Realist metaphor first used by Arnold Wolfers, *Discord and Collaboration: Essays on International Politics* (Baltimore: John Hopkins Press, 1962), 19–24.

81 Ibid., 507; Christian Reus-Smith, 'The Strange Death of Liberal International Theory' (2001) 12(3) *European Journal of International Law*, 573, 581–2.

82 Slaughter, above note 76, 507.

83 See A.M. Moravcsik, *Liberalism and International Relations Theory* (Center for International Affairs, Harvard University, Working Paper No. 92-6, 1992). See also Slaughter, above note 76 (endorsing Moravcsik's classification of the broad principles of liberalist theory), 508.

84 Moravcsik, above note 83, 6.

in state policy'.[85] This differs from the realist approach which divorces internal domestic matters from the factors that affect how a state will act in the international sphere. The third core liberalist assumption is that the behaviour of states – and hence levels of international conflict and cooperation – reflects 'the nature and configuration of state preferences'.[86]

1.4.2.2.1.3 REALISM AND LIBERALISM AS ALTERNATIVES The interplay between international law and politics became particularly pronounced during the Cold War. During this period, theories were advanced by scholars from both the United States and the USSR, which had the effect of justifying these political regimes' own respective and opposing ideologies. Policy-oriented schools of international legal theory during this period impacted significantly on global politics and therefore on the interpretation and development of international law.

However, while realism and liberalism were often used during this period in counteraction to the other, it is equally conceivable that the two are not truly alternatives, let alone mutually exclusive. Indeed, the better understanding of the interaction between these two theories is that liberalism is an offspring of realism. Liberalism, although in a sense more nuanced than realism, nonetheless remains rooted in the foundational principle that states act out of self-interest. The distinction lies in the fact that the range of interests considered to be of relevance by liberals is wider than those accepted by traditional realists.

1.4.2.2.1.4 CONSTRUCTIVISM The more plausible alternative to realism is constructivism. Although the term 'constructivism' was only coined in 1989, key tenets of constructivism can be found in the works of mainstream international political science theorists in the 1950s.[87] To constructivists, the international community is an environment of communication and learning in which states come to form expectations about others' behaviour. Whereas realism assumes that the interests of states are fixed and exogenous, constructivism views the interests and identities of states as endogenous and constituted through interaction with other states on the basis of shared norms.[88] International law, therefore, has a much more

---

[85] Ibid., 9.

[86] Ibid., 10.

[87] Jutta Brunee and Stephen J. Toope, 'International Law and Constructivism: Elements of an Interactional Theory of International Law', (2000–01) 39 *Columbia Journal of Transnational Law* 19.

[88] Anne-Marie Slaughter, Andrew S. Tulumello and Stepan Wood, 'International Law and International Relations Theory: A New Generation of

positive role to play in constructivist theory, cultivating a sense of shared identity and destiny, and engendering enhanced cooperation and trust between states.

1.4.2.2.2 Post-Cold War Two schools of political theory that shaped the polarized international law landscape during the Cold War were the New Haven and Soviet theories. The New Haven School was created by American scholars, and represented essentially an embrace of democratic values, growing out of the Second World War and the emergence of communism as an international political force.[89] This theory reflected an argument for 'clearly defined democratic values in all the areas of social life where lawyers have or can assert responsibility'.[90] In stark contrast, Soviet theory – developed by Soviet scholars during the Cold War period, particularly Tunkin – was a 'diametrical opposite to the New Haven School, both in its professed structure and envisaged political outcome.'[91]

The intense and obvious interplay between international law theory and politics during the Cold War period has since become more subtle, but is clearly still influential. While the age of diametrically opposed theories may have passed, states still utilize and rely upon international law theory to justify policy. A recent and relevant example of this was the use of the hegemonic theory by the US administration under George W. Bush to justify its treatment of 'enemy combatants' following the invasion of

Interdisciplinary Scholarship', (1998) 92 *American Society of International Law* 367, 373, 384; See, generally, Friedrich Kratochwil, *Rules, Norms and Decisions: On the Conditions of Practical and Legal Reasoning in International Relations and Domestic Affairs* (Cambridge: Cambridge University Press, 1989); Harold Hongju Koh 'Why do Nations Obey International Law?', (1997) 106 *Yale Law Journal* 2599.

89 Scobbie, above note 49, 93. Generally on the New Haven theory, see Hilary Charlesworth, 'Current Trends in International Legal Theory', in S.K.N. Blay, R.W. Piotrowicz and B.M. Tsamenyi, *Public International Law: An Australian Perspective* (Oxford: Oxford University Press, 1997), 403; Shaw, above note 4, 58–62.

90 Harold D. Laswell and Myers S. McDougal, 'Legal Education and Public Policy: Professional Training in the Public Interest', (1943) 52 *Yale Law Journal* 203, 207.

91 Scobbie, above note 49, 96 and 97 (referencing G.I. Tunkin, *Theory of International Law* (Cambridge, MA: Harvard University Press, 1974) and Lori Fisler Damrosch, Gennady M. Danilenko and Rein Mullerson, *Beyond Confrontation: International Law for the Post-Cold War Era* (Boulder, CO: Westview Press, 1995)).

Afghanistan in 2001. This theory, adopting a strongly dualist stance,[92] argues that a 'radical freedom of action' for the United States is to be put first and foremost before any form of international law. An unreconstructed advocate of this theory, John Bolton, argues:

> We should be unashamed, unapologetic, uncompromising American constitutional hegemonists. International law is *not* superior to, and does not trump the Constitution. The rest of the world may not like that approach, but abandoning it is the first step to abandoning the United States of America.[93]

This theory was used as a justification for US policy in the treatment of 'enemy combatants' at Guantanamo Bay and Abu Ghraib. By applying hegemonic theory and rejecting any form of law that has not been ratified by the US Congress, the Bush Administration was able to act in a way 'denying the applicability of the Geneva Conventions and international prohibitions on torture and inhumane treatment',[94] leading to wide-scale systematic human rights abuse.[95] This presents just one example, and a depressing one at that, of how international law theory is still used to justify the political behaviour of states.

Other theories of international law have a political content, in the broader sense of the term.

1.4.2.2.3 Marxist theory Marxist theory takes its name from Karl Marx, whose writings, along with Friedrich Engels', established an account of international law based upon a materialistic interpretation of history, criticism of capitalism and a theory of social change produced by economic conditions.[96] In general terms, Marxism is a description of the societal shift to communism, and an account of the inevitability of this shift, driven as it is by social inequality. The result is a broad-based social and political theory that encompasses multitudes of interpretations of Marx's

---

[92] For an explanation of 'monist' and 'dualist' theories of international law, see Chapter 3, section 3.1.

[93] John R. Bolton, 'Is There Really "Law" in International Affairs?' (2000) 10 *Transnational Law and Contemporary Problems*, 1, 48.

[94] Scobbie, above note 49, 106.

[95] See, e.g., George Aldrich, 'The Taliban, al Qaeda, and the Determination of Illegal Combatants', (2002) 96 *American Journal of International Law* 891.

[96] Susan R. Marks, 'Introduction', in Susan R. Marks (ed.), *International Law on the Left: Re-Examining Marxist Legacies* (Cambridge: Cambridge University Press, 2008), 1–3.

philosophy, producing categories such as 'Classical Marxism', 'Official Marxism', and 'Alternative Marxism'.[97]

Of the current incarnation of the school of Marxist theory, Chimni – who is at the forefront of current endeavours to recast mainstream accounts of international law in a Marxist mould – outlines the distinctive features of critical Marxist international law scholarship (CMILS).[98] First, the definition of 'national interest' is informed by historical phases, group and class interests.[99] Second, the democratic transformation of international law is recognized to be subject to structural constraints such as power-driven conceptions of sources of international law.[100] Thirdly, whereas mainstream theories contain notions of objectivity in interpretations of fact and law, and the New Haven School adopts a position of radical indeterminacy, CMILS occupies a middle-ground between the two.[101] Fourthly, CMILS attempts to take an inclusive approach to international law and acknowledges alternative theories rather than lending credence to the characterization of American and European perspectives as the universal story of international law.[102]

As it stands, proponents of Marxism remain engaged in the challenge to gain greater legitimacy as a more accurate and meaningful alternative to more mainstream theories of international law.

1.4.2.2.4 Critical legal studies Critical legal studies challenge accepted norms in the international community and question the assumptions 'common to most legal systems that they are rational, objective and supported by evidence'.[103] Regarding the current world order, critical legal theorists argue that the 'liberal underpinnings of western international law and the notion of universality based on the consensus of states, are

---

97 China Miéville, 'The Commodity Form Theory of International Law: An Introduction', (2004) 17 *Leiden Journal of International Law* 271, 276–9.

98 B.S. Chimni, 'An Outline of a Marxist Course on Public International Law', (2004) 17 *Leiden Journal of International Law* 1, 3–5; B.S. Chimni, 'Marxism and International Law: A Contemporary Analysis', (1999) 34 *Economics and Political Weekly* 337.

99 B.S. Chimni, 'An Outline of a Marxist Course on Public International Law', above note 98, 3.

100 Ibid., 4.

101 Ibid.

102 Ibid.

103 Gillian Triggs, *International Law: Contemporary Principles and Practices* (Sydney: LexisNexis Butterworths, 2011, 2nd edn), 13; Charlesworth, above note 89, 404.

illusory'.[104] This is due in part to the fact that 'liberalism tries constantly to balance individual freedom and social order and, it is argued, inevitably ends up siding with one or other of those propositions'.[105]

Critical legal studies have been described as a 'political location', lacking any essential intellectual component, and presently occupied by many fundamentally different and even sometimes contradictory subgroups, including various feminists, critical race theorists, post-modernists and political economists.[106] Nonetheless, several common themes can be discerned. The first is a strong view of the flaws in objectivism and formalism.[107] Another is the proposition that law is politics, that is, an analysis of the assumptions that form the foundation of the law will reveal that these assumptions operate to advance the interests of some political grouping.[108] Further, critical legal scholars stress the contradictions and indeterminacy inherent in legal rules.[109] Martii Koskenniemi, for example, argues that international legal analysis cannot provide an objective resolution of disputes because the recognition of sovereign states as the basic unit of international society is itself a normative, value judgement:[110]

> [I]nternational law is singularly useless as a means for justifying or criticizing international behaviour. Because it is based on contradictory premises it remains both over- and under-legitimizing: it is over-legitimizing as it can be ultimately invoked to justify any behaviour (apologism), it is under-legitimizing because it is incapable of providing a convincing argument on the legitimacy of any practices (utopianism).[111]

Koskenniemi attributes the inability of international legal analysis to objectively resolve disputes to the inherent 'reversibility' of international legal arguments. He argues that patterns of argument ostensibly appeal to autonomy (which is characterized as an ascending pattern of argument) or community (which is characterized as descending).[112] In international law, ascending patterns of argument are countered by descending patterns of

---

[104] Charlesworth, ibid., 404.

[105] Marttii Koskenniemi, *From Apology to Utopia: The Structure of International Legal Argument* (Cambridge: Cambridge University Press, 2005), 52.

[106] Mark Tushnet, 'Critical Legal Studies: A Political History', (1991) 100 *Yale Law Journal* 1515, 1516–18.

[107] See, generally, Roberto Mangabeira Unger, 'The Critical Legal Studies Movement', (1983) 96 *Harvard Law Review*, 561.

[108] Tushnet, above note 106, 1517.

[109] Shaw, above note 4, 63–4.

[110] Koskenniemi, above note 105, 192–3.

[111] Ibid., 48.

[112] Ibid., 503–4.

argument – for example, an argument for independence (ascending) will be countered by an argument for equality (descending). However, because the concept of independence can be justified by reference to principles of equality and vice versa, Koskenniemi argues that the characterizations of all legal arguments can be reversed.[113] Their underlying bases are fluid, inherently reversible concepts. Therefore, when making a decision as to the supremacy of one argument over another, there is no objective manner in which that decision can be made.[114] It cannot be said that one pattern of argument, or one particular conceptual category, should always be supreme. Such opinions emblematize the differing conceptions of international law and lead to the quintessential question of what is international law.[115]

1.4.2.2.5 Third World theory Third World theory presents a critical approach to international law that argues for change in the role and objectives of the current international order with particular regard for the perceived disempowerment of Third World states.[116] Third World theorists eschew attempts to define 'Third World' as having a distinct geographical definition, acknowledging lack of total cohesion amongst its members, and focusing instead on shared traits of under-development and marginalization.[117] This approach criticizes the role of international law in entrenching power imbalance between the developed and developing states, and assumptions of its universal application. Instead, it is argued that the rules of international law – which were conceived to serve the interests of the ruling powers of the time – should be re-evaluated given the emergence of developing Asian and African states,[118] and the radical changes in the make-up of the international community since the inception of international law. Third World theory is not a 'method' for an analysis of what is international law, per se. Rather, it is a framework within which legal scholars argue for the need for international law to

---

113 Ibid., 505.

114 Ibid., 508.

115 See discussion of this issue below at section 1.6.

116 See, generally, A.A. Fatouros, 'International Law and the Third World', (1964) 50 *Virginia Law Review* 783, and Maurice Flory, 'Adapting International Law to the Development of the Third World', (1982) 26 *Journal of African Law* 12.

117 Fatouros, above note 116, 785.

118 See, generally, Wolfgang Friedmann, 'The Position of Underdeveloped Countries and the Universality of International Law', (1963) 2 *Columbia Society of International Law*, 78, and R.P. Anand, 'Role of the "New" Asian-African Countries in the Present International Legal Order', (1962) 56 *American Society of International Law*, 383.

reflect a consensus amongst the international community, including newly emerged states.[119]

1.4.2.2.6 Feminist theory A feminist approach to international law is based on the same principles that underpin feminist theory at a domestic level. Feminist theory at the international level thus contends that the structure, actors and processes of international law fail adequately to take into account females and are inherently skewed towards a male gender bias. Feminist theory in relation to the international field has only gained significant traction since the early 1990s,[120] although feminist activism in the international sphere has been long established.

While there exist different feminist theories, a broad feminist approach at a national level is to question 'the claims of national legal systems to impartiality and objectivity, arguing that they deliver a sexed and gendered system of justice'.[121] Applying this to international law, feminists 'scrutinise international law and . . . challenge its universal basis'.[122] Charlesworth and Chinkin see feminist analysis of international law as having two main roles.[123] The first is the 'deconstruction of the explicit and implicit values of the international legal system, challenging their claim to objectivity and rationality because of the limited base on which they are built'.[124] This is based upon the idea that as women have been largely excluded from the 'construction' of international law, the values adopted by the international legal system do not have a female perspective and thus must be challenged, or deconstructed. The second role is that of reconstruction. This 'requires rebuilding the basic concepts of international law in a way that they do not support or reinforce the domination of women

---

119 Anand, above note 118, 387.

120 Charlesworth, above note 89, 407.

121 Ibid. For a history of the evolution of feminist theory, see Elizabeth Gross, 'What is Feminist Theory?', in Carole Pateman and Elizabeth Gross (eds), *Feminist Challenges: Social and Political Theory* (Sydney and London: Allen & Unwin, 1986), 190.

122 Charlesworth, above note 89, 407.

123 Hilary Charlesworth and Christine M. Chinkin, *The Boundaries of International Law: A Feminist Analysis* (Executive Park, NY: Juris Publishing Inc., 2000), 60. See also Hilary Charlesworth, Christine Chinkin and Shelly Wright, 'Feminist Approaches to International Law', in Robert J. Beck, Anthony Clark Arend and Robert D. Vander Lugt (eds), *International Rules: Approaches from International Law and International Relations* (Oxford and New York: Oxford University Press, 1996), 256; Christine Chinkin, 'Feminism, Approach to International Law', *Max Planck Encyclopedia of Public International Law* (2010); Charlesworth, above note 89, 407–9.

124 Charlesworth and Chinkin, above note 123, 60.

by men'.[125] It is argued that this would benefit not just women but also allow the major aims of the UN Charter 'to be defined in new, inclusive, ways'.[126]

Feminist theory has had some influence and success within the international system. The advancement of women has been given institutional support through the UN system, in particular through the Committee on the Elimination of Discrimination against Women (CEDAW), a body dedicated to investigating human rights abuses committed against women, and improving the human rights of women worldwide. Other examples are reflected in the area of international war crimes prosecutions, where radical developments have occurred in relation to both the role of women in armed conflict, and the recognition and more appropriate criminalizing of massive human rights violations against them as a group.[127]

1.5 SPECIALIST AREAS OF INTERNATIONAL LAW

1.5.1 The International Law of the Sea

The international law of the sea is the body of public international law concerned with defining permissible maritime activities, navigational rights, mineral rights, jurisdiction over coastal waters and the relationship between states and the seas.

From the seventeenth century until the mid-twentieth century, the international law of the sea was dominated by the concept of 'freedom of the seas' as promoted by Grotius in his Latin text, *Mare Liberum*.[128] During this time, states enjoyed freedom to pursue their interests unhindered in all areas of the sea, save for the three nautical miles from a state's coastline,

125 Ibid., 61.

126 Ibid.

127 See Charlesworth and Chinkin, above note 123, 330: 'The jurisdiction and emerging jurisprudence of the *ad hoc* Tribunals suggest that the silence about the suffering of women in all forms of armed conflict has been broken', and at 333: 'All these developments suggest that the international legal system has responded well in taking women's lives into account in the context of international criminal law. In some ways, however, the response has been very limited.'

128 Hugo Grotius, 'The Freedom of the Seas or The Right Which Belongs to the Dutch to Take Part in the East Indian Trade' (Ralph van Demen Magoffin trans., New York, Oxford University Press, 1916) [translation of *Mare Liberum* (1609)]; Edward W. Allen, 'Freedom of the Sea', (1966) 60 *American Journal of International Law* 814, 814.

which remained within the control of the coastal state (otherwise known as the 'cannon shot' rule).

This absolute freedom of activity began to give way as a result of a number of factors – which included a shift in geo-political priorities, the desire to extend national claims, concerns regarding the exploitation of the seabed's resources, protection of marine environments and fish stocks, and enforcement of pollution controls, migration laws and counter-terrorism. States began to conclude various lesser treaties to regulate limited aspects of maritime activity.[129]

The key milestone came in 1958 with the first United Nations Conference on the Law of the Sea in Geneva that aimed to produce a codification of the customary international law of the sea. It resulted in a series of multilateral treaties on the territorial sea and contiguous zone,[130] the high seas,[131] fishing and environmental conservation in the high seas,[132] the continental shelf,[133] and an optional protocol concerning the compulsory settlement of disputes.[134] However, the success of the conference was limited as states were able to pick and choose which conventions to participate in, with most ignoring the optional protocol, leaving the international law of the sea in a state of disunity. These issues remained unaddressed at the conclusion of the second United Nations Conference on the Law of the Sea, which failed to garner the necessary majority to effect any more than two minor procedural changes. This was changed, however, by the third and final United Nations Conference on the Law of the Sea, convened with an ambitious agenda and concluded in 1982. The result was a convention encompassing a range of rights and obligations – the 1982 United Nations Convention on the Law of the Sea (UNCLOS).[135] Participation in the convention is

---

[129] Such as the Convention for Regulating the Police of the North Sea Fisheries, 6 May 1882, 160 CTS 219; and the Convention for the Protection of Submarine Cables, 14 March 1884, 163 CTS 391.

[130] Convention on the Territorial Sea and the Contiguous Zone (adopted 29 April 1958, entered into force 10 September 1964) 516 UNTS 205.

[131] Convention on the High Seas (adopted 29 April 1958, entered into force 30 September 1962) 450 UNTS 11.

[132] Convention on Fishing and Conservation of the Living Resources of the High Seas (adopted 29 April 1958, entered into force 20 March 1966) 559 UNTS 285.

[133] Convention on the Continental Shelf (adopted 29 April 1958, entered into force 10 June 1964) 499 UNTS 311.

[134] The Optional Protocol of Signature Concerning the Compulsory Settlement of Disputes (adopted 29 April 1958, entered into force 30 September 1962) 450 UNTS 169.

[135] United Nations Convention on the Law of the Sea (adopted 10 December

'all-or-nothing'; to opt into the convention is to accept all entailing rights and obligations. With more than 160 ratifications,[136] the convention is arguably one of the most successful examples of customary law codification and international law-making.

The UNCLOS provides for compulsory dispute resolution through the International Tribunal for the Law of the Sea (ITLOS).[137] It prevails over the 1958 Conventions,[138] although where a party is not an UNCLOS signatory but is a signatory to the 1958 Convention, the 1958 Convention will prevail. Where a party is not a signatory to any convention, then the UNCLOS serves only as a source of customary law in the case of a dispute.[139]

A final note on the operation of the UNCLOS is its careful delimitation of areas of sea, and the apportioning of rights and obligations attached. The fundamental guiding principle is that the 'land dominates the sea' so that any delimitations of the sea are made with reference to the land territory of the coastal state.[140] Such delimitations include the continental shelf, the Exclusive Economic Zone (EEZ), the contiguous zone, archipelagic waters, territorial seas and internal waters. Internal waters are treated as territorial land.[141] The territorial sea, in most cases, constitutes the area of sea within 12 nautical miles measured from the coastal state's baselines.[142] The coastal state may exercise its sovereignty within this area, albeit subject to the right to innocent passage by vessels (although this may be suspended by the state if it deems it necessary for security reasons). The contiguous zone extends a further 12 nautical miles from the territorial sea.[143] In the contiguous zone a state may continue to set and enforce rules regarding pollution, taxation, customs and immigration. The EEZ covers an area of 200 nautical miles from the

---

1982, entered into force 16 November 1994) 1833 UNTS 397 (hereinafter 'UNCLOS').

136 United Nations, 'Chronological Lists of Ratifications of Accessions and Successions to the Convention and the related Agreements as at 15 November 2010', The United Nations, 15 November 2010, available at http://www.un.org/Depts/los/reference_files/chronological_lists_of_ratifications.htm.

137 UNCLOS, above note 135, Pt 15, Arts 279, 280, 281 and 284.

138 Ibid., Art. 311(1) states: 'this Convention shall prevail, as between the States Parties, over the Geneva Conventions on the Law of the Sea of 29 April 1958'.

139 Triggs, above note 103, 270.

140 Shaw, above note 4, 553.

141 See Chapter 6.

142 UNCLOS, above note 135, Arts 2, 3.

143 Ibid., Art 23.

baseline,[144] within which the coastal nation has exclusive rights to the exploitation of natural resources. Finally, the continental shelf is a geological ledge projecting from the continental land mass into the sea, covered by a typically shallow body of water. Where the continental shelf extends beyond the EEZ, it may correspondingly extend the area of state control up to a maximum of 350 nautical miles from the baseline of the coast.[145] Any areas of sea beyond the scope of state control are known as the high seas and are not open to acquisition by occupation by any state.[146]

1.5.2 International Trade Law

Public international trade law addresses the rules and customs regarding trade between states. For the most part, this area of law is governed by bilateral agreements, many of which exist beneath the overarching multilateral framework formed by the World Trade Organization (WTO)[147] (encompassing the General Agreement on Tariffs and Trade (GATT) 1947,[148] and the GATT 1994[149]). The WTO is based around principles of elimination of trade barriers and non-discrimination between trading states.[150]

This global approach to trade found its impetus in the ruins of the Second World War. As the Allies set about the task of rebuilding a devastated Europe and ensuring that such wars never occurred again, it was suggested that a liberal model of free trade would eliminate economic instability, which was considered to be one of the factors that leads to regional conflict. Accordingly, the GATT 1947 was established, providing an informal framework for international trade until its replacement by the WTO in 1995. The original GATT 1947 remains operational within the WTO structure, subject to the GATT 1994 amendments.[151]

---

144 Ibid., Arts 55, 57.

145 Ibid., Art. 76(1).

146 Ibid., Art. 86; Ian Brownlie, *Principles of Public International Law*, (Oxford: Oxford University Press, 2008, 7th edn), 224.

147 Marrakesh Agreement Establishing the World Trade Organization (adopted 15 April 1994, entered into force 1 January 1995) 1867 UNTS 3 (hereinafter 'the WTO Agreement').

148 General Agreement on Tariffs and Trade, 30 October 1947, 55 UNTS 194 (hereinafter 'GATT 1947').

149 General Agreement on Tariffs and Trade, 15 April 1994, Marrakesh Agreement Establishing the World Trade Organization (adopted for signature 15 April 1994, entered into force 1 January 1995) 1867 UNTS 3 (hereinafter 'GATT 1994').

150 Ibid., Arts 1(1), 3(1) and 11(1).

151 Ibid., Art. 1(b)(ii).

The fundamental aim of the WTO Agreement is the establishment of trade relations with a view to raising standards of living, ensuring full employment, increasing trade, pursuing an increase in trade and effective use of resources, sustainable development and environmental protection, in a manner consistent with the needs of different states.[152]

Similar to the UNCLOS, parties to the WTO Agreement are assenting to all annexed agreements. There are, however, some allowances for special agreements and measures for certain developing countries.[153]

By far the most significant development in international trade law has been the establishment of extensive and sophisticated procedures for the settlement of disputes under the WTO, in the form of the Dispute Settlement Understanding (DSU).[154] The DSU has extraordinary powers to hear disputes and impose decisions that are binding on all Member States. In the first ten years since its introduction, the number of disputes heard under the DSU exceeded the combined total of disputes heard by the International Court of Justice and the Permanent Court of International Justice in 85 years.[155] These statistics are a credit to the DSU as a powerful and compelling procedure for dispute resolution.

1.5.3 International Environmental Law

The issues of environmental management and transnational pollution pose unique and serious challenges to the international community. An increased awareness of risks to the environment in recent times has prompted a spate of bilateral, regional and multilateral measures targeting a wide range of areas from terrestrial to atmospheric pollution, wildlife conservation and sustainability.[156] Yet, because approaches to these issues are often informed by human and social priorities, disagreements about the level of responsibility of different states and the right to development,

---

152 WTO Agreement, above 147, preamble.

153 Ibid., Arts 11(2) and 20.

154 WTO Agreement, above 147, Annex 2.

155 Triggs, above note 103, 697.

156 For example, the Convention on the Conservation of Antarctic Marine Living Resources (adopted 20 May 1980, entered into force 7 April 1982) 1329 UNTS 47; Protocol on Environmental Protection to the Antarctic Treaty (adopted 4 October 1991, entered into force 14 January 1998) 30 ILM 145; the ILC, 'Draft Articles on Prevention of Transboundary Harm from Hazardous Activities' in ILC, 'Report of the International Law Commission on the Work of its Fifty-Third Session', UN Doc A/56/10(2001), adopted by the General Assembly in Res. 58/84, 12 December 2001; the UNCLOS, above note 135.

international environmental law lacks the focus and consensus seen in other areas of international law.[157]

The lack of a commonly accepted definition of 'environment' proves the first barrier to effective international action. 'Environment' was defined in the 1972 Stockholm Declaration as 'air, water, land, flora and fauna and especially representative samples of natural ecosystems'.[158] It has been noted, however, that no single definition of 'environment' exists, and its meaning often changes depending on the context in which it is used.[159]

The development of environmental law is guided by a number of general principles common to other areas of international law, such as sovereignty and state responsibility.[160] Other principles more specific to the area of environmental law include the precautionary principle, the concept of sustainable development, the polluter pays principle, common but differentiated responsibilities, and the common heritage principle.[161] The following provides an outline of some of the key recent developments in international environmental law.

The United Nations Framework Convention on Climate Change (UNFCCC), which opened for signature in 1992 at the Earth Summit in Rio de Janeiro, aimed to achieve 'stabilization of greenhouse gas concentrations in the atmosphere at a level that would prevent dangerous anthropogenic interference with the climate system'.[162] The approach taken critically emphasizes mitigation rather than cessation of pollution emission.

Following the Earth Summit, the international community yet again convened in Kyoto in December 1997, resulting in the Kyoto Protocol.[163] Exemplary of the differentiated responsibilities principle, developed countries agreed to reduce their aggregate levels of greenhouse gas emissions below 1990 levels by an average of 5.2 per cent during the period 2008 to

---

[157] Brownlie, above note 146, 275.

[158] Declaration of the UN Conference on the Human Environment, 16 June 1992, UN Doc. A/CONF/48/14/REV.1, Principle 2.

[159] Patricia Birnie and Allan Boyle, *International Law and the Environment*, (Oxford: Oxford University Press, 2002, 2nd edn), 3–4.

[160] *The Trail Smelter* (*United States v Canada*) *Arbitration* (1938–41) 31 RIAA 1905.

[161] See, generally, Brownlie, above note 146, 276–80.

[162] United Nations Framework Convention on Climate Change (adopted 4 June 1992, entered into force 21 March 1994) 1771 UNTS 164, Art. 2 (hereinafter 'UNFCCC').

[163] Protocol to the Framework Convention on Climate Change (opened for signature 11 December 1997, entered into force 16 February 2005) 37 ILM (1998) 22 ('Kyoto Protocol').

2012, while developing states were not bound to any particular reduction targets.

Since Kyoto, numerous conferences have been held in various places including The Hague, Copenhagen and Cancún. The running theme in the development of this vein of international law is the milieu of diverging interests and priorities. Developing states assert a right to prioritize their economic development and to increase their standard of living, demanding that developed states take responsibility for their historical contribution to transnational pollution. On the other hand, developing states are called upon to take responsibility for their projected future contributions. True cooperation will be difficult to attain at present, given the reluctance of global powers such as China and the United States to commit to binding targets. These disputes will continue to pose a major hurdle to effective international law-making in the future.

1.5.4 International Humanitarian Law

International humanitarian law (also known as the laws of war or the law of armed conflict)[164] emerges chiefly from the concept that conflict, being an inexorable part of human nature, is inevitable, and hence efforts should be made to create reasonable guidelines of conduct and to mitigate harm.[165] Primarily derived from international conventions,[166] it regulates the conduct and obligations of belligerent nations, neutral nations and individuals engaged in war. It also provides for the status and treatment of protected persons such as civilians.[167]

Much of international humanitarian law has been codified in the four Geneva Conventions of 1949,[168] which operate subject to amendments in

---

164 Shaw, above note 4, 1167.

165 Jean Pictet, *Humanitarian Law and the Protection of War Victims* (Leyden: Sijthoff; Geneva: Henry Dunant Institute, 1975), 30.

166 It has been suggested that international customary law principles exist over and above conventional rules. See Shaw, above note 4, 1167; and Theodor Meron, 'Revival of Customary Humanitarian Law' (2005) 99 *American Journal of International Law* 817.

167 Some discussion of the history of IHL can be found above at section 1.3.1. A more detailed discussion can be found in Boas et al., above note 42, Chapter 4, section 4.1.2.

168 The four Geneva Conventions of 12 August 1949, which entered into force on 21 October 1950 are: (1) Geneva Convention for the Amelioration of the Condition of the Wounded and Sick in Armed Forces in the Field, 75 UNTS 31 ('Geneva Convention I'); (2) Geneva Convention for the Amelioration of the Condition of Wounded, Sick and Shipwrecked Members of Armed Forces at

a further three protocols.[169] Today, the Conventions have an essentially universal participation rate, with 194 parties.[170]

In determining the applicability of the Geneva Conventions to a conflict, much rides on the characterization of the conflict. Common Articles 2 and 3 stipulate that the Conventions operate in relation to declared war or armed conflicts between nations that have ratified the Conventions.[171] Situations lacking the character of an 'armed conflict' would fall outside the scope of the Conventions. Similarly, if the armed conflict lacks an 'international character',[172] the Conventions will not apply, save for a list of minimum rules of war contained in Article 3.

The Geneva Conventions are supplemented by an extensive body of customary international law, which together give rise to a series of important principles relating to the protection of persons not directly participating in an armed conflict. These principles include the distinction between combatants and non-combatants, the prohibition on indiscriminate attacks, the requirement for proportionality in attacks, the respect and protection to be afforded to prisoners of war, and the prohibition of torture, medical experimentation and neglect endangering health.[173]

1.5.5 International Human Rights Law

International human rights law rests upon the foundation of universalism and egalitarianism and can trace its history back to the natural law philosophies of Roman Law. Its premise is that all humans are 'born free

---

Sea, 75 UNTS 85 ('Geneva Convention II'); (3) Geneva Convention relative to the Treatment of Prisoners of War, 75 UNTS 135 ('Geneva Convention III'); (4) Geneva Convention relative to the Protection of Civilian Persons in Time of War, 75 UNTS 287 ('Geneva Convention IV').

[169] Protocol Relating to the Protection of Victims of International Armed Conflicts (adopted 8 June 1977, entered into force 7 December 1978) 1125 UNTS 3; Protocol relating to the Protection of Victims of Non-International Armed Conflict (adopted 8 June 1977, entered into force 7 December 1978) 1125 UNTS 609; Protocol relating to the Adoption of an Additional Distinctive Emblem, conclusion date 8 December 2005 (not yet in force).

[170] International Committee of the Red Cross, 'Geneva Conventions of 12 August 1949' (2005), available at http://www.icrc.org/ihl.nsf/WebSign?ReadForm&id=375&ps=P.

[171] Geneva Conventions, common Arts 2 and 3.

[172] For a discussion of the customary rules of IHL, see generally the customary law study of the International Committee of the Red Cross: Jean-Marie Henckaerts and Louise Doswald-Beck, *Customary International Humanitarian Law* (Cambridge: Cambridge University Press, 2005).

[173] Ibid.

and equal in dignity and rights',[174] and are entitled to the protection and promotion of such rights. The human rights movement was galvanized in the wake of the atrocities of the Second World War.

The modern law of international human rights was founded upon the Universal Declaration of Human Rights 1948 (UDHR).[175] In strict terms it is a weak legal instrument and was never intended to be binding. Nevertheless the UDHR formed the platform for the promotion of such principles as the prohibition against slavery,[176] non-discrimination[177] and the right to life,[178] which provided a basis for the development of other related treaties. Such treaties include the International Covenant on Civil and Political Rights,[179] the International Covenant on Social and Cultural Rights,[180] the Convention against Torture,[181] the UN Convention on the Rights of the Child,[182] the Convention on the Elimination of All Forms of Racial Discrimination[183] and the Genocide Convention.[184]

Regional human rights treaties have followed, similar in form and function to the UN multilateral treaties. The UN also possesses the means to encourage compliance with human rights treaties at a domestic level through the Human Rights Council.[185] Particular areas of international human rights law are undergoing rapid change. The concept of human rights is becoming an increasingly extraterritorial one, while the notion of state responsibility to prevent human rights abuses is gaining traction.[186]

---

174 Universal Declaration of Human Rights, GA Res. 217A (III), UN Doc. A/810 at 71, Art. 1 (hereinafter 'UDHR').

175 Ibid.

176 Ibid., Art. 4.

177 Ibid., Art. 2.

178 Ibid., Art. 3.

179 GA Res. 2200A (XXI) 21 UN GAOR Supp. (No. 16) at 52, UN Doc. A/6316 (1966), entered into force 23 March 1976.

180 International Covenant on Social and Cultural Rights (adopted 16 December 1966, entered into force 3 January 1976) 993 UNTS 3.

181 United Nations Convention against Torture and Other Cruel, Inhuman or Degrading Treatment or Punishment (adopted 10 December 1984, entered into force 26 June 1987)1465 UNTS 85.

182 Convention on the Rights of the Child (adopted 20 November 1989, entered into force 2 September 1990) 1577 UNTS 3.

183 International Convention on the Elimination of All Forms of Racial Discrimination (adopted 21 December 1965, entered into force 4 January 1969) 660 UNTS 195.

184 Convention on the Prevention and Punishment of the Crime of Genocide (adopted 9 December 1948, entered into force 12 January 1951) 78 UNTS 277.

185 General Assembly, Resolution on the Human Rights Council, GA Res. 60/251, UN GAOR, 6th sess., 72nd plen. mtg, UN Doc. A/RES/60/251 (2006).

186 Shaw, above note 4, 276.

Furthermore, human rights law is becoming increasingly merged with international humanitarian law.

While the precise nature and role of international human rights law is the subject of uncertainty,[187] it is clear that international human rights law presents a new and dynamic front for the influence of international law to effect change in human interactions; its role, function and impact on the place of the individual in international law will be considered often in this book.

1.5.6 International Criminal Law

At the core of international criminal law are the concepts that individuals can be responsible for international crimes, that aggression is illegal, and the acknowledgement that international law has a role to play regarding criminality and armed conflict. International criminal law primarily deals with war crimes, genocide, crimes against humanity and possibly crimes against peace. The purpose of individual responsibility in international criminal law is to capture all of the methods and means by which an individual may contribute to the commission of a crime, or be held responsible for a crime under international law.[188]

Generally speaking, international criminal law provides an enforcement mechanism for the obligations and prohibitions created by international humanitarian law. Enforcement is by way of penal sanctions and may be achieved through reliance on domestic or international mechanisms.

Until the end of the Second World War, the concept of international crime was not well developed. Piracy and slave trading were arguably the only recognized crimes against international society. Provided that the accused was apprehended on the high seas or within the territory of the prosecuting state, states had universal jurisdiction to prosecute individuals for these crimes, regardless of the nationality of the accused or where the alleged crimes were committed.

After the First World War, the Treaty of Versailles provided for the punishment of German individuals who had violated the laws and

---

[187] Ibid., 265.

[188] See Gideon Boas, James L. Bischoff and Natalie L. Reid, *Forms of Responsibility in International Criminal Law* (Cambridge: Cambridge University Press, 2007), Chapter 1; see examples of this expressed in case law: *Prosecutor v Muvunyi*, Case No. ICTR-00-55A-T, Judgment, 11 September 2006, [459]–[460]; *Prosecutor v Gacumbitsi*, Case No. ICTR-2001-64-T, Judgment, 14 June 2004, [267]; *Prosecutor v Delalić, Mucić, Delić and Landžo* (Judgment) IT-96-21-T (16 November 1998) [321], [331].

customs of war – although only a few trials were actually held and within Germany itself.[189] Provision was also made to try Kaiser Wilhelm II before an international tribunal for 'a supreme offence against international morality and the sanctity of treaties'.[190] The clause was, however, never executed given that the Kaiser fled to the Netherlands, which refused to extradite him. It was only following the atrocities of the Second World War that the moral imperative to create an international tribunal was recognized. The first real international criminal tribunal was the Nuremburg Tribunal, created to prosecute prominent members of the German Nazi leadership.[191] The tribunal reasoned that its criminal findings were merely expressions of pre-existing customary international law, although some commentators have questioned the legal basis of this position.

The Nuremburg Tribunal affirmed numerous principles of international criminal law, including the rejection of the defence of superior orders and the criminality of aggressive war.[192] It also laid the foundation for the establishment of numerous subsequent international criminal tribunals, and prompted calls for a permanent international criminal court. Most of the subsequent tribunals have been specifically established in response to particular conflicts. For example, the International Criminal Tribunal for the former Yugoslavia and the International Criminal Tribunal for Rwanda were both ad hoc tribunals created by the United Nations Security Council,[193] and were followed by a host of internationalized (or hybrid) tribunals dealing with specific conflicts – for example, in East Timor,

---

[189] Treaty of Peace between the Allied and Associated Powers and Germany, and Protocol [1920] ATS 1 ('Treaty of Versailles'), Art. 228; C. Mullins, *The Leipzig Trials* (London: H.F. & G. Witherby, 1921). For a discussion of the abortive post-First World War trials, see Boas et al., above note 42, Chapter 2, section 2.1.1; Timothy L.H. McCormack, 'From Sun Tzu to the Sixth Committee: The Evolution of an International Criminal Law Regime', in Timothy L.H. McCormack and Gerry J. Simpson (eds), *The Law of War Crimes: National and International Approaches* (The Hague and Boston, MA: Kluwer Law International, 1997).

[190] Treaty of Versailles, above note 189, Art. 227.

[191] Allied Resolution on German War Crimes, *Inter-Allied Revue*, 15 January 1942.

[192] Shaw, above note 4, 400.

[193] Established by UN Security Council, Resolution 827 (1993), adopted by the Security Council at its 3217th meeting on 25 May 1993, S/RES/827 (1993), available at http://www.unhcr.org/refworld/docid/3b00f21b1c.html; and UN Security Council, Security Council Resolution S/RES/955 (1994), 8 November 1994, S/RES/955 (1994), available at http://www.unhcr.org/refworld/docid/3b00f2742c.html.

Sierra Leone and Cambodia.[194] In 2002, the International Criminal Court (ICC) was created.[195] The ICC is set up as a permanent court to prosecute individuals for international crimes. As of October 2010 the ICC has 114 member states, with a further 34 signatory countries that have yet to ratify the treaty. Importantly, a number of major states, including the US, China and India are not signatories to the Rome Statute. The absence of these states poses a significant problem to the legitimacy of ICC jurisdiction.

1.6 WHAT IS INTERNATIONAL LAW?

International law is primarily conceived of as a system of law that regulates the conduct of, and between, states in the exercise of their external relations with other states. The development in the relations between states, globalized trade, rules relating to recourse to armed conflict, and the increasing role of non-state institutions in the development and indeed creation of international law, means that it is no longer possible to simply talk of the 'law of nations' as synonymous with international law.

Before examining in detail the core principles that embody contemporary public international law in the remainder of this book, there is a key question that must be addressed: what is international law? This is at once a crucial, and a meaningless, question. All of the theories discussed or referred to already in this chapter offer some conception or perspective of what is international law. Many scholars have addressed this question, most acknowledging that it is a highly perplexing and subjective one.[196] Nonetheless, a book about international law can hardly avoid such a discussion.

A preliminary aspect to this question is whether international law as such even exists. Scholars at various periods have questioned the existence

---

[194] For a discussion of international criminal law, its institutions and functioning, see generally Gideon Boas, James L. Bischoff, Natalie L. Reid and B. Don Taylor III, *International Criminal Procedure* (Cambridge: Cambridge University Press, 2011); Boas et al., above note 42; Boas et al., above note 188; Robert Cryer, Håkan Friman, Darryl Robinson and Elizabeth Wilmshurst, *An Introduction to International Criminal Law and Procedure* (Cambridge: Cambridge University Press, 2007); Antonio Cassese, *International Criminal Law* (Oxford: Oxford University Press, 2008, 2nd edn).

[195] Rome Statute of the International Criminal Court (adopted 17 July 1998, entered into force 1 July 2002) 2187 UNTS 90.

[196] See, generally, Shaw, above note 4, 43–68; Kelsen, above note 45, 321–33; Oscar Schachter, *International Law in Theory and Practice* (Dordrecht; London: Martinus Nijhoff Publishers, 1991), 1–16; Higgins, above note 48, 2–12.

of international law at all, postulating that what we call international law is really no more than a system of international relations, lacking core aspects of a legal system as such.

H.L.A. Hart, for example, had this to say:

> [T]he absence of an international legislature, courts with compulsory jurisdiction, and centrally organised sanctions have inspired misgivings, at any rate in the breast of legal theorists. The absence of these institutions means that the rules for states resemble that simple form of social structure, consisting only of primary rules of obligation, which, when we find it among societies of individuals, we are accustomed to contrast with a developed legal system. It is indeed arguable . . . that international law not only lacks the secondary rules of change and adjudication which provide for legislature and courts, but also a unifying rule of recognition specifying 'sources' of law and providing general criteria for the identification of its rules. These differences are indeed striking and the question 'Is international law really law?' can hardly be put aside.[197]

A more recent and dangerous challenge to the existence, or at least legitimacy, of international law comes from critical legal studies. Simplistically put, this conception of international law sees it as essentially contradictory, invariably imbued with the social and political such that it cannot resolve crucial questions posed of it.[198] This view of international law recalls the positivism of John Austin, whereby international law is ostensibly the dictate of states and subject to the paradigms of power and control[199] – a paradigm in which powerful states hold all the cards. Such a perspective precludes a normative system of rules that can be legally defined, determined and developed.[200] Gerry Simpson explains Austin's conception of international law as essentially anarchic:

> Debate about the compatibility of law and anarchy is a permanent feature of the intellectual landscape in international law and relations. The question: 'Is international law, law?' derives from an assumed mismatch between conditions of anarchy and the existence of law. John Austin famously questioned the existence of public international law on precisely these grounds. In the

---

[197] H.L.A. Hart, *The Concept of Law* (Oxford: Clarendon Press, 1961), 209. For a discussion of Hart's statement, see Triggs, above note 103, 3. See also, J.L. Brierly, *The Outlook for International Law* (Oxford: Clarendon Press, 1944), 13; Thomas M. Franck, 'Legitimacy in the International System' (1988) 82 *American Journal of International Law* 705, 706.

[198] See for example, Koskenniemi, above note 105.

[199] See also Brierly, above note 197.

[200] See the development of these issues in Franck, above note 197.

> absence of a single over-arching world sovereign how could there be law among sovereigns?[201]

Thomas Franck defends the system of international law, while acknowledging that its defenders have been less than convincing:

> Why study the teleology of law? What are laws *for?* What causes obedience? Such basic questions are the meat and potatoes of jurisprudential inquiry. Any legal system worth taking seriously must address such fundamentals. J. L. Brierly has speculated that jurisprudence, nowadays, regards international law as no more than 'an attorney's mantle artfully displayed on the shoulders of arbitrary power' and 'a decorous name for a convenience of the chancelleries.' That seductive epigram captures the still dominant Austinian positivists' widespread cynicism towards the claim that the rules of the international system can be studied jurisprudentially. International lawyers have not taken this sort of marginalization lying down. However, their counterattack has been both feeble and misdirected, concentrating primarily on efforts to prove that international law is very similar to the positive law applicable within states. This strategy has not been intellectually convincing, nor can it be empirically sustained once divine and naturalist sources of law are discarded in favor of positivism.[202]

It is tempting to sweep aside theoretical perambulations about the existence or otherwise of international law as anachronistic. A pragmatic response to the debate might be to point to the explosion of international institutions and courts that are more or less universally recognized as creating, determining and/or applying 'international law'. The point is implicit in Franck's rhetorical questions: 'Why should rules, unsupported by an effective structure of coercion comparable to a national police force, nevertheless elicit so much compliance, even against perceived self-interest, on the part of sovereign states?'[203] If it is not international law then it is something so profoundly reflecting law in practice – and so clearly accepted as such by its subjects – that the question itself appears now to be nothing more than an abstraction. At the risk of being dismissive, to now question the existence of international law as a legal – and not purely political and social – system is to challenge the obvious. A century ago, Nys put it passionately, if not a little melodramatically: 'Law even if broken, even if

---

[201] Gerry Simpson, *Great Powers and Outlaw States: Unequal Sovereigns in the International Legal Order* (Cambridge; New York: Cambridge University Press, 2004), 63.

[202] Franck, above note 197, 706. See generally, Anthony D'Amato, *International Law: Process and Prospect* (Dobbs Ferry, NY: Transnational, 1987).

[203] Franck, above note 200, 707.

crushed under foot, is none the less law'.[204] Indeed, the recent notorious practice of the United States in relation to its Guantanamo Bay detention facility has exemplified how law crushed under foot is still law, and how threatening essential aspects of the international law system can give rise to a set of reactions and counter-reactions that reinforce its intrinsic value and character.

Another strong argument in favour of the existence of international law comes from even a cursory examination of history.[205] As Korff noted:

> The fact that the fundamental principles of international law intercourse always were and are even in our day identical all over the world . . . justifies the theory that international law is a necessary consequence of any civilization.[206]

If this was true in 1924, surely the extraordinary development of international law norms and institutions since makes it even truer today.

To assert that international law exists does not, however, answer the question of what it is. Rosalyn Higgins' view of international law is that of a normative system, rather than simply a system of rules that must be identified and applied to the exclusion of the 'extralegal', notably social and political factors.[207] This pragmatic view of international law stands in contrast to the more traditional, positivist view that sees international law as the ascertainment of objective rules, free of the interference of these 'extralegal' factors.[208]

In her book, *Problems and Process*, Higgins enters into a kind of dialogue with Martii Koskenniemi, with whom she disagrees. She views the argument – that where international law does more than apply rules, it risks opening itself to criticism as biased and partial, and open to the control of the powerful states – as overly simplistic. In certain crucial respects, international law is the same as domestic law; the social purpose of law is to regulate the behaviour and conduct of people and institutions

---

204 Nys, above note 2, 3.

205 See discussion above at section 1.3.

206 Korff, above note 2, 248.

207 See the views of Judges Fitzmaurice and Spender in the *South West Africa* cases (*Ethiopia v South Africa; Liberia v South Africa*) (Preliminary Objections) [1962] ICJ Rep 319, 466 (joint Dissenting Opinion). These views have, according to Higgins, been revived and developed in the more recent work of Martti Koskenniemi: see *From Apology to Utopia*, above note 105; 'The Politics of International Law' (1990) 1 *European Journal of International Law* (cited in Higgins, above note 48, 9).

208 See discussion of legal positivism above in section 1.4.2.1.

within a community for the common good.[209] There is discretion involved in all aspects of international law (as in all law), and to ignore a moral aspect to its identification, determination and application is naive, unrealistic and unnecessary.[210] Higgins makes a further – and important – point: by refusing to acknowledge the political and social factors involved in determining international law, we risk hiding what is a natural and inevitable aspect of the process.[211]

There is a distinct attraction to Higgins' conception of international law – for a start, it is an answer to the reductive perspective that critical theory brings to international law. An additional point needs, however, to be made about Higgins' approach. International law as a normative system that can be legitimately developed in the decision-making of institutions, as well as courts and tribunals, requires not just an openness about external influences (political or social) on decision-makers. A further step in reasoning needs to be made. It also demands an openness (and honesty) about the limitation of those rendering decisions and developing this law. One of the great myths of judicial decision-making, for example, is that judges, because they are professionals, are unaffected by context or emotion and are dispassionately discovering and applying defined rules, even if they are aware of and acknowledge the political and other extralegal contexts in which such decisions are made. The fiction of this position exists in all systems of law but is no better exposed than in the context of international criminal tribunals. An honest discussion about the competence, capacity and even integrity of these decision-makers is long overdue. Once again, this theme will re-emerge at different points throughout this book.

One point of departure between Higgins and Koskenniemi relates to the extent to which international law is equipped to resolve contradictions. For Higgins, one can make a rational choice between conflicting or contradictory principles or perspectives by making determinations for the 'common good'.[212] Rules are just past decisions of organs and courts; if international law is simply about finding and applying the law (formalism) then it cannot, in Higgins' view, contribute to and cope with a changing political world. Judges, legal advisers and others are not simply finding the rule in relation to a particular issue – part of their role is to determine what

---

[209] Higgins, above note 48, 2. She notes that most law, including international law, has nothing to do with the settlement of disputes – which is a discrete aspect of all legal systems.

[210] Ibid., 7.

[211] Ibid., 48.

[212] Ibid., 9.

the rule is and, in doing so, be aware of political and social context.[213] To Koskenniemi, such determinations require a foray into extralegal social and political matters not properly the domain of law; they also require choices to be made about the assertion of certain rights over others – and how does one exercise this choice?[214] An adherence to formal rules, he argues, lends greater protection to the rule of law and is better placed to protect the 'weak' in international law: 'from the instrumentalist perspective, international law exists to realize objectives of some dominant part of the community; from the formalist perspective, it provides a platform to evaluate behaviour, including the behaviour of those in dominant positions'.[215]

Koskenniemi views formalism as creating an objective basis for the achievement of the ultimate aims of international law, even if (or perhaps because) they reflect inflexible rules that are more resistant to political power paradigms:

> [I]nternational law exists as a promise of justice. The agnosticism of political modernity has made the articulation of this teleological view extremely difficult. For the justice towards which international law points cannot be enumerated in substantive values, interests, or objectives. It has no predetermined institutional form. All such languages and suggestions express inadequate and reified images, (partial) points of view. Even when acceptable in their general formulation, as soon as such principles are translated into particular policies, and start to prefer some interests or values over others, they become vulnerable to the critique of 'false universalism'.

Even if '[a] court's decision or a lawyer's opinion is always a genuinely political act, a choice between alternatives not fully dictated by external criteria',[216] one response to such a concern is: so what? The creation and interpretation of all law is in part an expression of both the internal and external influences upon the people forming opinions and rendering decisions. Whether considered through the prism of formalism (adherence to rules) or normativism (adherence to values and objectives based, say, on the idea of legitimacy), somebody makes the rules and somebody interprets, applies, ignores and reformulates them. Such is the nature of all human interaction. Any international lawyer who suggests that his or her discipline is somehow immune from this is quite misdirected.

---

213 Ibid., 2–3.
214 Ibid., 9–10, referring to the works of Koskenniemi cited at above notes 105 and 207.
215 Koskenniemi, above note 62, 68–9.
216 Ibid., 72.

These are important issues and reflect deep divisions in the understanding of the international legal system and what it can achieve. Whatever the theoretical lens through which one views international law, it is essential always to ask how it is to be conceptualized and applied to real problems. Theoretical debate about what international law is and whether it should be interpreted strictly as a defined set of legal rules exclusive of political context, or as a process that engages the inevitable extralegal context that a decision-maker must account for, are important questions. Positivism, formalism, instrumentalism, realism and other theoretical conceptions will continue to influence the debate about what is international law. One is left, however, with the sense that modern international law operates very much as a normative system of rules that can be ascertained and applied by courts and other institutions within its political and social context. Even Koskenniemi acknowledges, when considering 'what is international law for', that notions of 'peace', 'security' and 'justice' are acceptable notions of the purpose of international law, even if only because 'of their ability to gloss over existing disagreement about political choices and distributional priorities'.[217] Higgins' international law is an international law 'harnessed to the achievement of common values'[218] – a universal, all-embracing system that transcends rules complied with or breached. It is flawed to be sure, but nonetheless it is a normative system capable of delivering such abstract notions as peace, security and justice. Of course, the temptation towards the interpretation of international law as instrumentalism, as a normative system, as a pragmatic response to the question of what is international law, carries with it a set of problems beyond the theoretical. In examining the core principles of international law, this book will reveal how fraught and complex can be the application of international law in a world of competing needs and interests.

---

[217] Ibid., 58.
[218] Higgins, above note 48, 1–2.

2. International law-making: the sources of international law

In a national legal system, the identification of legal rules and their sources is a more or less straightforward process. While legal systems may differ in the way their vertical systems of rule-making function and apply (for example, common law systems will show a greater reliance on common law precedent than civil law systems, which rely on greater codification and eschew the operation of a doctrine of binding precedent), there is always a clear hierarchy to the sources of law. This hierarchical structure also lends a degree of certainty, stability and predictability to the legal process, in which the roles of the different institutions involved make the ascertainment of rules easier.

This certainty, stability and predictability can be sharply contrasted to the international law system, which has no single legislature, no executive and a disparate network of *sui generis* courts and tribunals that apply international law specific to their differing jurisdictions. This aspect of international law has 'inspired misgivings, at any rate in the breast of legal theorists'[1] and renders crucial the task of articulating what the sources of international law are and how they operate to guide and bind its subjects.

This chapter concerns the source of obligation in international law – the critical element that renders international law more than a system of international relations between states and other subjects. After discussing consent, obligation, fragmentation and the potential for conflicting norms within international law, this chapter will turn to Article 38(1) of the Statute of the International Court of Justice ('ICJ Statute') – a material source of almost constitutional significance, in the sense that its articulation of the sources of international law are universally accepted and applied. The primary sources of international law will then be examined: international conventions, or treaties; customary international law (including *jus cogens* and obligations *erga omnes*) and general principles

[1] H.L.A. Hart, *The Concept of Law* (Oxford: Clarendon Press, 1961), 209, where he raises the question 'Is international law really law?' This aspect of international law, and Hart's view, is discussed in Chapter 1, section 1.6.

of international law, as will the subsidiary sources of judicial decisions and the opinions of highly regarded publicists. As with all chapters in this book, contemporary issues and case studies will be discussed as they arise and the chapter will consider whether other sources of international law exist, outside the paradigm of Article 38 and its traditional interpretation.

2.1 THE SOURCE OF OBLIGATION IN INTERNATIONAL LAW

2.1.1 Derivation of the Sources of International Law and the Question of Hierarchy

Article 38(1) of the ICJ Statute authoritatively states that the sources of international law are (1) treaties, or conventions; (2) customary international law, or the consistent practice of states undertaken in the belief that the conduct is permitted, required or prohibited by international law; (3) the general principles of law recognized by and typically derived from the domestic legal systems of states; and, (4) as a subsidiary source, commentaries in judicial decisions and academic writings of the 'most highly qualified publicists'.[2]

International lawyers draw a distinction between 'formal' and 'material' sources of law. Formal sources are those giving a particular norm its validity or authority – treaty, custom and general principles. Thus, the reason why the Nuclear Test Ban Treaty is legally binding is that it is a norm laid down through the process of treaty-making. The prohibition on the commission of crimes against humanity, and the rights and obligations relating to the prosecution by states of offenders, is as a result of the existence of a rule of customary international law on the issue. The reason why *lex specialis derogat legi generali* (special words prevail over general words) applies to help to interpret a treaty,[3] or why circumstantial evidence may be relied upon in international law,[4] is because these are accepted general principles of international law.

---

[2] Statute of the International Court of Justice, Art. 38(1).

[3] See, e.g., International Law Commission, 'Conclusions of the Work of the Study Group on the Fragmentation of International Law: Difficulties Arising from the Diversification and Expansion of International Law' (2006), Conclusion (5), available at http://untreaty.un.org/ilc/texts/instruments/english/draft%20articles/1_9_2006.pdf ('Fragmentation Report').

[4] See *Barcelona Traction, Light and Power Company Ltd* (*Belgium v Spain*) [1970] ICJ Rep 3, 39.

Material sources, on the other hand, reflect evidence that may be referred to in order to prove that a particular norm has a formal source. For example, the UN Charter is a material source that evidences the content of the important treaty law it represents. The practice of states and their belief about that practice (*opinio juris*) are material sources for the proposition that particular customary norms exist – indeed, they are critical elements that establish the existence of such a norm. A piece of evidence can be used as a material source without regard to whether the source is itself norm-creating. Hence, judicial decisions and the writings of publicists, as subsidiary sources of law, can be relied upon to help form an opinion about whether a rule exists.

It is sometimes said that there is no 'hierarchy' among the formal sources of international law, in the sense that neither treaty, nor custom, nor general principles take precedence over each other. This contributes to the perception of international law as a horizontal, anarchic system of law without a sovereign that makes laws to which all members of the community of states must abide. This proposition is only partially true, as some norms do in practice 'trump' others. Generally, treaties and custom are hierarchically equal, in that the subsequent conclusion of a treaty will displace an inconsistent pre-existing customary norm as between the contracting parties and the emergence of a later customary norm can modify a treaty (for example, parties to a treaty may over time behave as if some of the treaty provisions are not obligatory). However, as will be discussed in detail below,[5] certain customary norms – referred to as *jus cogens* norms – are non-derogable and states may not 'contract out' of them, even by concluding a subsequent treaty.

In practice, general principles – listed after treaty and custom in Article 38(1) – perform a gap-filling function where there is no customary or treaty law on the issue, or where a principle is required to decide which hierarchically equal norm should prevail in the event of a clash.[6] Thus, treaty and custom have been said to be hierarchically superior to general

---

5 See discussion below at section 2.2.2.7.

6 See discussion below at section 2.2.3. It has been suggested that the ICJ has at times (e.g., in the *Reparations* and *Reservations* cases) used general principles to modify a pre-existing customary law: Hersch Lauterpacht, 'Sources of International Law', in Elihu Lauterpacht (ed.), *International Law: Being the Collected Papers of Hersch Lauterpacht* (Cambridge: Cambridge University Press, 1975), Vol. 2, 51, 88. However, it is more accurate to say that no pre-existing custom existed on the point and the Court was laying down a principle, which became a general principle of law when states did not protest: see discussion below at section 2.2.4.1.

principles,[7] although it might also be said that the gap-filling and tie-breaking function of general principles only indicates that this formal source operates in a different way and in a different sphere from that of treaty and custom. The issue is confused further when it is recognized that some general principles, such as *pacta sunt servanda* (the principle that agreements must be kept),[8] are also customary law.

There have, at various times in the recent history of international law, been attempts to create or define 'higher' sources of international law: sources that somehow go beyond or modify the content of Article 38(1) of the ICJ Statute. For example, the International Law Commission's (ILC) 1996 Draft Articles on Responsibility of States for Intentionally Wrongful Acts attempted to establish a principle of 'international crimes of states':

> An internationally wrongful act which results from the breach by a State of an international obligation so essential for the protection of fundamental interests of the international community that its breach is recognized as a crime by that community as a whole constitutes an international crime.[9]

This concept proved too divisive, as many states disagreed that the notion of state criminality should be part of international law.[10] Endeavours to identify some higher order of international law norms – usually derived from an over-thinking of language employed by the International Court of Justice (ICJ)[11] – have also led to conjecture as to the existence of 'fundamental principles' or principles of international 'constitutional' law that sit somehow above the accepted sources of international law.[12] Such

---

[7] Antonio Cassese, *International Law* (Oxford: Oxford University Press, 2005, 2nd edn), 188.

[8] See discussion of this below at section 2.2.1.2.3.

[9] Draft Articles on Responsibility of States for Intentionally Wrongful Acts 1996, Art. 19(2).

[10] For the five elements James Crawford identifies as giving rise to a criminal regime, see James Crawford, *The International Law Commission's Articles on State Responsibility: Introduction, Text and Commentary* (Cambridge: Cambridge University Press, 2002) 18–19, 36.

[11] See, e.g., *Military and Paramilitary Activities in and against Nicaragua* (*Nicaragua v United States*) [1986] ICJ Rep 14, [181] (referring to the use of force); *Applicability of the Obligation to Arbitrate under Section 21 of the United Nations Headquarters Agreement of 28 June 1947* (Advisory Opinion) [1988] ICJ Rep 12, [57] (referring to the relationship between municipal and international law).

[12] See, e.g., M. Virally, 'The Sources of International Law', in M. Sørensen (ed.), *Manual of Public International Law* (London: Macmillan; New York: St Martin's Press, 1968) 144–5; Georg Schwarzenberger, *The Inductive Approach to International Law* (London: Stevens, 1965), 89.

endeavours to augment or alter the traditional sources of international law were dealt with by the International Law Commission as long ago as 1976:

> [I]t is only by erroneously equating the situation under international law with that under internal law that some lawyers have been able to see in the 'constitutional' or 'fundamental' principles of the international legal order an independent and higher 'source' of international obligations, in reality there is, in the international legal order, no special source of law for creating 'constitutional' or 'fundamental' principles. The principles which come to mind when using these terms are themselves customary rules, rules embodied in treaties, or even rules emanating from bodies or procedures which have themselves been established by treaties.[13]

The simple fact is that the primary sources of international law are clear and defined: they are treaty, custom, or general principles of international law. While the behaviour of some international courts and the opinion of some scholars suggests otherwise, a binding set of international rules must be rooted in one of these sources.

2.1.2 The Consensual Basis of International Law

In any national legal system, laws derive their validity from norms superior in the hierarchy. For example, the local road regulations may stipulate that drivers must carry a driver's licence at all times. The regulations, promulgated by the executive branch as delegated legislation, derive their validity from a principal Act of Parliament, authorizing the responsible Minister to make such regulations. The Act of Parliament draws its validity from the fact that the constitution of the state grants the parliament powers to legislate in respect of roads. The constitution itself derives its validity from a fundamental assumption, what Kelsen termed the *Grundnorm* (basic norm), that the constitution is supreme and valid.[14]

In international law, such a rigid and binding hierarchical structure does not exist. But it is overly simplistic to characterize national law as a vertical system that derives legitimacy from binding layers of hierarchical norms and international law as an anarchical, horizontal system of norms. There is a consensual element to both national and international legal systems and the validity of the sources of international law (treaties,

13 'Draft Articles on State Responsibility', in Report of the International Law Commission on the Work of its Twenty-Eighth Session, UN Doc. A/31/10 (1976), Commentary to Article 17, [21].

14 Hans Kelsen, *General Theory of Law and State* (New York: Russell & Russell, 1961).

custom, general principles) also depends on fundamental assumptions about its structure.

Lauterpacht described consent as the foundation for international law.[15] Treaty law is self-evidently consensual in character. While it is true that custom and general principles can apply to states that have not even tacitly agreed to those *particular* norms, the validity and binding nature of such norms is a product of the common will of the international community that such sources bear a binding quality. If such communal consent to the sources of international law vanished, the sources would themselves disappear, to be replaced by a differently constituted international order, depending on the substance of the new prevailing will of the international community.

2.1.3 The Obligatory Nature of International Law

Implicit in the concept of an 'international community' is that international law is universal. No state, not even a 'rogue' state, is outside the international system. New states are immediately bound by general customary law and succeed to treaties of their predecessors. The international community under international law is not only open to but also obligatory for all states.

This was not always the case. The major part of modern international law derives from Western European civilization from the sixteenth and seventeenth centuries onwards.[16] The early law of nations grew out of the customary and treaty dealings between Christian states, with the dawn of the concept of state sovereignty after the Peace of Westphalia.[17] Insofar as non-Christian states and peoples were concerned, it was accepted by European states that principles of morality should be applied.[18] It was not until the League of Nations system following the First World War that the idea of an international law which included the contribution of the 'main forms of civilisation and principal legal systems of the world' took definite shape.[19] The United Nations, membership of which covers nearly the entire community of states, has as its first principle 'the sovereign equal-

---

[15] Lauterpacht, above note 6, 92.

[16] Robert Jennings and Arthur Watts (eds), *Oppenheim's International Law* (Harlow, UK: Longman, 1992, 9th edn) 87.

[17] See Chapter 1, section 1.3.2.

[18] James Crawford, *The Creation of States in International Law* (Oxford: Oxford University Press, 2006, 2nd edn), 176–84.

[19] Statute of the Permanent Court of International Justice, Art. 9.

ity of all its Members'.[20] Membership is open to all states that accept the obligations in the UN Charter,[21] but non-Members cannot escape these obligations either: one of the principles of the UN Charter is to 'ensure that states which are not Members . . . act in accordance with [the Charter] so far as may be necessary for the maintenance of international peace and security'.[22] This demonstrates that the international system has trended ever closer to universality, not only of law but of certain core obligations. As the editors of the ninth edition of *Oppenheim's International Law* state:

> A fully universal organisation of the international community, membership of which is not only open to all states but also compulsory for them, without possibility of withdrawal or expulsion, and which involves comprehensive obligations prescribed in the organisation's constitution, unavoidably implies far-reaching derogations from the sovereignty of states. They have so far been unwilling to relinquish their sovereignty to that extent, but the trend to universality over the second half of the twentieth century has nevertheless been marked.[23]

2.1.4 Fragmentation: the Relevance of Normative Frameworks given the Proliferation of *sui generis* Areas of International Law

The International Law Commission, in its recent study on the fragmentation of international law, defined 'fragmentation' as 'the splitting up of the law into highly specialized "boxes" that claim relative autonomy from each other and from the general law'.[24] With the development of the international community after the Second World War, a number of specialized areas of international law developed, with their own tribunals and substantive law that increasingly diverged from each other. Human rights, international criminal law and international environmental law are examples of *sui generis* 'boxes' that emerged only recently – the former two having their own dispute resolution system: the UN Human Rights Committee, and international criminal courts and tribunals respectively.[25]

---

20 Charter of the United Nations, Art. 2(1).

21 Ibid., Art. 4.

22 Ibid., Art. 2(6).

23 Jennings and Watts, above note 16, 90.

24 Fragmentation Report, above note 3, [13].

25 The major international courts and tribunals are: the International Criminal Tribunal for the former Yugoslavia (ICTY), the International Criminal Tribunal for Rwanda (ICTR) (collectively, the ad hoc Tribunals), the International Criminal Court (ICC), the Special Court for Sierra Leone (SCSL), the Extraordinary Chambers in the Courts of Cambodia (ECCC) and the Special Tribunal for Lebanon (STL).

When added to the burgeoning of other strands of international law – such as the law of the sea with its International Tribunal for the Law of the Sea, and international trade law with the Appellate Body of the World Trade Organization (WTO) – a complex patchwork of different tribunals emerges, each applying the overarching principles of international law to its specific subject area without any centralized coordination.

The resulting divergence of parallel strands of international law prompted the ILC to study the effect of this process on international law. Was this process weakening the sources of, and in turn the respect for, international law? The thrust of this argument is that different international law decision-making bodies might be applying the rules of international law differently; applying similar but not identical rules or construing and applying the same or analogous rules in a manner different from that of other tribunals. The ILC ultimately concluded that, while there was a tension between a universal coherence of rules and the place of pluralism in international law, the emergence of special regimes has 'not seriously undermined legal security, predictability or the equality of legal subjects'.[26] The ILC felt that international law provides 'a basic professional tool-box that is able to respond in a flexible way to most substantive fragmentation problems'.[27] Nevertheless, greater efforts need to be made to articulate the general principles of international law and the techniques for dealing with conflicts of norms – the subject of our next section.[28]

2.2 ARTICLE 38(1) ICJ STATUTE

Article 38(1) of the ICJ Statute is generally recognized as expressing the definitive sources of international law:[29]

> The Court, whose function is to decide in accordance with international law such disputes as are submitted to it, shall apply:
> a. international conventions, whether general or particular, establishing rules expressly recognised by the contesting states;
> b. international custom, as evidence of a general practice accepted as law;
> c. the general principles of law recognised by civilised nations;

---

[26] Fragmentation Report, above note 3, [492].

[27] Ibid.

[28] Ibid., [493] and Appendix.

[29] See, e.g., Georg Schwarzenberger, *International Law* (London: Stevens, 1957, 3rd edn) 26–7; G.M. Danilenko, *Law-Making in the International Community* (Dordrecht; London: M. Nijhoff Publishers, 1993), 30–36.

d. subject to the provisions of Article 59, judicial decisions and the teachings of the most highly qualified publicists of the various nations, as subsidiary means for the determination of rules of law.

This formulation succeeded a nearly identical provision in Article 38 of the Statute of the Permanent Court of International Justice,[30] which was modelled in 1920 by the Advisory Committee of Jurists on general understandings about the sources of international law. Of course, Article 38 is not itself the formal source of the rule it contains, but is merely a convenient material source that is in practice the starting point for any analysis of the sources of international law.[31] Nonetheless, it is now beyond question that its contents describe the sources of international law.

2.2.1 International Conventions: the Law of Treaties

2.2.1.1 The Vienna Convention on the Law of Treaties and its customary status

The Vienna Convention on the Law of Treaties 1969 ('Vienna Convention') is one of the most successful treaties ever concluded.[32] Although currently it has only 111 States Parties, the great majority of its provisions are accepted as reflecting customary international law.[33] Many of its provisions represented progressive developments at the time the Convention was signed, and these subsequently crystallized.[34] The success of the Vienna Convention is probably attributable to the fact that most of its provisions are not politically divisive, as they reflect commonly understood and largely universal notions of domestic contract law. Indeed, the ICJ has never held that a particular provision of the Vienna Convention does not reflect customary law.[35] Examples of important provisions held

---

[30] The only difference between the formulations is the inclusion of the words 'whose function is to decide in accordance with international law such disputes as are submitted to it'.

[31] See, e.g., Dissenting Opinion of Judge Tanaka in *South West Africa* cases (Second Phase) [1966] ICJ Rep 250, 300.

[32] D.J. Harris, *Cases and Materials on International Law* (London: Sweet & Maxwell, 2004, 6th edn), 786–7.

[33] See, e.g., *Gobčikovo-Nagymaros Project* (*Hungary v Slovakia*) [1997] ICJ Rep 7, [46]; *Kasikili/Sedudu Island* case (*Botswana v Namibia*) [1999] ICJ Rep 1045, [18]; *Fisheries Jurisdiction* case (*United Kingdom v Iceland*) [1973] ICJ Rep 3, [36]. See also Gillian Triggs, *International Law: Contemporary Principles and Practices* (Sydney: LexisNexis Butterworths, 2011, 2nd edn), 89.

[34] Jennings and Watts, above note 16, 1199.

[35] Triggs, above note 33, 90.

by the ICJ as constituting customary law include those relating to the rules of interpretation[36] and the articles on termination and suspension.[37] Even those provisions that reflect a choice made by the Vienna Convention between competing views of the time, such as those on reservations and breach, can be said to have attained general acceptance as rules of customary international law.[38]

The Vienna Convention was negotiated during the UN Conference on the Law of Treaties at Vienna in 1968–69. It was opened for signature on 23 April 1969 and entered into force on 27 January 1980. Its scope is limited to treaties between states,[39] in written form,[40] concluded after the Vienna Convention entered into force,[41] and it expressly disclaims application to state succession, state responsibility and the effect of hostilities on treaties.[42] Its provisions on interpretation have, however, often been applied analogously; for example the ad hoc Tribunals have referred to the Vienna Convention as applying to the interpretation of their statutes.[43]

Two subsequent treaties – the Vienna Convention on Succession of States in respect of Treaties 1978 and the Vienna Convention between States and International Organizations 1986 – were concluded to cover some of the few areas not dealt with in the 1969 Vienna Convention but it is only the 1969 Convention that will be discussed in this chapter, as it contains the general rules on the law of treaties. The other Conventions have implications for international personality, discussed in Chapters 4 and 5.

2.2.1.2 Formation

2.2.1.2.1 Intention to create international legal relations The existence of a treaty does not depend on nomenclature. This reflects the fact that

---

[36] *Kasikili/Sedudu Island* case, above note 33, [18].

[37] *Gobčikovo-Nagymaros Project* (*Hungary v Slovakia*), above note 33, [46].

[38] Harris, above note 32, 787.

[39] Vienna Convention on the Law of Treaties 1969, Art. 1. Note that the Vienna Convention applies to treaty relations between states notwithstanding that a non-state may also be party to the same convention: see Art. 3(c).

[40] Ibid., Art. 2(1)(a).

[41] Ibid., Art. 4.

[42] Ibid., Art. 73. See also Art. 3: the Vienna Convention does not affect the legal validity or application of any rule of law not covered by it. It does not purport to cover the whole field of the law of treaties.

[43] See, e.g., *Prosecutor v Milošević*, (*Amici curiae* Motion for Judgment of Acquittal Pursuant to Rule 98bis) IT–02–54–T (3 March 2004), Separate Opinion of Judge Patrick Robinson, [4].

international agreements have been given various titles – such as convention, protocol and agreement – without anything of substance turning on the use of any particular designation.[44] Article 2(1)(a) of the Vienna Convention defines a 'treaty' as 'an international agreement concluded between states in written form and governed by international law, whether embodied in a single instrument or in two or more related instruments and whatever its designation'.

The requirement that a treaty concluded by states be 'governed by international law' is central to the concept of treaty formation. The parties must have an intention to create international legal relations.[45] Such mutual assent, or intention, is ascertained objectively – a party cannot disclaim the assumption of an obligation if the other party was entitled to understand it as such in all the circumstances of the case.[46] There is no requirement that a party should provide consideration. Every state has the capacity to conclude treaties.[47]

These concepts, which codified customary international law, are illustrated in the 1933 case *Legal Status of Eastern Greenland* before the Permanent Court of International Justice (PCIJ).[48] The Court had to decide (1) whether Denmark had title to the territory of Eastern Greenland by occupation,[49] or (2) whether Norway had entered into a treaty with Denmark by the so-called 'Ihlen Declaration'. In a minuted conversation on 14 July 1919, the Danish Minister proposed to the Norwegian Foreign Minister, M. Ihlen, that if Norway did not oppose Denmark's claim to Eastern Greenland at the Paris Peace Conference, then Denmark would not object to Norway's claims on Spitzbergen. In a subsequent conversation, Ihlen declared that the Norwegian government 'would not make any difficulty' in respect of Denmark's claim. According to the PCIJ, the circumstances indicated that the two states had created a bilateral treaty whereby Norway agreed not to occupy or otherwise assert sovereignty over Eastern Greenland:

---

44 *South West Africa* cases (*Ethiopia v South Africa; Liberia v South Africa)* (Preliminary Objections) [1962] ICJ Rep 319, 331.

45 International Law Commission, Commentary (Treaties), Art. 2(6): (1966) *Yearbook of the International Law Commission*, II, 189; Fourth Report on the Law of Treaties (1965) *Yearbook of the International Law Commission*, II, 12.

46 See, e.g., *Legal Status of Eastern Greenland* (*Denmark v Norway*) (1933) PCIJ Rep (Ser. A/B) No. 53, 69. The extent to which other actors, such as international organizations, possess this capacity is discussed in Chapter 5.

47 Vienna Convention on the Law of Treaties 1969, Art. 6.

48 *Legal Status of Eastern Greenland*, above note 46.

49 See Chapter 4.

> The Court considers it beyond all dispute that a reply of this nature given by the Minister of Foreign Affairs on behalf of his Government in response to a request by the diplomatic representative of a foreign Power, in regard to a question falling within his province, is binding upon the country to which the Minister belongs.[50]

This case illustrates the centrality of the requirement of intention to create international legal relations, and shows that the courts will look to the substance rather than the form of any particular agreement.

2.2.1.2.2 Consent to be bound Under Article 11 of the Vienna Convention, 'the consent of a State to be bound by a treaty may be expressed by signature, exchange of instruments constituting a treaty, ratification, acceptance, approval or accession, or by any other means if so agreed'. This reflects the fact that treaties may be concluded in 'solemn form' or in 'simplified form'.

Many of the more important treaties have traditionally been concluded in 'solemn form', by which it is meant that at an international conference, after negotiation, the final text of the treaty is settled, or 'adopted' by the representatives (plenipotentiaries) of each state. Article 9 requires the treaty to be adopted unanimously or by consent of a two-thirds majority, unless otherwise specified within the treaty itself;[51] in some cases, the treaty must be adopted by all states.[52] The treaty is then authenticated – most commonly by signature.[53] Authentication requires the plenipotentiaries to produce appropriate 'full powers' – that is, a formal document emanating from the repository of the treaty-making power of the state authorizing the plenipotentiary to adopt and authenticate the treaty.[54]

By signing the treaty, the plenipotentiaries are not yet expressing the state's consent to be bound. In treaties concluded in 'solemn form', ratification is the means by which such consent is intended to be manifested. Ratification occurs after the plenipotentiaries have delivered a copy of the treaty to the repository of the treaty-making power of the state (for example, the minister for foreign affairs), who then ratifies the treaty and either notifies the other states or deposits the treaty with a depositary (a state or international organization tasked with record-keeping and admin-

---

[50] *Legal Status of Eastern Greenland*, above note 46.

[51] Vienna Convention on the Law of Treaties 1969, Art. 9(2).

[52] Ibid., Art. 9(1). If the treaty is drawn up within an international organization, the voting rule of the organization will apply: see Art. 5.

[53] Ibid., Art. 10.

[54] Ibid., Arts 2(1)(c), 7(1).

istration in respect of the treaty).[55] A state is not obliged to ratify a treaty. However, after signature, but before ratification or refusal of ratification, a state must not act to defeat the object or purpose of the treaty.[56] This obligation also applies after ratification, but before entry into force of the treaty, unless entry into force is 'unduly delayed'.[57] Partial or conditional ratifications (except to the extent that a state has made a lawful reservation) are counter-offers that require the assent of other states before they may be binding.[58]

For treaties in 'simplified form', an act other than ratification is intended by the parties to evidence their intention to be bound.[59] Also, the formal requirements of adoption, authentication, signature and ratification can be dispensed with. The *Legal Status of Eastern Greenland* case illustrates this, as consent to be bound was inferred from the circumstances to consist in the oral statement of Minister Ihlen that the Norwegian government would 'make no difficulty' over Denmark's claim to Eastern Greenland.[60] In practice it may be convenient for parties to conclude agreements, usually over more technical or trivial matters, by exchange of notes with signatures appended. It may be advantageous in some cases to avoid the constitutional requirements associated with ratification. For instance, the US Constitution requires the consent of a two-thirds majority of the Senate for ratification of a treaty;[61] the President has, however, an implied power to conclude 'executive agreements', which may equally express the state's consent to be bound.[62]

A person will only express a state's consent to be bound if that person has 'full powers' – otherwise the treaty is without legal effect unless subsequently confirmed by the state.[63] If, however, a state has placed a restriction on a plenipotentiary's otherwise full power to express the state's consent to be bound, the non-observance of the restriction will not render the treaty void, unless the state had notified the other States Parties of the restriction beforehand.[64] A treaty does not become voidable because it was made in breach of the state's domestic law relating to competence to

---

55 Ibid., Art. 16.
56 Ibid., Art. 18(a).
57 Ibid., Art. 18(b).
58 Jennings and Watts, above note 16, 1232–3.
59 Vienna Convention on the Law of Treaties 1969, Art. 11.
60 See *Legal Status of Eastern Greenland*, above note 46 and accompanying text.
61 United States Constitution, Art. 1, section 2, clause 2.
62 Jennings and Watts, above note 16, 2387.
63 Vienna Convention on the Law of Treaties 1969, Art. 8.
64 Ibid., Art. 47.

conclude treaties, unless the violation was 'manifest' and involved breach of a provision of 'fundamental importance'.[65] These provisions strike a balance between the principle that a state should not be bound by the acts of a renegade representative, and the principle that other states should be entitled to assume that the state's house is in order. As the state with the renegade representative is the party best placed to prevent the breach, the balance is struck in favour of other states contracting with it. As ratification is performed by the repository of the treaty-making power of the state, in practice these issues will only become relevant when consent to be bound is expressed by another act, such as by signature.[66]

A state that did not take part in the negotiating process can express its consent to be bound by a treaty through a formal process known as 'accession'.[67] For a state to join the treaty in this way, the treaty must so provide, or the parties must have so agreed.[68]

2.2.1.2.3 Pacta sunt servanda *and entry into force* The binding force of treaties is sourced in the principle of *pacta sunt servanda* (agreements must be kept). A customary norm that is by its very nature non-derogable, *pacta sunt servanda* is a *jus cogens* norm.[69] The Vienna Convention formulates the principle as follows: 'Every treaty in force is binding upon the parties to it and must be performed by them in good faith.'[70]

Thus, treaties become binding from the date on which they enter into force. If a treaty deals with matters to be performed before its entry into force, such as matters dealing with the permissibility of reservations,[71] then those provisions apply as from adoption of the text.[72] Treaties almost invariably specify the date on which they enter into force, usually after achieving a certain number of ratifications. Failing such specification, ratification (or other expression of consent to be bound) of all states is required for entry into force.[73] If a state expresses its consent to be bound

---

[65] Ibid., Art. 46(1). The requirement that the breach be 'manifest' requires that it be objectively evident to a state conducting itself in the matter in accordance with normal practice and in good faith: see Art. 46(2).

[66] Jennings and Watts, above note 16, 1222.

[67] Vienna Convention on the Law of Treaties 1969, Art. 15.

[68] Ibid.

[69] See Hans Wehberg, '*Pacta sunt servanda*' (1959) 53 *American Journal of International Law* 775; M. Janis, 'The Nature of *Jus Cogens*' (1988) 3 *Connecticut Journal of International Law* 359, 361.

[70] Vienna Convention on the Law of Treaties 1969, Art. 26.

[71] For a discussion of reservations to treaties, see section 2.2.1.4 below.

[72] Vienna Convention on the Law of Treaties 1969, Art. 24(4).

[73] Ibid., Art. 24(2).

after the treaty has entered into force, the treaty comes into force for that state on that day.[74]

2.2.1.2.4 Objects of treaties – jus cogens *and third states* States are generally free to select the objects, or subject-matter, of their treaty. However, any treaty concluded in breach of a *jus cogens* norm is void.[75] The general rule is also restricted by the principle, grounded in the sovereign equality of states[76] and arguably the flipside to *pacta sunt servanda*, that a treaty cannot create obligations or rights for non-states (called 'third states') without their consent: *pacta tertiis nec nocent nec prosunt*. A third state can assume an obligation under a treaty if it expressly accepts the obligation in writing[77] and it is presumed to assent to a right under a treaty unless and until it indicates a contrary intention.[78] No right or obligation will arise for a third state unless the parties to the treaty intended it to have this effect.[79] The consent of all the parties and the third state is required to revoke or modify an obligation that the third state has accepted, while the parties can unilaterally revoke a third state's right under the treaty unless the right was intended to be irrevocable.[80] Despite the provisions of the Vienna Convention, however, obligations and rights are imposed on third states against their will in exceptional cases. For instance, as a result of the importance and international personality of the UN, the provisions of the UN Charter, such as Article 33, are recognized as applicable to third states:

> The parties to any dispute, the continuation of which is likely to endanger the maintenance of international peace and security, shall, first of all, seek a solution by negotiation . . . or other peaceful means of their own choice.[81]

Other treaties that do not require the consent of third states include treaties creating new states, territories or international organizations,[82] or treaties imposing conditions on a defeated aggressor state.

---

74 Ibid., Art. 24(3).
75 Ibid., Art. 53.
76 Commentary (Treaties), Art, 30(1): (1966) *Yearbook of the International Law Commission*, II, 253–4.
77 Vienna Convention on the Law of Treaties 1969, Art. 35.
78 Ibid., Art. 36(1).
79 Ibid., Arts 35, 36.
80 Ibid., Art. 37.
81 See also Charter of the United Nations, Art. 2(6).
82 See Chapter 5.

2.2.1.3 Amendment and modification

The rules concerning the amendment and modification of treaties are also grounded in the principles of *pacta sunt servanda* and *pacta tertiis nec nocent nec prosunt*. 'Amendment' refers to a formal process of introducing changes to a treaty whereby every member is entitled to become a party to the treaty as amended.[83] 'Modification' is more informal and often does not involve all parties.[84] The legal treatment of both procedures is substantially the same. 'Revision' is the process whereby a new diplomatic conference comprehensively revises a treaty.[85]

Parties may amend or modify a treaty by agreement.[86] Where a multilateral treaty is amended by some states but not others, the amendments will not bind the non-consenting states.[87] Similarly, if states later accede to the treaty, the original version will govern the acceding state's relations with those parties that did not participate in the amendment.[88] A treaty modification must not affect the rights and obligations of other parties to the treaty or be incompatible with its object and purpose.[89]

A later treaty is taken to impliedly terminate or modify an earlier treaty to the extent of any inconsistency, but only insofar as parties to the later treaty are identical to the earlier one.[90] Where only some parties to an earlier treaty attempt to contract out of that treaty, they can only do so as between themselves.[91] The rights and obligations of states that are only party to the earlier treaty are not affected.[92]

Article 103 of the UN Charter states:

> In the event of a conflict between the obligations of the Members of the United Nations under the present Charter and their obligations under any other international agreement, their obligations under the present Charter shall prevail.

This provision is widely accepted as creating a hierarchy between treaties, although it is not settled whether an inconsistent provision of a

---

[83] Vienna Convention on the Law of Treaties 1969 Art. 40(3).
[84] Ibid., Art. 41.
[85] Malgosia Fitzmaurice, 'The Practical Working of the Law of Treaties', in Malcolm D. Evans (ed.), *International Law* (Oxford: Oxford University Press, 2006, 2nd edn) 187, 195.
[86] Vienna Convention on the Law of Treaties 1969, Arts 39 and 41(1).
[87] Ibid., Art. 40(4).
[88] Ibid., Art. 40(5).
[89] Ibid., Art. 41(1)(b).
[90] Ibid., Art. 30(3).
[91] Ibid., Art. 30(4).
[92] Ibid., Art. 30(4)(b).

treaty would be rendered void or merely unenforceable.[93] The Vienna Convention expressly states that it is subject to Article 103 of the Charter.[94]

2.2.1.4 Reservations

The more parties there are to a treaty, the more likely that some of them would seek to join the treaty only on condition that certain provisions are inapplicable to them or carry a certain interpretation. The Vienna Convention defines a reservation as:

> a unilateral statement, however phrased or named, made by a State, when signing, ratifying, accepting, approving or acceding to a treaty, whereby it purports to exclude or to modify the legal effect of certain provisions of the treaty in their application to that State.[95]

In the past, the rule was that every party's assent was required for a reservation to be effective. By their nature, reservations would be counter-offers if made to bilateral treaties. But the inflexibility of the rule, if applied to multilateral treaties, caused the ICJ to take a different approach in its Advisory Opinion in the *Reservations* case.[96] Upon certain reservations expressed by Soviet bloc countries to the jurisdiction of the ICJ in relation to the Genocide Convention, and other provisions such as immunity from prosecution, the UN General Assembly asked the ICJ to advise what the effect of reservations was when other states have objected to them. Although the Court was specifically dealing with the Genocide Convention, its views were of general purport. They were incorporated into the Vienna Convention and represent customary law today.[97]

Acceptance by a party of a reservation made by another party modifies the treaty as between them.[98] Objection by another party to a reservation does not prevent the treaty from entering into force as between the objecting and reserving states, unless the objecting state clearly indicates otherwise.[99] It merely renders the treaty inapplicable between the objecting and reserving states to the extent of the reservation.[100] A state is considered to

---

93 Jennings and Watts, above note 16, 1216.

94 Vienna Convention on the Law of Treaties 1969, Art. 30(1).

95 Ibid., Art. 2(1)(d).

96 *Reservations to the Convention on the Prevention and Punishment of the Crime of Genocide* (Advisory Opinion) [1951] ICJ Rep 15; see Jennings and Watts, above note 16, 1244–5.

97 See, e.g., *Temeltasch v Switzerland* (1983) 5 EHRR 417, 432.

98 Vienna Convention on the Law of Treaties 1969, Art. 20(4)(a), 21(1).

99 Ibid., Art. 20(4)(b).

100 Ibid., Art. 21(3).

have accepted the reservation if it has not objected within twelve months of being notified of the reservation, or from when it expressed its consent to be bound by the treaty, whichever occurred later.[101] This system allows as many states as possible to become party to a treaty the core principles of which are substantially agreed.[102] Reservations and objections to reservations may be withdrawn unilaterally by notice.[103]

A state's declaration that seeks to impute a particular interpretation to a provision may or may not be intended to make the state's acceptance of the provision conditional on the acceptance of its interpretation. Only if an interpretative declaration is intended to have this effect will it amount to a reservation.[104]

Reservations may not be made if the treaty expressly excludes them, or if they are incompatible with its object and purpose.[105] What constitutes an impermissible reservation contrary to the object and purpose of a treaty has become the subject of considerable disagreement in the context of human rights treaties. The UN Human Rights Committee has stated that human rights treaties 'are not a web of inter-State exchanges of mutual obligations. . . . They concern the endowment of individuals with rights'.[106] The Committee has complained that, in practice, states have often not seen any advantage to themselves of objecting to reservations that only affect the rights of citizens of other states.[107] Furthermore, the Committee has stated that, as human rights treaties are for the benefit of citizens within the jurisdiction of States Parties, provisions that codify customary international law may not be the subject of reservations.[108] More controversial was the following statement by the Committee:

> The normal consequence of an unacceptable reservation is not that the Covenant will not be in effect at all for a reserving party. Rather, such a reserva-

---

101 Ibid., Art. 20(5).

102 *Reservations to the Convention on the Prevention and Punishment of the Crime of Genocide* (Advisory Opinion) [1951] ICJ Rep 15, 24.

103 Vienna Convention on the Law of Treaties 1969 Art. 22.

104 Donald McRae, 'The Legal Effect of Interpretive Declarations' (1978) 49 *British Year Book of International Law* 155, 72–3.

105 Vienna Convention on the Law of Treaties 1969 Art. 19.

106 United Nations Human Rights Committee, 'General Comment 24 on Reservations to the International Covenant on Civil and Political Rights' (1995) 15 HRLJ 464; 2 IHRR10 ('General Comment 24'), [17].

107 Ibid., [17].

108 Ibid, [8].

> tion will generally be severable, in the sense that the Covenant will be operative for the reserving party without the benefit of the reservation.[109]

The Committee's attempt to establish the different application of the law of treaties in relation to human rights sparked strong objections from several states,[110] leading the ILC to subsequently affirm that a human rights object will not affect the application of the Vienna Convention regime.[111]

A reservation to a provision that expresses a *jus cogens* norm is inadmissible under customary international law. For example, in the *North Sea Continental Shelf* cases,[112] the ICJ considered whether Article 6 of the Geneva Convention on the Continental Shelf had crystallized as a rule of customary law. One issue was the significance of the faculty of making reservations. Three of the judges saw fit to state that *jus cogens* rules codified in a treaty could not be the subject of reservations.[113] Indeed, the UN Human Rights Committee pointed out the incongruity in a state reserving the right, for instance, to engage in slavery.[114]

2.2.1.5 Interpretation

Traditionally, there have been three schools of treaty interpretation: (1) the textual school, which looked to the 'ordinary' meaning of the text; (2) the intentionalist school, which attempted to ascertain the intention of the drafters; and (3) the teleological school, which preferred an interpretation that best fulfilled the object and purpose of the treaty. Article 31(1) of the Vienna Convention incorporates elements of all three schools in stating the general rule: 'A treaty shall be interpreted in good faith in accordance with the ordinary meaning to be given to the terms of the treaty in their context and in light of its object and purpose.'[115]

---

[109] Ibid, [18].

[110] 'Observations on General Comment 24 by France' (1997) 4 IHRR 6; 'Observations on General Comment 24 by the United Kingdom' (1996) 3 IHRR 261; 'Observations on General Comment 24 by the United States' (1996) 3 IHRR 265.

[111] 'Report of the International Law Commission on its Forty-Ninth Session', UN Doc. A/52/10 (1997) 126–7.

[112] *North Sea Continental Shelf* cases (*Federal Republic of Germany v Denmark and the Netherlands*) [1969] ICJ Rep 3. For a discussion of the facts and relevance of this seminal case on the formation of custom, see below sections 2.2.2.2 and 2.2.2.3.

[113] Ibid., 97 (Separate Opinion of Judge Padilla Nervo), 182 (Dissenting Opinion of Judge Tanaka), 248 (Dissenting Opinion of Judge Sørensen).

[114] General Comment 24, above note 106, [8].

[115] Article 31(1) has attained the status of customary law: see *Kasikili/Sedudu Island* case, above note 33, [18].

For these purposes, the 'context' includes the text of the treaty and any instrument made by the parties relevant to its conclusion.[116] Although the Vienna Convention does not presuppose a hierarchy as between the interpretive tools, the ICJ has emphasized that the textual interpretation is central. In the *Territorial Dispute* case, the Court stated that interpretation 'must be based above all upon the text of a treaty'.[117] The Vienna Convention does not countenance the stretching of the wording beyond breaking point to satisfy, for example, a perceived need to bring the provision in line with the treaty's object and purpose. Indeed, what the object and purpose of a treaty requires can be notoriously slippery and thus an unreliable tool of interpretation.[118] Any subsequent agreement about the interpretation of a treaty – for instance, as part of the acceptance by States Parties of an interpretative declaration that amounts to a reservation – must be taken into account.[119]

As a 'supplementary' means of interpretation, regard may be had to the preparatory work (*travaux préparatoires*) of the treaty.[120] At first blush, this seems to relegate the full-blooded intentionalist approach to a minor role, but the *travaux préparatoires* of the Vienna Convention itself, coupled with the jurisprudence of international tribunals, suggest that the word 'supplementary' should not be viewed as a significant obstacle.[121] Indeed, the Vienna Convention itself allows recourse to a treaty's *travaux* even if it is to 'confirm' the meaning arrived at via Article 31.[122]

In addition to the rules set out in the Vienna Convention, treaties are to be interpreted in accordance with various well-established maxims of interpretation. The principle of effectiveness, *ut res magnis valeat quam pereat*, is derived from the teleological approach.[123] In case of ambiguity, an interpretation should be preferred that enables the treaty to have appropriate effect, as the parties are presumed not to create an ineffective instrument. Similarly, the rule against surplusage stipulates that an inter-

---

[116] Vienna Convention on the Law of Treaties 1969, Art. 31(2).

[117] *Territorial Dispute* (*Libya v Chad*) [1994] ICJ Rep 6, [41].

[118] Fitzmaurice, above note 85, 202.

[119] Vienna Convention on the Law of Treaties 1969, Art. 31(3).

[120] Ibid., Art. 32.

[121] Herbert W. Briggs, 'The *Travaux Préparatoires* of the Vienna Convention on the Law of Treaties' (1971) 65 *American Journal of International Law* 705, 708, 712.

[122] Vienna Convention on the Law of Treaties 1969, Art. 32.

[123] International Law Commission, (1966) *Yearbook of the International Law Commission*, II, 219; Hugh Thirlway, 'The Law and Procedure of the International Court of Justice, 1960–1989: Part Three' (1992) 63 *British Year Book of International Law* 1.

pretation giving effect to every provision in the treaty is to be preferred.[124] As limitations on sovereignty are not to be presumed,[125] the meaning that is less onerous to the party assuming an obligation is to be preferred.[126] This is the principle of *in dubio mitius*. Furthermore, exceptions or provisos to principal provisions are interpreted strictly.[127] An ambiguous provision should be interpreted against the party who drafted the provision.[128] Another important maxim is *lex specialis derogat legi generali* – specific words prevail over general words to the extent of any inconsistency. Finally, a treaty is to be interpreted in the light of general rules of international law at the time it was concluded, unless a concept in the treaty is intended to be evolutionary – this is the 'rule of the inter-temporal law'.[129] Other maxims commonly used in the legal systems of the world may also be applied – for example, grammatical rules such as *ejusdem generis* (general words following special words are limited to the same type as the special words).[130]

If a treaty is authenticated in more than one language, the text is equally authoritative in each language and it is presumed to have the same meaning in each.[131]

2.2.1.6 Invalidity

Invalidity will be dealt with separately from termination and suspension because of their differing nature and legal effects. Invalidity may be either *relative* or *absolute*.

Relative invalidity makes the treaty voidable: after becoming aware of the facts, the state whose consent has been affected may elect to consider the treaty invalid, either expressly or by conduct.[132] The first two grounds of invalidity have been discussed above: where the representative expresses the state's consent to be bound in manifest breach of a provision of the state's internal law on entering into treaties of fundamental

---

124 Fitzmaurice, above note 85, 202.

125 *SS 'Lotus'* (*France v Turkey*) (1927) PCIJ (Ser. A) No. 10, 18–19.

126 *Nuclear Tests* cases (*Australia and New Zealand v France*) [1974] ICJ Rep 253, 267.

127 Case No. 7/68 *Commission of the European Communities v Italy* [1968] ECR 423. Note that where there is a clash between *in dubio mitius* and the principle that exceptions should be construed strictly, the latter takes precedence: see Jennings and Watts, above note 16, 1279.

128 *Brazilian Loans* case (1929) PCIJ (Ser. A) Nos 20–21, 114.

129 *Namibia (Legal Consequences) Advisory Opinion* [1971] ICJ Rep 31.

130 Jennings and Watts, above note 16, 1280.

131 Vienna Convention on the Law of Treaties 1969 Art. 33.

132 Ibid., Art. 45.

importance;[133] and where the representative has concluded the treaty in breach of an express restriction imposed by the repository of the treaty-making power of the state, where the other parties knew of the restriction.[134] Error is the third ground of invalidity. A state can consider its consent to be bound vitiated if it was in error about a fact or situation that was assumed by the state to exist at the time and formed an essential basis of its consent,[135] although this ground is not available if the state contributed to the error or was put on notice of the error.[136] It would be rare for a state to successfully invoke this ground.[137] Equally rare is the ground of fraud. If a negotiating state induces, by fraudulent conduct, another state's representative to express the state's consent to be bound, the latter state may consider its consent to be invalidated.[138] Corruption by a negotiating state of another state's representative may also make the treaty voidable at the suit of the latter state.[139] 'Corruption' requires something calculated to exercise a substantial influence on the representative.[140] Where multilateral treaties are concerned, a treaty would only be void as between the state whose consent was vitiated and other states.[141]

The following three are grounds of *absolute invalidity*, by which it is meant that states may not elect to validate the treaty, and multilateral treaties will be irrevocably void as between all states.[142] First, coercion by acts or threats directed against state representatives to force them to express the state's consent to be bound, whether or not perpetrated by a negotiating state, also renders the treaty void.[143] Similarly, coercion of the state through the threat or use of force in violation of the UN Charter has the same legal effect.[144] However, recourse to purely political or economic pressure would not invalidate a treaty, despite the fact that a declaration was appended to the Vienna Conference condemning such pressure.[145] Thus, the so-called 'unequal treaties' concluded

---

133 Ibid., Art. 46.
134 Ibid., Art. 47.
135 Ibid., Art. 48(1).
136 Ibid., Art. 48(2).
137 S.E. Nahlik, 'Grounds of Invalidity and Termination of Treaties' (1971) 65 *American Journal of International Law* 736, 741.
138 Vienna Convention on the Law of Treaties 1969, Art. 49.
139 Ibid., Art. 50.
140 Jennings and Watts, above note 16, 1290.
141 Vienna Convention on the Law of Treaties 1969, Art. 69(4).
142 Ibid.
143 Vienna Convention on the Law of Treaties 1969, Art. 51.
144 Ibid., Art. 52.
145 Declaration on the Prohibition of Military, Political and Economic

between former colonial powers and their colonies are not invalidated by the Vienna Convention.[146] What is required is procuring the state's consent to be bound through the application of force; 'a vague general charge unfortified by evidence in its support'[147] will not suffice. Finally, a treaty that, when it is concluded, conflicts with a norm of *jus cogens* is void.[148] Article 44(5) of the Vienna Convention states that, in the above cases of absolute invalidity, an offending provision cannot be severed from the treaty itself. To Antonio Cassese, it is illogical that, if only one provision in a treaty is contrary to *jus cogens*, the whole treaty is invalid; he suggests that the Vienna Convention does not reflect customary law on this point.[149] Another way of looking at the effect of Article 44(5), however, is that it contributes to the deterrent effect of *jus cogens* norms, which can be said to be their primary purpose.[150] For relative invalidity, where the ground relates to particular clauses, they may be struck out without impairing the validity of the treaty as a whole, unless those clauses formed the essential basis of the state's consent to be bound.[151]

The consequence of establishing invalidity is the legal rescission of the treaty from its date of conclusion. The parties should, as far as possible, be put in the position in which they would have been had the treaty not been concluded. This means that any performance of the treaty undertaken before it was declared void should be undone.[152] In cases of fraud, corruption or coercion, however, the offending party cannot take the benefit of this provision.[153] Offending conduct may also attract international responsibility of states.[154]

2.2.1.7 Termination and suspension

Termination allows the parties to consider the treaty discharged, or permanently ineffective, from the date of termination. Suspension makes the treaty temporarily ineffective.

Termination or suspension can take place, first, in accordance with an

---

Coercion in the Conclusion of Treaties, Annexed to the Final Act of the Vienna Conference on the Law of Treaties, UN Doc. A/CONF 39/26.

146 Harris, above note 32, 855.

147 *Fisheries Jurisdiction* case, above note 33, 14 [24].

148 Vienna Convention on the Law of Treaties 1969, Art. 53.

149 Cassese, above note 7, 206.

150 See discussion below at section 2.2.2.7.

151 Vienna Convention on the Law of Treaties 1969, Art. 44(3).

152 Ibid., Art. 69(2).

153 Ibid., Art. 69(3).

154 See Chapter 9.

express provision in the treaty, or with the consent of all parties.[155] Such consent can be express, or it may be implied – for example, when the parties later conclude another treaty inconsistent with the previous treaty remaining on foot.[156] Otherwise, a party may not denounce or withdraw from a treaty unless the parties intended to admit this possibility, or such a right is implied from the nature of the treaty.[157] 'Denunciation' and 'withdrawal' are cognate terms. Both relate to a declaration by a party that it no longer wishes to be bound by the treaty. 'Denunciation' is used when a treaty is thereby terminated and 'withdrawal' when the departure of a party from a multilateral treaty does not put an end to the effect of the treaty as between the remaining parties.[158]

The other main grounds of termination or suspension are material breach, supervening impossibility of performance and fundamental change of circumstances. Other grounds are termination of a treaty from the date of crystallization of an inconsistent *jus cogens* norm[159] and desuetude (obsolescence).[160]

Material breach by a party gives another party grounds for terminating the treaty or suspending it in whole or part.[161] Material breach occurs when the defaulting party repudiates the treaty or violates a provision essential to the accomplishment of its object or purpose.[162] Repudiation occurs when it appears, by words or conduct, that the defaulting party has an intention not to perform the treaty or one of its essential provisions. The ICJ decision in the *Hungarian Dams* case[163] is a case in point. Through a bilateral treaty, Hungary and Czechoslovakia undertook to construct a series of locks diverting the Danube River along a new channel to produce hydroelectricity, improve navigation and protect against flooding. In 1989, Hungary stopped work on the project because of local protest at its environmental impact, whereupon Czechoslovakia began to construct a bypass canal (known as Variant C) for its own benefit. However, it did not take irreversible steps until it dammed the river in October 1992. Hungary had

---

155 Vienna Convention on the Law of Treaties 1969, Arts 54 and 57.

156 Ibid., Art. 59.

157 Ibid., Art. 56.

158 For the difficulties associated with these terms, see Nahlik, above note 137, 749–50.

159 Vienna Convention on the Law of Treaties 1969, Art. 64.

160 Obsolescence is not expressly mentioned by the Vienna Convention, but it is well established in customary law: Jennings and Watts, above note 16, 1297.

161 Vienna Convention on the Law of Treaties 1969, Art. 60(1). The consequences of breach for state responsibility are discussed in Chapter 9.

162 Ibid., Art. 60(3).

163 *Gobčikovo-Nagymaros Project* (*Hungary v Slovakia*), above note 33.

purported to terminate the treaty in May 1992, ostensibly in response to Variant C. The Court held that Czechoslovakia only committed a material breach in October 1992, when it took the irreversible steps to dam the river. Hungary had, therefore, prematurely repudiated the treaty in May 1992. Furthermore, given Hungary's own breaches in unilaterally suspending the treaty, its purported termination was not in good faith and had prejudiced its right to subsequently terminate.[164] The Court stated:

> The Court would set a precedent with disturbing implications for treaty relations and the integrity of the rule of *pacta sunt servanda* if it were to conclude that a treaty in force between States, which the parties have implemented in considerable measure and at great cost over a period of years, might be unilaterally set aside on grounds of reciprocal non-compliance.[165]

Another well-established ground of termination or suspension is supervening impossibility of performance. The impossibility must result from the permanent (in the case of termination) or temporary (in the case of suspension) disappearance or destruction of an object indispensable for the execution of the treaty.[166] A commonly cited example is the sinking of an island that was the object of a treaty. The obligations can no longer be carried out. This ground is not available to a party who brought about the impossibility by a breach of the treaty or any other international obligation owed to a party to the treaty.[167]

More contentious is the ground of fundamental change of circumstances, or *rebus sic stantibus*. Given the broad disagreement about the scope and even validity of this ground before the Vienna Convention was drafted, the drafters had to choose between views.[168] In the event, Article 62 harmonizes the approaches somewhat by acknowledging the existence of the ground, but confining it within strict limits. A fundamental change of circumstances with regard to those that existed at the conclusion of the treaty may be invoked only if it was unforeseen by the parties; the circumstances were an essential basis of the consent of the parties to be bound; and the change radically transforms the extent of executory obligations that is, those still to be performed under the treaty.[169] The ground does not apply to treaties establishing a boundary and a party cannot invoke it if it

164 Ibid., [110].
165 Ibid., 68.
166 Vienna Convention on the Law of Treaties 1969, Art. 61(1).
167 Ibid., Art. 61(2).
168 Nahlik, above note 137, 748; Hans Kelsen, *Principles of International Law* (New York: Holt, Rinehart and Winston, 1966, 2nd edn), 497–8.
169 Vienna Convention on the Law of Treaties 1969 Art. 62(1).

brought about the changed circumstances by breach of the treaty or other international obligations owed to a contracting party.[170] This formulation goes a way towards ensuring that, in the context of limited enforcement mechanisms at international law, this ground would not be invoked by a state as a pretext for jettisoning treaty obligations. Indeed, Kelsen has observed that 'it is the function of the law in general and treaties in particular to stabilize the legal relations between states in the stream of changing circumstances'.[171] Thus the emphasis in Article 62 on a 'radical' transformation of the extent of executory obligations should ensure that a valid claim of *rebus sic stantibus* would be rare.

Fundamental change of circumstances was one of Hungary's arguments in the *Hungarian Dams* case. However, the Court felt that the change in the political situation in Hungary and Czechoslovakia after the lifting of the iron curtain, greater knowledge about the environmental impact of the project and blowouts in its cost were:

> not of such a nature, either individually or collectively, that their effect would radically transform the extent of the obligations still to be performed in order to accomplish the Project. A fundamental change of circumstances must have been unforeseen; the existence of the circumstances at the time of the Treaty's conclusion must have constituted an essential basis of the consent of the parties to be bound by the Treaty. The negative and conditional wording of Article 62 of the Vienna Convention on the Law of Treaties is clear indication moreover that the stability of treaty relations requires that the plea of fundamental change of circumstances be applied only in exceptional cases.[172]

The consequences of termination are that the parties are released from performing executory obligations, but the termination does not affect the validity of executed obligations – that is those performed prior to termination.[173] In the case of suspension, the parties are freed from performing the treaty during the suspension period only.[174] Dispute resolution clauses often survive the termination or suspension of a treaty, as one of the purposes of such clauses is to test the validity of a purported termination or suspension.[175]

---

[170] Vienna Convention on the Law of Treaties 1969 Art. 62(2).

[171] Kelsen, above note 168, 498.

[172] *Gobčikovo-Nagymaros Project* (*Hungary v Slovakia*), above note 33, 65. See also *Fisheries Jurisdiction* case, above note 33, 20–21; *Free Zones* case (1932) PCIJ (Ser. A/B) No. 46, 156–8.

[173] Vienna Convention on the Law of Treaties 1969, Art. 70.

[174] Ibid., Art. 72.

[175] *Appeal Relating to the Jurisdiction of the ICAO Council* [1972] ICJ Rep 46. The Vienna Convention itself contemplates this, as it states that the provisions

2.2.1.8 Some contemporary issues in treaty law

2.2.1.8.1 Codification and progressive development of international law: the role of multilateral treaties Since the late nineteenth century, states have come together to conclude multilateral treaties on matters of global importance. Significant early examples are the 1899 and 1907 Hague Conventions, which laid down much needed laws on war and neutrality. It was not, however, until the formation of the United Nations that codification and progressive development acquired an institutional character. Under Article 13 of the UN Charter, the UN General Assembly created the International Law Commission. The ILC was to be composed of representatives from all of the major legal systems of the world appearing in their personal capacity with a mandate to promote the 'codification' and 'progressive development' of international law. Thus, in addition to treaties negotiated between states directly, the United Nations Treaty Series is replete with important texts, usually on the more traditional matters such as state responsibility,[176] prepared by the ILC. The Vienna Convention on the Law of Treaties was itself a product of the work of the ILC. The Rome Statute of the International Criminal Court is another example, following several formulations over 40 years of the Draft Code on Offences against the Peace and Security of Mankind. The ILC has defined 'progressive development' as 'the drafting of a convention on a subject which has not yet been highly developed or formulated in the practice of states' and 'codification' as 'the more precise formulation and systematization of the law in areas where there has been extensive state practice, precedent and doctrine'.[177]

For states seeking to establish binding legal regimes, the treaty is their material source of choice. The black and white text of a treaty is more certain than the often uncollated state practice and *opinio juris* that constitute the material source of custom. But treaties can be vital to the development not only of international law between the parties, but international law in general. As discussed below,[178] a treaty can influence the subsequent development of customary law in that it can constitute *opinio juris* of the customary norm. Further, instead of merely constituting *opinio juris*

---

relating to the legal effect of termination or suspension do not apply to the extent that the 'treaty otherwise provides or the parties otherwise agree': see Vienna Convention on the Law of Treaties 1969, Arts 70 and 72.

[176] Cassese, above note 7, 167.

[177] Cited in Robert Jennings, 'The Progressive Development of International Law and Its Codification' (1947) 24 *British Year Book of International Law* 301, 12.

[178] See discussion below at section 2.2.2.3.

which contributes to the later crystallization of custom, the conclusion of a treaty may itself trigger the crystallization of an emergent custom. An example is the decisive effect of the UN Convention on the Law of the Sea 1982 (UNCLOS) on the crystallization of most concepts embodied in the Convention.[179] The negotiation and conclusion of UNCLOS had allowed the majority of states to express *opinio juris* on this issue, providing a potent vehicle for the crystallization of custom that was merely aspirational beforehand.

Besides crystallizing a custom and influencing subsequent crystallization, a treaty may 'codify' pre-existing custom, giving it a definite wording. In practice, however, this may also amount to 'progressive development', as the aim of codification is to 'resolve differences and to fill in the gaps'; indeed, the very act of reducing a custom to writing lends it a somewhat different colour.[180] Judge Sørensen stated in his Dissenting Opinion in the *Fisheries* case:[181]

> It has come to be generally recognized, however, that this distinction between codification and progressive development may be difficult to apply rigorously to the facts of international legal relations. Although theoretically clear and distinguishable, the two notions tend in practice to overlap or to leave between them an indeterminate area in which it is not possible to indicate precisely where codification ends and progressive development begins. The very act of formulating or restating an existing customary rule may have the effect of defining its contents more precisely and removing such doubts as may have existed as to its exact scope or the modalities of its application.

Quite apart from the question of the influence of treaties on custom, treaty-making is a useful tool in the progressive development between the parties of more 'radical' obligations, or where state practice is frustratingly slow to form. Although there is no 'international legislation' or 'instant custom'[182] upon the conclusion of treaties, those multilateral treaties with widespread state representation, such as the UN Charter, exert a significant influence on restructuring the prevailing international legal order.

As Gabriella Blum has pointed out, to focus entirely on the positives of the proliferation of multilateral treaties, as restricting the scope for unilateral state conduct and enhancing interdependence and *communitas*, is to

---

[179] Triggs, above note 33, 63–4.

[180] Robert Jennings, 'The Progressive Development of International Law and Its Codification' (1947) 24 *British Year Book of International Law* 301, 302, 304.

[181] *Fisheries Jurisdiction* case, above note 33, 242–3.

[182] See discussion below at section 2.2.2.4.

take a 'universalist' view.[183] There is, however, a competing 'unilateralist' view, emanating particularly from the United States, that a state's independence, flexibility and freedom of action in choosing its international obligations, uninfluenced by international 'peer pressure', is something that should not be sacrificed on the altar of the homogenizing influence of a global order.[184] Thus, there is a certain push-back, emphasizing the role bilateral and regional treaties still play in defending state interests. It is perhaps a cause for concern that such unilateralist thinking may, if taken too far, undermine the stability of international law in times of crisis – the failure of the United States to properly observe the Geneva Convention in its treatment of detainees at Guantanamo Bay stands as a notorious recent example.[185]

2.2.2 Customary International Law

2.2.2.1 The origins and dynamic nature of international custom

Customary law is the oldest source of international law and all law generally.[186] Humans have a natural predilection toward the reasoning that, because we have always done things a certain way, it must therefore be the right way.[187] As discussed in Chapter 1, the modern concept of customary international law as the *jus gentium*, or the natural or common law among nations, developed from the Roman Empire's dealings with foreigners. Thereafter, customary law in various forms complemented the slowly emerging system of nation states by recognizing the legitimate expectations created in other states by consistent conduct.[188] It was not, however, until 1899 that the concept of *opinio juris sive necessitatis* was coined and

---

183 Gabriella Blum, 'Bilateralism, Multilateralism, and the Architecture of International Law' (2008) 49(2) *Harvard International Law Journal* 323, 324.

184 Ibid., 325. Blum noted that the United Nations Treaty Series contained 3500 multilateral treaties and 50 000 bilateral treaties, which indicates the significant role bilateral treaties still play in ordering relations in modern international society: ibid., 326.

185 See George Aldrich, 'The Taliban, al Qaeda, and the Determination of Illegal Combatants' (2002) 96 *American Journal of International Law* 891.

186 Jennings and Watts, above note 16, 25.

187 See also Kopelmanas, cited in I.C. MacGibbon, 'Customary International Law and Acquiescence' (1957) *British Year Book of International Law* 115, 133: '[The] formation and existence of a custom depend on its conformity with the social needs of a legal order. The custom results from acts of the same character because those who do them cannot do otherwise.'

188 Hugh Thirlway, 'The Sources of International Law', in Evans, above note 85, 121.

assumed its current character as the subjective element of custom, as distinct from the earlier conception that this element expressed a 'spirit of the nation'.[189] Thus custom ostensibly caught up with the positivist spirit of the times, which eschewed natural law concepts of a pre-existing law in favour of a view grounded in the empirically verifiable opinions of states. State practice also had to change as a result of the explosion of states that marked the era of decolonization in the twentieth century.[190] The change from a mere handful of states to a diverse community of close to 200 states has gradually led to a loosening of the requirement of uniformity of state practice, so that it need only be 'widespread and representative'.[191]

The durability of custom over the ages may have something to do with its flexibility, for the existence and content of custom can change over time without the practical difficulties that attend the creation and modification of treaties.[192] Treaties must be expressly negotiated and, especially in the case of multilateral treaties with many States Parties, achieving consensus is rarely straightforward. The final wording must align the political, economic and social interests of the various parties.[193] The treaty text itself is fixed and, except in the case of open-textured obligations discussed above,[194] relatively definite in meaning. Conversely, the formation (commonly referred to as 'crystallization') of custom does not even require the *tacit* consent of all states.[195] The norm may emerge and change simply by virtue of the customary acts (and omissions) of state organs. Thus, no great effort is necessarily required to develop custom. The content of the custom is itself ordinarily more fluid and open to shifting interpretation than black and white treaty text.

In this sense, customary norms tend to be more dynamic (less rigid) than treaty norms. The very quality, however, that gives the norm durability can also be perceived as a weakness, in that it makes determining what custom requires at any particular time difficult to ascertain. The following discussion will show that the elements of custom – state practice and *opinio juris* – are by no means easy to apply.

---

[189] Jörg Kammerhofer, *Uncertainty in International Law: A Kelsenian Perspective* (London: Routledge, 2010) 534. *Opinio juris sive necessitatis* is widely said to have been coined by the French jurist François Gény in *Methode d'interpretation et sources en droit privé positif* (Paris, 1899).

[190] Kelsen, above note 168, 452; Cassese, above note 7, 165.

[191] *North Sea Continental Shelf* cases, above note 112, [73].

[192] See, e.g., MacGibbon, above note 187, 116.

[193] Cassese, above note 7, 156.

[194] See discussion at section 2.2.

[195] Kelsen, above note 168, 444.

It is, however, appropriate to first dispose of an argument that is occasionally raised to suggest that custom is essentially rigid and difficult to change. To replace an existing custom with a new custom, states must, for some time before the emergence of the new custom, act in a way that is consistent with the nascent norm but inconsistent with the pre-existing norm. Some commentators have suggested that this involves a logical contradiction, since law cannot be created by breach of its own provisions.[196] However, this objection is fallacious, as behaviour inconsistent with a custom is only a breach of that custom, not a breach of the formal source of custom. As discussed above,[197] the formal source of custom is the norm that custom is created through state practice and *opinio juris*, the material source of which is Article 38(1)(b) of the ICJ Statute.

This point is illustrated by the *Anglo-Norwegian Fisheries* case,[198] which concerned the issue of whether Norway's practice over a 60-year period of using the straight baseline system to delimit its territorial waters had crystallized into custom. The new delimitation expanded Norway's territorial sea so as to cover economically important stretches of the high seas. The ICJ held that the custom had crystallized even though, prior to its crystallization, Norway had acted in breach of the freedom of the high seas by excluding British fishing interests from what were international waters. Norway had been acting in breach of the previous custom, but it was engaging in conduct (state practice and *opinio juris*) that was formative of new custom.

The following sections examine the twin elements required for the formation of custom. They are (1) consistent state practice, and (2) *opinio juris* – the belief that the practice is required by law.

2.2.2.2 State practice: the first element of custom

2.2.2.2.1 Consistency of state practice The *North Sea Continental Shelf* cases[199] concerned the delimitation as between several states of the areas of the continental shelf in the North Sea. In the course of holding that there was no rule of custom specifying how such delimitation should occur, the ICJ formulated the following oft-cited principle:

---

[196] See, e.g., G.J.H. van Hoof, *Rethinking the Sources of International Law* (Deventer; London: Kluwer Law and Taxation, 1983) 99, quoted in Kammerhofer, above note 189, 531. See also Rosalyn Higgins, *Problems and Process: International Law and How We Use It* (Oxford: Clarendon Press, 1994) 19.

[197] See discussion above at section 2.2.

[198] *Anglo-Norwegian Fisheries* case (*United Kingdom v Norway*) [1951] ICJ Rep 116.

[199] *North Sea Continental Shelf* cases, above note 112.

> [A]n indispensable requirement would be that within the period in question, short though it might be, State practice, including that of States whose interests are specially affected, should have been both extensive and virtually uniform.[200]

In the *Asylum* case, the ICJ also spoke of state practice, or 'usage', having to be 'constant and uniform'.[201] References to uniformity were never intended to suggest that every state must have engaged in the relevant practice for the norm to emerge. It is not the common consent of the international community that crystallizes a norm, but the consent of a 'widespread and representative'[202] part of it.[203] Indeed, a land-locked state can hardly participate in creating a maritime custom as it is not specially affected. If, however, the state subsequently acquires a stretch of coastline, it will be bound by the customary law of the sea. So too will a new state, which is born into a world of laws and cannot pick and choose which laws it will observe.[204]

Even state practice directly opposed to the norm will not necessarily constitute divergent practice such as to destroy it. In *Military and Paramilitary Activities in and against Nicaragua* ('*Nicaragua* case'),[205] the ICJ considered whether the United States had violated, *inter alia*, the customary norm against the use of force other than in self-defence. In a claim brought in 1984, Nicaragua claimed that the United States, in actions taken against the left-wing Sandinista government, mined Nicaraguan internal and territorial waters and gave assistance to the *contras* guerrilla forces fighting against the government. Although applicable treaties existed between the countries governing the issue, a US reservation to the jurisdiction of the ICJ under Article 36(2) of the ICJ Statute restricted the Court's jurisdiction to customary law. Nevertheless, the Court held that the United States had contravened several customary norms, including the norm against the use of force.[206] In a highly influential judgment, the Court recognized the following principle:

> The Court does not consider that, for a rule to be established as customary, the corresponding practice must be in absolutely rigorous conformity with the rule. . . . If a State acts in a way prima facie incompatible with a recognized rule,

---

[200] Ibid., [74].
[201] *Asylum* case (*Colombia v Peru*) [1950] ICJ Rep 266, 276.
[202] *North Sea Continental Shelf* cases, above note 112, [73].
[203] Kelsen, above note 168, 445.
[204] Jennings and Watts, above note 17, 29.
[205] *Military and Paramilitary Activities in and against Nicaragua*, above note 11.
[206] The implications of the *Nicaragua* case for the law of state responsibility and the use of force are discussed in Chapters 9 and 10 respectively.

> but defends its conduct by appealing to exceptions or justifications contained within the rule itself, then whether or not the State's conduct is in fact justifiable on that basis, the significance of that attitude is to confirm rather than to weaken the rule.[207]

A striking example of this is the customary – indeed *jus cogens* – norm against torture. Despite reliable evidence indicating that many states have engaged in systematic torture, frequent breaches of the *jus cogens* norm prohibiting torture have never been justified on the basis that it is lawful.[208]

2.2.2.2.2 Kinds of state practice – acts, omissions and acquiescence The kinds of act that constitute state practice include the exclusion of others from territory, the institution of legal action, positive acts of state officials and armed forces, financial and material assistance to individuals or groups and actions intended to have legal effect, such as recognition of another state.[209] While the identification of the positive acts of states may seem relatively straightforward, as revealed in the decision-making of international courts and tribunals, in practice it can be extremely difficult to identify state practice among the states of the world sufficient to arrive at a considered opinion on a matter of international law.

Omissions, as evidence of state practice, are more difficult to characterize. In the 1996 *Nuclear Weapons* Advisory Opinion,[210] the ICJ was asked to determine whether there was a customary norm prohibiting the threat or use of nuclear weapons. The Court held, first, that there was no specific custom banning nuclear weapons. Secondly, the Court stated that it 'could not decide' whether any conceivable use of nuclear weapons would be contrary to the customary norms of the laws of armed conflict. This second ruling amounted to a *non liquet* (a refusal to decide), which will be discussed in more detail below.[211] However, its first finding that there was no specific custom banning nuclear weapons was made even though no state had used nuclear weapons since 1945, 50 years before the decision. The Court appeared to accept that this was state practice consistent with

---

[207] *Military and Paramilitary Activities in and against Nicaragua*, above note 11, [186].

[208] Higgins, above note 196, 20.

[209] *Anglo-Norwegian Fisheries* case, above note 198; *SS 'Lotus'* (*France v Turkey*), above note 125; *Military and Paramilitary Activities in and against Nicaragua*, above note 11.

[210] *Legality of the Threat or Use of Nuclear Weapons* (Advisory Opinion) [1996] ICJ Rep 226 ('*Nuclear Weapons* (Advisory Opinion)').

[211] See discussion below at section 2.2.3.3.

the prohibition of nuclear weapons, but focused its attention on whether *opinio juris* could be inferred from this omission.[212]

This approach is consistent with an early decision of the Permanent Court of International Justice in the *Lotus* case. This case concerned a collision on the high seas between a French and Turkish steamer in which eight Turkish nationals were killed. The Permanent Court of International Justice had to decide whether Turkey had jurisdiction to prosecute the French officer of the watch at the time of the collision for involuntary manslaughter under Turkish law. One of the French submissions was that states had, in practice, abstained from prosecuting unless the alleged crime occurred on a ship flying that state's flag. The Court, however, held that 'only if such abstention were based on their being conscious of having a duty to abstain would it be possible to speak of an international custom'.[213] The Court went on to find that no such *opinio juris* existed to convert the practice into custom.

In the foundation case for the principle of acquiescence, the *Anglo-Norwegian Fisheries* case,[214] the ICJ, refusing the claim of the United Kingdom, held:

> The notoriety of the facts, the general toleration of the international community, Great Britain's position in the North Sea, her own interest in the question, and her prolonged abstention would in any case warrant Norway's enforcement of her system against the United Kingdom.[215]

The absence of protest by a state affected by another state's practice, where the former has actual or constructive knowledge of the latter's practice, would convert an omission – otherwise neutral in effect – into passive practice supporting the latter's active practice.[216] It is interesting to note that acquiescence need not be coupled with *opinio juris* of the acquiescing state in the strict sense; only to the extent that *opinio juris* is inferred from the omission can it be said to exist. Therefore, the United Kingdom's absence of protest or other conduct in reaction to Norway's use for 60 years of the straight baseline system is grounded more in justice than consent.[217] The holding in *Anglo-Norwegian Fisheries* therefore develops and expands the effect of omissions as formulated in the *Lotus* case. As

---

212 *Nuclear Weapons* (Advisory Opinion), above note 210, 253–4.
213 *SS 'Lotus' (France v Turkey)*, above note 209, 28.
214 For the facts of this case, see the discussion above at section 2.2.2.1.
215 *Anglo-Norwegian Fisheries* case, above note 198, 138.
216 Kammerhofer, above note 189, 529.
217 MacGibbon, above note 187, 145.

noted by MacGibbon, acquiescence will be more relevant where a state is directly affected by a right exercised by another state, as opposed to where the other state is performing an obligation.[218]

2.2.2.2.3 Quantity of state practice The amount of state practice required for the creation of custom varies, depending on the nature of the norm. Rosalyn Higgins has raised the following problem:

> Applying the same tests that it enunciated in the *Continental Shelf* cases to the question of genocide, would the Court have determined that there were relatively few ratifying parties to the Genocide Convention, that they did not include most of the potential butchers, and that the basis of the practice of most states in not committing genocide has to remain 'entirely speculative'?[219]

It may be responded that with essentially proscriptive norms, such as the norm against genocide, *opinio juris* becomes central and state practice, though still indispensable, becomes secondary.[220] Conversely, norms allocating rights between states, such as a custom specifying the extent of a state's territorial sea, refocus the analysis on how consistent or divergent state practice has been. In yet another field, space law, it has been suggested that customary norms in respect of outer space developed in a very short period of time, simply from a UN Resolution on Outer Space, given that at the time only the United States and the Soviet Union were capable of reaching that realm.[221] This view – of 'instant custom' – has been implicitly rejected by the ICJ.[222] Indeed, it runs counter to the orthodoxy of Article 38(1)(b) of the ICJ Statute and is arguably a contradiction in terms.[223] Some state practice must occur for at least a 'short'[224] period of time before one can speak of a 'custom'. There is, however, no strict rule on this, as Judge Tanaka stated in his Dissenting Opinion in the *North Sea Continental Shelf* cases:

---

218 Ibid, 129, 131, 144–5. See section 2.2.2.3 for further discussion of acquiescence in the context of *opinio juris*, though the issues are somewhat intertwined.

219 Higgins, above note 196, 30–31.

220 Cassese, above note 7, 158.

221 B. Cheng, 'United Nations Resolutions on Outer Space: "Instant" International Customary Law?' (1965) 5 *Indian Journal of International Law* 23.

222 *Military and Paramilitary Activities in and against Nicaragua*, above note 11, [188].

223 Peter Malanczuk and Michael Barton Akehurst, *Akehurst's Modern Introduction to International Law* (London; New York: Routledge, 1997, 7th edn), 46.

224 *North Sea Continental Shelf* cases above note 112, [74].

> The repetition, the number of examples of State practice, the duration of time required for the generation of customary law cannot be mathematically and uniformly decided. Each fact requires to be evaluated relatively according to the different occasions and circumstances.[225]

The Court in the *North Sea Continental Shelf* cases makes it clear that, in the traditional orthodoxy, state practice is an 'indispensable' requirement. Nevertheless, in practice, the distinction between state practice and *opinio juris* has become blurred, especially when statements (as opposed to actions and omissions) are relied on to constitute state practice. Some commentators maintain a rigid distinction between state practice and *opinio juris* – to them, 'a claim is not an act'.[226] The very concept of 'custom' requires a course of conduct, and statements are not custom unless they produce effects in the physical world, such as a state's recognition of another state, or the giving of a notice or order.[227] This view has much to commend it in that it is logically consistent. The alternative view is less coherent, but it may more accurately reflect the reality of how custom is 'found' by international courts and tribunals. This view is that the state can only act through its organs and, in fact, most of the 'acts' of a state are statements issued to its organs, such that it would be 'artificial to distinguish between what a state does and what it says'.[228]

2.2.2.3 *Opinio juris*: the second element of custom

2.2.2.3.1 General sources of evidence of opinio juris *Opinio juris sive necessitatis* is the second and more complex element of custom. In requiring that states undertake state practice out of a sense of legal obligation, *opinio juris* serves to distinguish practice that is custom and practice that is mere 'comity'. For example, the practice of saluting ships flying a different flag is not customary law, since states do this merely out of courtesy – they do not consider it to be legally obligatory. In the seminal *North Sea Continental Shelf* cases judgment, the ICJ stated:

---

[225] Ibid., 176.

[226] Anthony D'Amato, *The Concept of Custom in International Law* (Ithaca; London: Cornell University Press, 1971), cited in Kammerhofer, above note 189, 525.

[227] For other examples of statements with legal effect, see Cassese, above note 7, 184–5.

[228] Michael B. Akehurst, 'Custom as a Source of International Law' (1977) 47 *British Year Book of International Law* 1, cited in Kammerhofer, above note 189, 526.

> The States concerned must therefore feel that they are conforming to what amounts to a legal obligation. The frequency, or even habitual character of the acts is not in itself enough. There are many international acts, e.g., in the field of ceremonial and protocol, which are performed almost invariably, but which are motivated only by considerations of courtesy, convenience or tradition.[229]

There are certain conceptual difficulties with the notion of *opinio juris*. Customary law is formed only when state practice and *opinio juris* exist in a sufficient number of states. This presupposes a period before the crystallization of the custom when some states possess the requisite *opinio juris* but other states do not. Hence, the seemingly counter-intuitive conclusion follows that custom is formed by states possessing a mistaken belief that the practice is already legally obligatory.[230] This apparent paradox has led Kelsen to suggest: 'They must believe that they apply a norm, but they need not believe that it is a legal norm which they apply. They have to regard their conduct as obligatory or right.'[231] However, this formulation insufficiently distinguishes custom from comity. The view that best reflects international reality is that states initially engage in divergent practice out of a sense of political, social or economic necessity (*opinio necessitatis*),[232] coupled with a feeling that the practice *should* be legally obligatory.[233] It constitutes an invitation to other states to do the same.[234] Only if this does not meet with consistent opposition over time and other states have taken up the invitation does the belief that the practice amounts to law (*opinio juris*) develop. Even then, it is probably more accurate to say that states merely 'claim' that it amounts to law and their subjective belief, being presumably cognizant of the current state of the law, remains that the norm *should* be law.[235] Of course, once the norm crystallizes, its continuing existence is sustained by consistent state practice and *opinio juris*, otherwise a counter-norm might emerge.

It is hardly surprising that one of the more difficult aspects in the ascertainment of *opinio juris* is how exactly to deduce a state's 'opinions'. *Opinio juris* can be derived from the conclusion of treaties, attitudes to the activities of international organizations (such as resolutions of the UN

---

229 *North Sea Continental Shelf* cases, above note 112, 44 [77].

230 See, e.g., Thirlway, above note 188, 122.

231 Kelsen, above note 168, 440.

232 Cassese, above note 7, 156–7.

233 Raphael Walden, 'Customary International Law: A Jurisprudential Analysis' (1978) 13 *Israel Law Review* 86, 97; Hugh Thirlway, *International Customary Law and Codification* (Leiden: A.W. Sijthoff, 1972) 55.

234 Harris, above note 32, 39.

235 Thirlway, above note 233, 55.

General Assembly), legislation, press releases, the jurisprudence of international and national tribunals, diplomatic correspondence, opinions of national legal advisers, government policies, official manuals (for example, relating to conduct of the armed forces), executive practices and comments on drafts written by the ILC.[236]

In practice, these sources are often insufficient to found a robust attribution of *opinio juris*. Thus, *opinio juris* may be inferred from the state practice itself,[237] though this is not always a fruitful exercise. It may be impossible to deduce whether a state is engaging in conduct out of a sense of obligation, or whether it is merely doing so out of expediency or convenience.[238] For example, in the *North Sea Continental Shelf* cases, 'no inference could legitimately be drawn as to the existence of a rule of customary law' from practice consistent with the Geneva Convention on the Continental Shelf by the States Parties to it.[239] Not even the consistent practice of states not party to the Convention indicated *opinio juris*: there was 'not a shred of evidence' that 'they believed themselves to be applying a mandatory rule of customary international law'.[240] However, the ICJ did not appear to reject the possibility that inferences of *opinio juris* might be drawn from state practice, given its conclusion that state practice 'must also be such, or carried out in such a way, as to be evidence of a belief that this practice is rendered obligatory by the existence of a rule of law requiring it'.[241]

Having set out a relatively rigid regime for the determination of the elements of custom, the ICJ has at times itself – indeed, one might say increasingly – sourced relevant *opinio juris* purely from past judicial decisions of the Court and that of other international tribunals. In the *Gulf of Maine* case,[242] for example, the ICJ was asked to delimit the maritime boundary between Canada and the United States. In drawing the boundary, a Chamber of the Court stated that the ICJ's judgment in the *North*

---

236 International Law Commission, 'Documents of the Second Session including the Report of the Commission to the General Assembly' (1950) *Yearbook of the International Law Commission*, II, 368–72; Ian Brownlie, *Principles of Public International Law* (Oxford: Oxford University Press, 2008, 7th edn), 6; *Military and Paramilitary Activities in and against Nicaragua*, above note 11, 99–101.

237 Brownlie, ibid., 8; Thirlway, above note 188, 123.

238 Kelsen, above note 168, 450.

239 *North Sea Continental Shelf* cases, above note 112, [76].

240 Ibid., [76].

241 Ibid., [77].

242 *Delimitation of the Maritime Boundary on the Gulf of Maine Area* (*Canada v United States of America*) [1984] ICJ Rep 246. See also discussion below at section 2.2.2.5: Treatment by international courts and tribunals.

Sea Continental Shelf cases is 'the judicial decision that has made the greatest contribution to the formation of customary law in this field' and proceeded to apply its finding that the delimitation must, in the absence of agreement between the parties, be drawn 'according to equitable principles'.[243] To confirm the norm in the *North Sea Continental Shelf* cases, the Court cited another of its own decisions and the decision of an arbitral tribunal.

In the *Arrest Warrant* case,[244] the ICJ stated that it had 'carefully examined state practice', including 'decisions of national higher courts, such as the House of Lords or the French Court of Cassation', to reach the conclusion that there is no exception in customary international law to the rule of immunity from domestic criminal process of incumbent ministers for foreign affairs, even when they are suspected of war crimes or crimes against humanity.[245] No actual state practice or *opinio juris* was cited.

Finally, in the *Israeli Wall* case,[246] the ICJ cited solely from its previous decisions to determine that it had jurisdiction to render an Advisory Opinion on the legal consequences of Israel building a wall in occupied Palestinian territory.[247]

This process of determining the existence of a customary rule by reference to judicial determinations gives rise to serious questions. Such a reliance on previous decisions – whether it is bare or substantial – may amount to a breach of Article 59 of the ICJ's own Statute, which states that previous decisions of the Court are not binding upon it in cases other than that under consideration.[248] In other words, there is no system of binding precedent in international law. The Court may not rely upon its own determinations as to the existence or content of a rule as evidence of the existence of that rule. Rather, it must rely upon material evidence of the existence of *opinio juris*, state practice or indeed both.

As discussed above, omissions can amount to state practice, whether as practice relating to a prohibition, such as genocide or crimes against humanity, or in the form of acquiescence when a right is invoked by

---

243 Ibid., [91]–[94].

244 *Arrest Warrant of 11 April 2000* (*Democratic Republic of Congo v Belgium*) [2002] ICJ Rep 3. For a discussion of the facts of this case, see text accompanying note 316 below.

245 Ibid., [58]. Compare the difference in approach of Judge van Wyngaert in her Dissenting Opinion: ibid., [9]ff.

246 *Legal Consequences of the Construction of a Wall in the Occupied Palestinian Territory* (Advisory Opinion) [2004] ICJ Rep 136.

247 Ibid., [36]–[45].

248 See section 2.2.4.1 below.

another state, such as that which occurred in *Anglo-Norwegian Fisheries*. Although a state's silence in respect of the former class of omission (performance of an obligation) is not evidence of *opinio juris*, lack of protest at another state's exercise of a claimed right constitutes *opinio juris* so long as the acquiescing state has actual or constructive knowledge of the other state's practice.[249] For example, in *Anglo-Norwegian Fisheries*, the United Kingdom complained that it did not know of the Norwegian practice in relation to maritime delimitation. The ICJ rejected this argument, as the United Kingdom was 'greatly interested' in the fisheries in the area and, as an important maritime power, 'could not have been ignorant' of the Norwegian practice, 'nor, knowing of it, could it have been under any misapprehension as to the significance of its terms'.[250]

2.2.2.3.2 Treaty obligations as evidence of opinio juris A treaty can interact with customary law in three ways. The treaty may (1) codify a pre-existing custom; (2) crystallize an emerging custom; or (3) constitute evidence of *opinio juris* that might contribute to the formation of a customary norm in the future.[251] Importantly, the existence of a treaty as a material source of custom does not 'supervene' the custom itself, even if the terms are identical. Thus, even if a treaty declaratory of customary law is terminated, or otherwise cannot be relied upon, the customary rule is not affected.[252] This situation arose in the *Nicaragua* case. The United States had made a reservation to the Court's jurisdiction in respect of 'multilateral treaties', which included Article 2(4) of the UN Charter relating to the use of force. Therefore, to determine whether the US had impermissibly engaged in the use of force, the ICJ had to revert to the non-use of force as an analogous customary rule of international law.

The third kind of interaction was argued by the Netherlands and Denmark in the *North Sea Continental Shelf* cases. These states claimed that the equidistance method of delimitation[253] contained in Article 6 of

---

249 *Anglo-Norwegian Fisheries* case, above note 198.

250 Ibid., 138–9.

251 Codification and progressive development of treaties is discussed above at section 2.2.1.8.1.

252 *Military and Paramilitary Activities in and against Nicaragua*, above note 11, [177].

253 Equidistance is explained in Article 6(1) of the Geneva Convention on the Continental Shelf as follows: 'Where the same continental shelf is adjacent to the territories of two or more States whose coasts are opposite each other, the boundary of the continental shelf appertaining to such States shall be determined by agreement between them. In the absence of agreement, and unless another boundary line is justified by special circumstances, the boundary is the median line, every

the Geneva Convention on the Continental Shelf, which entered into force a mere three years before the institution of proceedings,[254]

> is, or must now be regarded as involving, a rule that is part of the *corpus* of general international law; – and, like other rules of general or customary international law, is binding on the Federal Republic automatically and independently of any specific assent, direct or indirect, given by the latter. . . . As a matter of positive law, it is based on the work done in this field by international legal bodies, on State practice and on the influence attributed to the Geneva Convention itself, – the claim being that these various factors have cumulatively evidenced or been creative of the *opinio juris sive necessitatis*.[255]

For a treaty provision to constitute *opinio juris*, the provision must, 'at least potentially, be of a fundamentally norm-creating character'.[256] This is not a reference to *jus cogens*, but to whether the treaty provision is expressed in such a manner as to be laying down a rule of law. The Court determined that several factors indicated that Article 6 was not 'fundamentally norm-creating'. First, the obligation to use the equidistance method was made contingent on failure of a primary obligation to effect delimitation by agreement. Secondly, there was significant ambiguity about the 'exact meaning and scope' of the qualification of 'special circumstances' relative to the treatment of equidistance. Finally, parties had the ability to make reservations to Article 6.[257] These factors, though not by themselves enough, were cumulatively effective in denying the 'fundamentally norm-creating character' of Article 6. Additionally, the Court found that the practice of parties and non-parties to the Convention in acting consistently with the treaty was not unequivocally indicative of *opinio juris*.[258]

The Court in the *North Sea Continental Shelf* cases stated that the eventual creation of a customary norm as a result of the influence of a treaty provision is 'not lightly to be regarded as having been attained'.[259] However, as mentioned above in the context of state practice,[260] customary law seems to apply differently to proscriptive norms, such as the norm against genocide. Where such a proscriptive norm is concerned, it is less

---

point of which is equidistant from the nearest points of the baselines from which the breadth of the territorial sea of each State is measured.'

254 *North Sea Continental Shelf* cases, above note 112, [74].

255 Ibid., [77].

256 Ibid., [72].

257 Ibid., [72].

258 Ibid., [76].

259 Ibid., [71].

260 See discussion above at section 2.2.2.2.

likely that states are taken to be acting merely in the application of a treaty, such as the Genocide Convention.[261] It is more readily to be concluded that states are foregoing the acts proscribed in such treaties because they believe a norm of international law independent of the treaty compels such forbearance. This position appears to be starker where *jus cogens* norms, such as the proscription against genocide, are concerned.

A related point is the significance of dispute resolution and other procedural clauses in a treaty. Such clauses are by definition not of a 'fundamentally norm-creating character' and cannot therefore express customary law.[262] Thus one reason why a state would conclude a treaty on a matter already covered by customary law might be to create procedural mechanisms for the monitoring, enforcement and other resolution of disputes relating to pre-existing customary norms. Looked at in this way, the notion that states conclude a particular treaty precisely because of their belief that there is no pre-existing law on the matter may in any given circumstance be quite wrong.[263]

The influence of treaties on customary law is complex and allows courts, tribunals and states significant leeway in considering whether a customary norm has crystallized as a result of the existence of a relevant treaty regime.

2.2.2.3.3 UN General Assembly resolutions as evidence of opinio juris The ICJ has often used UN General Assembly resolutions as evidence of *opinio juris*. In the *Nicaragua* case, the United States had made a reservation to the jurisdiction of the ICJ in respect of Article 2(4) of the UN Charter, making it necessary to determine whether there was a customary norm against the use of force. The ICJ found that such *opinio juris* existed, but in doing so relied exclusively on a series of General Assembly resolutions. The Court stated:

> The *opinio juris* may, though with all due caution, be deduced from, *inter alia*, the attitude of the Parties and the attitude of States towards certain General Assembly resolutions. . . . The effect of consent to the text of such resolutions . . . may be understood as an acceptance of the validity of the rule or set of rules declared by the resolution by themselves.[264]

---

261 Higgins, above note 196, 30–31; Cassese, above note 7, 158.

262 *Military and Paramilitary Activities in and against Nicaragua*, above note 11, [178].

263 See further Thirlway, above note 188, 131.

264 *Military and Paramilitary Activities in and against Nicaragua*, above note 11, [188].

The value of *opinio juris* in General Assembly resolutions should not be overstated. It depends on the degree of consensus achieved by particular resolutions, as well as the number of times the norm has been reaffirmed in subsequent resolutions.[265] Although such resolutions can be a 'very concentrated focal point'[266] for *opinio juris*, there are limits to their effectiveness. In the *Nuclear Weapons* Advisory Opinion, evidence of numerous General Assembly resolutions expressly condemning as illegal the use of nuclear weapons – several by very large majorities – was not effective to constitute *opinio juris* amounting to a prohibition on nuclear weapons. Starting with GA Resolution 1653 (XVI),[267] overwhelming majorities in the General Assembly have passed numerous resolutions – 49 by 1996[268] – asserting that the use of nuclear weapons is unlawful.[269] The Court, however, considered that the consistent reservation of the nuclear weapons states of the right to use nuclear weapons in self-defence, pursuant to a policy of deterrence, prevented the formation of the custom.[270]

Rosalyn Higgins explained the 'obsessive interest' in UN Resolutions as a basis for *opinio juris* as reflecting two things: first, the relative ease with which a court can ascertain what is in the minds of states, as opposed to the complex and sometimes impossible task of searching for evidence of this in more traditional ways; and, secondly, a growing sense that a rigorous search for evidence of states' belief about the existence of a binding rule is less important.[271] Recent seminal ICJ rulings indicate increasing reliance upon UN Resolutions and other more easily ascertainable evidence of state practice and *opinio juris* for the determination of the existence and content of a rule of custom. Examples include the *Nicaragua* case, where such evidence was used to ascertain that common Articles 1 and 3 of the Geneva Conventions of 1949 reflect customary international law and are therefore binding on all states, whether or not they are parties to those treaties, without ever examining evidence of the existence and content of customary rules reflecting the content of these provisions.[272] Another

---

[265] Higgins, above note 196, 22–8.

[266] Rosalyn Higgins, *The Development of International Law through the Political Organs of the United Nations* (London: Oxford University Press, 1963) 2.

[267] Declaration on the Prohibition of the Use of Nuclear and Thermo-nuclear Weapons, GA Resolution 1653 (XVI), UN GAOR, 16th sess., 1063rd plen. mtg, UN Doc. A/5100 (1961).

[268] See *Nuclear Weapons* (Advisory Opinion), above note 210, 532.

[269] Ibid., 255.

[270] Ibid., 248–53, 255.

[271] Higgins, above note 196, 23.

[272] *Military and Paramilitary Activities in and against Nicaragua*, above note 11, [220].

example was in the *Israeli Wall* case where it was used to confirm the prohibition on the use of force and the principle of self-determination.[273]

The ICJ has, at least on one occasion, expressed the need for caution in the use of these declaratory resolutions of the UN General Assembly. In the *Nuclear Weapons* case, the ICJ stated that, to ascertain whether a particular UN General Assembly resolution has normative force, 'it is necessary to look at its content and the conditions of its adoption'.[274] As discussed above, while the Court noted that there were numerous General Assembly resolutions condemning the use of nuclear weapons, they did not show a 'gradual evolution' of customary law, as many of the resolutions were adopted with substantial numbers of negative votes and abstentions.[275] Such reticence might also be read in light of the politically delicate question under consideration – a conclusion supported by the ultimate non-finding in the case. Considered overall, the contemporary practice of the Court clearly indicates employment of these resolutions without a genuine attempt to explain whether the resolution is evidence of state practice, *opinio juris* or both.

As with any declaration by a state, it is always necessary to consider what states actually mean when they vote for or against certain resolutions in international fora. States often vote in a particular way not because they believe the issue in question to give rise to a binding rule, or even because they necessarily agree with the content of the resolution. Their vote may well be an expression of nothing more than political compromise designed to achieve a goal partly or entirely distinct from the issue under vote.[276] While it is tempting to simplify the process of identifying the existence of *opinio juris* in relation to a question of custom under consideration, it is important to carefully consider the context and purpose of any expression of a state's belief, particularly before international fora, where questions of politics and diplomacy are accentuated.

Some scholars have gone even further and suggested that General Assembly resolutions can evidence both state practice as well as *opinio juris*, thereby giving rise to a self-contained source of custom.[277] This approach was implicitly rejected in the *Nicaragua* case, where the Court

---

[273] *Legal Consequences of the Construction of a Wall in the Occupied Palestinian Territory*, above note 246, [87]–[88].

[274] *Nuclear Weapons* (Advisory Opinion), above note 210, 254–5.

[275] Ibid., 255.

[276] See G. Arangio-Ruiz, 'The Normative Role of the General Assembly of the United Nations and the Development of Principles of Friendly Relations'(1972 III) *Recueil des cours*, 431; Higgins, above note 196, 26.

[277] Blaine Sloan, *United Nations General Assembly Resolutions in Our Changing*

expressly linked its analysis of General Assembly resolutions only to *opinio juris*.[278]

2.2.2.4 Challenges to the traditional elements of custom

In 1993, Grigory Tunkin suggested that the exponential growth of general multilateral treaties since 1945 has changed the international paradigm to such a degree that treaties should now also be regarded as formal sources of general international law – in other words, some treaties should, like general custom, apply to all states, even those not parties to the treaty.[279] Tunkin's invitation went largely unanswered. Recently, however, Rudy Baker provocatively asserted that the jurisprudence of international criminal courts and tribunals has been elevated to the status of customary law and hence 'the debate over whether consistent state practice and *opinio juris* are the only building blocks of customary international law is over, because clearly, for better or for worse, they no longer are'.[280]

Baker seeks to substantiate this proposition by reference to three case studies. First, he cites the International Criminal Tribunal for the former Yugoslavia (ICTY) judgment of the Appeals Chamber in the *Tadić* case, which applies a variant of the control test set out by the ICJ to determine whether, for the purposes of armed conflict, one state can be said to be acting as an agent of another. [281] The ICTY 'overall control test', which expressly differs from the 'effective control test' formulated by the ICJ, it is argued, may be taken to express new customary international law.[282]

Baker's second example relates to the suggestion by commentators that the law on state immunity is now in flux, given the jurisprudence of the ICTY and the International Criminal Tribunal for Rwanda (ICTR) based on their Statutes, which expressly reject the application of the dispositional custom of state immunity in respect of their jurisdictions.[283] The suggestion is that the different treatment of the issue of immunity in the

---

World (Ardsley-on-Hudson, NY: Transnational Publishers, 1991) 71–5; Cheng, above note 221.

[278] *Military and Paramilitary Activities in and against Nicaragua*, above note 11, [188].

[279] Grigory Tunkin, 'Is General International Law Customary Law Only?' (1993) 4 *European Journal of International Law* 534.

[280] Roozbeh (Rudy) B. Baker, 'Customary International Law in the 21st Century: Old Challenges and New Debates' (2010) 21(1) *European Journal of International Law* 173, 175.

[281] *Prosecutor v Tadić* (Appeals Chamber Judgment) IT-94-1-A (15 July 1999), [40]–[62] (setting out the relevant test).

[282] Baker, above note 280, 187.

[283] Ibid., 189; Statute of the International Criminal Tribunal for the former

context of the ad hoc international criminal tribunals creates, by virtue of these provisions and endorsement by the Courts of their content, a separate customary law rule.

Thirdly, Baker refers to the application of the doctrine of superior responsibility before the modern international criminal courts and tribunals – an ancient doctrine which was given a modern voice in the jurisprudence of the International Military Tribunals at Nuremberg and Tokyo.[284] Baker argues that such a doctrine, which has since become accepted as customary law, could only be sourced in general principles of law,[285] while concluding that the 'had reason to know' element of command responsibility, as articulated by the tribunals,[286] is not reflected in the domestic law of major legal systems.

The argument that the jurisprudence of the international criminal tribunals has created a new form of custom, rendering state practice and *opinio juris* as no longer indispensable to the formation of custom, is quite wrong. First, Baker acknowledges that 'the majority of ICTY and ICTR jurisprudence follows generally accepted international law'.[287] Secondly, the 'overall control' test in *Tadić* was said by that Court to be expressly founded in custom. The manner in which the ICTY and ICTR go about determining the existence of a customary international law rule is the subject of considerable concern and may call into question the reliability of some of its rulings.[288] However, while the tribunals' methods of identifying state practice and *opinio juris* are at times highly questionable, they are very far from repudiating the need to base custom in those elements – indeed, they confirm the need to do so, in principle if not always in practice. Thirdly, the fact that the customary position of state immunity appears to be 'in flux' suggests only that state practice and *opinio juris* may be developing to change the customary law on this point. Indeed, it was not by judicial determination of a couple of international tribunals that the immunity exception was created; rather it was created by the Security

Yugoslavia ('ICTY Statute'), Art. 7(2); Statute of the International Criminal Tribunal for Rwanda ('ICTR Statute'), Art. 6(2).

[284] See ICTY Statute, Art. 7(3); ICTR Statute, Art. 6(3).

[285] See discussion below at section 2.2.3.

[286] See, e.g., *Prosecutor v Delalić et al. (Čelebići)* (Appeals Chamber Judgment) IT-96-21-A (20 February 2001), [226].

[287] Baker, above note 280, 184.

[288] An example of this unsatisfactory identification of custom can be found in a case before the ICTY concerning privilege attaching to a former ICRC employee: see *Prosecutor v Simić* (Trial Chamber Decision on the Prosecution Motion under Rule 73 for a Ruling Concerning the Testimony of a Witness) IT-95-9-PT (27 July 1999), [73]–[74]. This decision is discussed further in section 2.2.2.5 below.

Council under Chapter VII of the UN Charter.[289] Finally, even assuming a dubious birth in general principles for the doctrine of superior responsibility, state practice and *opinio juris* subsequent to (and indeed including) the Nuremberg and Tokyo trials is the professed basis for the current customary norm.

Despite such flirtations with the idea of a modified doctrine concerning the creation of custom, the twin elements of state practice and *opinio juris* are enduring requirements. At the same time, a lack of rigour in their identification by courts or tribunals may call into question how and when a rule has come into existence. It may even threaten the confidence of states and other subjects of the international legal regime in the identification of customary rules by such bodies. This is the subject of the following section.

2.2.2.5 Treatment by international courts and tribunals

As a subsidiary source, decisions of international courts and tribunals do not make international law. Nevertheless, as these fora constitute the enforcement mechanism for international law, it is vital that they apply the correct methodology when pronouncing on customary law. Some recent decisions of international criminal tribunals and the ICJ have suggested a disturbing trend away from a rigorous approach toward the identification of state practice and *opinio juris*.

A stark example of this in the context of international criminal law was the case of *Prosecutor v Simić*[290] tried before the ICTY. This case concerned the trial of three accused for crimes against humanity and violations of the laws and customs of war, for events that occurred during the Bosnian armed conflict. An interlocutory issue that arose in the proceedings concerned whether or not there was a customary norm granting absolute immunity to employees of the International Committee of the Red Cross (ICRC) from testifying about matters they learnt in the course of their employment. In addressing the issue, the Trial Chamber emphasized the importance of the right of non-disclosure to the ICRC's mandate, before stating:

> The ratification of the Geneva Conventions by 188 States can be considered as reflecting the *opinio juris* of these State Parties, which, in addition to the general practice of States in relation to the ICRC as described above, leads the Trial

---

[289] Itself, the most important multilateral treaty in existence. All the international criminal courts and tribunals containing effectively the same provision are created by or in agreement with the UN, save for the International Criminal Court, which is created by virtue of a multilateral treaty.

[290] *Prosecutor v Simić*, above note 288.

> Chamber to conclude that the ICRC has a right under customary international law to non-disclosure of information.[291]

As Judge Hunt noted in his Separate Opinion, 'it is an enormous step to assume' that states had contemplated an absolute immunity for employees of the ICRC before international courts, especially given the role of these courts in enforcing the Geneva Conventions.[292] Not only do the Conventions themselves not recognize anything like such an immunity of the ICRC, it had not been expressly reflected upon at any of the Red Cross and Red Crescent International Conferences[293] such that states could be said to have expressed views about this specific issue. Also, no real evidence of state practice and *opinio juris* was referred to in support of the Chamber's determination. The decision shows the risks involved in using the decisions of courts on the existence of a customary rule as precedent for the existence of that rule. It is critical to look at what evidence the court specifically identified as establishing a rule. Verification and application of that *evidence*, as opposed to poorly substantiated assertion, may be of some use.

While more understandable – and perhaps less dangerous – in *sui generis* tribunals where there is a variation in the competence and international law experience of judges and where decisions are being rendered on discrete subjects, this attenuated practice has also appeared in judgments of the ICJ. As discussed above, the ICJ has increasingly relied on its own prior judgments as evidence of customary law without independently articulating the basis for the law, despite the injunction in Article 59 of its own Statute that previous decisions have no binding force.[294] A similarly dubious practice has been the mere assertion by the Court in its judgments that it has considered state practice without referring expressly to what this practice is. In the *Arrest Warrant* case,[295] for example, the ICJ did precisely this:

> The Court has carefully examined state practice, including national legislation and those few decisions of national higher courts, such as the House of Lords

---

[291] Ibid., [74].

[292] Ibid., (Separate Opinion of Judge Hunt), [23].

[293] The International Conference of the Red Cross and Red Crescent Movement is the gathering of all the states that have signed up to the Geneva Conventions of 1949 (virtually all states), at which core issues and strategic direction for the Movement are discussed.

[294] See discussion of the *Gulf of Maine* case and other cases, above at section 2.2.2.3.1.

[295] *Arrest Warrant of 11 April 2000*, above note 244.

> or the French Court of Cassation. It has been unable to deduce from this practice that there exists under customary international law any form of exception to the rule according immunity from criminal jurisdiction and inviolability to incumbent Ministers for Foreign Affairs, where they are suspected of having committed war crimes or crimes against humanity.[296]

Voices from the bench of the ICJ itself echo concerns about the manner in which customary international law rules are determined and applied. Judge van Wyngaert in her dissent in the *Arrest Warrant* case described the Court's inverted logic in determining the question of immunity before it: 'In a surprisingly short decision, the Court immediately reaches the conclusion that such a rule exists. A more rigorous approach would have been highly desirable.'[297] Judge Buergenthal has issued a scathing attack on the majority decision of the Court for its determinations in the *Israeli Wall* Advisory Opinion for reaching determinations about Israel's actions without the availability of evidence to enable that conclusion.[298] The relaxed practice of the Court in identifying custom has also been noted by scholars.[299]

2.2.2.6 The persistent objector exception

Once a custom of general international law forms, it is prima facie binding on all states, notwithstanding lack of consent on the part of particular states. Many scholars assert that there is a narrow exception to this rule.[300]

---

[296] Ibid., [58]. Cf the meticulous analysis of state practice and *opinio juris* in the *Nicaragua* case, where the Court established the content of the prohibition against the use of force in customary international law: *Military and Paramilitary Activities in and against Nicaragua*, above note 11, [180]–[210].

[297] *Arrest Warrant of 11 April 2000*, above note 244, [11] (Dissenting Opinion of Judge van Wyngaert).

[298] See *Legal Consequences of the Construction of a Wall in the Occupied Palestinian Territory*, above note 246, Declaration of Judge Buergenthal, in which his Excellency criticizes the Court for reaching determinations based upon UN information in the absence of crucial information which Israel refused to provide to the Court. Judge Buergenthal concludes (at [10]) that, as this was an Advisory Opinion and not a contentious case, Israel was not obliged to produce any evidence and its failure to do so could not prejudice its position.

[299] See Mark Weisburd, 'American Judges and International Law' (2003) 36 *Vanderbilt Journal of Transnational Law* 1475, 1505ff; Prosper Weil, 'Towards Relative Normativity in International Law?' (1983) 77 *American Journal of International Law* 413; Anthony D'Amato, 'Trashing Customary International Law' (1987) 81 *American Journal of International Law* 101.

[300] See, e.g., Brownlie, above note 236, 11; Thirlway, above note 188, 127; *Restatement (Third) of the Foreign Relations Law of the United States*, (1987), Vol. 1, [102], comment 26.

When, during the custom's formative period, a state consistently objects to the application of the customary rule to itself, the custom that eventually crystallizes will not bind that state. This is known as the 'persistent objector exception'.

Commonly cited to support this rule are the *obiter dicta* of two ICJ cases. The first of these is the *Asylum* case which, as discussed below, was arguably concerned only with the doctrine of regional custom.[301] A more cogent argument is based on the *Anglo-Norwegian Fisheries* case.[302] One of the United Kingdom's arguments in that case was that a 'ten-mile rule' of delimitation of territorial waters was a rule of customary international law and thus binding on Norway. The ICJ found that, although some states did apply the ten-mile rule, other states did not and thus state practice was insufficiently widespread. It then added: 'In any event, the ten-mile rule would appear to be inapplicable as against Norway inasmuch as she has always opposed any attempt to apply it to the Norwegian coast.'[303]

Barring these cases, however, there do not appear to be many international judicial pronouncements in support of the persistent objector rule, and state practice on the issue is minimal.[304] Thus, if the persistent objector rule – necessarily a customary norm – exists at all, its scope would be narrow. It would certainly not be applicable to exclude a state from the application of a *jus cogens* norm, as the general disregard of South Africa's opposition to the *jus cogens* norm of apartheid shows.[305]

On a consensualist view, the persistent objector rule is desirable because it prevents international law degenerating into a tyranny of the majority.[306] The sovereign equality of states demands that there be some limits to the ability of the majority to bind the minority, especially since the persistent objector rule only concerns dispositional custom. On a communitarian view, the more integrated, less anarchic nature of modern international society means that in practice states find it more difficult to resist the will of the overwhelming majority.[307] It is a natural consequence of modern

---

[301] See discussion below at section 2.2.2.9.

[302] *Anglo-Norwegian Fisheries* case, above note 198.

[303] Ibid., 131.

[304] Thirlway, above note 188, 127; Cassese, above note 7, 163.

[305] Louis Henkin, *International Law: Politics and Values* (Dordrecht; London: Martinus Nijhoff, 1995) 39; see discussion below at section 2.2.2.7.

[306] Thirlway, above note 188, 127; *Restatement (Third) of the Foreign Relations Law of the United States*, above note 300. The Restatement admits such exemption has been rare.

[307] Cassese, above note 7, 155, 163.

international society that all states are bound by the same set of rules. Those who hold this opinion stress the flimsiness of the evidence that the consensualists are able to drum up of the existence of the persistent objector rule, pointing out that all customary international law automatically applies to a new state, even though it may not have consented to particular norms, putting the lie to any unified consensualist theory.[308]

Although the issue is far from settled, it appears that opposition by states to an emergent custom will, in virtually all cases, amount to nothing more than evidence that the customary rule may not yet be supported by enough states for it to crystallize. If the persistent objector rule does exist, its narrowness would at very least require strong and consistent opposition, both before and after the crystallization of the norm, for a state to hope to invoke it.

2.2.2.7 *Jus cogens*

The debate over the basis and content of *jus cogens* is one of the most contentious in international legal scholarship.

As treaty law and customary law are usually hierarchically equal, a subsequent treaty rule will ordinarily override, as between the States Parties to the treaty, the operation of any inconsistent customary rule. This is true for *jus dispositivum*, or 'yielding' custom, but not so for *jus cogens* – 'peremptory' norms of international law. Such norms sit at the top of the hierarchy of international law sources and cannot therefore be derogated from by states, either by international agreement or national legislative action.[309] Article 53 of the Vienna Convention on the Law of Treaties provides:

> A treaty is void, if, at the time of its conclusion, it conflicts with a peremptory norm of general international law. For the purposes of the present Convention, a peremptory norm of general international law is a norm accepted and recognised by the international community of States as a whole as a norm from which no derogation is permitted and which can be modified only by a subsequent norm of general international law having the same character.[310]

---

[308] Patrick Dumberry, 'Incoherent and Ineffective: The Concept of Persistent Objector Revisited' (2010) 59 *International and Comparative Law Quarterly* 779, 794; Jonathan Charney, 'Universal International Law' (1993) 87 *American Journal of International Law* 529, 541. But see MacGibbon, above note 187, 137.

[309] See Michael Akehurst, 'The Hierarchy of the Sources of International Law' (1974–75) 47 *British Yearbook of International Law* 273; Malcolm N. Shaw, *International Law* (Cambridge; New York: Cambridge University Press, 2008, 6th edn) 115–19.

[310] Similarly, Article 64 of the Vienna Convention on the Law of Treaties

It is widely recognized that this provision, which deals with the consequences rather than the content of *jus cogens*, has attained the status of custom.[311] This is despite the fact that some delegates at the Vienna Conference only agreed to the adoption of this provision after insisting on the inclusion of Article 66(a), which obliges parties to a dispute under Article 53 to submit the matter to the ICJ. The delegates were concerned that, as the *jus cogens* norms were themselves left undefined – precisely because many of them were highly controversial – the stability of treaties might be impaired.[312] Yet, as a dispute resolution provision, Article 66(a) is not part of custom, unlike its substantive counterpart in Article 53,[313] and given that there are currently only 111 parties to the Vienna Convention, it is conceivable that a non-party could claim that a treaty contravenes *jus cogens* without having to resolve the dispute before the ICJ. In practice, however, legal disputes about *jus cogens* have not arisen. This is largely because, as the ICTY stated in the *Furundžija* case, in convicting a member of the Croatian Defence Council of torture and rape:

> [T]he *jus cogens* nature of the prohibition against torture . . . is designed to produce a deterrent effect, in that it signals to all members of the international community and the individuals over whom they wield authority that the prohibition of torture is an absolute value from which nobody must deviate.[314]

Indeed, Antonio Cassese has gone so far as to assert that deterrence is the *primary* purpose of the *jus cogens* concept and that it has achieved its goal, given the diplomatic and psychological motivations that have largely dissuaded states from contravening a rule that the rest of the community considers to be fundamental.[315] There are also suggestions that the ICJ has been reluctant to apply the *jus cogens* concept. In the *Arrest Warrant* case,[316] the ICJ considered whether the incumbent Congolese Foreign

provides: 'If a new peremptory norm of general international law emerges, any existing treaty which is in conflict with that norm becomes void and terminates.'

[311] Cassese, above note 7, 206.

[312] I. Sinclair, *The Vienna Convention on the Law of Treaties* (Manchester, UK: Manchester University Press, 1984, 2nd edn), 66; Egon Schwelb, 'Some Aspects of International *Jus Cogens* as Formulated by the International Law Commission' (1967) 71 *American Journal of International Law* 946, 972–3.

[313] Cassese, above note 7, 205.

[314] *Prosecutor v Furundžija* (Trial Chamber Judgment) IT-95-17/1-T (10 December 1998), [154].

[315] Cassese, above note 7, 209; Dinah Shelton, 'Normative Hierarchy in International Law' (2006) 100 *American Journal of International Law* 291, 305.

[316] *Arrest Warrant of 11 April*, above note 244.

Minister (Yerodia) was immune from domestic Belgian criminal process, even though he was accused of war crimes and crimes against humanity. In the absence of any link between Belgium and the accused, Belgium argued that it had universal jurisdiction to try him. As the Democratic Republic of the Congo did not ultimately contest this latter claim, the sole question before the ICJ was whether, assuming Belgium otherwise had jurisdiction, the accused was immune by virtue of his position as Foreign Minister during the alleged crimes. In a controversial and highly criticized ruling, the Court held that the dispositional custom of immunity of foreign ministers from the criminal process of other states[317] was unaffected even when the crimes charged contravened *jus cogens* norms.[318]

The other reason for considering Article 53 of the Vienna Convention to be a material source of custom, notwithstanding the non-customary nature of Article 66(a), is that the concept of *jus cogens* pre-dates the Vienna Convention. The most uncontroversial *jus cogens* norm is *pacta sunt servanda* – that promises must be kept. This norm is of truly ancient pedigree, as it is the machinery without which treaty-making would be entirely meaningless.[319] The institution of treaty-making relies on a hierarchically superior norm enabling states to bind themselves in the future in exchange for the same from the other parties to the compact. State practice and *opinio juris* on *pacta sunt servanda* exists 'from time immemorial'.[320] That Article 53 codified an existing norm finds ample support. For example, during the *Krupp* trial in 1948, the United States Military Tribunal sitting in Nuremberg considered whether 12 directors of the Krupp Group of companies were guilty, inter alia, of the war crime of using French prisoners of war in the German armaments industry. In the course of convicting the accused, the Tribunal stated that any treaty between Germany and the Vichy government authorizing Germany to engage French prisoners of war in German armament production would

---

[317] See Chapter 6 for further discussion of state immunity.

[318] *Arrest Warrant of 11 April*, above note 244, [58]. The case has been the subject of much scholarly criticism: Neil Boister, 'The ICJ in the Belgian *Arrest Warrant* Case: Arresting the Development of International Criminal Law' (2002) 7(2) *Journal of Conflict and Security Law* 293; Steffen Wirth, 'Immunity for Core Crimes? The ICJ's Judgment in the *Congo v Belgium* Case' (2002) 13(4) *European Journal of International Law* 877.

[319] Wehberg, above note 69, 782–3. The modern formulation is Article 26 of the Vienna Convention on the Law of Treaties: 'Every treaty in force is binding upon the parties to it and must be performed by them in good faith.' See discussion above at section 2.2.1.

[320] Wehberg, above note 69, 783.

have been void as manifestly *contra bonos mores*[321] – against good morals. This idea underscores the deductive, even natural law, basis of *jus cogens*. Further evidence can be found in the prohibition against genocide. Judge Elihu Lauterpacht has stated that 'genocide has long been regarded as one of the few undoubted examples of *jus cogens*'.[322]

Rather than arising from the consent of states, *jus cogens* appears to spring from the core ethics of international society. It expresses, in the words of the ICTY, an 'absolute value from which nobody must deviate' and runs counter to the old orthodoxy that international rules 'binding upon States . . . emanate from their own free will as expressed in conventions or by usages generally accepted as expressing principles of law'.[323]

Some commentators have erroneously suggested that the requirement in Article 53 that the norm be 'recognized by the international community of States *as a whole*' means that it should be a norm that *every* state recognizes, such that if there is one deviant, the norm is defeated.[324] This interpretation would make the norm logically inconsistent, as it would merely reflect international reality – something that law is, by definition, designed to regulate. In other words, a state could defeat the norm by refusing to recognize it and engaging in practice incompatible with it. Ambassador Yasseen, the President of the Drafting Committee of the Vienna Convention, stated:

> [I]f one State in isolation refused to accept the peremptory character of the rule, or if that State was supported by a very small number of States, the acceptance and recognition of the peremptory character of the rule by the international community as a whole would not be affected.[325]

---

[321] Cited in Schwelb, above note 312, 950–1. This was also the view of the International Law Commission in its Commentary on the precursor to Article 53, although governments seemed reluctant to recognize it as such in their comments on the draft: ibid., 970.

[322] *Application of the Convention on the Prevention and Punishment of the Crime of Genocide* (*Bosnia and Herzegovina v Yugoslavia*) [1993] ICJ Rep 325, Separate Opinion of Judge ad hoc Elihu Lauterpacht, 440. See also *Barcelona Traction, Light and Power Co. Ltd* (*Belgium v Spain*) above note 4, [33]–[34]; William A. Schabas, *Genocide in International Law* (Cambridge: Cambridge University Press, 2000), 445–6.

[323] *SS 'Lotus'* (*France v Turkey*), above note 209,18.

[324] See Martti Koskenniemi, *From Apology to Utopia: The Structure of International Legal Argument* (Cambridge: Cambridge University Press, 2005), 324.

[325] UN Conference on the Law of Treaties, 1st session, Vienna, 26 March to 24 May 1968, *Official Records*, Summary Records of the Plenary Meetings and of the

As *jus cogens* can only be modified by a 'subsequent norm of general international law having the same character', contrary dispositional custom and the persistent objector rule are inapplicable. So, too, are reservations to *jus cogens* norms contained in multilateral treaties.[326] Besides limiting the validity of international acts of states, *jus cogens* may also impugn the validity of domestic legislative or executive acts, insofar as they are inconsistent with the *jus cogens* norm.[327] Laws bestowing amnesty on perpetrators of international crimes that have the character of *jus cogens* can thus be declared invalid in an international forum or even in a domestic forum if international law is part of the law of the land.[328] A striking example of such incorporation is the inclusion in 1999 of provisions of the Swiss Constitution giving the Federal Assembly the duty to invalidate an attempt at reform of the Constitution that violates '*les règles imperatives du droit international*'.[329]

The above has briefly sketched the potential operation of *jus cogens*. Of course, the secondary norm codified in Article 53 is itself meaningless without identification of the content of the primary norms the consequences of which it purports to regulate. Hugh Thirlway has argued that the crystallization of a specific *jus cogens* norm would, according to traditional concepts of custom formation, require an attempt by a state to enforce a treaty in breach of customary law, followed by universal condemnation asserting that the custom was non-derogable.[330] However, as mentioned above, disputes over *jus cogens* are rare in practice, given the deterrent effect that attends the widespread belief that a norm is 'fundamental' to international public order. Nevertheless, while such heinous acts as genocide, slavery and torture are universally recognized as *jus cogens*, it appears then that there is an abundance of *opinio juris* but very little state practice. This has implications for the traditional conception of custom as a rigid separation of its two elements, discussed above.[331] Dinah Shelton has even stated:

> Although it may be appropriate today to recognize fundamental norms deriving from an international public order, the extensive assertions of peremptory

Meetings of the Committee of the Whole, Doc. A/Conf.39/11 (1969), 472, cited in Cassese, above note 7, 201.

326 *North Sea Continental Shelf* cases, above note 112, 97, 182, 248.
327 *Prosecutor v Furundžija*, above note 314, [154]–[157].
328 See Chapter 3.
329 The fundamental rules of international law.
330 Thirlway, above note 233, 138.
331 See discussion above at section 2.2.2.2.

> norms made by some writers and international tribunals, without presenting any evidence to support the claimed superior status of the norms under consideration, pose risks for the international legal order and the credibility of the authors and tribunals.[332]

Indeed, the first time the ICJ stated that a specific norm was *jus cogens* was in 2006, in the *Armed Activities on the Territory of the Congo* case, in which it bluntly asserted that the prohibition of genocide was 'assuredly' a peremptory norm of international law, without adducing any supporting evidence.[333] Interestingly, the lack of any resistance to or substantive criticism of such a proposition increases the sense that such proscribing norms have a place somehow above the normative framework of international law, once again evoking a natural law sensibility in relation to certain norms.[334]

Although the list of *jus cogens* norms seems to be as long as the particular commentator's foot,[335] the peremptory nature of the following seven norms appears to be settled:

- *pacta sunt servanda*;
- piracy – the oldest international crime;
- use of force other than in self-defence, as expressed in Article 2(4) of the UN Charter;
- genocide – arguably the most abhorrent of international crimes;
- crimes against humanity;
- slavery – universally considered an anathema after the American Civil War; and
- torture – the frequent breaches of this rule have never been justified on the basis that torture is lawful.[336]

Additionally,

- the laws of armed conflict, a great many of which, in the opinion of the ICJ, are 'so fundamental to the respect of the human person and

---

332 Shelton, above note 315, 292.

333 *Armed Activities on the Territory of the Congo* (*Democratic Republic of Congo v Rwanda*) [2005] ICJ Rep 168. Note that the point about *jus cogens* was not central to the Court's decision, as it held that its jurisdiction did not depend on whether the norm invoked had the character of *jus cogens*: ibid.

334 Norms relating to 'laws of humanity and the requirements of the public conscience'. For a discussion of natural law theory and its place in the development of international law, see chapter 1, section 1.4.2.1.

335 See, e.g., Shelton, above note 315, 303.

336 Higgins, above note 196, 20.

"elementary considerations of humanity" . . . [that] they constitute intransgressible principles of international customary law';[337]

- apartheid or systemic racial discrimination, given the South African experience; and
- international terrorism

also seem settled *jus cogens*, even though there is no consensus as to the exact meaning of the latter or where to draw the line separating a 'terrorist' from a 'freedom fighter'.[338]

2.2.2.8 *Erga omnes* obligations

A sibling of *jus cogens* is the concept of obligations *erga omnes* – obligations owed 'towards all' states. Like *jus cogens*, *erga omnes* lays down a procedural consequence flowing from the importance of certain substantive norms to the international public order. If an obligation is *erga omnes*, then it is owed to the whole community of states, such that any state has standing under international law to enforce compliance with it.

In the 1949 *Reparations* case, the ICJ formulated the general rule of standing in international law: 'only the party to whom an international obligation is due can bring a claim in respect of its breach'.[339] This mirrors the general principle of national public law in the major systems of the world, that persons whose interests are not affected (that is, mere busybodies) cannot sue.

The seminal case in this area is the *Barcelona Traction* case before the ICJ.[340] The question before the Court was whether Belgium had standing to sue Spain in carrying out its duty of diplomatic protection of Belgian nationals who had sustained economic damage as a result of Spain's activities towards a Canadian company in which the Belgian nationals were shareholders. The Court began by stating:

> [A]n essential distinction should be drawn between the obligations of a State towards the international community as a whole, and those arising vis-à-vis another State in the field of diplomatic protection. By their very nature the former are the concern of all States. In view of the importance of the rights

---

337 *Nuclear Weapons* (Advisory Opinion), above note 210, 257.

338 Ben Saul, *Defining Terrorism in International Law* (Oxford: Oxford University Press, 2006) 182, 186, 188, 200–201, 254, 258, 270.

339 *Reparation for Injuries Suffered in the Service of the United Nations* (Advisory Opinion) [1949] ICJ Rep 174, 180–81.

340 *Barcelona Traction, Light and Power Co. Ltd* (*Belgium v Spain*), above note 4.

> involved, all States can be held to have a legal interest in their protection; they are obligations *erga omnes*.[341]

Although the Court did not expressly say so, it made it clear that only those norms the importance of which approached that of *jus cogens* would give rise to obligations owed *erga omnes*:

> Such obligations derive, for example, in contemporary international law, from the outlawing of acts of aggression, and of genocide, as also from the principles and rules concerning basic rights of the human person including protection from slavery and racial discrimination.[342]

If, however, there exists a specific international body monitoring compliance with treaty provisions relating to an obligation *erga omnes* – such as the UN Committee against Torture – standing would be accorded to such a body in preference to states. The ICTY has held that 'these bodies enjoy priority over individual states', so as to make it possible 'for compliance with international law to be ensured in a neutral and impartial manner'.[343]

Despite the conceptual similarities, there is no necessary identity between obligations *erga omnes* and *jus cogens*. To be captured by both concepts, a norm must attain a certain level of importance. However, the *way* in which a norm must be important differs. For *jus cogens*, it is the norm's non-derogability that must be of fundamental importance to the international community, such that it must apply to every state, even against its will. For obligations *erga omnes*, it is the norm's ability to be enforced that must be of fundamental importance. Hence, international public order is more likely to demand that a norm be *erga omnes* if the norm regulates the internal behaviour of the state, with the consequence that no other state is directly affected.[344] Thus, there is more scope to argue that certain human rights obligations possess an *erga omnes* character. In this sense, *erga omnes* can be wider than *jus cogens*, though the area is far from settled.[345]

2.2.2.9 Regional custom

The custom of states need not be of general application to be normative. While general international law does bind every state in the international

---

341 Ibid., [33].
342 Ibid., [34].
343 *Prosecutor v Furundžija*, above note 314, [152].
344 Shelton, above note 315, 318.
345 Note that the ICJ considers *erga omnes* and *jus cogens* as separate concepts: *East Timor* (*Portugal v Australia*) [1995] ICJ Rep 90, [29].

community, except possibly persistent objectors,[346] a custom can also develop as between a group of states, or even between two states.[347] Like general custom, regional custom requires practice by states that are sought to be bound by the norm, and *opinio juris* whereby they consider the norm to be legally obligatory. There is, however, a further requirement for the creation of regional custom: a state will not be bound by it unless it has *itself* manifested at least tacit consent to the norm.[348] This differs from general custom, which does not insist on uniformity of state practice or *opinio juris*.[349]

Some commentators have stated that *opinio juris* for a regional custom, as opposed to a general custom, cannot be inferred solely from consistent state practice.[350] This is a claim unsupported by judicial decisions and arguably is not a necessary corollary of the requirement that the practice be opposable to the state sought to be bound. A better view is that state practice can occur in circumstances that strongly compel the inference of *opinio juris* – for example, state A may continuously grant state B access to lucrative gold mines on state A's territory. In the absence of any evidence suggesting that state A is being compensated with, for example, political or military protection, the inference is open that state A is granting state B a right of passage because it believes itself legally obliged to do so. In the *Right of Passage* case,[351] Portugal claimed that it was entitled to the benefit of a regional custom with India whereby Portugal had a right of passage through Indian territory in order to practically exercise its sovereignty over Portuguese enclaves on the subcontinent. The Court found considerable state practice consistent with such a right. On *opinio juris* it had only the following to say:

> This practice having continued over a period extending beyond a century and a quarter unaffected by the change of regime in respect of the intervening territory which occurred when India became independent, the Court is, in view of all the circumstances of the case, satisfied that that practice was accepted as law by the Parties and has given rise to a right and a correlative obligation.[352]

Thus, the Court was inferring *opinio juris* from a veritable mountain of state practice. Note that this finding was restricted to the passage of

---

346 See section 2.2.2.6 above.

347 *Right of Passage* case (*Portugal v India*) [1960] ICJ Rep 6, 39.

348 Jennings and Watts, above note 16, 30; Cassese, above note 7, 164.

349 See discussion above at sections 2.2.2.2 and 2.2.2.3.

350 Brownlie, above note 236, 11. For discussion about the inference of *opinio juris* from general custom, see discussion above at section 2.2.2.3.

351 *Right of Passage* case, above note 347.

352 Ibid., 40.

civilian persons and goods. In respect of military forces, police, arms and ammunition, the Court considered that 'the course of dealings established between the Portuguese and the British authorities with respect to the passage of these categories excluded the existence of any such right'.[353]

Perhaps the most significant case on regional custom is the ruling of the ICJ in the *Asylum* case.[354] In 1948, the leader of a failed rebellion in Peru sought asylum at the Colombian Embassy. While under general international law this was an unlawful intervention by Colombia in the sovereign affairs of Peru, Colombia argued that there was a regional custom among Latin American states to the contrary. It relied upon the principle that where a regional custom and a general dispositional custom conflict, the regional custom is preferred to the extent of the inconsistency, applying the general principle *lex specialis derogat legi generali* – special laws prevail over general laws. The ICJ did not consider it a barrier that Article 38(1)(b) of the ICJ Statute uses the words 'international custom, as evidence of a *general* practice accepted as law'.[355] The Court held:

> The Party which relies on a custom of this kind must prove that this custom is established in such a manner that it has become binding on the other Party. The Colombian Government must prove that the rule invoked by it is in accordance with a constant and uniform usage practised by the States in question, and that this usage is the expression of a right appertaining to the State granting asylum and a duty incumbent on the territorial State.[356]

In holding that the practice of Latin American states had not been uniform or supported by *opinio juris*, the Court denied the existence of the local custom. Even if a custom had crystallized, in the Court's view, 'it could not be invoked against Peru which, far from having by its attitude adhered to it, has on the contrary repudiated it'.[357] Although some commentators have seen this latter statement as a formulation of the persistent objector rule,[358] the better view is that the Court was applying the rule that regional custom is only opposable against states that have consented to it. Also, as the extracts from the judgment indicate, the burden of proving that another state is bound by the regional custom rests on the state seeking to

---

[353] Ibid., 43. Note that when India became independent from Britain in 1947, it succeeded Britain's international obligations incurred in respect of the territory, in accordance with the law of state succession, discussed in Chapter 4.

[354] *Asylum* case, above note 201.

[355] Emphasis added.

[356] Ibid., 276.

[357] Ibid., 277–8.

[358] Thirlway, above note 188, 126–7; see discussion above at section 2.2.2.6.

have the court recognize the custom. This is in contrast to general custom, which is a matter the decision-maker must positively determine without recourse to burden of proof principles.[359]

2.2.3 General Principles of Law

2.2.3.1 The nature and role of general principles of law

The third source of international law in Article 38(1)(c) of the ICJ Statute is referred to as 'general principles of law recognised by civilised nations'. The term 'civilised' is at best old-fashioned, at worst a hangover of colonialist thinking. Despite the wording of the ICJ Statute, this source has more commonly been considered as 'general principles of law recognised by the community of nations', excising the qualifier altogether,[360] although it seems that the term 'civilised' should be transmuted to mean 'nations with a mature legal system'.[361] For example, in the *Abu Dhabi* arbitration,[362] the arbitrator considered whether there were general principles of law dealing with oil concessions. In doing so, he disregarded the law of Abu Dhabi, as it had no principles that could be applied to modern commercial instruments.

Although listed as a source proper, rather than a 'subsidiary' source like judicial decisions and learned publicists, general principles tend to perform a gap-filling function, where there appears to be no settled custom or treaty on the question.[363] Although international courts and tribunals had applied general principles before the source's material appearance in Article 38(1)(c) of the ICJ Statute (and its precursor in the Permanent Court of International Justice Statute), its continued acceptance as a source of law relied on the perception that international law – being an anarchic, horizontal legal system – required a formal source other than treaty and custom to function.[364] Rules such as those on circumstantial evidence[365] were unlikely to be the subject of state practice and *opinio*

---

[359] Cassese, above note 7, 164. Note that in international criminal trials, the burden always rests on the prosecution to prove the existence of a customary norm.

[360] See, e.g., Cassese, above note 7, 188.

[361] Thirlway, above note 188, 128.

[362] *The Sheikh of Abu Dhabi* [1951] 18 ILR 144.

[363] Cassese, above note 7, 128.

[364] Hersch Lauterpacht, 'Some Observations on the Prohibition of "*Non Liquet*" and the Completeness of the Law', in Elihu Lauterpacht (ed.), *International Law: Being the Collected Papers of Hersch Lauterpacht* (Cambridge: Cambridge University Press, 1975), Vol. 2, 213, 220–21.

[365] See *Corfu Channel* (*United Kingdom v Albania*) (Merits) [1949] ICJ Rep 4, 18.

juris, or be important enough to be the subject of an applicable treaty. Thus, recourse to 'general principles' would be required to prevent decision-makers from either pronouncing a *non liquet* (failure to decide) or, worse, deciding the issue according to their personal whim. An example of the latter occurred in 1831 when the King of the Netherlands, acting as arbitrator in a boundary dispute between the United States and Great Britain, found that the law of nations contained insufficient rules on the subject and proceeded to draw the boundary in a way that seemed to him 'most appropriate'.[366] The nature of a *non liquet* will be further discussed below.[367]

The question remains how such 'general principles' should be derived, and it appears that there are two sources for these principles. First, a court may find that there is a principle that is, in substance,[368] recognized by the domestic legal systems of the world. The process is thus one of induction: the general principle at international law is deduced from the separate instances at domestic law. The reason why a general review of legal systems is required is that, as Lord Asquith has stated, 'almost any national system is a mixture of modern and antiquated principles, of those of general applicability and those of historic or national peculiarity'.[369] Not all principles are in substance shared among domestic orders and a principle may not, by its nature, be translatable into international law, at least without adjustment. Judge Cassese stated in his Dissenting Opinion in the ICTY Appeals Chamber decision in *Prosecutor v Erdemović*:[370]

> [N]ormally it would prove incongruous and inappropriate to apply in an inter-State legal setting a national law concept as such, that is, with its original scope and purport. The body of law into which one may be inclined to transplant the national law notion cannot but reject the transplant, for the notion is felt as extraneous to the whole set of legal ideas, constructs and mechanisms prevailing in the international context. Consequently, the normal attitude of international courts is to try to assimilate or transform the national law notion so as to adjust it to the exigencies and basic principles of international law.

At first blush, it might be thought difficult to derive general principles from across the diverse cross-section of legal systems of the world. However,

---

366 Lauterpacht, above note 364, 219.

367 See discussion below at section 2.2.3.3.

368 Wolfgang Friedmann, 'The Uses of "General Principles" in the Development of International Law' (1963) 57 *American Journal of International Law* 279, 284–5.

369 Quoted in Friedmann, ibid., 284.

370 *Prosecutor v Erdemović* (Appeals Chamber Judgment) IT-96-22-A (7 October 1997), Dissenting Opinion of Judge Cassese, [3].

many principles – such as the principle that a party cannot take advantage of its own wrong[371] – are rooted in fairness and logic and hence suggest that there are areas of significant similarity in substance between the national legal systems of the world. Additionally, the course of history has seen many of the major European legal systems attain dominance in most of the world, thus lessening the chance of a fundamental clash of principles. Domestic principles potentially of use to international law – those of a 'jurisdictional' or 'incidental' character – are precisely those which are most likely to be substantially homogenous among domestic orders.[372]

The second form of general principles does not depend on any process of induction from domestic law. General principles may be derived directly from international legal relations and legal relations generally. The suite of interpretive principles used by international courts fall into this category, for example, the principle that special laws prevail over general laws (*lex specialis derogat legi generali*). Interestingly, this very principle can be applied to assert that general principles derived specifically from international legal relations prevail over those induced from domestic law.[373] Foundational principles of the international community – such as the sovereign equality of states, and core principles of certain areas of law such as 'elemental considerations of humanity'[374] in the field of international humanitarian law – are more than gap-fillers and provide a standard according to which conflicting norms, where two outcomes are reasonably open, can be resolved.

Many of these principles, such as *pacta sunt servanda* (that promises must be kept) also have the character of customary law.[375] In *Prosecutor v Furundžija*,[376] the ICTY had to decide what the specific elements were of rape as a war crime or crime against humanity. Having found no unanimity in the domestic legislation of states regarding whether forced oral penetration constituted rape, the Court found that the 'general principle of respect for human dignity is the basic underpinning and indeed the very *raison d'être* of international humanitarian law and human rights law' and

---

371 *Factory at Chorzów* (*Germany v Poland*) (Jurisdiction) (1927) PCIJ (Ser. A) No. 9, 31.

372 Jennings and Watts, above note 16, 95; Hersch Lauterpacht, 'Decisions of Municipal Courts as a Source of International Law', in Elihu Lauterpacht (ed.), *International Law: Being the Collected Papers of Hersch Lauterpacht* (Cambridge: Cambridge University Press, 1975), Vol. 2, 245–6.

373 Cassese, above note 7, 194.

374 *Nuclear Weapons* (Advisory Opinion), above note 210, 257; *Corfu Channel* case, above note 365, 22.

375 Brownlie, above note 236, 19; Thirlway, above note 188, 128.

376 *Prosecutor v Furundžija*, above note 314.

hence it was 'consonant with this principle that such an extremely serious sexual outrage as forced oral penetration should be classified as rape'.[377] This case illustrates that customary law (for example, that relating to rape) may at times only provide the broad legal doctrine to be applied and that general principles are thus essential for fleshing out and putting into practical effect such customary norms.

2.2.3.2 The identification of general principles by international courts and tribunals

When deriving a general principle from the domestic legal systems of the world, international courts and tribunals do not undertake an exhaustive comparative study. Generally, judgments cite from a few major Western legal systems, and then presume that these principles are self-evidently universal.

Examples abound before the international criminal tribunals of reference to general principles derived from national legal systems, where a handful of sources from a small sample of states (usually traversing the common and civil law legal systems) are considered.

Adding to the sense that general principles are being derived from a limited pool of states is the sometimes confusing terminology employed to describe general principles as a source of international law. The following statement by the Trial Chamber in the *Kupreškić* case before the ICTY serves as a prime example:

> [A]ny time the Statute does not regulate a specific matter, and the *Report of the Secretary-General* does not prove to be of any assistance in the interpretation of the Statute, it falls to the International Tribunal to draw upon (i) rules of customary international law or (ii) general principles of international criminal law; or, lacking such principles, (iii) general principles of criminal law common to the major legal systems of the world; or, lacking such principles, (iv) general principles of law consonant with the basic requirements of international justice.[378]

The reference to customary international law in the extract is meaningful as a primary source of international law itself. However, the reference to the three forms of general principles does not facilitate any comprehension of their meaning or relationship with the 'general principles of law'

---

377 Ibid., [183].

378 *Prosecutor v Kupreškić, Kupreškić, Kupreškić, Josipović, Papić and Šantić* (Judgment) IT-95-16-T (14 January 2000), [591]. Similarly confusing is a passage in *Prosecutor v Furundžija* (Trial Chamber Judgment) IT-95-17/1-T (10 December 1998) ('*Furundžija* trial judgment'), [182].

as it is enshrined as a source of international law in Article 38 of the ICJ Statute.

2.2.3.3 *Non liquet* in international law

The gap-filling function of general principles was designed to prevent courts from pronouncing a *non liquet* – that the law is 'not clear' – and thus refusing to decide the case, or deciding it according to arbitrary whim.[379] This view, of the 'completeness' of international law,[380] was one firmly held by Lauterpacht:

> [T]he principle of completeness of international law – the prohibition of *non liquet* – constitutes one of the most indisputably established rules of positive international law as evidenced by an uninterrupted continuity of international arbitral and judicial practice.[381]

Nonetheless, at least in respect of Advisory Opinions, the ICJ has accepted that a *non liquet* may be declared. In its controversial decision in the *Nuclear Weapons* Advisory Opinion, the Court ultimately held:

> [I]n view of the present state of international law viewed as a whole, as examined above by the Court, and of the elements of fact at its disposal, the Court is led to believe that it cannot reach a definitive conclusion as to the legality or illegality of the use of nuclear weapons by a state in an extreme circumstance of self-defence, in which its very survival would be at stake.[382]

The prohibition against declaring *non liquet* most likely still holds good in contentious proceedings. The general rule in the *Lotus* case that 'restrictions upon the independence of states cannot . . . be presumed'[383] operates to place the burden of proof on the claimant. Hence, when uncertain or ambivalent about the outcome, the Court may declare that the case is 'not proven' instead of declaring that the law itself is 'not clear'. However, practice suggests that the Court must determine for itself questions relating to whether particular customary rules exist, without reference to

---

[379] See discussion above at section 2.2.3.1.

[380] Lauterpacht, above note 364.

[381] Lauterpacht, ibid., 217. See also the Dissenting Opinion of Judge Higgins in the *Nuclear Weapons* (Advisory Opinion), above note 210; Lauterpacht, above note 6, 97.

[382] *Nuclear Weapons* (Advisory Opinion), ibid., 263. See Timothy McCormack, 'A *Non Liquet* on Nuclear Weapons – The ICJ Avoids the Applications of General Principles of International Humanitarian Law' (1997) 316 *International Review of the Red Cross* 92.

[383] *SS 'Lotus' (France v Turkey)*, above note 209, 18–19

burden of proof principles.[384] A more solid foundation for the prohibition of *non liquet* in contentious proceedings is Article 38(1) of the ICJ Statute, which states that the Court's 'function is to *decide* in accordance with international law such *disputes* as are submitted to it'.[385] By its nature a failure to decide, a *non liquet*, seems inapplicable to disputes.

It may be said that the function of any court is to make an authoritative pronouncement on legal questions that are submitted to it – whether the proceedings are advisory or contentious. A strong argument can be made that the *Nuclear Weapons* Advisory Opinion was an abdication of the judicial function. The implications are even more troubling in the context of the subject matter of that case. Given the destructive power of nuclear weapons, Judge Shahabuddeen considered in his Dissenting Opinion that 'it would, at any rate, seem curious that a World Court should consider itself compelled by the law to reach the conclusion that a state has the legal right, even in limited circumstances, to put the planet to death'.[386]

2.2.4 Judicial Decisions and Highly Regarded Publicists – Subsidiary Sources

2.2.4.1 Judicial decisions

2.2.4.1.1 No precedent in international law: Article 59 ICJ Statute Article 38(1)(d) of the ICJ Statute recognizes that, 'subject to the provisions of Article 59, judicial decisions . . . are a subsidiary means for the determination of rules of law'. The reference to 'subsidiary' means that judicial decisions are only material and not formal sources of law. Reinforcing this restriction is the reference to Article 59 of the ICJ Statute: 'The decision of the Court has no binding force except between the parties and in respect of that particular case'. This Article is the material source for the principle that international law knows no doctrine of precedent (*stare decisis*) as it is understood in common law, and less so in certain civil law, systems.[387]

---

[384] Cassese, above note 7, 164. Note that in international criminal trials the burden always rests on the prosecution to prove the existence of a customary norm.

[385] Emphasis added.

[386] *Nuclear Weapons* (Advisory Opinion), above note 210, 34 (Dissenting Opinion of Judge Shahabuddeen).

[387] For a discussion of the differing approaches across common and civil law systems, as well as the position in international criminal law, see Gideon Boas, 'The Case for a New Appellate Jurisdiction for International Criminal Law', in Göran Sluiter and Sergey Vasiliev (eds), *International Criminal Procedure: Towards A Coherent Body of Law* (London: Cameron May Ltd, 2008).

The reasoning in previous judgments, even if it constitutes an essential step leading to the ultimate outcome in those judgments (*ratio decidendi*), will not inescapably bind subsequent decision-makers, regardless of their place in the international system.

The reference to 'judicial decisions' includes decisions of both international and national courts and tribunals.[388] Given the relative sparseness of international decisions, the ICJ has examined the decisions of national courts where they provide useful commentary on the existence and scope of an international norm. This is not to be confused with the other (albeit limited) role of domestic decisions as evidence of state practice and *opinio juris*. The *Arrest Warrant* case[389] provides an example of where the ICJ has considered the views of national courts as a material source of a rule of international law. In argument, the Democratic Republic of the Congo raised several decisions of higher national courts in support of its claim that an incumbent Foreign Minister was immune from the criminal process of national courts, even where the minister was suspected of war crimes or crimes against humanity. For instance, the Congo cited Lord Browne-Wilkinson's statement in the UK House of Lords decision in *Pinochet No.3*[390] that 'a complete immunity attached to the person of the head of state or ambassador . . . rendering him immune from all actions or prosecutions'.[391] The ICJ agreed with the Congo's submission, after examining 'state practice, including national legislation and those few decisions of national higher courts, such as the House of Lords or the French Court of Cassation'.[392]

The position of judicial decisions in the determination of international law is clearly far more complex than simply saying that there is no doctrine of binding precedent and that such decisions may assist a Court in identifying evidence of a rule or principle. As discussed in respect of the determination of the existence of customary international law rules by the ICJ, a troubling practice of referring to the Court's own past rulings as support for the existence of a rule – as opposed to reference to *evidence* of a rule – has started to creep into the practice of the

---

[388] Lauterpacht, above note 372; Donald Anton, Penelope Mathew and Wayne Morgan, *International Law: Cases and Materials* (Oxford: Oxford University Press, 2005) 243.

[389] *Arrest Warrant of 11 April 2000*, above note 244.

[390] *R v Bow Street Metropolitan Stipendiary Magistrate, ex parte Pinochet Ugarte (No. 3)* [2000] 1 AC 147.

[391] *Arrest Warrant of 11 April 2000*, above note 244, [57].

[392] Ibid., [58]. Compare the difference in approach of Judge van Wyngaert in his Dissenting Opinion: ibid., [9]ff.

Court.[393] This may be indicative of a weakening of the requirements for the identification of sufficient state practice and *opinio juris* for the identification of a rule of custom.

2.2.4.1.2 A de facto *normative system of precedent at international law?* Although ostensibly only a material source of international law that is not of precedential value, decisions of the ICJ are highly persuasive and have done much to clarify norms of international law. For example, the decision of the ICJ in the *North Sea Continental Shelf* cases[394] has laid down invaluable guidelines for the derivation of custom.[395] Other cases have arguably assumed normative significance, such as the ICJ's decision in the *Reservations* case,[396] breaking with the traditional doctrine that the consent of all contracting states is necessary for a reservation to be admissible, as well as the Court's broad formulation in the *Reparations* case[397] of the nature of the international personality of intergovernmental organizations as being related to the purposes of the particular organization. Insofar as the ICJ has made new law (and hence, in effect, binding precedent) in judgments such as these, Cassese points out that the international community of states have acquiesced to them, such that they have acquired the status of general principle.[398]

More routinely, the ICJ cites profusely from its own previous decisions, sometimes even at the expense of examining actual evidence of state practice. For example, in the *Israeli Wall* case,[399] the ICJ relied almost exclusively on its previous decisions, in preference to finding relevant custom by its own endeavours.[400]

Other international courts and tribunals have also followed this trend of citing previous decisions, perhaps none more so than the international

---

[393] See *Legal Consequences of the Construction of a Wall in the Occupied Palestinian Territory*, above note 246; *Delimitation of the Maritime Boundary on the Gulf of Maine Area*, above note 242. See also discussion above at sections 2.2.2.3.1 and 2.2.2.5.

[394] *North Sea Continental Shelf* cases, above note 112.

[395] See discussion at section 2.2.2.

[396] *Reservations to the Convention on the Prevention and Punishment of the Crime of Genocide*, above note 96.

[397] *Reparation for Injuries Suffered in the Service of the United Nations*, above note 339. See Chapter 5.

[398] Cassese, above note 7, 196.

[399] *Legal Consequences of the Construction of a Wall in the Occupied Palestinian Territory*, above note 246.

[400] See also the discussion above at section 2.2.2.5.

criminal tribunals. In *Prosecutor v Kupreskić et al.*,[401] the ICTY Trial Chamber was assessing the international criminal responsibility of accused parties charged with war crimes and crimes against humanity perpetrated against the village of Ahmići during the Bosnian war. The ICTY openly defended its pervasive use of its own prior judgments and those of other international tribunals:

> The Tribunal's need to draw upon judicial decisions is only to be expected, due to the fact that both substantive and procedural criminal law is still at a rudimentary stage in international law. In particular, there exist relatively few treaty provisions on the matter. By contrast, especially after World War II, a copious amount of case law has developed on international crimes. Again, this is a fully understandable development: it was difficult for international law-makers to reconcile very diverse and often conflicting national traditions in the area of criminal law and procedure by adopting general rules capable of duly taking into account those traditions. By contrast, general principles may gradually crystallise through their incorporation and elaboration in a series of judicial decisions delivered by either international or national courts dealing with specific areas. This being so, it is only logical that international courts should rely heavily on such jurisprudence.[402]

Indeed, the ad hoc criminal tribunals for the former Yugoslavia and Rwanda have expressly determined that a strict form of binding precedent operates in those institutions[403] – a point that is less certain at the permanent International Criminal Court.[404]

Thus it appears that there is at least a *de facto* system of precedent at international law, in the sense that international courts and tribunals often take what was said in earlier cases at face value where it would require the expenditure of a considerable amount of resources to properly examine

---

[401] *Prosecutor v Kupreskić, Kupreškić, Kupreškić, Josipović, Papić and Šantić*, above note 378.

[402] Ibid., [537].

[403] For ICTY, see *Prosecutor v Delalić, Mucić, Delić and Landžo* (Appeals Chamber Judgment) IT-96-21-A (20 February 2001) ('*Čelebići* Appeal Judgment'), [8]; *Prosecutor v Aleksovski* (Appeals Chamber Judgment) IT-95-14-1-A (24 March 2000) ('*Aleksovski* Appeal Judgment'), [112]–[113]. For ICTR, see *Prosecutor v Semanza* (Appeals Chamber Judgment) ICTR-97-20-A (20 May 2005) ('*Semanza* Appeals Judgment'), [92]. For a discussion of precedent in international criminal law, see generally Boas, above note 387.

[404] See Statute of the International Criminal Court, entered into force 1 July 2002, UN Doc. A/CONF. 183/9 (1998) ('Rome Statute'), Art. 21(1). See also *Prosecutor v Bemba* (Decision on the Evidence Disclosure System and Setting a Timetable for Disclosure between the Parties) ICC-01/05-01/08-424 (31 July 2008), [14]. It would appear that there is at least an informal system of precedent as between decisions of the Appeals Chamber and lower chambers.

state practice and *opinio juris* every time a case comes up for decision. It may be suggested that this *de facto* doctrine of precedent is the product of a need to accommodate the divide in the international community largely between common law and civil law legal systems. As the editors of the ninth edition of *Oppenheim's International Law* state:

> [A]pparent differences in basic notions and methods of approach resulting from divergences in national systems and traditions have been satisfactorily bridged by an assimilation and mutual approximation of apparently opposed concepts. This is shown, for instance, in the manner in which the practice of the Permanent Court of International Justice and its successor have combined formal disregard of the doctrine of judicial precedent with constant and fruitful regard for their previous decisions.[405]

Nonetheless, the lack of a frank and honest discussion by some of these courts about the reliance on precedent, and the effect of this on the basic principle expressed in Article 59 of the ICJ Statute, leaves a sense of uncertainty about the meaning and scope of such developments and their impact on the sources of international law.

2.2.4.2 Writings of publicists

The influence of academic writers has diminished markedly over the course of the history of international law. Until the second half of the twentieth century, writers such as Grotius, Vattel, Lauterpacht and Oppenheim were central to the development of an area of law that was mostly customary and the subject of few treaties or judicial decisions. Indeed, these publicists were instrumental in affirming and building the legitimacy of international law as a system of law.[406]

However, with the increasing proliferation of international organizations, the development of a world order based around the UN Charter, the explosion of treaty-making, the birth of *sui generis* areas of law producing a breadth of judicial, administrative and quasi-judicial opinion (such as in the areas of human rights, trade, law of the sea and international criminal law) and the advent of globalization, heralding technological change and a flatter, more interconnected world, international courts and tribunals have seen less need for the opinions of publicists, which are often tainted with bias.[407] It is ironic that the growth of international law, which has contrib-

---

[405] Jennings and Watts, above note 16, 95.

[406] Harris, above note 32, 54–5. See Chapter 1.

[407] See, e.g., C. Parry, *The Sources and Evidences of International Law* (Manchester, UK: Manchester University Press, 1965) 103–5.

uted to the proliferation of academic writing on international law, is also responsible for the diminution in importance of such works as a material source of law.

This is not to say that international courts and tribunals ignore extra-judicial commentary altogether. It is inevitably relied on by judges (and, far less visibly, judges' assistants) to familiarize themselves with the law and to conduct research, though such reliance – however deep – may not make it into their judgments because of the perceived lessening of their legitimacy and authoritative voice.[408] There are, however, some publicists who still exert considerable influence. For instance, the three-volume study undertaken by the ICRC in finding and collating voluminous evidence on state practice relating to international humanitarian law[409] is often cited in the judgments of international criminal tribunals. The ILC's Draft Articles on Responsibility of States for Intentionally Wrongful Acts (2001) has also been cited by the ICJ in the *Hungarian Dams* case,[410] among others.

In this way, while the golden era of the international law scholar's significance may be over, they continue to exert considerable influence on the development of international law through sometimes less visible means. This may be, as explained above, through reliance by international decision-makers and their staff upon such writings. It may also be seen in the engagement of such scholars in the process of international law interpretation and even law-making. For example, the appointment of highly regarded scholars to the Bench of the ICJ or other international courts, to the ILC or as UN Rapporteurs or other consultants may extend their influence from scholarly opinion into the realm of hard international law.

2.3 CONCLUSIONS

The extraordinary development of international law over the past century has invariably impacted upon the nature of international law sources, as well as how they are defined, applied and of course developed. From a nascent global system of law with relatively few treaties and areas of specialization, international law has grown exponentially in size and complexity. Indeed, the velocity at which international law had developed by

---

408 Brownlie, above note 236, 24–5.

409 Jean-Marie Henckaerts and Louise Doswald-Beck, *Customary International Humanitarian Law* (Cambridge: Cambridge University Press, 2005) Vols 1–3.

410 *Gobčikovo-Nagymaros Project (Hungary v Slovakia)*, above note 33.

the end of the twentieth century led some to fear that it was 'in crisis', even on the verge of collapse.[411] The ILC's fragmentation study explored this concern and found that the proliferation of semi-autonomous strands of international law – human rights, international criminal law, international environmental law, to name a few – did not put an unbearable strain on the integrity of the system. Judges had plenty of sources from which to derive tie-breaker principles, such as *lex specialis*, and they had the foresight to emphasize harmonization over conflict where two norms ostensibly covered the same ground.[412]

The establishment of a new international public order under the United Nations system catalyzed a number of enduring trends that have changed the fabric of the international system. One of these trends has been the codification and progressive development of international law. Once dominated by relatively uncertain and in many cases inadequate customary law, the international plane has seen the proliferation of an increasingly cohesive network of treaties – bilateral and multilateral – regulating diverse aspects of relations between nations. The Vienna Convention on the Law of Treaties 1969 did much to regularize and facilitate the harmonization of national interests that only treaty-making can achieve. There exist today a vast number of multilateral treaties, including the constitutive instruments of international organizations – such as the UN and the WTO – which have assisted in the pursuit of the common interests of states and act as fora for diplomatic dialogue and even the expression of *opinio juris*.[413]

Custom as a source of international law has not remained static either. Ever since the classical formulation of this source of law in the *North Sea Continental Shelf* cases,[414] successive attempts by the ICJ to grapple with the once uncertain concepts of *opinio juris* and state practice have lent them greater content.[415] It is, however, a cause for concern that the ICJ and international criminal tribunals have occasionally indulged in an over-reliance on their past decisions instead of undertaking an open and comprehensive analysis of *opinio juris* and state practice in each case.[416] There is also latent uncertainty about the content of *jus cogens* and the troubling advent of decisions such as the *Nuclear Weapons* Advisory Opinion, which can only be explained as placing politics over law. Some

---

411 See Fragmentation Report, above note 3.
412 Ibid. See also discussion above at section 2.1.4.
413 See discussion above at section 2.2.2.3.3.
414 *North Sea Continental Shelf* cases, above note 112.
415 See discussion above at sections 2.2.2.2 and 2.2.2.3.
416 See discussion above at section 2.2.2.5.

commentators have suggested that the sources of customary international law are undergoing a fundamental methodological change.[417] However, these developments have stopped short of jettisoning the traditional elements of customary law as the courts still acknowledge that state practice and *opinio juris* are indispensable, even though they may show a laxity in articulating evidence of the establishment of these elements in certain cases.[418]

Today's increasingly integrated international society has its own challenges and the mechanisms for determining the sources of international law, as developed over the course of the last century, contribute to the unity and coherence of the system. The key to overcoming future challenges could be the continuing general rejection of confusing appeals to 'relative normativity' – that is, obscuring what the sources of law recognize as binding and not binding. As Dinah Shelton observes:

> [F]or practitioners, governments, and intergovernmental organizations, there is not a continuum of instruments from soft to hard, but a binary system in which an instrument is entered into as law or not-law. The not-law can be politically binding or morally binding, and expectations of compliance with the norms contained in the instrument can be extremely strong, but the difference between a legally binding instrument and one that is not appears well understood and acted upon by government negotiators. . . . Such instruments may express trends or a stage in the formulation of treaty or custom, but law does not come with a sliding scale of bindingness, nor does desired law become law by stating its desirability, even repeatedly.[419]

At several points in this chapter, the attenuation of formal requirements for the identification of a rule of customary international law has been discussed. The ICJ rulings in the *Gulf of Maine* and *Israeli Wall* cases provide two examples of the World Court relying on its own past rulings as automated evidence of the existence of a customary rule, in apparent contradiction to Article 59 of its Statute relating to precedent.[420] The Court has also been criticized for over-reliance upon General Assembly Resolutions and for the identification of customary rules without providing any evidence of such a rule's existence.[421] The consequence of this may well be a watering down of the rigorous requirements for the establishment of

---

[417] See discussion above at section 2.2.2.4.
[418] See discussion above at section 2.2.4.1.2.
[419] Shelton, above note 315, 321.
[420] See above section 2.2.4.1.1.
[421] See *Arrest Warrant of 11 April 2000*, above note 244, [58] and text accompanying note 392.

custom by pointing to sufficient state practice and *opinio juris*. It may also signal a greater role for judicial (and perhaps arbitral) decisions on the formation of international law.

Whether these developments are desirable depends considerably on one's point of view and may differ from case to case. It does invoke consideration of the discussion in Chapter 1 about the nature of international law (what it is and what it is used for) and the different theoretical perspectives about how international law functions.[422] Critical theorists like Koskenniemi see this lack of formalism in the application of international law as precisely what is wrong with the international legal system.[423] Viewed more as a normative system, international law is invariably developed by courts and tribunals, as well as other decision-makers and actors in the international community. In this way, international law is more a process;[424] variations and changes in the identification of rules, more or less desirable, are inevitable aspects of the reality of a functioning international law system.

Higgins argues that a normative system can legitimately be developed in the decision-making of institutions, as well as courts and tribunals, so long as there is openness about external influences (political or social) on decision-makers. I have argued in Chapter 1 that, while there is merit in this view, it also requires a frank discussion about the competence and capacity of these decision-makers in a given context. The treatment of the sources of international law by some of the international tribunals discussed in this chapter, including the approach to the question of custom by the ICJ, accentuates some of these concerns. Are the requirements for the identification and articulation of rules of customary international law attenuating? Or should we take such rulings by international courts as an aberration? It is difficult to assess the impact of this judicial practice, both upon the substantive process of identifying rules, as well as upon the role of courts and judicial decisions in the norm creating process. What can be said with certainty is that courts should be frank about what they are doing in this respect. A failure to do so suggests that either a relaxed approach is being taken to the identification of binding international law, or that a normative shift is taking place beneath the disapproving eyes of the primary subjects of international law – states – as well as other stakeholders.

---

422 See Chapter 1, section 1.4.

423 See Koskenniemi, above note 324.

424 See Higgins, above note 196.

3. The relationship between international and national law

A fundamental issue in international law is the nature of the relationship that exists between international and national law.[1] Monism and dualism (as well as transformation and incorporation) are important theoretical frameworks that speak to the relationship between the state as an internal entity and the state as a member of the international legal community and how this impacts on the international legal system.

As well as theoretical considerations, the relationship between national and international law gives rise to a host of practical considerations and the resolution of a dispute may differ considerably depending upon which legal regime applies. At the essence of the interplay between these differing systems of law is a critical question: where they cover a common field, and there is a dispute between them, which should be supreme over the other?[2]

This chapter addresses both the theoretical and practical implications of the relationship between international and national law. Different conceptions of this relationship from an international law perspective are expressed in the monist and dualist theories, which will be discussed first, as will contemporary perspectives on these theoretical frameworks. The relationship between national and international law naturally suggests two opposing perspectives. This chapter will first examine the operation of national law in international law, exploring practical implications and the use of national law as a source of international law, either as general principles of international law or as evidence of state practice in relation to a principle of international law. How international law is implemented into, and influences, national law will then be examined. As this varies across states and legal traditions, examples of these jurisdictions will be

[1] Reference in the cases and literature is made interchangeably to the terms 'national', 'domestic' and 'municipal' in relation to the internal law of a state. Reference in this book is largely made to 'national law', although any use of other synonymous terms holds no technical significance.

[2] See, e.g., Ian Brownlie, *Principles of Public International Law* (Oxford: Oxford University Press, 2008, 7th edn), 31.

considered and themes explored in relation to this important aspect of the international legal system.

3.1 DIFFERENT CONCEPTIONS OF THE RELATIONSHIP BETWEEN INTERNATIONAL AND NATIONAL LAW

The relationship between international law and national law is one that is fiercely debated.[3] At a theoretical level, there exist two dominant theories for explaining this relationship: monism and dualism.

3.1.1 Dualism

The dualist approach views international and national law as two separate systems that exist independently of one another. This theory is based upon the 'assumption that international law and municipal legal systems constitute two distinct and formally separate categories of legal orders'[4] because they 'differ as to their sources, the relations they regulate and their legal content.'[5] Therefore, these two systems are seen to be firmly independent from one another, as neither can claim supremacy.[6] Where international law is incorporated into national law by the state, this is seen as an exercise of authority by the state, rather than international law imposing itself into the domestic sphere.[7] From a practical perspective, if a national court in a dualist state is considering a case and there is a conflict between international and national law, the court (in the absence of any legislative guidance to the contrary) would apply domestic law.[8]

---

[3] For an early discussion of the monist/dualist debate, see Edwin M. Borchard, 'The Relation between International Law and Municipal Law' (1940–41) 27 *Virginia Law Review* 137; see also Hans Kelsen, *General Theory of Law and State* (New York: Russell & Russell, 1961), 363–88.

[4] Antonio Cassese, *International Law* (Oxford: Oxford University Press, 2005, 2nd edn), 214.

[5] Gillian D. Triggs, *International Law: Contemporary Principles and Practices* (Sydney: LexisNexis Butterworths, 2011, 2nd edn), 153, referring to H. Lauterpacht and L. Oppenheim, *International Law: A Treatise*, Vol. I, 'Peace' (London: Longmans Green, 1955, 8th edn), 35.

[6] Malcolm Shaw, *International Law* (Cambridge; New York: Cambridge University Press, 2008, 6th edn), 132–3; Brownlie, above note 2, 32.

[7] Brownlie, ibid., 32.

[8] Ibid., 32; Cassese, above note 4, 214. See also discussion below at sections 3.4.1 and 3.4.2 on the transformation and incorporation approaches.

3.1.2 Monism

The monist theory, developed by Kelsen, asserts that there is a relationship between national and international law, with international law being supreme.[9] Monists argue that as law ultimately regulates the conduct of individuals, there is a commonality between international and national law which both ultimately regulate the conduct of the individual. Therefore, each system is a 'manifestation of a single conception of law'.[10] Hersch Lauterpacht was a great proponent of the monist approach, by which a single, superior order of law could better protect fundamental legal principles and values, particularly in the area of human rights:

> The main reason for the essential identity of the two spheres of law is, it is maintained, that some of the fundamental notions of international law cannot be understood without the assumption of a superior legal order from which the various systems of municipal law are, in a sense, derived by way of delegation. It is international law that determines the jurisdictional limits of the personal and territorial competence of states. Similarly, it is only by reference to a higher legal rule in relation to which they are all equal that the equality and independence of a number of sovereign states can be conceived.[11]

This final assertion by Lauterpacht – that only by reference to a higher legal rule can the fundamental principle of the equality of states be achieved – has attraction, although it has to be acknowledged that it is somewhat conclusory. It suggests a preference for the predominance of international law and views the effectiveness of the system as a dominant concern of states. While protecting – or at least promoting – the equality of states seems a desirable goal, it risks attracting the countervailing argument that if international law is not solid enough to ensure fulfilment of its own fundamental principles then it may not be a stable legal system.

The monist/dualist theoretical conception of international law is of clearly practical significance. Ian Brownlie provides the following hypothetical example that illustrates the importance that adopting a monist or dualist approach can have in a concrete dispute:

---

[9] Hans Kelsen, *Pure Theory of Law* (Berkeley, CA: University of California Press, 1967), 332–4. This concept was first outlined by the German scholar W. Kaufmann in 1899 (W. Kaufmann, *Die Rechtskraft des Internationales Rechtes und das Verhältnis der Staastsgesetzgebungen und der Staastorgane zu demselben* [Stuttgart: F. Enke, 1899]).

[10] Lauterpacht and Oppenheim, above note 5, 38.

[11] Ibid., 36–7.

> An alien vessel may be arrested and the alien crew tried before a municipal court of the arresting authority for ignoring customs laws. The municipal law prescribes a customs enforcement zone of x miles. The defendants argue that international law permits a customs zone of x–4 miles and that the vessel, when arrested, had not yet entered the zone in which enforcement was justified under international law.[12]

Should national law or international law apply in such a dispute? Applying a dualist approach, domestic law would apply; applying a monist approach, international law should prevail. Either approach would lead to a very different practical outcome for the alien crew in this instance.

3.1.3 An Alternative Approach

An alternative theory to monism and dualism has been advanced by Fitzmaurice and Rosseau.[13] They argue that international law and national law lack a common field of operation, never operating within the same sphere, or dealing with the same subject matter.[14] Therefore, they do not come into conflict as systems. This formulation, at least in relation to its relevance to contemporary international law, has been criticized by scholars on the basis that the Fitzmaurice approach is 'essentially dualist', and has been 'overtaken by thc extensive contemporary interaction' between international and national law.[15] On the other hand, Brownlie notes that 'if one has to choose between the theories . . . then the views of Fitzmaurice and Rosseau might be preferred as coming close to the facts. Each system is supreme *in its own field*, and neither has a hegemony over the other'.[16]

---

[12] Brownlie, above note 2, 41.

[13] G. Fitzmaurice, 'The General Principles of International Law Considered from the Standpoint of the Rule of Law'(1957-II) 92 *Hague Recueil* 68–94; Shaw, above note 6, 132–3; Brownlie, ibid., 33.

[14] Shaw, ibid., 132–3; Martin Dixon, *Textbook on International Law* (Oxford: Oxford University Press, 2005, 5th edn), 83; Brownlie, ibid., 33.

[15] Triggs, above note 5, 154.

[16] Brownlie, above note 2, 53.

3.2 NATIONAL LAW IN INTERNATIONAL LAW

3.2.1 International Law Is Supreme in its Domain

Breaches of international law cannot be justified by reference to a state's own internal laws.[17] A state cannot legitimately argue that it has behaved in a manner contrary to international law because its conduct was permissible, or even required, under its own law. In this way, international law, from the perspective of international courts, tribunals and arbitral bodies, is supreme.[18]

There exists much authority to support this proposition. In the *Greco-Bulgarian Communities* Advisory Opinion[19] – which concerned the Greco-Bulgarian Convention created in the aftermath of the First World War to provide for the reciprocal emigration of persecuted minorities between the two states – one of the questions considered by the Court was, in the case of a conflict between the application of the Convention and the national law of one of the two signatory powers, which provision should be preferred?[20] The Court replied by clearly articulating the supremacy of international law in its domain:

> It is a generally accepted principle of international law that in the relations powers who are contracting parties to a treaty, the provisions of municipal law cannot prevail over those of the treaty.[21]

Similar statements were made in the *Free Zones* case,[22] and the principle has more recently been affirmed in leading cases of the International Court of Justice.[23] It is also reflected in Article 27 of the Vienna Convention on the Law of Treaties, which states that a party 'may not invoke the

---

[17] See, e.g., Art. 27 of the Vienna Convention on the Law of Treaties (adopted 23 May 1969, entered into force 27 January 1980) 1155 UNTS 331; Draft Declaration on Rights and Duties of States (1949), *Yearbook of the International Law Commission 1949*, Art. 13; Brownlie, above note 2, 34–5; Shaw, above note 6, 133; Eileen Denza, 'The Relationship between International and National Law', in Malcolm Evans (ed.) *International Law* (Oxford: Oxford University Press, 2010), 424.

[18] Shaw, above note 6, 133–4.

[19] *Greco-Bulgarian Communities* case (1930) PCIJ (Ser. B) No. 17.

[20] Ibid., 32.

[21] Ibid., 32.

[22] *Free Zones* case, (1932) PCIJ (Ser. A/B) No. 46, 167.

[23] See, e.g., *Applicability of the Obligation to Arbitrate* case [1988] ICJ Rep 12, 34; Judge Shahabuddeen's judgment in *Questions of Interpretation and Application of the 1971 Montreal Convention arising from the Aerial Incident at Lockerbie* (*Provisional Measures*), (*Libya v United States*; *Libya v United Kingdom*) (1992) ICJ Rep 3, 32; *LaGrand* (*Federal Republic of Germany v United States of America*)

provisions of its internal law as justification for its failure to perform a treaty'.[24] Many international law scholars also agree that this principle is established law.[25]

3.2.2 The Application of National Law within International Law

As a corollary, the fact that an act may be illegal in national law does not necessarily mean it is in breach of international law.[26] However, this does not mean that there is no role for national law within the international sphere. Indeed, cases in which an international tribunal in dealing with matters of pertinence to international law also give rise to an examination of the internal laws of one or more states, are far from exceptional.[27] As Shaw notes:

> [E]xpressions of the supremacy of international law over municipal law in international tribunals do not mean that the provisions of domestic legislation are either irrelevant or unnecessary. On the contrary, the role of internal legal rules is vital to the workings of the international legal machine.[28]

There exists a growing body of academic literature supporting the approach of an enhanced recognition of national law by international courts and tribunals.[29] From a practical perspective, there are a number of reasons why international courts utilize national law. If there is a

---

[2001] ICJ Rep 466, 497–8; *Avena* case (*Mexico v United States of America*) [2004] ICJ Rep 12, 65. See also Shaw, above note 6, 135.

[24] Vienna Convention on the Law of Treaties, above note 17, Art. 27. Art. 46 provides for very limited circumstances in which a state may utilize its internal law to invalidate its consent to an international treaty, Art. 46(1) stating: 'A State may not invoke the fact that its consent to be bound by a treaty has been expressed in violation of a provision of its internal law regarding competence to conclude treaties as invalidating its consent unless that violation was manifest and concerned a rule of its internal law of fundamental importance.'

[25] Brownlie, e.g., states: 'The law in this respect is well settled. A state cannot plead provisions of its own law or deficiencies in that law in answer to a claim against it for an alleged breach of its obligations under international law': Brownlie, above note 2, 34. See also Dixon, above note 14, 84; Cassese, above note 4, 217–8; C Wilfred Jenks, *The Prospects of International Adjudication* (London: Stevens & Sons, 1964), 556.

[26] *Elettronica Sicula S.p.A* case (*United States of America v Italy*) [1989] ICJ Rep 15, 73–4. See also *Compania de Aguas del Aconquija v Argentine Republic* (2002) 41 ILM 1135, 1154; Shaw, above note 6, 136.

[27] See, e.g., Jenks, above note 25, 547–603; Brownlie, above note 2, 36.

[28] Shaw, above note 6, 126.

[29] See e.g., James Crawford, 'International Law and the Rule of Law' (2003) 24 *Adelaide Law Review* 3, 10; André Nollkaemper, 'Internationally

dispute relating to an area where no satisfactory international law exists, and there exists a well-developed and relevant principle at the national level, the court may choose to use that principle.[30] The court may also use a state's law in an evidentiary sense, to determine the state's internal legal position on a disputed issue before the court.[31] Of course, reference to the national laws of states can, given consistency and breadth of practice, give rise to a general principal of international law,[32] or act as evidence of state practice in the determination of customary international law.[33]

3.2.3 Use of National Law by International Tribunals to Resolve Disputes

In a number of cases, issues have come before the courts for which there exists no relevant or applicable legal principle at the international level. In these circumstances, the courts have shown a willingness to borrow relevant national law concepts to apply within the international sphere.[34] The authority for courts to apply national law in the international sphere is found in Article 38(1)(c) of the Statute of the Permanent Court of International Justice,[35] which provides that 'the general principles of law recognized by civilized nations', typically being those derived from the domestic legal systems of states, may be utilized as a source of international law.[36] Thus, a general legal principle that exists at the national level may be imported into the international system, where it is appropriate to do so. Where there is consistency in practice, this can lead to the creation of a general principal of international law. In the *Barcelona Traction* case, the Belgian government sought reparations for damage caused to

---

Wrongful Acts in Domestic Courts' (2007) 101 *American Journal of International Law* 799.

[30] See, e.g., *Barcelona Traction, Light and Power Co. Ltd* (*Belgium v Spain*) (Second Phase) [1970] ICJ Rep, 3, discussed in detail below at 3.2.3.

[31] See, e.g., *Anglo-Iranian Oil Co.* case (*United Kingdom v Iran*) [1952] ICJ Rep 93, discussed in detail below at 3.2.4.

[32] For a discussion of general principles as a source of international law, see the discussion in Chapter 2, section 2.2.3.

[33] For a discussion of custom as a source of international law, see the discussion in Chapter 2, section 2.2.2.

[34] See generally Jenks, above note 25, and in particular 547.

[35] Statute of the Permanent Court of International Justice (adopted 16 December 1920) 6 LNTS 380, Art. 38.

[36] See Rosalyn Higgins, *Problems and Process: International Law and How We Use It* (Oxford: Clarendon Press, 1994), 208, 218; Triggs, above note 5, 162–3. For a detailed discussion of this source of international law, see Chapter 2, particularly section 2.2.3.1.

Belgian nationals (who were shareholders in the Canadian company Barcelona Traction, Light & Power Co. Ltd) from the Spanish government who caused the damage, as the company carried out its operations in Spain.[37]

The Court, in considering the dispute, emphasized the role played by national law:

> If the Court were to decide the case in disregard of the relevant institutions of municipal law it would, without justification, invite serious legal difficulties. It would lose touch with reality, for there are no corresponding institutions of international law to which the Court could resort. Thus the Court has, as indicated, not only to take cognizance of municipal law but also to refer to it. It is to rules generally accepted by municipal legal systems which recognize the limited company whose capital is represented by shares, and not to the municipal law of a particular State, that international law refers. In referring to such rules, the Court cannot modify, still less deform them.[38]

The Court clearly regarded the use of domestic law as an essential element in the resolution of the dispute before it. Interestingly, it was also noted that where domestic law rules are imported, they cannot be modified or altered in the process of applying them to international disputes. An international tribunal may, therefore, import domestic law. Indeed, it may need to do so in the resolution of an international dispute – but may not alter it in the process.

In the *Trail Smelter* arbitral case,[39] the United States brought an action against Canada for alleged air pollution caused by a smelter operated in Canada. The arbitral tribunal noted:

> No case of air pollution dealt with by an international tribunal has been brought to the attention of the Tribunal, nor does the Tribunal know of any such case . . . There are, however, as regards both air pollution and water pollution, certain decisions of the Supreme Court of the United States which may legitimately be taken as a guide in this field of international law.[40]

The Court then relied upon a number of judgments from the US Supreme Court, and imported into international law the national law principle established in these cases that 'no State has the right to use or permit the use of its territory in such a manner as to cause injury by fumes in or to

---

37 *Barcelona Traction* case, above note 30.
38 Ibid., 50.
39 *Trail Smelter Arbitration* (*United States v Canada*) (1941) 3 RIAA 1911.
40 Ibid., 1963–4.

the territory of another';[41] this has since become an established principle in international law.

Again, the approach of the tribunal to the incorporation of national law into international law so as to make sense of and resolve a dispute reveals a pragmatic, more than a principled, approach. In this case, the tribunal had regard to US case law. This in itself is not objectionable; the general principles of law, as a legitimate source of international law, are often determined in decisions of international courts by reference to a range of practice across a number of relevant national legal jurisdictions. Examples of this process include recognition by the International Court of Justice of the principle of 'good faith' in the creation and performance of international legal obligations,[42] and the acceptance in international decision-making of circumstantial evidence;[43] recognition by the US-Iran Claims Tribunal of the principle of 'unjust enrichment' in international law;[44] and the finding by the International Criminal Tribunal for the former Yugoslavia of the definition of rape as a crime against humanity resulting from the convergence of the principles of the major legal systems of the world.[45]

What may be questionable in the *Trail Smelter* arbitral case is the exclusive reference to US case law which, no matter how sensible or authoritative in its domestic jurisdiction, cannot in itself amount to a rule of international law. The role of national law in international law as mapped out in the *Barcelona Traction* and *Trail Smelter* cases raises an interesting theoretical problem. While the judicial reasoning seems entirely rational and perhaps essential to the proper functioning of the international legal system, it does raise what critical legal scholars would identify as the contradictions and indeterminacy inherent in legal rules. In other words, simply saying that an international court needs to apply national law to resolve an international law dispute does not explain what the legal justification is for doing so. Courts need to be more open and referential to the traditional sources of international law, and their proper application, in

---

41 Ibid., 1965.

42 See *Nuclear Tests* cases (*Australia and New Zealand v France*) [1974] ICJ Rep 253.

43 See *Corfu Channel* (*UK v Albania*) [1949] ICJ Rep 4 ('this indirect evidence is admitted in all systems of law, and its use is recognized by international decisions').

44 See *Sea-Land Service* case [1984] 6 Iran–USCTR 149, 168–9: recognizing that the principle of 'unjust enrichment' is 'widely accepted as having been assimilated into the catalogue of general principles of law available to be applied by international tribunals'.

45 *Prosecutor v Furundžija* (Judgment) IT-95-17/1-T (10 December 1998), [178]–[186].

determining disputes, lest the legitimacy of the system of international law be called into question.[46]

Indeed, while national law principles may be applicable in international law, considerable authority cautions against such a practice in the absence of an express or implied requirement to utilize these principles.[47] For example, in the *Exchange of Greek and Turkish Populations* case,[48] an Advisory Opinion was sought from the Permanent Court of International Justice over the interpretation of a Convention concerning the exchange of Greek and Turkish citizens at the end of a conflict between these two states. Specifically, the Court was asked to consider the meaning of the word 'established' as set out in the treaty. In certain cases where persons were not deemed 'established', they were subject to compulsory exchange between the two states; but where they were deemed to be 'established', they were exempt from exchange. The interpretation of the term was thus of crucial importance to the affected people.

The Court took a restrictive approach to the incorporation of national legal principles into the international sphere. It began by noting that there was no express reference to national legislation in determining the definition of 'established', before determining that the Convention made no implicit reference to national legislation. Therefore, the Court rejected Turkey's submission to interpret the Convention as taking into account domestic interpretations of the term, instead relying upon the natural meaning of the word. This had the effect of a broader definition of 'established' and thus allowed for a greater number of people to be excluded from the compulsory exchange between the two states. The Court justified its approach, stating:

> It is a well-known fact that the legislation of different States takes into account various kinds of local personal ties and deals with them in different ways. The application of Turkish and Greek law would probably have resulted in uncertainties, difficulties and delays incompatible with the speedy fulfilment always regarded as essential to the Convention under consideration. Moreover, it might well happen that a reference to Turkish and Greek legislation would lead to the division of the population being carried out in a different manner in

---

[46] These cases are far from isolated examples of this problem. Reliance on sparse national law references to resolve aspects of international law is also discussed in Chapter 2, at section 2.2.3.2. For a theoretical discussion on the purpose and legitimacy of international law, see Chapter 1, section 1.4.

[47] See, e.g., the *Exchange of Greek and Turkish Populations* case (1925) PCIJ (Ser. B) No. 10, 19–21. See also the Separate Opinion of Judge McNair in the *South West Africa* case [1950] ICJ Rep 148.

[48] *Exchange of Greek and Turkish Populations* case, above note 47.

> Turkey and in Greece. This, again, would not be in accordance with the spirit of the Convention, the intention of which is undoubtedly to ensure, by means of the application of identical and reciprocal measures in the territory of the two States, that the same treatment is accorded to the Greek and Turkish populations. Nor is there any indication that the authors of the Convention, when they adopted the word which has given rise to the present controversy, had in mind national legislation at all. Everything therefore seems to indicate that, in regard to this point, the Convention is self-contained and that the Mixed Commission in order to decide what constitutes an established inhabitant must rely on the natural meaning of the words as already explained.[49]

The way in which international law borrows from national law is not by means of importing private law institutions 'lock, stock and barrel', ready-made and fully equipped with a set of rules.[50] It would be difficult to reconcile such a process with the application of 'the general principles of law'. The better view of the duty of international tribunals is to regard any feature or terminology which is reminiscent of the rules and institutions of national law as an indication of policy and principles rather than as directly importing these rules and institutions. Therefore, while there are circumstances in which national law will be imported into international law, it should not be an automatic process, nor one to be taken lightly by the international courts and tribunals.

However, where there exist applicable and well-developed principles at the national level, there is clearly scope – where the right circumstances exist and traditional sources of international law are appropriately considered – for these principles to be used in the resolution of a dispute before an international tribunal. As the cases discussed above disclose, there is clearly an element of the pragmatic at work when it comes to interpreting and applying national laws in international law cases.

3.2.4 Use of National Law to Resolve a State's Position on a Question of International Law

Another way in which national law is used by international courts is to ascertain a state's legal position on a given issue.[51] In the *Anglo-Iranian Oil* case,[52] a conflict arose between the Iranian Government, which sought

49 Ibid., 20. See also 18–23.

50 Judge McNair uses this phrase in his Separate Opinion in the *South West Africa* case, above note 47, 148.

51 *Anglo-Iranian Oil Co.* case, above note 31; Shaw, above note 6, 126; Jenks, above note 25, 577.

52 *Anglo-Iranian Oil Co.* case, ibid., 93.

to nationalize its oil industry, and the Anglo-Iranian Oil Company, which argued that this nationalization breached an existing treaty. In deciding the issue, a question arose as to whether the International Court of Justice had jurisdiction over treaties or conventions entered into by Iran prior to the ratification of a Declaration made by both the UK and Iran granting the ICJ jurisdiction, or only after this date. The Court's answer to this question would determine whether it had jurisdiction to hear the case before it. While the UK argued that the Court should have jurisdiction over all treaties and conventions entered into by Iran, the Court held that Iran only intended the Court to have jurisdiction over treaties and declarations entered into after the ratification of the Declaration. In coming to this conclusion, the Court looked at existing Iranian domestic law as evidence to support Iran's legal position on the relevant issue, but stated:

> It is contended that this evidence [the relevant Iranian domestic law] as to the intention of the Government of Iran should be rejected as inadmissible and that this Iranian law is a purely domestic instrument, unknown to other governments . . . The Court is unable to see why it should be prevented from taking this piece of evidence into consideration.[53]

By looking at the national law of a state, an international tribunal may be able to determine how the state views various issues including jurisdiction, conditions of nationality, treaty interpretation and territorial sea boundaries.[54] A state's stance on these issues, as evidenced through its domestic legislation, can be of crucial importance in determining a dispute.[55]

National law can also be used to determine whether a state is complying with international obligations (treaty or customary law).[56] The Permanent Court of International Justice, in the *Certain German Interests in Polish Upper Silesia* case, considered an allegation by Germany that Poland had unlawfully taken over a German-controlled nitrate factory based in Chorzow, and had also appropriated agricultural property owned by the company.[57] One of Germany's arguments was that the relevant Polish national law breached the Geneva Convention providing for certain standards relating to the expropriation of property. The Court stated:

---

53 Ibid., 107.

54 Shaw, above note 6, 136.

55 See *Serbian Loans* case (1929) PCIJ (Ser. A) No. 20; *Brazilian Loans* case (1929) PCIJ (Ser. A) No. 21.

56 Brownlie, above note 2, 38; Shaw, above note 6, 126.

57 *Certain German Interests in Polish Upper Silesia* (1925) PCIJ (Ser. A) No. 6.

> From the standpoint of International Law and of the Court, which is its organ, municipal laws are merely facts which express the will and constitute the activities of States, in the same manner as do legal decisions or administrative measures. The Court is certainly not called upon to interpret the Polish law as such; but there is nothing to prevent the Court's giving judgment on the question whether or not, in applying that law, Poland is acting in conformity with its obligations towards Germany under the Geneva Convention.[58]

The Court ostensibly opted to use Poland's domestic law to help determine whether or not that state had breached an international obligation, determining that a number of breaches of this convention had in fact occurred.[59]

Rosalyn Higgins points out that the reference to judicial decisions as a subsidiary source of law in Article 38(1) of the ICJ Statute is not limited to decisions of the ICJ itself:[60]

> Of course, we think of the judgments of the International Court of Justice and its advisory opinions as being the judicial decisions there referred to. But there is nothing in the wording of Article 38 that limits the reference to the International Court of Justice at The Hague. And it is not specified that the judicial decision be an international one at all. Although it is natural that the judicial decisions of the International Court of Justice will have a great authority, it is also natural in a decentralized, horizontal legal order that the courts of nation states should also have a role to play in contributing to the norms of international law.[61]

Naturally, there are limits on the use by international tribunals of national legislation. For example, they may not declare national rules invalid, as this would impermissibly cross over into the state's domain. Thus in the *Interpretation of the Statute of Memel Territory*, the Permanent Court of International Justice decided that an act by the Governor of Memel in dissolving its Chamber of Representatives was invalid in respect of the relevant treaty. The Court was careful to note, however, that this finding did 'not thereby intend to say that the action of the Governor in dissolving the Chamber, even though it was contrary to the treaty, was of no effect

---

58 *Certain German Interests in Polish Upper Silesia,* (1926) PCIJ (Ser. A) No. 7, 19.

59 Ibid., 80–82.

60 See generally Chapter 2 on the sources of international law. See also Jenks, above note 25, 553, 547; Dixon, above note 14, 84.

61 Higgins, above note 36, 208. Higgins notes at 218 that the scope for courts to examine international law matters is 'substantially reduced in dualist systems whereby interpretation and application of treaties is broadly permissible only when the treaty has been incorporated'.

in municipal law'.[62] This principle thus recognizes the practical reality that situations will arise where, while an act may be in breach of a treaty at the international level, it will nonetheless be treated within the national sphere as if it is a legal act, provided it is in accordance with that state's own laws.[63]

Furthermore, interpretation of a state's laws by its own courts is binding on any international tribunal.[64] As Brownlie notes, this principle is based partially on the 'concept of the reserved domain of domestic jurisdiction' and partially on the need to avoid contradictory interpretations of the law of a state from different sources.[65]

3.3 INTERNATIONAL LAW IN NATIONAL LAW

In an age of increased globalization and evolving interconnectedness between people, states and institutions across borders, the role of international law within states is a developing and important one. In many states, for international rules to become operative, they must be implemented into the national law of a state.[66] As already discussed, states cannot rely upon national law to escape their international law obligations.[67] While there also exists some support for a general principle requiring states to bring their national law in line with their international obligations,[68] whether this principle does in fact exist at the level of customary international law is doubtful,[69] particularly when a multitude of states clearly choose not to bring some or all of their national law in line with their international obligations.

There has been a relatively modern development in this area, concerning treaty obligations and *jus cogens* norms that require states to take positive steps towards implementation of a whole or part of a treaty into their domestic legislation. Examples of this include the four Geneva Conventions of 1949 concerning the victims of war. The Statutes of the

---

[62] *Interpretation of the Statute of the Memel Territory* (1932) PCIJ (Ser. A/B) No. 49, 336.

[63] See also Brownlie, above note 2, 39.

[64] *Serbian Loans* case, above note 55, 46; Brownlie, ibid., 39.

[65] Brownlie, ibid., 39.

[66] See Cassese, above note 4, 217.

[67] See above section 3.2.1.

[68] *Exchange of Greek and Turkish Populations* case, above note 47, 20; Brownlie, above note 2, 35.

[69] See, Cassese above note 4, 218.

International Criminal Tribunal for the former Yugoslavia (ICTY) and International Criminal Tribunal for Rwanda (ICTR)[70] require all states to cooperate with and assist requests made by these courts – an obligation which flows from their status as creations under Chapter VII of the UN Charter (which carries with it the authority of the Security Council).[71] The International Criminal Court (ICC) also requires all Member States to provide cooperation to the Court.[72] A range of multilateral treaties regarding the issues of terrorism, international and transnational crime and certain human rights abuses, require states to implement legislation, as well as to prosecute or extradite persons in their jurisdiction.[73]

A key issue that arises in implementing international law at the national level is that of compliance. There exists a general unwillingness on the part of states to criticize one another for failing to implement international law obligations at the domestic level. This stems from the desire by states to be free to conduct their internal affairs without interference from other states or international bodies. This unwillingness extends to the courts of states, as Chief Justice Fuller stated in an oft-cited passage in *Underhill v Fernandez*: 'Every sovereign state is bound to respect the independence of every other sovereign state, and the courts of one country will not sit in judgment on the acts of the government of another within its own territory.'[74]

---

[70] Statute of the International Tribunal for the Former Yugoslavia, annexed to SC Res. 827, UN SCOR 48th sess., 3217th mtg, UN Doc. S/25704 (1993), Art. 29; Statute of the International Criminal Tribunal for Rwanda, annexed to SC Res. 955, UN SCOR, 49th sess., 3453rd mtg, UN Doc. S/RES/955 (1994), Art. 28.

[71] These ad hoc tribunals were created by the Security Council under its authority to maintain or restore international peace and security – an unusual and controversial exercise of this power (see generally Gabriël H. Oosthuizen, 'Playing Devil's Advocate: the United Nations Security Council is Unbound by Law' (1999) 12 *Leiden Journal of International Law* 549.

[72] Rome Statute of the International Criminal Court, UN Doc. A/CONF. 183/9; 37 ILM 1002 (1998), Art. 88.

[73] See, e.g., International Convention for the Suppression of Terrorist Bombings (adopted 15 December 1997, entered into force 23 May 2001) A/RES/52/164; International Convention for the Suppression of Acts of Nuclear Terrorism (adopted 13 April 2005, not yet entered into force) A/RES/59/766; Convention on the Prevention and Punishment of the Crime of Genocide (adopted 9 December 1948, entered into force 12 January 1951) 78 UNTS 277; Convention against Torture and Other Cruel, Inhuman or Degrading Treatment or Punishment (adopted 10 December 1984, entered into force 26 June 1987) 1465 UNTS 85. For a discussion of the principle of *aut dedere aut judicare* (the duty to prosecute or extradite), see Chapter 6, section 6.3.5.2.

[74] *Underhill v Fernandez* 168 US 250 (1897), [252]. For criticism of this approach, see Higgins, above note 36, 217: 'Should we expect this understandable

Even so, there do exist a number of monitoring mechanisms designed to encourage compliance with international law in a range of areas, in particular international human rights and global trade law. In the field of international human rights, for example, the Human Rights Council exists to encourage domestic compliance with the provisions of the International Covenant on Civil and Political Rights (ICCPR).[75] The Council came about from a recognized need to reform its previous incarnation (the Human Rights Committee), which was described by then UN Secretary-General Kofi Annan as facing 'declining credibility and professionalism'.[76]

The Council is made up of independent human rights experts, and is granted a number of powers to assist it in the task of encouraging compliance with human rights. These include a requirement for parties to the ICCPR to submit regular reports on the implementation of the Convention in their state, a complaints process, and the ability to make recommendations to the relevant state. A new power that was previously not available to the Council is that of 'universal periodic review', which allows for the review of all of the UN Member States in four-year cycles, which means that 48 states are reviewed every year.[77] As Sarah Joseph notes, however, whilst the broad mechanisms themselves have been retained, the content of these mechanisms has been altered, some strengthening and some weakening the human rights protection that the powers grant.[78] The overall success of the Council is debatable, given that

---

principle to apply when the acts of the foreign state are manifestly in violation of international law?'

[75] See International Covenant on Civil and Political Rights (adopted 16 December 1966, entered into force 23 March 1976), 999 UNTS 171 ('ICCPR'), Art. 28. For further information on the role of the Committee, see Arts 40 and 41 ICCPR; Optional Protocol to the International Covenant on Civil and Political Rights (adopted 16 December 1966, entered into force 19 December 1966) 999 UNTS 171. The Human Rights Council was created by resolution of the General Assembly: Resolution on the Human Rights Council, GA Res. 60/251, UN GAOR, 6th sess., 72nd plen. mtg, UN Doc. A/RES/60/251 (2006). The predecessor to the Council, the Human Rights Committee, was abolished, taking effect on 1 June 2006, by resolution of the Economic and Social Council: Implementation of GA Res 60/251, ESC Res. 2/2006, UN ESCOR, 62nd sess., UN Doc. E/RES/62/2 (2006).

[76] Secretary-General Kofi Annan, 'In Larger Freedom: Toward Development, Security and Human Rights for All', UN Doc. A/59/2005 (21 March 2005), [182].

[77] For further information on the Universal Periodic Review process, see http://www.upr-info.org.

[78] Sarah Joseph, 'The United Nations and Human Rights', in Sarah Joseph and Adam McBeth (eds), *Research Handbook on International Human Rights Law* (Cheltenham, UK; Northampton, MA: Edward Elgar, 2010), 10.

its findings and recommendations are not binding and in many countries it has enjoyed limited effectiveness.[79]

Another example of mechanisms encouraging compliance with international law is seen at the World Trade Organization (WTO). The WTO was designed as the world's first global international trade organization, with 149 members.[80] The WTO has an extensive process for resolving disputes between states, through the Dispute Settlement Understanding (DSU).[81] The DSU is a powerful dispute resolution tool, as it establishes compulsory and binding procedures applicable to all members, thus ensuring that their international obligations accrued through the WTO are enforceable. There is a complex and detailed procedure for the resolution of disputes, eventually leading to recommendations made by the panel or Appellate Body that decides the dispute, which generally takes the form of compensation.

If the penalized party fails to comply with these recommendations, an application may be made to request the suspension of various concessions or other obligations that the party may have, in principle in the same trade sector in which the violation took place.[82] By 31 August 2010, over 411 complaints had been notified to the WTO,[83] 98 reports of panels and the Appellate Body had been adopted,[84] and the suspension of concessions

---

[79] See, e.g., in relation to Australia, the case of *A v Australia* (560/1993) 30 March 1997, UN Doc. CCPR/C/59/D/560/1993: even though human rights breaches by Australia were found by the Human Rights Committee, it could only make recommendations on how to respond to the situation to Australia, which Australia simply dismissed, resulting in a lack of effective remedy provided by the Committee: Official Records of the General Assembly, 53rd sess., UN Doc. CCPR/A/53/40, Vol. 1 (1998). See also Hilary Charlesworth, 'Human Rights: Australia versus the UN', Discussion Paper 22/06, Democratic Audit of Australia, Australian National University, August 2006, available at http://democraticaudit.anu.edu.au/papers/20060809_charlesworth_aust_un.pdf .

[80] Marrakesh Agreement Establishing the World Trade Organization, opened for signature 15 April 1994, 1867 UNTS 3 (entered into force 1 January 1995) ('WTO Agreement').

[81] Annex 2, WTO Agreement. Generally, on the DSU, see *Handbook on the WTO Dispute Settlement System by World Trade Organization* (2004); Federico Ortino & Ernst-Ulrich Petersmann (eds), *The WTO Dispute Settlement System, 1995–2003* (The Hague; New York: Kluwer Law International, 2004). For information on the legal documents relating to the WTO, see http://www.wto.org/english/docs_e/legal_e/legal_e.htm.

[82] World Trade Agreement, Annex 2, Understanding on Rules and Procedures Governing the Settlement of Disputes, Art. 22.1.

[83] Statistics available at http://www.wto.org/english/tratop_e/dispu_e/dispu_status_e.htm.

[84] Statistics available at http://www.wto.org/english/tratop_e/dispu_e/stats_e.htm.

had been authorized in 17 cases. The DSU can therefore be described as a highly effective and compelling process for ensuring that states comply with their WTO obligations, considering that 393 out of the total 411 complaints were resolved without the need for concessions to be placed on a state. As well as illustrating the effectiveness of the DSU at the international level, determinations by the DSU will also directly impact on national law. Whilst they are not binding in the sense in which a statute is binding, the decisions will nonetheless have a direct influence upon domestic jurisprudence.[85]

3.4 DIFFERENT APPROACHES TO THE IMPLEMENTATION OF INTERNATIONAL LAW IN NATIONAL LAW

There are two main theories which govern how international law becomes a part of the national law of states: transformation and incorporation. This section will first consider the theories themselves, before examining examples of the practical implementation process of international law within a sample of states. There are apparent differences between the implementation of customary international law (represented largely by the incorporation approach), and treaty law (which generally is implemented through a process of transformation). Regardless of which theoretical approach is adopted, from a practical perspective there are growing calls for national courts, in light of globalization, to take a more 'aggressive' approach to the implementation of international law into national law.[86]

3.4.1 Transformation

The principle of transformation provides that before international law can become part of a state's national law, the state must implement legislation to 'transform', or implement, the international law into national law.[87]

---

[85] See, e.g., in relation to the USA, John H. Jackson, *The Jurisprudence of the GATT and WTO: Insights on Treaty Law and Economic Relations* (Cambridge: Cambridge University Press, 2000), 167.

[86] See, e.g., Benvenisti and Downs, 'National Courts, Domestic Democracy, and the Evolution of International Law' (2009) 20(1) *European Journal of International Law* 65–8.

[87] For a theoretical consideration of the implementation of international law into national law, see Kelsen, above note 3, 378–83, 388; F Morgenstern 'Judicial Practice and the Supremacy of International Law' (1950) 27 *British Yearbook of International Law* 42.

Transformation is the dominant approach among states in relation to treaty law, which is generally transformed through an Act of Parliament. The content of such an Act of Parliament will normally take one of two forms. The first is a legislative Act setting out all of the relevant treaty provisions within the Act itself, which then becomes part of the domestic law. An example of this is the Australian International Criminal Court Act 2002 (Cth),[88] which aims to 'facilitate compliance obligations' under the Rome Statute of the International Criminal Court, and sets out at length all of the relevant substantive Rome Statute provisions within the domestic Act.[89]

The second approach involves the legislative Act simply acknowledging that the treaty is to become part of the domestic law, without setting out the treaty provisions within the Act itself, but instead annexing the treaty as a schedule. Once the treaty is transformed, it becomes a part of the state's domestic law.[90] An example of this is the Australian Geneva Conventions Act 1957 (Cth),[91] which does not include the provisions of the relevant Geneva Conventions within the Act, but instead attaches them as Schedules to be used in the interpretation of the Act.[92]

3.4.2 Incorporation

The doctrine of incorporation is based on the principle that, in the absence of conflicting domestic legislation, international law should *automatically* become part of a state's law without any need for a specific Act to be passed 'transforming' the international law into national law.[93] The incorporation doctrine can be described as the dominant doctrine in relation to customary international law, although the 'pure' concept of incorporation is altered, and in some cases heavily modified, in the context of each individual state.

The incorporation doctrine is traditionally only employed in relation

---

[88] Australian International Criminal Court Act 2002 (Cth), assented to 27 June 2002, all parts commenced operation 26 September 2002.

[89] For a discussion of this process, see, e.g., Gideon Boas, 'An Overview of Implementation by Australia of the Statute of the ICC' (2004) 2 *Journal of International Criminal Justice*, 179.

[90] See Brownlie, above note 2, 44.

[91] Australian Geneva Conventions Act 1957 (Cth), assented to 18 December 2002, commenced operation 1 September 1959.

[92] Ibid. See also Human Rights and Equal Opportunity Act 1986 (Cth), which incorporates a range of human rights treaties in schedules to the Act.

[93] Brownlie, above note 2, 41; Cassese, above note 4, 220; Shaw, above note 6, 140.

to customary international law, not treaty law. The reason for this is that generally the power to negotiate and enter into treaties is given to a state's executive, not its legislature.[94] This would mean that, in the absence of a transformation requirement, the executive could enter into or exit treaties, with all the obligations these actions would entail and without any input from the legislature. These treaties would then be automatically incorporated into the state's national law, bypassing the legislature almost entirely.[95]

An important qualification to the incorporation doctrine is that international law generally only applies insofar as it is not inconsistent with domestic legislation. The practical effect of the incorporation doctrine being applied within a state is thus less powerful than it may initially appear, for in a modern state which has a sophisticated and developed legal framework, the areas on which it would not have legislated, and in which international law would therefore claim substantial influence, are limited. In those areas where the state's domestic law and international law are predominantly in accord it will be the state's domestic law that would take precedence in any dispute between the two areas of law (assuming the absence of any incorporating legislation by the state).

3.4.3 The Implementation of Customary International Law into National Law

For customary international law, the principal approach, particularly in countries that follow the English common law system,[96] is that of automatic incorporation into domestic law, subject to the proviso that these rules are only incorporated to the extent that they are not inconsistent with the state's existing law.[97]

3.4.3.1 Common law states

3.4.3.1.1 The United Kingdom In the United Kingdom, the doctrine of incorporation is generally followed with respect to customary inter-

---

[94] This is the case in states based upon the British common law system, including the United Kingdom and Australia. This can be contrasted with states such as the United States, where the executive is given the power to enter into treaties, in light of its more substantive role within the constitutional framework.

[95] There have, however, been some interesting contemporary developments contrary to this traditional approach, in relation to Russia and East Timor (see below section 3.4.4.3).

[96] Shaw, above note 6, 166.

[97] Brownlie, above note 2, 47.

national law.[98] Thus the approach is largely that international law will automatically become part of the law of the UK in the absence of any domestic law to the contrary.[99] There is an extensive line of authority in support of this principle, an early example being the eighteenth century case of *Buvot v Barbuit*, in which Lord Talbot held that 'the law of nations in its full extent was part of the law of England'.[100] More recently, the case of *Trendtex Trading Corporation v Central Bank of Nigeria*[101] endorsed the incorporation approach. In the course of determining the case, involving a complex contractual arrangement for Trendtex to supply cement to Nigeria, Lord Denning made the following comments:

> A fundamental question arises for decision. What is the place of international law in our English law? One school of thought holds to the doctrine of incorporation. It says that the rules of international law are incorporated into English law automatically and considered to be part of English law unless they are in conflict with an Act of Parliament. The other school of thought holds to the doctrine of transformation . . . Under the doctrine of incorporation, when the rules of international law change, our English law changes with them. But, under the doctrine of transformation, the English law does not change. It is bound by precedent. It is bound down to those rules of international law which have been accepted and adopted in the past. It cannot develop as international law develops.[102]

After considering the historical development of these two theories, Lord Denning then went on to reverse his position in an earlier decision that the doctrine of transformation was to be preferred[103] and, instead, endorsed the doctrine of incorporation:

> Which is correct? As between these two schools of thought, I now believe that the doctrine of incorporation is correct. Otherwise I do not see that our courts could ever recognise a change in the rules of international law. It is certain that international law does change. I would use of international law the words

---

[98] Brownlie, ibid., 41; Shaw, above note 6, 141; Dixon, above note 14, 97. See generally David Feldman, 'Monism, Dualism and Constitutional Legitimacy' (1999) 20 *Australian Yearbook of International Law* 105.

[99] Shaw, above note 6, 141–8; Brownlie, ibid., 42–4. Note also that there exists a presumption that domestic legislation does not run counter to international law.

[100] (1736) 3 Burr 1481, as cited by Lord Denning in *Trendtex Trading Corporation v Central Bank of Nigeria* [1977] QB 529, 553–4.

[101] [1977] QB 529. See also J.G. Collier, 'Is International Law Really Part of the Law of England?' (1989) 38 *International & Comparative Law Quarterly* 924, 926.

[102] *Trendtex* case, above note 101, 553.

[103] *R v Secretary of State for the Home Department, ex parte Thakrar* [1974] 1 GB 684, 701.

which Galileo used of the earth: "But it does move." International law does change: and the courts have applied the changes without the aid of any Act of Parliament.[104]

In the more recent *Pinochet* rulings, including those of the House of Lords, the doctrine of automatic incorporation was endorsed.[105] In *Ex parte Pinochet (No. 1)* Lord Lloyd endorsed the incorporation doctrine, referring to the 'principles of customary international law, which principles form part of the common law of England'.[106] This approach was affirmed in *Ex parte Pinochet (No. 3)*, in which Lord Millett reached a similar conclusion, holding that 'customary international law is part of the common law'.[107]

However, doubt has recently arisen as to whether the traditional incorporation approach is still applicable. In the case of *R v Jones*,[108] a question as to whether the customary international law crime of aggression was automatically incorporated into UK law was considered. According to the traditional incorporation approach, in the absence of any domestic legislation (there being no domestic legislation in this case), it would normally automatically become part of the law of the UK. Yet the House of Lords unanimously held that the incorporation doctrine did not apply to the crime of aggression, stating two key reasons. First, it was accepted that UK courts no longer had the power to create new crimes, following a unanimous recent House of Lords decision to that effect,[109] and thus in the absence of statutory guidance they were unable to incorporate the customary international law crime of aggression. As Lord Hoffmann stated: 'While old common law offences survive until abolished or superseded by statute, new ones are not created. Statute is now the sole source of new criminal offences.'[110]

Secondly, Lord Hoffmann stated that 'when it is sought to give domestic effect to crimes established in customary international law, the practice is to legislate.'[111] He then referred to a number of examples where legislation was implemented to address crimes established under customary

---

[104] *Trendtex* case, above note 101, 553. The incorporation doctrine was also accepted by the other two judges in this case, Stephenson and Shaw LJJ.

[105] See also Brownlie, above note 2, 41, listing an extensive list of authority in support of this principle.

[106] [2000] 1 AC 61, 98.

[107] [2000] 1 AC 147, 276.

[108] [2006] UKHL 16. See also Shaw, above note 6, 146.

[109] *Knuller (Publishing, Printing and Promotions) Ltd v DPP* [1972] 2 All ER 898, [1973] AC 435.

[110] *R v Jones*, above note 108, [28].

[111] Ibid.

international law, in particular the International Criminal Court Act 2001 (UK),[112] giving effect to the Rome Statute. He noted that this legislation, whilst including crimes such as genocide, crimes against humanity and war crimes, excluded the crime of aggression, which was present in the original Rome Statute. Thus, he stated, '[i]t would be anomalous if the crime of aggression, excluded (obviously deliberately) from the 2001 Act, were to be treated as a domestic crime, since it would not be subject to the constraints applicable to the crimes which were included'.[113] Lord Hoffmann did state that the principle was not absolute, although it could only be departed from where 'very compelling reasons' existed.[114]

Where does that leave the UK's approach to customary international law? Whilst *R v Jones* may not appear to follow the incorporation approach, this can be explained by the specific facts of that case. Thus, it appears that the approach taken in *Trendtex* is still good law, and that the incorporation approach remains dominant. This approach has been adopted and revised to suit the particular circumstances of a number of other states, including the United States and Australia.

3.4.3.1.2 The United States The United States also has an incorporation-based approach similar to that of the United Kingdom, with the added proviso that the incorporation of international law is additionally subject to the US Constitution.[115] In a clear endorsement of the place of international law, the US Supreme Court has held:

> As a general proposition, it is of course correct that the United States has a vital national interest in complying with international law. The Constitution itself attempts to further this interest by expressly authorizing Congress '[t]o define and punish Piracies and Felonies committed on the high Seas, and Offenses against the Law of Nations'.[116]

The Court, however, noted that international law could only be enforced to the extent that it was not incompatible with the Constitution, stating

---

[112] International Criminal Court Act 2001 (UK), assented to 11 May 2001, general commencement from 1 September 2001.

[113] Ibid. It is unclear what effect recent amendments to the Rome Statute, to include the crime of aggression (with effect from some time after 2017), will have on this argument.

[114] Ibid., [29].

[115] For an early example of this see *The Schooner Exchange v McFadden*, 11 US (7 Cranch) 116 (1812), 146. See also John Marshall Rogers, *International Law and United States Law* (Aldershot, UK: Ashgate, 1999), 36.

[116] *Boos v Barry,* 485 US 312 (1988) 323.

that, 'at the same time, it is well established that no agreement with a foreign nation can confer power on the Congress, or on any other branch of Government, which is free from the restraints of the Constitution'.[117]

The contemporary status of customary international law in the US is subject to some controversy and debate;[118] however, as a general proposition, it can be said that it is treated as federal law, and any determination made by the federal courts is binding upon state courts.[119] As with the UK, the doctrine of incorporation is subject to any existing domestic statute to the contrary, as well as the doctrine of precedent.[120] However, as is also the case in the UK, there exists a presumption that domestic legislation is to be read as being in accordance with international law, 'unless it unmistakably appears that congressional act was intended to be in disregard of a principle of international comity'.[121]

There has been some renewed discussion of the approach taken by the United States in relation to customary law, particularly in the area of human rights. This has arisen from a uniquely American historical peculiarity, in the form of the Alien Tort Statute.[122] This statute provides that '[t]he district courts shall have original jurisdiction of any civil action by an alien for a tort only, committed in violation of the law of nations'.[123] Thus the Act allows for non-nationals to bring an action for a tort committed against them in violation of international law, even outside the jurisdiction of the US. In *Filartiga v Peña-Irala*,[124] a case came before the US Court of Appeals for the Second Circuit involving an action brought by Paraguayans against a fellow Paraguayan for the torture and death of the plaintiff's son. The Court held that torture constituted a violation of the law of nations, as a breach of customary

---

117 Ibid., citing *Reid v Covert,* 354 US 1, 16 (1957).

118 See, e.g., Ernest A. Young, 'Sorting out the Debate over Customary International Law' (2002) 42 *Virginia Journal of International Law* 365; Curtis Bradley and Jack Goldsmith, 'Customary International Law as Federal Common Law: A Critique of the Modern Position' (1997) 110 *Harvard Law Review* 815; Harold Koh, 'Is International Law Really State Law?' (1998) 111 *Harvard Law Review* 1824.

119 *United States v Belmont* 301 US 324, 331; *Restatement (Third) of the Foreign Relations Law of the United States*, (1987), Vol. I, 48–52. See also *Kadić v Karadžić* 70 F.3d 232, 246 (2d Cir. 1995).

120 *Schroeder v Bissell* 5 F.2d 838, 842 (1925); *Committee of United States Citizens Living in Nicaragua v Reagan*, 859 F.2d 929 (1988).

121 *Schroeder* case, above note 120.

122 28 USC §1350,

123 Ibid.

124 630 F.2d 876 (1980).

international law,[125] and was thus actionable under the Alien Torts Claims Act.

Subsequent cases involving the Alien Torts Claims Act have seen mixed results in incorporating customary international law provisions into US domestic law. In *Kadić v Karadžić*,[126] the US Court of Appeals for the Second Circuit held that the Act applied to genocide and war crimes committed by Karadžić as a state actor. On the other hand, in the case of *Sosa v Alvarez-Machain*,[127] it was held that the Alien Torts Claims Act did not create new causes of action, and was restricted only to violations of the laws of nations that existed at the time the Act came into effect.

3.4.3.1.3 Australia The Australian approach differs markedly from the UK and US approaches, resembling more of a transformative approach. Such an approach follows the comments of Justice Dixon in the High Court decision of *Chow Hung Ching v The King* where he found 'that international law is not a part, but is one of the sources, of English law'.[128]

In more recent High Court authority, the acceptance of international law as a source of law and influence on national law has been confirmed. In the *Mabo No. 2* decision,[129] Justice Brennan held that, in the event of a clash between domestic binding precedent and international customary law, the court may elect to adopt customary international law. This echoed Lord Denning's statement in the *Trendtex* case that domestic law must adapt to the changing nature of international law. In reconsidering the long-held view that indigenous Australians did not exercise lawful ownership over their land when Europeans originally arrived in Australia, Justice Brennan found that it was no longer acceptable to uphold the international law notion that inhabited land could be classified as *terra nullius* in light of modern developments in international law, including Australia's ratification of the ICCPR, leading to his view that:

> A common law doctrine founded on unjust discrimination in the enjoyment of civil and political rights demands reconsideration. It is contrary both to international standards and to the fundamental values of our common law to entrench a discriminatory rule which, because of the supposed position on the scale of social organisation of the indigenous inhabitants of a settled colony, denies them a right to occupy their traditional lands.[130]

---

125 Ibid., 884–5.
126 70 F.3d 232 (1995).
127 542 US 692 (2004), 71ff.
128 (1948) 77 CLR 449.
129 *Mabo v Queensland (No. 2)* 175 CLR 1.
130 Ibid., 42.

Whilst international law appears to operate as an influence on Australian law, the doctrine of automatic incorporation was squarely rejected by the Federal Court in the case of *Nulyarimma v Thompson*.[131] In that case, the majority acknowledged that genocide, the relevant crime in this case, was a peremptory norm (*jus cogens*) of international law but, as genocide was not a defined crime within Australian statutory or common law, it could not be incorporated into Australian law. In this way, the Court adopted the transformative approach, and from a practical perspective based this decision on the *nullen crimen sine lege* maxim (there exists no crime unless expressly created by law).[132] Other recent cases reinforce this distinct lack of clarity in the Australian approach to the implementation of customary international law.[133]

3.4.3.2 Civil law states

3.4.3.2.1 Italy, Germany and Japan A number of states following the Second World War provided for automatic incorporation of customary international law through constitutional provisions.[134] Article 10 of the 1947 Italian Constitution states: 'Italian law shall be in conformity with the generally recognized rules of international law.'[135] However, this does not affect the validity of legislation passed prior to the creation of the constitution.[136]

As required by the Allied countries following the War, Germany and Japan enacted provisions recognizing customary international law. Thus the 1949 Basic Law for the Federal Republic of Germany states, in Article 25, that 'the general rules of public international law are an integral part of federal law. They shall take precedence over the laws and shall directly

---

131 (1999) FCR 153.

132 Ibid., Wilcox J at [26], [32], Whitlam J at [54].

133 See, e.g., *Ahmed Ali Al-Kateb v Godwin* 219 CLR 562, [63]: Justice McHugh strongly denounced the use of international law in interpreting the constitution. But see Justice Kirby in the same case at [190] (advocating the use of international law in interpreting the constitution: 'opinions that seek to cut off contemporary Australian law (including constitutional law) from the persuasive force of international law are doomed to fail').

134 Whilst a general outline of a number of constitutional provisions is provided below, it must be remembered, as is the case with the states above, that states seldom adopt a pure form of incorporation, and instead modify it to fit within their particular legal framework. Thus the practical implementation of customary international law in states through national courts will vary.

135 Constitution of the Italian Republic, enacted 22 December 1947, Art. 10.

136 Brownlie, above note 2, 48.

create rights and duties for the inhabitants of the federal territory'.[137] The wording of this article has caused some controversy and confusion,[138] an ongoing debate being whether customary international law could take precedence over the German Constitution.[139]

Article 98(2) of the Constitution of Japan states, somewhat less comprehensively than the Germany Basic Law, that the '[t]reaties concluded by Japan and established laws of nations shall be faithfully observed'.[140] This has been interpreted as incorporating customary law into the domestic legal system.[141]

3.4.3.2.2 Portugal and the Netherlands The 1989 Constitution of the Portuguese Republic, Article 8(1), states that customary international law is an integral part of national law.[142] Whilst the 1983 Netherlands Constitution does not address customary law specifically, commentators have noted that customary international law will automatically apply internally, but will be trumped by statute in the case of conflict.[143]

3.4.3.3 Contemporary developments: growing constitutional recognition of the primacy of customary international law

Leading into the 1990s, a number of states expressly recognized international law in their constitutions. Following the collapse of the Communist regime, the Russian Federation adopted a new constitution in 1993, Article 15(4) of which provides:

> [T]he generally recognized principles and norms of international law and the international treaties of the Russian Federation shall constitute part of its legal

---

137 Basic Law for the Federal Republic of Germany, promulgated on 23 May 1949, Art. 25.

138 For example, see *German Consular Notification* case (*Individual Constitutional Complaint Procedure*), BVerfG, 2 BvR 2115/01, 19 September 2006. See also A. Drzemczewski, *The European Human Rights Convention in Domestic Law* (Oxford: Clarendon Press, 1983) and Amos J. Peaslee, *Constitutions of Nations* (The Hague: Nijhoff, 1950), Vol. III, 361.

139 Shaw, above note 6, 171.

140 Constitution of Japan, enacted 3 May 1947, Art. 98(2).

141 See Y. Iwasawa, 'The Relationship Between International Law and National Law: Japanese Experiences', (1993) 64 *British Yearbook of International Law* 333.

142 Constitution of the Portuguese Republic, promulgated 2 April 1976, Art. 8(1).

143 See, e.g., H.F. van Panhuys, 'The Netherlands Constitution and International Law: A Decade of Experience', 58 *American Journal of International Law*, 1964, 88–108.

> system. If an international treaty of the Russian Federation establishes other rules than those stipulated by the law, the rules of the international treaty shall apply.[144]

In 1996, following the fall of apartheid, the South African Constitution (one of the most progressive) was enacted, section 232 providing: 'Customary international law is law in the Republic unless it is inconsistent with the Constitution or an Act of Parliament.'[145]

Moving into the twenty-first century, a number of new state constitutions have recognized the supremacy of customary international law. The 2002 Constitution of the Democratic Republic of East Timor states in Article 9(1): 'The legal system of East Timor shall adopt the general or customary principles of international law.'[146] Similarly, the 2008 Kosovo Constitution, recognizes in Article 19(2): 'Ratified international agreements and legally binding norms of international law have superiority over the laws of the Republic of Kosovo.'[147]

These developments have had the result of strengthening the role that customary law plays within a state's domestic legal system through its increased automatic acceptance. As a consequence, the growing acceptance of automatic incorporation has also led to potentially enhanced consequences arising from the decision to deem the crystallization of a customary international law norm. This is because the creation of a norm will now have instantaneous and potentially wide-ranging legal effects within the growing number of countries that adopt the approach of automatic incorporation.

3.4.4 The Implementation of Treaty Law into National Law

While there is a large body of states that adhere to the incorporation doctrine in relation to customary international law, treaty law reveals a far greater divergence among states between transformation and incorporation approaches.[148]

---

[144] Constitution of the Russian Federation, ratified 12 December 1993, Art. 5.

[145] Constitution of the Republic of South Africa, certified by the Constitutional Court on 4 December 1996.

[146] Constitution of the Democratic Republic of East Timor, entered into force 20 May 2002, Art. 9(1).

[147] Constitution of the Republic of Kosovo, ratified 9 April 2008, Art. 19(2).

[148] See generally Higgins above note 36, 209–10.

3.4.4.1 Common law states

3.4.4.1.1 The United Kingdom While adhering to an incorporation approach in the implementation of customary law, with respect to treaties the UK adopts a transformative approach.[149] This approach requires an Act of Parliament to integrate a treaty into England's domestic law before that instrument will have any effect on domestic law. The reasoning behind such a view is that, while customary international law develops over a period of time through the actions of many states, treaty law can lead to the instant creation of new obligations or laws through the action of a state's executive in choosing to ratify a treaty. In the case of the UK, this would mean that if an incorporation approach were to be adopted in relation to treaty law, the Crown would be handed considerable new powers. In this way, the unelected Crown would be able to ratify and incorporate treaties into English national law, bypassing entirely the legislature.[150] Because of this, as Shaw notes:

> [A]ny incorporation theory approach to treaty law has been rejected. Indeed, as far as this topic is concerned, it seems to turn more upon the particular relationship between the executive and legislative branches of government than upon any preconceived notions of international law.[151]

Once a treaty is ratified in the UK, the question then turns to the interplay between the treaty and UK domestic legislation. There exists a rule of legal construction which provides that where domestic legislation is passed to give effect to an international convention, it is presumed that Parliament intended to uphold its international obligations.[152] This, however, must be read in conjunction with the constitutional principle that, in the case of conflict between a treaty and a later Act of Parliament, the later Act

---

[149] See, e.g., Rosalyn Higgins, 'United Kingdom', in Francis G. Jacobs and Shelley Roberts (eds), *The Effect of Treaties in Domestic Law* (London: Sweet & Maxwell, 1987), Ch. 7, 125; Dixon, above note 14, 93. See also Brownlie, above note 2, 44–7.

[150] This can be contrasted with the US, as discussed below, where the executive is elected and plays a very active as opposed to ceremonial role, as is intended by the American Constitution.

[151] Shaw, above note 6, 148. See also Brownlie, above note 2, 45 (noting that 'if a transformation doctrine were not applied, the Crown could legislate for the subject without parliamentary consent'); *Maclaine Watson v Department of Trade and Industry* [1989] 3 All ER 523.

[152] Brownlie, above note 2, 45. See, e.g., *Salomon v Commissioners of Customs and Excise* [1967] 2 QB 116, 141 (Lord Denning MR).

of Parliament will prevail. This constitutional principle has the effect of potentially limiting the legal impact a treaty can have, since any ratified treaty is always subject to the possibility of being overruled by Parliament.

3.4.4.1.2 The United States The United States also subscribes to a transformative approach in relation to treaties, although one that differs substantially from that of the UK. For a treaty to become law, it must be approved by a two-thirds majority in the Senate (the legislature) before being ratified by the President (the executive).[153] The interplay between the legislature and executive is more pronounced than it is in the UK because of the largely ceremonial role played by the Crown compared with the far more substantive role of the President within the US system. Unlike the UK, where the ratification of a treaty is a mere formality carried out by the Monarch, in the US the decision of the President to ratify is a substantive one. Once a treaty is ratified, Article VI, section 2 of the Constitution provides that:

> All Treaties made or which shall be made with the authority of the United States shall be the supreme law of the land and the Judges in every state shall be bound thereby, anything in the Constitution or Laws of any state to the contrary notwithstanding.[154]

There is an exception to the requirement of Senate approval for a treaty to come into force, through the medium of executive agreements. These agreements are usually made by the President (without the requirement for Senate approval) but nonetheless constitute valid treaties within the international sphere. These agreements are not explicitly mentioned in the Constitution, but their existence has been implied and they enjoy considerable use.[155]

As to the impact of treaties upon domestic law, there is a distinction between 'self-executing' and 'non self-executing' treaties.[156] This is a somewhat artificial distinction drawn in certain states, including the US, which whilst having no effect upon the ratification process of the treaty, do have an effect upon its use in the domestic sphere. Self-executing treaties do not

---

153 United States Constitution, adopted 17 September 1787, Art. II s. 2. See also Cassese, above note 4, 226; Shaw, above note 6, 161.

154 United States Constitution, ibid., Art. VI s. 2.

155 See, e.g., *United States v Pink* 315 US 203 (1942), 48. See also Shaw, above note 6, 161–2.

156 Brownlie, above note 2, 48–9, Shaw, above note 6, 161–2. See also Benedetto Conforti, *International Law and the Role of Domestic Legal Systems* (Dordrecht; London: Martinus Nijhoff, 1993), 25.

require domestic legislation to come into effect and thus are automatically incorporated, whereas non self-executing treaties do require an enabling act, and consequently must be transformed to become the law of the land. Generally, a self-executing treaty will be one that sets out clear and definable rights and obligations that will arise under the treaty. By contrast, a non self-executing treaty is generally harder to quantify, and can be described more as 'aspirational'.

3.4.4.1.3 Australia The Australian approach to treaty law is largely consistent with the UK approach, adopting a transformation approach that requires an Act of Parliament before a treaty can become law. This was demonstrated in *Nulyarimma v Thompson*,[157] in which an action was brought against a number of government Ministers and Members of Parliament who, it was alleged, had engaged in genocide against Australia's indigenous people. One of the key issues in the case turned on whether the *jus cogens* norm of genocide could be automatically incorporated into Australian law through Australia's ratification of the Genocide Convention, without the need for transformation through domestic legislation – a proposition answered by the majority of the Court in the negative.[158]

A ratified but unincorporated treaty did, however, play a crucial role in the *Teoh* case before the High Court of Australia.[159] In this case, the applicant claimed to have a legitimate expectation that Australia would take into account the interests of his children. This expectation was founded on the UN Convention on the Rights of the Child (UNCRC),[160] which Australia had ratified but not implemented into national law through an Act of Parliament. He argued that if his legitimate expectation was not taken into account, he would be denied procedural fairness. The High Court held that there was a 'legitimate expectation' that arises where a treaty is ratified.[161] In an oft-quoted passage, Mason CJ and Deane J set out the relevant principles governing their decision:

---

157 (1999) 96 FCR 153.

158 Ibid., Wilcox J at [20], Whitlam J at [54].

159 *Minister of State for Immigration and Ethnic Affairs v Teoh* (1995) 183 CLR 273. For a discussion of this case, see Margaret Allars, 'One Small Step for Legal Doctrine, One Giant Leap towards Integrity in Government: Teoh's Case and the Internationalisation of Administrative Law' (1995) 17 *Sydney Law Review* 204.

160 UNGA, Convention on the Rights of the Child (adopted 20 November 1989, came into force 2 September 1990) 1577 UNTS 3 (UNCRC).

161 (1995) 183 CLR 273.

> The provisions of an international convention to which Australia is a party, especially one which declares universal fundamental rights, may be used by the courts as a legitimate guide in developing the common law . . . Much will depend upon the nature of the relevant provision, the extent to which it has been accepted by the international community, the purpose which it is intended to serve and its relationship to the existing principles of our domestic law.[162] [R]atification of a convention is a positive statement by the Executive Government of this country to the world and to the Australian people that the Executive Government and its agencies will act in accordance with the Convention.[163]

The *Teoh* case is authority for the principle that ratification of a treaty is not a 'merely platitudinous or ineffectual act', and that a ratified treaty can and should be applied by domestic Australian courts, where appropriate. While this ruling seems to be a step away from the transformative approach that is generally adopted by Australia, it prompted a significant political backlash and led to a number of legislative attempts to reduce the impact of the *Teoh* decision in both 1995 and 1997, although both of these attempts failed.[164]

While *Teoh* has been endorsed in a number of international jurisdictions, including the United Kingdom,[165] it would appear that its potential scope has been reduced in light of subsequent High Court decisions, in particular *Lam*, in which a number of judges considered unfavourably the *Teoh* interpretation of a legitimate expectation and expressed strong reservations against it.[166]

As with its relationship with customary international law, Australia's approach to treaty law is perplexing. With the exception of *Teoh*, the Australian High Court has resisted intervention by international law in domestic law in the absence of a domestic incorporation of the relevant treaty. The combined effect of the approach taken by the High Court

---

162 Ibid., 286–7.

163 Ibid., 291.

164 See Boas, above note 89, 182–3.

165 *Teoh* was endorsed in principle by the Court of Appeal in *R v Secretary of State for the Home Department, ex parte Ahmed and Patel* [1998] INLR 570. On this point see Feldman, 'Monism, Dualism and Constitutional Legitimacy' (1999) 20 *Australian Yearbook of International Law* 105, 106.

166 *Re Minister for Immigration and Multicultural and Indigenous Affairs; Ex parte Lam* (2003) 214 CLR 1, [140] (Callinan J), [81–106] (McHugh and Gummow JJ). Meanwhile, rulings in other jurisdictions within Australia seem to adhere more closely to the approach in *Teoh*, although they tend not to make direct reference to that case (see, e.g., *DPP v TY (No. 3)* [2007] VSC 489 (Victorian Supreme Court)).

and by successive Australian governments is to severely limit the effect of unincorporated treaties upon domestic law, in contrast to the UK and US, both of which have mechanisms through which unincorporated treaties can play a substantive role in the domestic sphere.

3.4.4.2 Civil law states

There is divergence among civil law states as to how treaty law is implemented. Generally, states with constitutional provisions will require treaties to be implemented by an Act of Parliament, unless they are construed as self-executing.

3.4.4.2.1 Germany In Germany, under the Basic Law, power to conduct treaties is granted to the President (executive) by Article 59(1).[167] With regard to the implementation of these treaties, they are regarded by German federal courts as taking precedence over domestic legislation, but must be in accord with the constitution.[168] Once the federal law has been passed, treaties that fall under Article 59(2) will be treated as incorporated but will only be given the status of a federal law (not a higher status).[169]

3.4.4.2.2 Japan Article 73(3) of the 1946 Japanese Constitution gives Cabinet the power to enter into treaties, with the prior or subsequent approval of the Diet (legislature).[170] Article 98 of the Constitution states that 'the treaties concluded by Japan . . . shall be faithfully observed'.[171] This is clearly a vague statement and does not provide a great deal of guidance. It has, however, been interpreted as incorporating international law (both customary law, as discussed above, and treaty law) into Japan's legal system.[172]

3.4.4.2.3 The Netherlands Article 91(1) of the 1983 Netherlands Constitution[173] requires Parliamentary approval before treaties become binding. Once approved, the treaty will take precedence over existing statute law. A treaty can generally not conflict with the Constitution, although if it does conflict it may be passed through a restrictive

---

167 Basic Law for the Republic of Germany, above note 137, Art. 59(1).
168 Shaw, above note 6, 172.
169 Ibid.
170 Constitution of Japan, above note 140, Art. 73(3).
171 Ibid., Art. 98.
172 H. Oda, *Japanese Law* (Oxford: Oxford University Press, 1999, 2nd edn), 49–50; Iwasawa, above note 141.
173 Constitution of the Netherlands, adopted 17 February 1983, Art. 91(1).

procedure, the requirement being a two-thirds majority in both chambers of parliament.[174]

3.4.4.3 Contemporary developments: automatic incorporation of treaty law into domestic law

The constitutions of a number of states, and especially those of Russia and East Timor, have adopted a less conventional transformation-based approach to the implementation of treaty law into domestic law. Whilst self-executing treaties traditionally do not require implementing legislation, and this position has not changed, it will be seen that in relation to non self-executing treaties, these states adopt a more progressive approach.

Under Article 15(4) of the Russian Constitution, and Article 5 of the Federal Law on International Treaties of the Russian Federation of 1995, ratified treaties are considered part of Russia's legal system.[175] If a treaty does not require 'the publication of intra-state acts' it will be directly imported into Russian law. If the treaty requires a legal act, Russia is under an obligation to implement the necessary legislation. This is a significant trend away from the traditional position, whereby states maintain a discretion to determine, after ratifying a treaty, whether or not they will then implement it into domestic law through an Act of Parliament. Under Russia's constitution, once ratified, treaties appear to have the scope to be incorporated directly into Russian law.

Similarly, the 2002 Constitution of East Timor allows for treaties to be automatically applied internally.[176] Considering the broad scope of its provisions, East Timor appears to be adopting a purely incorporation-based approach to both customary and treaty law.

Article 19(1) of the 2008 Kosovo Constitution[177] provides that, upon ratification, treaty law becomes part of the internal law of Kosovo.[178] Treaty law is directly applicable, except in the case of a non self-executing treaty, where application requires the promulgation of a law. In Article 19(2), it is stated that ratified international agreements, as well as norms of international law, take superiority over the laws of Kosovo. While this

---

[174] See generally J. Klabbers, 'The New Dutch Law on the Approval of Treaties' (1995) 44 *International and Comparative Law Quarterly* 629.

[175] Constitution of the Russian Federation, above note 144, Art. 15(4).

[176] Constitution of the Democratic Republic of East Timor, above note 146, s. 9(1–3).

[177] Constitution of Kosovo, ratified 9 April 2008, Art. 19(1).

[178] After their publication in the Official Gazette of the Republic of Kosovo.

Constitution is not as broad as that of East Timor, it nonetheless represents a highly progressive approach to international law.

Contemporary developments suggest an increasing challenge to the traditional approach to the implementation of treaty law by states. Particularly in the cases of Russia, East Timor and Kosovo, the automatic incorporation of treaty law upon ratification by the executive[179] sets a highly progressive precedent. It does appear, however, that widespread adoption of the approach taken by these states is unlikely. This is largely because of the constitutional interplay that exists between the legislature and the executive in English common law states, and the strong shift in power towards the executive that would result from allowing for the automatic incorporation of treaty law.

3.5 CONCLUSIONS

The theoretical debate between monism and dualism in many ways frames a key practical issue facing the international legal order today: where national and international law overlap, which should prevail? Before international fora, there is no question that international law is supreme. That is not to say that domestic law does not have a role to play; clearly it does, but it is a secondary role, to supplement international law where it is deficient, and to cast light on complex issues of fact upon which an international tribunal will pass judgment.

The real dilemma arises when considering the role that international law should play within the domestic sphere. The choice between incorporation or transformation, and how these models are implemented, varies considerably between states, and there is hardly uniformity of practice. With respect to customary international law, incorporation approaches seem predominant both in the common law and civil law states, but practice is by no means uniform.

With respect to treaty law, the variation of approach by states is even greater. However, to make sense of the divide, it may be helpful not to view the question as a choice between transformation and incorporation, but one involving the role of the executive. In states where the executive plays a largely ceremonial role, such as the UK, Australia and the Netherlands, a transformative approach tends to be adopted in order not to grant the executive substantive power by allowing it to enter into

179 In the case of Kosovo this is stated expressly only to extend to self-executing treaties.

treaties unilaterally. In states where the executive plays a more substantive role, such as the USA and Germany, an incorporation approach tends to be preferred. This is, of course, subject to the distinction drawn in some states between self-executing and non self-executing treaties.

Contemporary developments suggest an interesting shift toward a greater supremacy of international law. In the most recently created or amended constitutions – Russia, East Timor and Kosovo, for example – the supremacy of international customary and treaty law over domestic law is explicitly emphasized. As in other areas of international law and relations (such as human rights, international criminal justice, and the developing power and number of international and regional organizations), the unilateral power of states within their own domains is shifting. This should not be seen as an 'assault on the citadel of state sovereignty',[180] for it is the states themselves, acting individually or collectively, that cede such authority. Nonetheless, the extent of this acknowledgement of international law, and its place in the internal fabric of a state's legal and social life, is not entirely clear, as is revealed by the varying practice between states in relation to these issues.

---

180 To quote Orentlicher in a different context, see Dianne F. Orentlicher, 'The Law of Universal Conscience: Genocide and Crimes against Humanity', available at http://www.ushmm.org/genocide/analysis/details/1998-12-09-01/orentlicher.pdf, 11.

4. The subjects of international law: states

Who or what are the subjects of international law? What exactly is required to cross the threshold of legal personality and become a participant on the international legal plane? In what ways do the rights and obligations – capacities – differ as between those privileged participants in the international legal system? These questions are crucial to an understanding of how the international legal system functions, and they will be the subject of this and the following chapter.

When faced with the question of whether the United Nations possessed the requisite capacity to bring a claim for reparations before the International Court of Justice (ICJ) in 1949, the Court famously remarked that, to be an international person, an entity must be 'a subject of international law and capable of possessing international rights and duties'; it must also have 'the capacity to maintain its rights and duties by bringing international claims'.[1] While this formulation of international legal personality has stood the test of time and remains undisputed, its circular nature is striking. As Ian Brownlie observed: 'All that can be said is that an entity of a type recognized by customary law as capable of possessing rights and duties and of bringing international claims, and having these capacities conferred upon it, is a legal person.'[2] From this uncertainty, it might be said that the measure of international legal personality is the actual, rather than the potential, exercise of rights and duties. Indeed, to properly appreciate the nature of personality it is necessary to go further than merely comprehending that personality is concerned with the incidence of international legal rights and duties. In international law, personality is a relative phenomenon, and accordingly its measure in any given

---

1 *Reparation for Injuries Suffered in the Service of the United Nations*, (Advisory Opinion) [1949] ICJ Rep 174, 179.

2 Ian Brownlie, *Principles of Public International Law* (Oxford: Oxford University Press, 2008, 7th edn), 57. See also Neyire Akpinarli, *The Fragility of the 'Failed State' Paradigm: A Different International Law Perspective of the Absence of Effective Government* (Leiden: Brill, 2010), 105.

case will depend on a variety of factors – only some of which are strictly legal in nature.

Legal personality is a *conditio sine qua non* for participation in a legal system. It is a threshold that must be crossed, for without legal personality entities do not exist in law.[3] As Kelsen notes, law cannot be considered only in terms of rights and duties – it must also be able to point to someone or something that possesses those rights and duties.[4] Even so, the concept of personality in international law is ambiguous; how does this decentralized legal system identify which entities can have rights or duties and under what conditions?

To begin at the beginning: states are the primary and universally accepted subjects of international law.[5] Since the Peace of Westphalia, signed in 1648, effectively legitimized the nation-state as the sole legal entity in international relations, the role of sovereign states as the masters of international law has not been profoundly challenged. Of course, the fact of the privileged position that states hold in international law tells only part of the story about its subjects, nature and content. The essence of legal personality, and the rights and responsibilities held by the myriad of entities in any legal system, vary and evolve – at times incrementally, at other times with a meteoric speed. The period since the creation of the United Nations in 1945 has heralded some extraordinary examples of this.

This and the following chapter will address both the traditional position of the subjects of international law, as well as contemporary developments in their nature and capacity. This chapter focuses on states. It begins by considering the international personality of states and the nature of sovereignty. The traditional criteria for statehood, set out in Article 1 of the Montevideo Convention on the Rights and Duties of States,[6] will be

---

[3] Jan Klabbers, 'The Concept of Legal Personality' (2005) 11 *Ius Gentium* 35.

[4] Hans Kelsen, *General Theory of Law and State* (Cambridge, MA: Harvard University Press, 1945), 93.

[5] See Christian Walter, 'Subjects of International Law', in Rüdiger Wolfrum (ed.), *Max Planck Encyclopedia of Public International Law* (Heidelberg: Max-Planck-Institut, 2010), 1; M.P. Vorster, 'The International Legal Personality of Nasciturus States' (1978) 4 *South African Year Book of International Law* 1, 2; Rosalyn Higgins, *Problems and Process: International Law and How We Use It* (Oxford: Clarendon Press, 1994), 39; Rebecca M.M. Wallace and Olga Martin-Ortgea, *International Law* (London: Sweet & Maxwell, 2009, 6th edn), 63; Vaughan Lowe, *International Law* (Oxford: Oxford University Press, 2007), 14–15, 122–3.

[6] Montevideo Convention on the Rights and Duties of States (adopted 26 December 1933, entered into force 26 December 1934) 49 Stat. 3097; Treaty Series 881, Art. 1.

considered, as will examples of their application. Apart from the specific requirements for the creation of statehood, the process of recognition of a state by other states within the international community is a critical aspect of statehood, and the different elements and theories of recognition will be discussed.

The chapter will then consider the relevance of additional criteria to the process of statehood – the willingness to observe international law, in particular human and peoples' rights, and the impact of this on the evolution in the understanding of statehood. The importance of territory to the concept and operation of sovereignty is difficult to understate and the principles and operation of territorial sovereignty will be discussed. Finally, this chapter will address a fundamental aspect of statehood in the context of the post-Second World War period. The principle of self-determination, which has heralded an exponential growth in the number of states and a radical shift in the international legal and political landscape, will be given detailed attention.

In considering the creation and place of states within international law, certain recent developments since the break-up of the former Yugoslavia suggest a shift in the manner and circumstances in which states may manifest. Contemporary developments will be discussed, as will emergent themes that may suggest either a future direction – or simply some degree of confusion – in the complex realm of international law.

4.1 THE NATURE OF THE PERSONALITY OF STATES IN INTERNATIONAL LAW

As has always been the case in international law, it is only states that have international legal personality to the fullest extent.[7] They are the most obvious and universally accepted subjects of international law[8] and, as such, the conclusion that they have legal personality for the purposes of international law, giving them certain rights and duties, is uncontroversial.[9] While there is little doubt that the participants are diversifying, the position of states as sovereigns with primary control over the creation

---

[7] Higgins, above note 5, 39; Anthony Aust, *Handbook of International Law* (Cambridge: Cambridge University Press, 2005), 16; Oleg I. Tiunov 'The International Legal Personality of States: Problems and Solutions' (1992–1993) 37 *St Louis University Law Journal*, 326–7; Vorster, above note 5, 2.

[8] Walter, above note 5, 1; Vorster, above note 5, 2.

[9] M.N.S. Sellers, 'International Legal Personality' (2005) 11 *Ius Gentium* 67; Tiunov, above note 7, 323.

and development of international law sets them apart from all other participants.

Since the establishment of the United Nations system, there has been a dramatic increase in the number of entities calling themselves states. This has largely been a consequence of the process of decolonization and the increasing recognition of new or reconstituted states based on the right of peoples to self-determination. The increase in the number of states, from 75 prior to the Second World War[10] to 192[11] today, has had a profound impact on the nature of modern international law.[12] The growth in the number of state-entities following the Second World War led the International Court of Justice as early as 1970 to note that, in this context, the interpretation of international law 'cannot remain unaffected by the subsequent development of law, through the Charter of the United Nations and by way of customary law'.[13]

To be sure, the law has developed considerably in this area over the past few decades such that the idea of statehood, as well as when and how it might arise, has become something of a changing dynamic.

4.2 SOVEREIGNTY

To appreciate the meaning of statehood and its relationship with international law, one must consider the fundamental principle of state sovereignty. The notion of sovereignty is one of the oldest concepts in

---

[10] James Crawford, *The Creation of States in International Law* (Oxford: Oxford University Press, 2006, 2nd edn), 4.

[11] There are currently 192 members of the United Nations. This does not include the Holy See or claims by the territories of Taiwan and Palestine to the right of statehood. Nor does it include the potentially new or developing states of Kosovo, South Sudan, Abkhazia, Nagorno-Karabakh or Northern Cyprus. Of these, certainly South Sudan and Kosovo seem most likely to be first to join the list of the world's states.

[12] Recent examples include the new statehood of Kosovo, Montenegro and East Timor.

[13] *Legal Consequences for States of the Continued Presence of South Africa in Namibia (South West Africa) notwithstanding Security Council Resolution 276* (Advisory Opinion) [1971] ICJ Rep 16, 53. See generally Robert Jennings and Arthur Watts (eds), *Oppenheim's International Law* (Harlow, UK: Longman, 1992, 9th edn); Ti-Chiang Chen, *The International Law of Recognition* (New York: Frederick A. Praeger Inc., 1951); John Dugard, *Recognition and the United Nations* (Cambridge, UK: Grotius Publications, 1987); T.D. Grant, *The Recognition of States: Law and Practice in Debate and Evolution* (Westport, CT; London: Praeger, 1999).

international law. Article 2(1) of the Charter of the United Nations reflects the continued relevance of the principle to modern international law and the significance of the sovereign equality of all states.[14] However, the criteria necessary to make a state 'sovereign' – always the subject of some degree of confusion – has become increasingly complex, as a variety of stated and unstated indicia seem to have developed in recent years.

The principle of the sovereign equality of states in international law far predates the United Nations Charter. Its origins can be traced to the Peace of Westphalia, after which the hierarchical system organized around the Church and the Holy Roman Empire was disbanded in preference to a horizontal system based on the recognition of the equality of nation states. Emerich de Vattel, an eminent eighteenth-century international law scholar, famously stated: 'A dwarf is as much a man as a giant is; a small Republic is no less a sovereign state than the most powerful kingdom.'[15]

For Hans Kelsen, '[s]overeignty in its original sense means "highest authority"'.[16] As such, developments in the national organization of states and, as a corollary, the development of international law, have established the principle of the exclusive competence of the state with regard to its own territory. The Permanent Court of Arbitration noted in 1928 that sovereignty involves not only the exclusive right to display the activities of a state,[17] but 'sovereignty in the relations between states signifies independence'.[18]

Judge Shahabuddeen stated in the *Nauru* case, 'whatever the debates relating to its precise content in other respects, the concept of equality of states has always applied as a fundamental principle to the position of states before the Court'.[19] Indeed, in contemporary usage, the concept of sovereignty has both political and legal connotations. Despite sovereignty and equality representing a basic doctrine of the law of nations, in reality 'the history of the international system is a history of inequality *par*

---

[14] United Nations, Charter of the United Nations (24 October 1945) 1 UNTS XVI.

[15] Emerich de Vattel, *Le droit des gens, ou principes de la loi naturelle, appliqués a la conduite et aux affaires des Nations et Souverains* (Washington, DC: Carnegie Institution of Washington, 1916).

[16] Kelsen, above note 4, 189.

[17] *Island of Palmas* case *(or Miangas)* (*United States of America v Netherlands*) (1928) 2 RIAA 829, 9.

[18] Ibid., 8.

[19] *Certain Phosphate Lands in Nauru* (Preliminary Objections) [1992] ICJ Rep 240, 270–1; see also Ram P. Anand, 'New States and International Law', in *Max Planck Encyclopedia of International Law* (Heidelberg: Max-Planck-Institut, 2010), 1; Tiunov, above note 7, 327–9.

excellence'.[20] Formal equality exists only in a legal sense before the judicial organs in the international system.

Despite the legal fiction that all states possess sovereign equality, it is clear from history that the Great Powers (whoever they happen to be at a given time) 'impose limits on the application of the law' based on political decisions.[21] The 'haves' in the international system are not just materially advantaged, but have correspondingly greater capacity to influence and shape the content of the rules that govern all states.[22] The distinction between states referred to as the Great Powers and a large mass of middle and smaller powers (including those who have at times been referred to as 'rogue' or 'pariah' states) is that the Great Powers police the international order from a position of assumed cultural, material and legal superiority.[23] A key prerogative of this position has been a right to intervene in the affairs of other states in order to promote some proclaimed enlightened goal. This was illustrated most recently in the invasion of Iraq by the Coalition of the Willing led by the United States (as well, perhaps, as the use of force against Gaddafi's regime in Libya[24]), but also much earlier in history in the colonial projects of, amongst others, England, France, Germany and Italy, and earlier still in the religious quest of the Crusades. Indeed, whether one goes back as far as Rome, ancient Greece or Babylonia,[25] the story has been much the same.

While sovereign equality remains enshrined in international law as a quality possessed by all states, these examples illustrate that the vagaries of international politics render sovereign equality something of a compromised ideal. Sovereign equality is not necessarily reflected in international practice, at least not in the traditional sense that prevailed after the Peace of Westphalia. Arguably, political considerations weigh more heavily on the shoulders of states than do legal considerations, when states are

---

[20] R.W. Tucker, *The Inequality of Nations* (New York: Basic Books, 1977), 8. See also discussion concerning John Austin's conception of sovereignty in Chapter 1.

[21] Oscar Schachter, *International Law in Theory and Practice* (Dordrecht; London: Martinus Nijhoff, 1991), 9.

[22] Ngaire Woods, 'Order, Globalization and Inequality in World Politics', in Andrew Hurrell and Ngaire Woods (eds), *Inequality, Globalization and World Politics* (Oxford: Oxford University Press, 1999), 21.

[23] Gerry Simpson, *Great Powers and Outlaw States: Unequal Sovereigns in the International Legal Order* (Cambridge; New York: Cambridge University Press, 2004), 5.

[24] See Security Council Resolution 1973 (2011).

[25] For a discussion of the place of international law in history, see Chapter 1, section 1.3.

required to reaffirm their 'faith in fundamental human rights, in the dignity and worth of the human person, in the equal rights of men and women and of nations large and small'.[26] The variety of responses from different states to different circumstances that engage these fundamental values certainly bears out this view.

Political double standards might be cited in the UN's response to apartheid in South Africa and white rule in Rhodesia (now Zimbabwe) beginning in 1966, where a link was first made between internal state practices and status in the international community. The forerunners of today's pariah states were South Africa and, to a lesser extent, Rhodesia. For example, as a response to the all-white minority Smith regime's Unilateral Declaration of Independence in the British colony of Southern Rhodesia in 1965, the Security Council called on states to break off relations with Rhodesia and applied a sanctions regime that became increasingly punitive.[27] In South Africa, clearly an independent state and member of the League of Nations, a similar process occurred.[28] These prohibitions had the enlightened goal of ending apartheid, deemed the most egregious form of racism in existence at the time. However, the failure to seriously sanction Pol Pot's Kampuchea, Idi Amin's Uganda or Guatemala, for example, reflects the vagaries of international politics.[29]

4.3 TRADITIONAL CRITERIA FOR STATEHOOD

In essence, for a state to be a state, it must be sovereign and characterized by the recognized features of statehood. As the Arbitration Commission of the European Conference on Yugoslavia rather blandly put it, a state may be defined as 'a community which consists of a territory and a population subject to an organized political authority . . . such a state is characterized by sovereignty'.[30] This tells an important part of the story – but not the whole story. While contemporary developments in this area of law have rendered opaque the circumstances in which statehood may be said to have been established (perhaps this has always been the case), the primary

---

26 Charter of the United Nations, Preamble.

27 SC Res. 221 (9 April 1966); SC Res. 232 (16 December 1966); SC Res. 277 (15 March 1970); Lowe above note 5, 159.

28 SC Res. 418 (4 November 1977).

29 Simpson, above note 23, 300.

30 Cited in M. Craven, 'The EC Arbitration Commission on Yugoslavia' (1994) 65 *British Yearbook of International Law* 333.

legal basis for establishing a legitimate title to statehood remains the four main criteria set out in Article 1 of the 1933 Montevideo Convention:

- a permanent population;
- a defined territory;
- a government; and
- the capacity to enter into relations with other states.[31]

While it is not clear precisely at which point in history these four fundamental elements were first accepted as forming the basic test for statehood in international law, the signing of the Convention on 26 December 1933 is commonly viewed as amounting to a crystallization of the then prevailing and widely held practice. Article 1 has since been regarded as setting down '[t]he best known formulation of the basic criteria for statehood',[32] and – as Rosalyn Higgins has noted – '[n]o further serious attempts at definition have been essayed'.[33]

Strictly speaking, in order for a state to come into existence, all four criteria of the Montevideo Convention must be present to a certain extent. Legally these criteria are discrete requirements, although in practice it is helpful to view them as existing in an interconnected relationship where no element is mutually exclusive. For example, to have a permanent population, there must be a defined territory; in order to enter into relations with other states there must be a recognized government, in control of a permanent population, in a defined territory. Looked at in this way, the criteria become more than mere legal rhetoric and instead provide a concrete basis for determining a state's international legal capacity and legitimacy. The criteria are, perhaps, a rare happy marriage between formal legal requirements and the irresistible logic of the rational world; although, as we shall see, that is not to say the marriage is not at times considerably strained by the external forces of politics and other extralegal considerations.

4.3.1 First Criterion: Permanent Population

The first Montevideo criterion requires that the state entity exhibit a permanent population, and that this population can be defined as a 'stable

---

[31] Montevideo Convention, above note 6, Art. 1.
[32] Crawford, above note 10, 45.
[33] Higgins, above note 5, 39.

community'.[34] As such, the population does not have to be homogeneous in nature, but it must be settled. This requirement illustrates the basic need for some form of stable human community capable of supporting the superstructure of the state. This means that the people must have the intention to inhabit a specific territory on a permanent basis. Mere occupation of a territory will not be sufficient to legally fulfil this criterion. The presence of inhabitants who are traditionally nomadic will not necessarily affect the requirement of permanence.[35] This point was reflected in the ICJ's Advisory Opinion on the Western Sahara where – while it was a territory sparsely populated mostly by people of a nomadic nature – it was still considered by the Court to have a permanent population, possessing the right to self-determination.[36]

Nonetheless, it seems logical that to fulfil this criterion, there remains a requirement for some permanence, if not in living arrangements then at least such as to suggest the viability of the community over time. This does not necessarily mean that any particular measure of longevity or extended pedigree is required before a population can form the basis of a state. There is also no requirement as to the size of the population, as evidenced by the existence of states with very small populations, such as the Vatican City (under 1000), Nauru and Tuvalu (both under 11000).[37]

4.3.2 Second Criterion: Territory

In order to satisfy the second Montevideo criterion, control must be exercised over a certain portion of territory. This criterion is a critical precondition for statehood.[38] Exclusive control of territory remains a fundamental prerequisite for the competence and authority required by any state to administer and exercise its state functions both in fact and in law. As Cassese puts it, states have paramountcy in international law by virtue of their stable and permanent control over territory.[39]

It is not a requirement that the precise delimitations of this territory be defined. The ICJ noted in the *North Sea Continental Shelf* cases:

---

34 Brownlie, above note 2, 71–6.

35 Aust, above note 7, 15–16.

36 *Western Sahara* (Advisory Opinion) [1975] ICJ Rep 2, [70], [162]; GA Res. 3292 (XXIX).

37 John H. Currie, *Public International Law* (Toronto: Irwin Law, 2008), 21.

38 Ibid., 22.

39 Antonio Cassese, *International Law* (Oxford: Oxford University Press, 2005, 2nd edn), 74.

> The appurtenance of a given area, considered as an entity in no way governs the precise determination of its boundaries, any more than uncertainty as to boundaries can affect territorial rights. There is, for instance, no rule that the land frontiers of a State must be fully delimited and defined, and often in various places and for long periods they are not.[40]

Israel is one such example. It achieved statehood in 1948, even though the whole of its territory was in dispute.[41] Similarly, Kuwaiti sovereignty was restored and recognized before its borders were finally demarcated by the UN in 1992 in accordance with its 1963 agreement with Iraq.[42] The size or wealth of the territory is also not important. The Vatican City is considered a sovereign state despite, 'whatever domain it may have elsewhere', occupying less than 100 acres on earth.[43] Since 1990, despite their small size, Andorra, Liechtenstein, Monaco, Nauru, San Marino and Tuvalu have all joined the United Nations.[44]

What is important in relation to territory is that an exclusive right is established in that area to display state power – that is, effective government (the third Montevideo criterion). The 'obsession by states with territory'[45] is in this sense quite understandable, as territorial sovereignty is dependent upon territorial control over a certain portion of the globe to the exclusion of any other state.[46] During a civil war, for example, a state may lose effective control of a portion of its territory to a rebel government. Even so, while the conflict continues, and until the borders of the area under rebel control become static, the rebel group will not be able to show a sufficiently defined territory to support a claim to statehood.[47]

The ICJ, in its ruling in the *Military and Paramilitary Activities in Nicaragua* case, confirmed the link between a state's territorial integrity

---

40 *North Sea Continental Shelf* cases (*Federal Republic of Germany v Denmark and the Netherlands*) [1969] ICJ Rep 3, [46].

41 See Lawyers Committee for Human Rights, 'Comments Relating to the Combined Initial and First Periodic Report of the State of Israel before the UN Human Rights Committee' (1998); *Legal Consequences of the Construction of a Wall in the Occupied Palestinian Territory* (Advisory Opinion) [2004] ICJ Rep 136, 121; Lowe, above note 5, 156.

42 Wallace and Martin-Ortgea, above note 5, 65.

43 David Harris, *Cases and Materials on International Law* (London: Sweet & Maxwell, 2004, 6th edn), 100.

44 Crawford, above note 10, 52.

45 Peter Hilpold, 'The Kosovo Case and International Law: Looking for Applicable Theories' (2009) 8 *Chinese Journal of International Law* 58.

46 *Island of Palmas* case, above note 17, 8.

47 Lowe, above note 5, 156.

and its sovereignty.[48] In the case regarding South Africa's presence in Namibia, the Court was emphatic that it was the '[p]hysical control of territory, and not sovereignty or legitimacy of title' that formed the basis for a state's liability for acts affecting other states.[49]

4.3.3 Third Criterion: Government

The third Montevideo criterion requires that a state-entity must have a central government operating as a political body within the law of the land and in effective control of the territory.[50] The population in question must be constituted by a coercive, relatively centralized legal order; there must exist central organs for the creation and the application of the norms of that order, especially that organ which is called government.[51] The requirement for government is not tied to any particular form or style of government, but is instead concerned with a coherent, stable and effective political organization.[52] The mere existence of a government will not be sufficient to satisfy the requirement of an *effective government*. To do this it must be sovereign and independent, so that within its territory it is not subject to the authority of another state.[53] The importance of government as a criterion for statehood in international law is best understood by appreciating the need for stability and effectiveness both within a state and in a state's international relations.

The traditional example often referred to in relation to this is the 1920

---

[48] *Military and Paramilitary Activities in and against Nicaragua* (Merits) [1986] ICJ Rep 14, 106 ('*Nicaragua* case'); Jennifer L. Czernecki, 'The United Nations Paradox: The Battle between Humanitarian Intervention and State Sovereignty' (2002–03) 41 *Duquesne Law Review* 396.

[49] *Legal Consequences for States of the Continued Presence of South Africa in Namibia (South West Africa) notwithstanding Security Council Resolution 276*, above note 13, 54; Jochen A. Frowein, 'De Facto Regime', in Rüdiger Wolfrum (ed.), *Max Planck Encyclopedia of Public International Law* (Heidelberg: Max-Planck-Institut, 2010), 1.

[50] Aust, above note 7, 16.

[51] Hans Kelsen, 'Recognition in International Law, Theoretical Observations' (1941) 35 *American Journal of International Law* 605, 607–8.

[52] *Nicaragua* case, above note 48, [263]; Letter of 20 November 1991 (issued as UN Doc. A/46/844 and S/23416) in which Libya emphasized that the Charter 'guarantees the equality of peoples and their right to make their own political and social choices, a right that is enshrined in religious law and is guaranteed by international law' (quoted in *Questions of Interpretation and Application of the Montreal Convention arising from the Aerial Incident at Lockerbie* (*Libya v United Kingdom*) (Provisional Measures), Dissenting Opinion of Judge Oda, [30]).

[53] Aust, above note 7, 16.

Aaland Islands case, which concerned the claim to self-determination of a population living on a group of islands (the Aaland Islands) in the Baltic Sea. An International Committee of Jurists was entrusted by the League of Nations to give an Advisory Opinion on the legal aspects of the claim. The case turned on whether the Islanders were under the domestic sovereignty of Finland (in which case the principle of state sovereignty would render it an internal state matter), or whether at the relevant time Finland did not possess the relevant qualities of statehood (in which case the Islanders might have a right to claim self-determination[54]). The 1920 report of the Committee stated:

> It is . . . difficult to say at what exact date the Finnish Republic, in the legal sense of the term, actually became a definitely constituted sovereign State. This certainly did not take place until a stable political organization had been created, and until the public authorities had become strong enough to assert themselves throughout the territories of the State without the assistance of foreign troops.[55]

In other words, for a state to come into being, the requirement for an effective government is closely associated with the notion of self-sufficiency and non-reliance, especially with respect to primary state functions such as the maintenance of internal peace and stability.

However, recent developments arguably contradict the principle set down in the *Aaland Islands* case. Scholars have pointed to state practice emerging from the break-up of the former Socialist Federal Republic of Yugoslavia that suggests the permissibility of entities to declare statehood *before* the criteria for an effective government has been substantially met.[56] In 1992, when Croatia and Bosnia and Herzegovina were both embroiled in a series of brutal armed conflicts, and when non-government forces and the forces of other state entities controlled substantial areas of their respective territories, both were admitted as independent Member States

---

[54] The relevance of this case to self-determination is discussed below at section 4.9.1.1.

[55] LNOJ Sp. Supp. No. 4 (1920), 8–9.

[56] Malcolm N. Shaw, *International Law* (Cambridge; New York: Cambridge University Press, 2008, 6th edn), 200–201; Roland Rich 'Recognition of States: The Collapse of Yugoslavia and the Soviet Union' (1993) 4 *European Journal of International Law* 36, 51. Consider also Afghanistan, Sierra Leone, Somalia and the Democratic Republic of the Congo, which have been classified at varying times as 'failed states' in that, in spite of possessing legal capacity on the international plane, they were unable to exercise it in the absence of an effective governing regime.

into the United Nations. This appears to reflect a shift in the traditional necessity for the effective exercise of control by a government throughout its territory. However, when considered in the context of the development and evolution of the principle of self-determination throughout the twentieth century, it is possible that the position with respect to Croatia and Bosnia and Herzegovina reflects a relaxation of the traditional requirement for effective control.[57]

4.3.4 Fourth Criterion: Capacity to Enter into Legal Relations

The final traditional criterion for statehood – the capacity to enter into legal relations with other states – is discrete, but in practice is often treated as being closely connected to the third requirement of effective government. This is because the capacity to enter into relations with other states is primarily concerned with the emergent entity having the relevant political and legal machinery with which to engage in the complex sphere of international relations. The critical consideration attaching to this criterion is one of the *capacity* to act independently in international legal relations, rather than proof of action.

For example, while 'states' or provinces within federated countries – such as Victoria (in Australia), Texas (in the USA) or Ontario (in Canada) – have permanent populations, defined territory and effective governments, they are not considered to be sovereign states. This is because the capacity to act on the international plane is the preserve of federal governments of these countries, and not of their provincial governments. As Article 2 of the Montevideo Convention stipulates, 'the federal state shall constitute a sole person in the eyes of international law'. Thus, although political subdivisions within a state may meet the first three criteria, they will not meet the fourth.[58] Of course, the fact that some provincial entities do, in fact, maintain international dealings only reinforces the vagaries of international law in this area. Examples of this include the government of Quebec, which maintains overseas delegations and has extensive dealings with foreign governments, as well as the present government of California's relations with other governments on the Pacific Rim, particularly in relation to its Renewable Energy Program.[59]

---

[57] This is discussed further below in relation to the break-up of the former Yugoslavia – see section 4.9.3.

[58] Lowe, above note 5, 158.

[59] The California Energy Commission, 'California's Renewable Energy Program'; available at http://www.energy.ca.gov/renewables/index.html (accessed on 7 November 2010).

4.4 RECOGNITION

In 1941, Hans Kelsen wrote that '[t]he problem of recognition of states and governments has neither in theory nor in practice been solved satisfactorily'.[60] Seventy years later, one could reasonably make precisely the same statement. Fulfilment of the Montevideo criteria tells only part of the story of the process of achieving statehood. Claims of statehood are inevitably affected by the greater number – and nature – of states prepared to treat a new entity as a state and enter into relations with it.[61] This is because, unless an entity is accorded recognition as a state by a sufficiently large number of other states, it cannot realistically claim to be a state with all the corresponding rights and obligations.[62] Participation in international organizations and regional groupings is also of considerable importance in the assertion of legal capacity,[63] and will often flow from broader recognition.

Recognition is a manifestation of the will of a state whereby it expresses the legitimacy of the existence of the nascent state entity.[64] Recognition is relevant if the legality of a title or situation is doubted.[65] In the past the term 'recognition' in international law has been used mainly in connection with the recognition by existing states of new states, of new heads of government of existing states, and of belligerent communities. A satisfactory, if general, articulation of the role of recognition is as a procedure 'whereby the governments of existing states respond to certain changes in the world community'.[66] Indeed, recognition has frequently been sought by both new state entities seeking admission to the family of nations as well as from states that have acquired, by occupation or annexation, some new piece of territory in the belief that the grant of recognition by important states will strengthen its title over the newly acquired territory.[67]

---

60 Kelsen, above note 51, 605.

61 Christopher J. Borgen, 'The Language of Law and the Practice of Politics: Great Powers and the Rhetoric of Self-Determination in the Cases of Kosovo and South Ossetia' (2009) 10 *Chicago Journal of International Law* 2, 15; Wallace and Martin-Ortgea, above note 5, 67.

62 Aust, above note 7, 17; Lowe, above note 5, 157.

63 Borgen, above note 61, 2.

64 Alexander Orakhelashvili, *Peremptory Norms in International Law* (Oxford: Oxford University Press, 2006), 372.

65 Hersch Lauterpacht, *Recognition in International Law* (Cambridge: Cambridge University Press, 1947), 411.

66 Grant, above note 13, xix.

67 Arnold D. McNair, 'The Stimson Doctrine of Non-Recognition: A Note on its Legal Aspects' (1933) 14 *British Yearbook of International Law* 66; Higgins,

States seek recognition from other states of a change in the international order because legal recognition has the ability to confer legitimacy and make it a subject of international law.[68] This is because the legal status of state as a state is intimately tied to the willingness of other states to recognize and deal with it. Therefore, once the Montevideo criteria have been adequately established, appropriate recognition is the most straightforward means of achieving the required mantle of statehood. Despite the broadly held view that recognition is purely a question of policy and not of law,[69] in practice political and legal recognition work in unison, for unless an entity is accorded recognition as a state by a sufficiently large number of other states, it cannot participate as a state in international law.

While the formation, altered territorial status, dissolution or extinction, or changing control of states are on one view matters of fact, they are materially and invariably affected by the process by which the community of nations is prepared to recognize and accept such changes. As is shown by the differing responses to the Turkish Federated State of Cyprus, the dissolution of the former Yugoslavia and creation of the new states of Slovenia, Croatia and Bosnia-Herzegovina – and, more recently, Kosovo, South Ossetia and Abkhazia – the process of altering statehood is one very much dependent on whether such changes receive support and recognition, and by whom, within the international community.

4.4.1 Political Recognition of Statehood

A distinction must be made between recognition of states and recognition of governments. The recognition of a government is no more than an acknowledgement that it is the representative organ of the state, and has the consent or at least the acquiescence of its people.[70] The recognition of a state, however, is the establishment of the fact that a state is a subject

above note 5, 39–55; Q. Wright, 'Some Thoughts About Recognition' (1950) 44 *American Journal of International Law* 548–59.

[68] Kelsen, above note 51, 608; Merrie Faye Witkin 'Transkei: An Analysis of the Practice of Recognition – Political or Legal?' (1977) 18 *Harvard International Law Journal* 606.

[69] *Accordance with International Law of the Unilateral Declaration of Independence in respect of Kosovo* (Advisory Opinion), 22 July 2010, ICJ General List No. 141, 26; McNair, above note 67, 66; Philip Marshal Brown, 'The Legal Effects of Recognition' (1950) 44 *American Journal of International Law* 617; M. Kaplan and N. Katzenbach, *The Political Foundations of International Law* (New York: Wiley, 1961), 109; Shaw, above note 56, 445.

[70] Stefan Talmon, *Recognition of Governments in International Law* (Oxford: Clarendon Press, 1998), 5–6.

of international law.[71] Recognition of a state may consist of a legal act or a political act. This means that an act of recognition can have purely political (and thus, non-legal) consequences, or recognition can have legal consequences by establishing the fact of the existence of a state in the sense of international law. Thus, recognition can be both political and legal in nature and effect.[72]

Political recognition occurs where a recognizing state or government expresses a *willingness* to enter into political and other relations with the recognized state or government.[73] A political act of recognition is 'declaratory' in the sense that it is an act without legal consequences.[74] The declaration of willingness by a state or government to enter into political relations with the recognized state or government in itself has no legal consequences, although it may be of great importance politically to the prestige of the nascent state or government seeking to be recognized.

Recognition of a new state of affairs in international relations can be established at any time regardless of the date on which, in the opinion of the state doing the recognizing, the new participant began to fulfil the Montevideo criteria.[75] Political recognition may hinge on certain conditions being fulfilled by the new entity, such as the degree of independence or an undertaking to adhere to international law.[76] However, this is unimportant from a legal point of view since the declaration of willingness to enter into political and other relations with a state or government does not constitute any legal obligation in itself.[77] Existing states are only empowered, not obligated, to perform the act of recognition. Refusal to recognize the existence of a new state is not a violation of international law and is often used as a persuasive political tool.[78]

With existing states, a political policy of non-recognition can be employed as a sanction and deterrent for preventing breaches of the international order. However, once a state has become a legal entity by virtue of its relations with other states, non-recognition has no legal effect on its statehood. This is illustrated in the case of the United States of America

---

[71] Kelsen, above note 51, 607, 609.

[72] Ibid., 605; see Shaw, above note 56, 445, 470–72.

[73] Kelsen, above note 51, 605; Rich, above note 56, 36, 43, 65.

[74] Kelsen, above note 51, 605.

[75] Kelsen, ibid., 613.

[76] McNair, above note 67, 67.

[77] Kelsen, above note 51, 605; Wallace and Martin-Ortgea, above note 5, 76.

[78] See, Lowe, above note 5, 164; Akpinarli, above note 2, 137. Examples include the non-recognition by many Arab states of the state of Israel, the non-recognition of Turkey's control over Northern Cyprus, or the non-recognition by the international community of Somaliland.

and the Islamic Republic of Iran which, since the Islamic Revolution in Iran in 1979 overthrowing the US-backed Shah Reza Pahlavi and replacing him with an overtly hostile Shi'a regime, have not conducted diplomatic relations. Further economic sanctions have been imposed recently in an attempt to dissuade Iran from its nuclear programme. On 19 March 2009, US President Barack Obama spoke directly to the Iranian people in a video saying that, '[t]he United States wants the Islamic Republic of Iran to take its rightful place in the community of nations. You have that right – but it comes with real responsibilities.'[79] As Obama suggests, Iran already has a rightful place among the community of nations as a result of its fulfilment of the Montevideo criteria and by virtue of its recognition by other states. He is also correct in stating that this right conveys certain responsibilities, in this case to abide by the Nuclear Non-Proliferation Treaty (NPPT). However, the diplomatic non-recognition of the Iranian government by the United States is purely political in nature and does not affect Iran's legality as a state.

Non-recognition, sometimes referred to as the Stimson doctrine,[80] can occur when the international community is faced with breaches of international law by one of its members, such as the case of Iran and the NPPT, the acquisition of the West Bank and East Jerusalem by force by the state of Israel, or the international isolation experienced by South Africa under the apartheid regime. The Stimson doctrine of non-recognition arises when the conduct of a state becomes so objectionable that a severe diplomatic response is considered necessary. Examples of this have included the possession of armaments in contravention of international agreements, acts of external aggression, or the resort to war or any other non-pacific means used for the solution of an international dispute.[81] Because political recognition is always accompanied by further and more concrete evidence of support,[82] non-recognition affects commercial treaties, extradition treaties, diplomatic protection, protection of industrial, literary and artistic property, etc.[83] It must be distinguished from cases where recognition is withheld for legal reasons, such as where the entity in question does not

---

79 'Obama offers Iran "new beginning"', *BBC News,* 20 March 2009, available at http://news.bbc.co.uk/2/hi/7954211.stm

80 Named after US Secretary of State Henry Stimpson. The Stimpson Doctrine is a policy of the United States federal government, enunciated in an identic note of 7 January 1932, to Japan and China, of non-recognition of international territorial changes that were executed by force.

81 McNair, above note 67, 67.

82 Ibid., 69.

83 Ibid., 72–3.

possess the attributes of statehood outlined in the Montevideo Convention and recognition of it as a state would be premature, as occurred with Palestine or Taiwan.[84]

4.4.2 Declaratory and Constitutive Theories of Recognition

Two distinct theories exist that explain the role of recognition in the formation of states: declaratory and constitutive. The *declaratory* theory of recognition treats recognition as a mere political or symbolic act, with no legal ramifications. To proponents of this theory, statehood can be achieved without recognition from other pre-existing states. The establishment of statehood in international law is regarded as a question of fact. Once certain facts come into existence (usually the criteria for statehood established by the Montevideo Convention although, as discussed below, at section 4.5, other criteria may be relevant), international personality and statehood are conferred on the newly emergent state. Thus, any decision to recognize a newly emerging state is merely an acknowledgement that the new state has already satisfied the requisite criteria of statehood. The state in question does not have to wait for recognition.[85]

In contrast, under the *constitutive* theory, recognition by existing states is a fundamental precondition for the attainment of statehood for a newly emerging state. Statehood, as a legal status, springs from the act of recognition itself.[86] Given the nature of general international law, it is the states that are empowered to determine violations of general international law. Thus, it is said the constitutive theory reflects the legal system itself determining its own subjects with certainty.[87] It is the recognition by an existing state of a newly emerging state that, according to the constitutive model, creates a state and determines its legal personality.[88] Jennings and Watts explain the constitutive theory of recognition as follows:

> [I]t is a rule of international law that no new state has a right as against other states to be recognised by them; that no state has a duty to recognise a new state; that a new state before its recognition cannot claim any right which a member of the international community has as against other members; and

---

[84] Vera Gowlland-Debbas, *Collective Responses to Illegal Acts in International Law: United Nations Action in the Question of Southern Rhodesia* (Dordrecht; London: M. Nijhoff, 1990) 275; Shaw, above note 56, 469–70.

[85] See generally Currie, above note 37, 31; Shaw, above note 56, 445–6; Wallace and Martin-Ortgea, above note 5, 75.

[86] Witkin, above note 68, 607.

[87] Crawford, above note 10, 20; Kelsen, above note 51, 607.

[88] Wallace and Martin-Ortgea, above note 5, 76.

> that it is recognition which constitutes the new state as a member of the international community'.[89]

One consequence of the constitutive theory is that the legal status of statehood is inherently relative in character.[90] The existence of a state is not absolute: a 'state exists only in its relations to other states'.[91] It is the legal act of recognition from existing states that enables the new state to exist on the international legal plane.[92]

In 2006, Crawford expressed the view that '[n]either theory of recognition satisfactorily explains modern practice' – the declaratory theory confuses fact with law, and the constitutive theory denies the possibility that new states may come into existence by virtue of general rules or principles, 'rather than on an ad hoc, discretionary basis'.[93] In 2008, however, Shaw noted that while states have, in the past, refused recognition to other states for political reasons, it is rarely contended that the unrecognized state is denied any rights or obligations under international law. This is regarded by Shaw to indicate that the declaratory theory is stronger.[94] Modern practice in 2011 suggests that a range of (sometimes variable) factual requirements impact upon the rules relating to whether statehood may be said to exist. The question of recognition (and by whom) continues to affect how the new state can demonstrate that it fulfils these rules as required, before it will be welcomed into the community of nations.

4.4.3 *De Facto* and *De Jure* Recognition

The significance of a *de jure* or *de facto* recognition in international law is not entirely clear. In general, it is believed that *de jure* recognition is final, whereas *de facto* recognition is only provisional and may be withdrawn.[95] From a juristic point of view, the distinction is of little importance.

In the 1970s, a number of states recognized the *de facto* incorporation of East Timor into Indonesia as a *fait accompli.* For example, believing that it was unrealistic to continue to refuse to recognize the effective control

---

89 Jennings and Watts, above note 13, 129.

90 Kelsen, above note 51, 609; Crawford, above note 10, 21.

91 Kelsen, ibid., 609.

92 See generally, Currie, above note 37, 30–31; Shaw, above note 56, 446–8; Wallace and Martin-Ortgea, above note 5, 5.

93 Crawford, above note 10, 5.

94 Shaw, above note 56, 447.

95 Kelsen, above note 51, 612; Wallace and Martin-Ortgea, above note 5, 79; Shaw, above note 56, 459–60.

Indonesia exercised over East Timor, the Australian government stated at the time that the incorporation of East Timor into Indonesia was a reality and that the Indonesian government was the authority in effective control.[96] However, Australia and other states remained sceptical of the legal validity or the method of East Timor's incorporation. They also maintained that the people of East Timor continued to possess the right to self-determination.[97] Whatever the pretext of recognition, the subsequent independence of East Timor confirms that *de jure* or *de facto* recognition of the incorporation into Indonesia was ultimately devoid of legal validity.[98]

4.4.4 Current Recognition Practice

The question of the legal effect of state recognition practice in international law has been a source of controversy and continuous debate in international law for much of the twentieth century. This unease was exemplified in an editorial comment in the *Washington Post* in 1992, stating that 'no element of international policy has gone more askew in the break-up of Yugoslavia than recognition – whether, when, how, under what conditions – of the emerging parts'.[99] In large part, this has stemmed from the divergence and often incongruous body of state practice on the matter. Those subscribing to the traditional positivist school in international law advanced the constitutive model. The emergence of new states into the international community meant that existing members of the international community would owe new obligations to them. Therefore, it was desirable that the consent of these existing states to be so bound was necessary in order for a new state to come into existence. This was to occur through the voluntary practice of state recognition.

However, with the rapid process of decolonization and the self-determination of so many states during the second half of the twentieth century, a new body of state practice began to form. Along with this, heavy criticism was pointed at the constitutive theory. Central to this criticism was the argument that the process of determining statehood in international law is so important that it should not be permitted to rest on the isolated,

---

[96] *Case concerning East Timor (Australia v Portugal) Counter Memorial of the Government of Australia* (1 June 1992) ICJ, Ch. 2, see http://www.icj-cij.org/docket/files/84/6837.pdf. See also Wallace and Martin-Ortgea, above note 5, 79; Shaw, above note 56, 445.

[97] C. Antonopoulos, 'Effectiveness v the Rule of Law Following the East Timor Case', (1997) 27 *Netherlands Yearbook of International Law*, 97.

[98] Alexander Orakhelashvili, above note 64, 381–2.

[99] Quoted in Rich, above note 56, 37.

sometimes conflicting and politically motivated recognition of existing members of the international community.[100]

The Institut de Droit International had emphasized in its resolution on recognition of new states and governments as early as 1936 that the 'existence of the new state with all the legal effects connected with that existence is not affected by the refusal of one or more states to recognise'.[101] While the position remained (and probably still remains) unclear, in 1991, with the beginning of the disintegration of the Socialist Federal Republic of Yugoslavia, the Arbitral Commission of the Conference of Yugoslavia (the Badinter Commission) was asked to determine the status of the emerging entities in the region.[102] In its first opinion of 29 November 1991, the Commission stated that 'the effects of recognition by other States are purely declaratory',[103] a statement that has been heralded as important support for the declaratory model as the applicable modern doctrine.

While the position taken by the Badinter Commission has been considered to be influential, without clarification from the International Court of Justice there continues to be some uncertainty. The ICJ had just such an opportunity in its recent Advisory Opinion on the *Accordance with International Law of the Unilateral Declaration of Independence in respect of Kosovo*.[104] Regrettably, it declined to shed further light on the question of the primacy of the declaratory or constitutive theories of recognition. Citing the wording of the question posed to it by the General Assembly, the Court confined its opinion to whether or not the declaration of independence by Kosovo itself was in accordance with international law (which it answered in the affirmative),[105] and did not concern itself with

---

[100] Crawford, above note 10, 20; Rich, above note 56, 56; Shaw, above note 56, 460–62.

[101] 39 Annuaire de L'Institut de Droit International (1936), 300. See also, Shaw, above note 56, 445–50.

[102] The Badinter Commission was set up by the Council of Ministers of the European Economic Community on 27 August 1991 to provide the Conference on Yugoslavia with legal advice. See below, section 4.9.3, for a detailed discussion of the break-up of Yugoslavia and its effect on the development of international law relating to self-determination.

[103] Opinion 1, Badinter Commission, 29 November 1991, 92 ILR 165; cf 'Declaration on the Guidelines on Recognition of the New States in Eastern Europe and the Soviet Union', *Focus* (Special Issue), Belgrade, 14 January 1992, at 149 where the European Community outlined that it thought that recognition as a simple declaration of an ascertainable fact did not provide sufficient means to allow the EC to influence the situation in Eastern Europe.

[104] *Accordance with International Law of the Unilateral Declaration of Independence in Respect of Kosovo*, above note 69.

[105] Ibid., 79.

the legal consequences of that declaration. In particular, the Court did not consider whether or not Kosovo had achieved statehood. Nor did it enquire about the validity or legal effects of the recognition of Kosovo by the states which recognized it as an independent state.[106] Therefore, it appears that, for the time being at least, the report by the Badinter Commission remains the most authoritative statement on the role of recognition in international law.

4.5 CONTEMPORARY DEVELOPMENTS AND THE ROLE OF OTHER CRITERIA IN THE DEVELOPMENT OF STATEHOOD

In this light, it is apparent that, while the four traditional criteria of the Montevideo Convention remain integral to the concept of statehood, contemporary developments in international law have raised the possibility that additional criteria – such as recognition by other states and a willingness to adhere to international law – may now also be necessary elements for statehood. In practice, however, it seems that the interpretation and application of the criteria for statehood will depend on the particular circumstances and context in which the claim for statehood is made. As discussed above, recent developments in international law suggest that while a prospective state must still exhibit the four Montevideo criteria, unless an entity is accorded recognition as a state by a sufficiently large number of other states (particularly powerful ones), it cannot realistically claim to be a state with all the corresponding rights and obligations.[107] Additionally, a willingness to observe international law, or at the very least the principles set out in Article 2 of the UN Charter, are increasingly seen as essential.[108]

4.5.1 Willingness to Observe International Law and Fundamental Rights

The observance of international law has frequently been referred to as an additional criterion in determining the admission of states into the international legal arena. Signatories to the UN Charter have agreed, pursuant to

---

[106] Ibid., 51.

[107] Christopher J. Borgen, 'The Language of Law and the Practice of Politics: Great Powers and the Rhetoric of Self-Determination in the Cases of Kosovo and South Ossetia' (2009) 10 *Chicago Journal of International Law* 2, 2; Wallace and Martin-Ortgea, above note 5, 76.

[108] Brownlie, above note 2, 71–6.

Article 2 of the Charter, to 'settle their international disputes by peaceful means in such a manner that international peace and security, and justice, are not endangered'. In cases such as Cyprus, Israel and Kosovo, recognition by other states of the new entity has been held to be contingent upon the observance of international legal norms. Because the Charter of the United Nations still only accepts states as its primary constituents, it is becoming increasingly necessary for entities seeking admission to the UN to recognize the importance of the pacific settlement of disputes, international human rights and fundamental freedoms which all UN members have agreed to promote and respect.[109]

State practice seems to suggest that an attempt to create new states, or extend the territory of existing states, by the use of force is unlikely to lead to the widespread recognition of statehood necessary. For example, the Turkish Republic of Northern Cyprus, located in the northern portion of the island of Cyprus, came about through military means. The result was a partitioning of the island, resettlement of many of its inhabitants, and a subsequent unilateral declaration of independence by the north, which was controlled by Turkey, in 1983. The Turkish Republic of Northern Cyprus has received recognition from only one state – Turkey, upon which it is entirely dependent for economic, political and military support. Northern Cyprus has so far been denied recognition before the UN on the basis that it was established by the illegal use of force and is in violation of the territorial integrity of the Republic of Cyprus.[110] In the circumstances, it is difficult to count the Turkish Republic of Northern Cyprus, as far as international law is concerned, as anything more than an illegal occupation.

The state of Israel's forcible acquisition and subsequent occupation of the West Bank and East Jerusalem in 1967 has led to the non-recognition of Israeli sovereignty over these areas, based on the impermissibility of the use of force to acquire the territory.[111] The same holds true for the Israeli annexation of the Golan Heights in 1981.[112] Despite attempts by the US in the 1990s to alter the legal status of these areas through diplomatic statements,[113] such state views cannot, and have not, generated a change in their legal status as occupied territory. This has been most recently

---

[109] Sellers, above note 9, 2; Charter of the United Nations (1945), Arts 55 and 56.

[110] UNSC Resolutions 541 (1983), 550 (1984); *Loizidou v Turkey*, EctHR, Series A-310, 23 March 1995.

[111] UNSC Resolutions 242 (1967), 252 (1968), 267 (1969), 465 (1980).

[112] UNSC Resolution 497 (1981).

[113] Orakhelashvili, above note 64, 383.

confirmed in the ICJ's Advisory Opinion on the *Legal Consequences of the Construction of a Wall in the Occupied Palestinian Territory.*[114]

In contrast, the unilateral declaration of independence by the provisional government of Kosovo on 17 February 2008 states at Article 2 that:

> We declare Kosovo to be a democratic, secular and multi-ethnic republic, guided by the principles of non-discrimination and equal protection under the law. We shall protect and promote the rights of all communities in Kosovo and create the conditions necessary for their effective participation in political and decision-making processes.

In its 2010 Advisory Opinion regarding the legality of this declaration, the ICJ considered that the claim by the authors of the declaration to statehood for Kosovo was reinforced by the fact that they 'undertook to fulfil the international obligations of Kosovo'.[115] While the Court made no determination as to whether the declaration actually brought about a new state, its comments do seem to suggest that the willingness of the Kosovo government to abide by international law certainly supported the legality of its unilateral declaration of independence.

Of course, Kosovo's independence can be viewed also from a somewhat different perspective – in some respects the inverse to that of Northern Cyprus. The history of Kosovo's developing claim to statehood has to be understood by reference to the persecution of its ethnic majority population by Serbia, the war Slobodan Milošević waged against the Kosovo Albanian population of the (then) province of Serbia, the Rambouillet Peace Agreement which Serbia refused to accept and NATO's subsequent bombing of Serbia – all of which set up the inevitable support by the US and many states within western Europe of Kosovo's claim to statehood.[116]

Given that the statehood of Kosovo was only made possible by a campaign of NATO bombing of Serbia – an armed attack unsanctioned by the

---

[114] *Legal Consequences of the Construction of a Wall in the Occupied Palestinian Territory*, above note 41.

[115] *Accordance with International Law of the Unilateral Declaration of Independence in Respect of Kosovo*, above note 69, 105–6.

[116] Despite the categorical denial of the US and NATO that this was to be the result of international interference in Serbia and Kosovo: see Security Council Resolution 1244 (1999), 10 June 1999, forming the legal basis for international administration, which reaffirmed the commitment of all UN Member States 'to the sovereignty and territorial integrity of the Federal Republic of Yugoslavia'; J. Norris, *Collision Course: NATO, Russia, and Kosovo* (Westport, CT; London: Praeger, 2005), 33.

UN Security Council – and subsequent massive entity building under the auspices of the United Nations,[117] one must remark that the use of armed force in the development of independent statehood very much depends upon who is using it and in what context. It is possible to view Kosovo's independence as something of a punishment to Serbia for its role in the wars of the former Yugoslavia and its long-standing persecution of the Kosovo Albanian people. While justification and legality of the use of force by NATO countries in Serbia will be discussed in Chapter 8, it seems reasonable to conclude that the international community, however selectively or hypocritically, puts considerable emphasis on a certain observance of fundamental aspects of international law relating to human and peoples' rights.

At the very least, these examples illustrate the importance of the willingness of states to abide by international law as a potential additional criterion for admission to statehood. One might regard the Badinter Commission's opinions, and its treatment of the question of recognition, as a political expedient particular to the break-up of the former Yugoslavia, the finalization of which has been realized by Kosovo's apparently successful claim to independent statehood.[118] Another way of regarding these events is as the development of a new approach by the international community to statehood.[119] But what is that approach? Should we take its stated support for the declaratory theory at face value? Or is the acceptance of Croatia and Bosnia-Herzegovina into the community of nations before they fulfilled all the Montevideo criteria evidence that the constitutive theory is of greater weight to the development of statehood (a conclusion possibly supported by the independence of Kosovo)? It is difficult to determine at this point whether Russia's support for claims of independence by South Ossetia and Abkhazia – despite its

---

117 Created by Security Council Resolution 1244 (1999), 10 June 1999.

118 Kosovo's declaration of independence and its path towards successful secession from Serbia is in some ways a scenario without precedent: see Report of the Special Envoy of the Secretary-General on Kosovo's Future Status, S/2007/168, 26 March 2007 ('Ahtisaari's Report'). On the other hand, it has a clear relationship with the atypical approach of the Badinter Commission (and, in turn Europe and the UN) to the creation of statehood that emerged out of the disintegration of the former Yugoslavia.

119 See, e.g., Crawford, above note 10, 91–2; Rob Dickinson, 'Twenty-First Century Self-determination: Implications of the Kosovo Status Settlement for Tibet' (2009) 26 *Arizona Journal of International and Comparative Law* 547, 558; *Case concerning the Frontier Dispute* (*Burkina Faso/Mali*) [1986] ICJ Rep 554; Rich, above note 56, 62; Lowe, above note 5, 161.

claim that this does not serve as any kind of precedent[120] – reflects further evidence of such a trend.

What is clear is that the law regarding what it takes to fulfil the criteria for statehood and recognition is changing in ways that are yet to be entirely understood.

4.6 THE PRINCIPLE OF TERRITORIAL SOVEREIGNTY

Put simply, a state cannot exist without territory.[121] This is a fundamental paradigm of international law, the importance of which cannot be overstated.[122] As the international community comprises states, and the existence of states and the scope of their activities are defined by their territories, rules regarding territory are at the heart of international law. Indeed, Jennings suggests that the very 'mission and purpose of traditional international law has been the delimitation of the exercise of sovereign power on a territorial basis'.[123] Shaw, too, sees the central aim of many of the fundamental principles of international law as the 'protection and preservation of the dominant statist order founded upon territorial exclusivity'.[124] As such, an understanding of the rules governing territorial sovereignty, its acquisition, disposal and scope, are fundamental to any appreciation of the character and operation of international law.

Before examining the principle of territorial sovereignty in detail, it is worth noting that the territorially based state has not always been the conduit through which humans have conducted their interactions. The post-Roman era, for example, saw the organization of human societies centred upon individual and tribal allegiances rather than territory.[125] It was the signing of the Peace of Westphalia that marked a significant mile-

---

[120] 'Abkhazia, S. Ossetia no precedents for other rebel regions – Lavrov', *RIA Novosti*, 18 September 2008, cited in Rein Müllerson, 'Precedents in the Mountains: On the Parallels and Uniqueness of the Cases of Kosovo, South Ossetia and Abkhazia' (2009) 8 *Chinese Journal of International Law* 1, 4.

[121] Jennings and Watts, above note 13, 563; Malcolm N. Shaw, *Title to Territory* (Aldershot, UK: Ashgate, 2005), 3; R.Y. Jennings, *The Acquisition of Territory in International Law* (Manchester, UK: Manchester University Press, 1963), 2.

[122] Cf. Kelsen who sees territory as little more than the space in which states may act: Kelsen, above note 4, 308.

[123] Jennings, above note 121, 2.

[124] Shaw, above note 121, 11.

[125] Ibid., 4.

stone in the establishment of a world order based on defined territorial groupings, conferring exclusivity of state action within such territory. This emphasis on territory as the basis of legal rights, duties and immunities has been the dominant trend for the past 300 years and has come to form the basis of modern international law.[126]

4.6.1 Territory, Title and Sovereignty

Territory is a geographical concept. It includes land and subterranean areas, rivers, lakes, reefs, rocks, islets, islands, territorial sea and airspace.[127] Territory can be subject to one of four possible types of regime, of which territorial sovereignty is one. The other three regimes are:

- *res nullius* – territory that may be acquired by states but has not yet been placed under territorial sovereignty;
- *res communis* – territory not capable of being placed under state sovereignty, such as the high seas, the exclusive economic zones and outer space; and
- territory not subject to the sovereignty of any other state, but which possesses a status of its own (such as trust territories).[128]

Territorial sovereignty is best understood as a legal nexus, and has been defined variably as 'the relationship between the state and the physical area it encompasses',[129] and 'the framework within which the public power is exercised'.[130] In classical international law territorial sovereignty is thought to comprise both rights and duties.[131] These aspects were

---

[126] Sharma notes that 'despite pressing integrationist trends contemporarily in operation in the world arena, the traditional model of territorial order based on the principle of state sovereignty stands firm. This underscores the continuing importance of the concepts of territory, independence and territorial sovereignty to the development of international law': Surya P. Sharma, *Territorial Acquisition, Disputes and International Law* (The Hague; London: M. Nijhoff, 1997), 327.

[127] But not the exclusive economic zone, or airspace above the exclusive economic zone or continental shelf: Shaw, above note 121, 8–9; Gillian D. Triggs, *International Law: Contemporary Principles and Practices* (Sydney: LexisNexis Butterworths, 2011, 2nd edn), 272.

[128] Brownlie, above note 2, 105.

[129] Shaw, above note 121, xii. See also Andrea Brighenti, 'On Territory as Relationship and Law as Territory' (2006) 21(2) *Canadian Journal of Law and Society* 65.

[130] *Nationality Decrees in Tunis and Morocco* (French Pleadings) (1923) PCIJ (Ser. C) No. 2, 106.

[131] *Island of Palmas* case, above note 17, per Judge Huber, 838.

recognized respectively by Judge Huber in the *Island of Palmas* case when he referred to 'the exclusive competence of the State in regard to its own territory', and 'the obligation to protect within the territory the rights of other States'.[132] Territorial sovereignty constitutes the scope of state jurisdiction, to the end that within its territory, a state exercises its supreme, and normally exclusive, authority.[133]

When we speak of title to territory, on the other hand, we are referring to 'the vestitive facts which the law recognises as creating a right'.[134] These are the factual circumstances required for a change in the legal status in international law of some area of territory. As Salmond puts it,

> every right (using the word in a wide sense to include privileges, powers and immunities), involves a title or source from which it is derived. The title is the de facto antecedent, of which the right is the de jure consequent.[135]

The very rules regarding acquisition of territory constitute no more than the circumstances in which a state is granted title and *ipso facto* acquires sovereignty (and its consequential legal rights and obligations) over that territory.[136] In the *Burkina Faso/Republic of Mali* case the ICJ recognized that the term 'title' has multiple accepted meanings, and that 'the concept of title may also, and more generally, comprehend both any evidence which may establish the existence of a right, and the actual source of that right'.[137]

4.6.2 The Role of Territorial Sovereignty

As already noted, territorial sovereignty serves as a fundamental characteristic of statehood, possession of which confers the necessary status to gain entry into the international community. However, territorial sovereignty also serves extralegal purposes. As Gottman has observed:

> If a territory is the model compartment of space resulting from partitioning, diversification and organization, it may be described as endowed with two main

---

132 Ibid.

133 Brighenti, above note 129, 82–3; Jennings and Watts, above note 13, 564. For a discussion of territorial jurisdiction, see Chapter 6, section 6.3.1.

134 Triggs, above note 127, 271. Jennings, above note 121, 4.

135 Glanville Williams, *Salmond on Jurisprudence* (London: Sweet & Maxwell, 1957, 11th edn), 378.

136 Jennings and Watts, above note 13, 679.

137 *Frontier Dispute* (*Burkina Faso and Republic of Mali*), above note 119, 564.

> functions: to serve on one hand as a shelter for security, and on the other hand as a springboard for opportunity.[138]

Furthermore, by apportioning an area of the globe in which a group of people through their governing body has exclusivity of action, territorial sovereignty can entrench and enforce a people's sense of belonging and identity. While this traditional construct of international society may be under something of a challenge by an increasingly globalized world, it remains a quintessential aspect of international social, political and legal life.

4.6.3 Territory and the State

What exactly is the nature of the relationship between a state and territory? The oldest theory, patrimonial theory, claims sovereignty to be the result of an assumed natural right of the state to exercise power over territory. This theory eventually evolved into the object theory, or property theory. Both theories draw heavily upon the analogy of private law property owners exercising their right over possessions, and have been dismissed by contemporary authors for confusing the concepts of sovereignty and property,[139] known alternatively in Roman law as *imperium* and *dominium*. Such confusion appears to have arisen during the feudal era when a ruler was seen to own territory in a property law sense. These theories also cannot properly account for the concept of federal states; nor can it explain why a state ceases to exist upon disposal of all of its territory.[140]

The subjectivist doctrine, otherwise known as the space and quality theory,[141] is of the view that territory is not separate from the state. Rather, territory is seen as a crucial part of the personality of the state.[142] A major criticism of this theory is that it appears to suggest that change in the territorial composition or territorial extent of a state seriously affects its personality. Furthermore, like the patrimonial theory, this approach is difficult to reconcile with concepts of federal states, condominiums and leases.[143]

---

138 Jean Gottmann, *The Significance of Territory* (Charlottesville, VA: University Press of Virginia, 1973), 14.

139 Shaw, above note 121, 17.

140 W. Schoenborn, 'La Nature Juridique du Territoire', 30 *Hague Recueil* (1929 V) 108–12.

141 Ibid., 114.

142 J.H.W. Verzijl, *International Law in Historical Perspective*, Vol. III (Leiden: Sijthoff, 1970), 12–13.

143 Shaw, above note 121, 18.

This can be contrasted with the objectivist or competence theory, which diminishes the importance of territory to merely the geographic space in which a state may rightfully exercise its jurisdiction.[144] This theory, however, is deficient in the sense that it fails to recognize that territory may be viewed not only as the sphere of jurisdiction, but also the legal underpinning for that jurisdiction.[145]

Shaw suggests, instead, that a 'composite approach' is the most acceptable explanation for the relationship between a state and territory.[146] Such an approach synthesizes the three major doctrines, views territorial sovereignty as a divisible element, and acknowledges that territory is both the basis upon which, and the area in which, jurisdiction is exercised.

4.6.4 The Acquisition of Territorial Sovereignty

While many writers still mould their analysis of the relevant rules around the traditional categories or 'modes' of acquisition formulated in the Middle Ages, it is now generally acknowledged that these categories are deficient in many respects.[147] For a start, these categories as laid out by Grotius and subsequent legal writers rely heavily on analogy with Roman laws regarding private property ownership.[148] The rules of territorial acquisition have evolved considerably since, and today such clear-cut categorization misstates the complex interplay of broad, overlapping principles at work in the acquisition of territory. Nor does such categorization accord with the realities of tribunal practice. Rarely, if ever at all, do today's tribunals engage in the artificial exercise of squeezing the facts before them into a traditional mode of acquisition.[149] Instead, they focus on principles such as effective occupation and administration.[150]

---

[144] As Kelsen puts it, 'there is no relation at all between the State, considered as a person, and its territory, since the latter is only the territorial sphere of validity of the national legal order': Kelsen, above note 4, 218.

[145] Ibid.; Benedetto Conforti, 'The Theory of Competence in Verdross' 5 *European Journal of International Law* (1994) 1, 2.

[146] Shaw, above note 121, 19.

[147] See generally Brownlie, above note 2, 127; Shaw above note 56, 495; Triggs, above note 127, 212–3. Jennings and Watts, above note 13, 678–9.

[148] See generally Hersch Lauterpacht, *Private Law Sources and Analogies of International Law (with Special Reference to International Arbitration)* (New York: Longmans, Green & Co., 1927).

[149] What Brownlie refers to as a 'preoccupation' with orthodox 'labels': Brownlie, above note 2, 127.

[150] For example, in the *Island of Palmas* case, although the United States and the Netherlands made respective claims to territory based on discovery, cession,

Nonetheless, while traditional conceptions of territorial sovereignty are simplistic and misleading in terms of modern practice, it is important to understand them for two simple reasons. First, the doctrine of intertemporal law demands that a state's title to territory be judged in the context of the law of the time. In this way, historical acts of territorial acquisition remain relevant to many territorial disputes today. Secondly, modern practice has evolved out of traditional practice, so that perhaps in this area more than some others 'the old is necessary to an understanding of the new'.[151]

4.6.5 The Former Modes of Acquisition

There are five classical modes of acquisition: (i) occupation, (ii) accretion, (iii) cession, (iv) conquest (otherwise known as subjugation), and (v) prescription. Some writers also include adjudication as a sixth mode of acquisition.[152] It must also be noted that boundary treaties and boundary awards also constitute a root of title.[153] Such treaties will typically deal with the acquisition or loss of territory by the delineation or clarification of state borders.

4.6.5.1 Accretion

Accretion, erosion and avulsion (the abandonment of a river channel and the formation of a new channel) refer to the natural geological processes that result in an increase or decrease in the territory and are relatively uncontroversial as modes of acquisition of territorial sovereignty.[154] For example, where the erosion of land that once comprised the territory of

---

contiguity and prescription, Judge Huber's decision did not directly analyse the facts in terms of any one of the traditional modes of acquisition, and most noticeably refrained from using the language of the former modes of acquisition. Rather, what was emphasized was the importance of 'the actual continuous and peaceful display of state functions' evidenced in the Netherlands' administrative acts over the territory: above note 17, 867–71. See also the *Legal Status of Eastern Greenland* (1933) PCIJ (Ser. A/B) No. 53 and the *Minquiers and Ecrehos* case [1953] ICJ Rep 47.

151 Jennings and Watts, above note 13, 679.

152 See generally A.L.W. Munkman, 'Adjudication and Adjustment – International Judicial Decision and the Settlement of Territorial and Boundary Disputes' (1972–73) 46 *British Yearbook of International Law* 20.

153 In the *Eritrea/Yemen* arbitration, the Tribunal found that boundary treaties made between two parties 'represents a legal reality which necessarily impinges upon third States, because they have effect *erga omnes*': 114 ILR 1, 48. Brownlie, above note 2, 129; Shaw above note 56, 495–6.

154 Jennings and Watts, above note 13, 696; Brownlie, above note 2, 145.

a state upstream results in the extension of a river bank of a state downstream, the territories of both states are correspondingly diminished or enlarged. Artificial formations such as man-made islands, embankments and so on do not enlarge a state's territory. Accordingly, no state may deliberately alter its own territory to the detriment of another state without former agreement.[155]

4.6.5.2 Cession

Cession occurs when an owner state transfers sovereignty over territory to another state. A state may cede any part of its land territory, and by ceding all its territory it will completely merge with the other state. Rivers and the maritime belt may not be ceded on their own, as they are an inalienable appurtenance of the land.[156] In order to effect a cession of territory, it must be intended that the owner state transfers sovereignty, and not merely governmental powers short of sovereignty. Cessions of territory are usually effected by a treaty. Examples can be found in the cessions of Hong Kong and Kowloon by China to the United Kingdom following the Opium Wars, and the United States' purchase of Alaska from Russia in 1867.

4.6.5.3 Occupation

Occupation as a mode of acquisition of territory historically only occurred when a state intentionally acquired sovereignty over territory that was not subject to the sovereignty of another state.[157] In other words, the territory in question at the time must have been uninhabited, or inhabited by persons whose community was not considered to be a state. This was the crux of the *Western Sahara* case, in which it was determined that territory inhabited by a people with a political or social structure is not *terra nullius* and thus cannot be occupied.[158]

For occupation to have successfully founded title to territory, the acquiring state first had to take possession of the territory. This required both physical possession and the requisite intent to acquire sovereignty.[159] Secondly, an administration had to be established over the territory in the name of the acquiring state. If the acquiring state failed to establish some responsible authority which exercised governing functions within

---

[155] Jennings and Watts, ibid., 696–7.

[156] Brownlie, above note 2, 118.

[157] Occupation was recognized as an 'original means of peaceably acquiring sovereignty' in *Legal Status of Eastern Greenland*, above note 150, 21, 44 and 63.

[158] *Western Sahara* (Advisory Opinion), above note 36.

[159] *Legal Status of Eastern Greenland*, above note 150 42–3; Brownlie above note 2, 133–5; Jennings and Watts, above note 13, 689.

a reasonable time after taking possession, then there was no effective occupation as no sovereignty had been exercised.[160] Lastly, there had to be some intent to act as sovereign, an *animus possidendii*.[161] It was also required that the activities of the state be referable to it and not unauthorized natural persons.[162]

Today, it is conceivable that the acquisition of new territory through occupation is nigh impossible given that little to no *terra nullius* land remains on this planet. However, that is not to say that occupation is irrelevant to modern international law. For example, for the purposes of resolving a current territorial dispute, it may be necessary to look back in time to see whether title was, in fact, validly acquired through effective occupation in the first place, for the reason of *nemo dat quod non habet* – none may pass better title than they have.

4.6.5.4 Prescription

Although there has always been a school of thought that questioned whether acquisitive prescription even constitutes a mode of acquisition,[163] it had generally been accepted that territory could be acquired through prescription as a matter of practice.[164] Acquisitive prescription involved the transfer of territory to an acquiring state through open possession by continuous and undisturbed acts of sovereignty over a prolonged period of time, adverse to the original state.[165] No concrete rules existed that set

---

160 Jennings and Watts, ibid., 688–9.

161 Brownlie above note 2, 134–5.

162 Humphrey Waldock (ed.), *Brierly's Law of Nations: An Introduction to the Law of Peace* (Oxford: Clarendon Press, 1963, 6th edn), 163.

163 For example, in his Separate Opinion delivered in the *Land, Island and Maritime Frontier* case, Judge Torres Bernandez referred to acquisitive prescription as 'a highly controversial concept which, for my part, I have the greatest difficulty in accepting as an established institute of international law': [1992] ICJR 629, 678. A similar position was adopted by Judge Moreno Quintana in his Dissenting Opinion in *Right of Passage over Indian Territory* (*Portugal v India*) (Merits) [1960] ICJ Rep 6, 88. Also see generally A.W. Heffter, *Le Droit international de l'Europe* (Berlin: H.W. Müller; Paris: A. Cottilon 1883, 4th edn, by Geffcken) s. 12.

164 See generally D.H.N. Johnson, 'Acquisitive Prescription in International Law' (1950) 27 *British Yearbook of International Law* 332; Jennings and Watts, above note 13, 706.

165 The definition given by Johnson is 'the means by which, under international law, legal recognition is given to the right of a state to exercise sovereignty over land or sea territory in cases where that state has, in fact, exercised its authority in a continuous, uninterrupted and peaceful manner over the area concerned for a sufficient period of time, provided that all other interested and affected states . . . have acquiesced in this exercise of authority': Johnson, ibid., 353.

out a minimum length of time or requisite acts of sovereignty in order to have successfully acquired title by prescription. Such matters were dictated by the individual circumstances of each case.[166] It is important to note that such definitions of acquisitive prescription, as with occupation, which emphasizes the passage of time, are now outdated. What is more important is the establishment of effective control.[167]

The best example of title founded by prescription can be found in the *Island of Palmas* case.[168] In this case, Judge Huber found that even if it were accepted that, as the United States claimed, Spain had title to the island by discovery, such title did not prevail in the face of a 'continuous and peaceful display of sovereignty'.[169] In this case it was required that there exist acts attributable only to sovereignty, and the will to act as sovereign and, furthermore, acquiescence on the part of the original sovereign.

4.6.5.5 Subjugation

Lastly, subjugation was the acquisition of territory by military force, followed by annexation.[170] While this mode of acquisition was traditionally a predominant feature of the acquisition of territory by states and empires, the use of force for the purpose of acquisition has, for some time, been unlawful in international law.[171] Accordingly, the purported annexation of Kuwait by Iraq in 1990 was invalid, as it was acquired by unlawful force.[172] The principle of inter-temporal law subjugation may still be relevant, however, in determining title in the context of the law as it stood at the time of the relevant acts.[173]

Of course, use of force is not unlawful if exercised in self-defence.[174] This

---

166 Jennings and Watts, above note 13, 698.

167 See 4.6.6.3 for a discussion of effective occupation and administration.

168 Though it is important to note that the decision was not expressly decided on the basis of prescription or any of the former modes of occupation.

169 *Island of Palmas* case, above note 17, 840.

170 See generally Sharon Korman, *The Right of Conquest: Acquisition of Territory by Force in International Law and Practice* (Oxford: Clarendon Press, 1996); Shaw, above note 56, 500–502.

171 Charter of the United Nations, above note 14, Art. 2(4) stipulates that Member States must refrain from the threat or use of force against the territorial integrity or political independence of any state. See also Article 5(3) of the Consensus Definition of Aggression adopted in 1974 by UN General Assembly, and Article 52 of the Vienna Convention on the Law of Treaties 1969.

172 E. Lauterpacht, C.J. Greenwood, M. Weller and D. Bethlehem (eds) *The Kuwait Crisis – Basic Documents* (Cambridge, UK: Grotius, 1991), 90.

173 See section 4.6.6.2 for a discussion of inter-temporal law.

174 See Charter of the United Nations, above note 14, Art. 51; and Chapter 8.

raised the question of whether territory could have been validly acquired by annexation following the use of force in self-defence – for example, if, in response to an act of aggression, a state acted in self-defence and in doing so found it necessary to occupy part of the territory of an aggressor. The vast weight of authority, however, suggests doubt that such an annexation would ever have been valid in today's context.[175]

4.6.6 Departure from the Traditional Modes of Acquisition – Guiding Principles

As noted above, in modern international law, such neat doctrinal categories are difficult to apply and are rarely done so by tribunals in determining a territorial dispute. They serve, rather, as a broad framework from which arise many complex and sometimes overlapping principles. These guiding principles have their roots in the former modes of acquisition, but are also founded in the underlying concepts that are fundamental to the international order, such as the need for territorial stability in international relations, preventing state rights from arising from illegal acts, ideals of international justice and equity, political reality and the need for certainty, and the growing spheres of influence of human rights and the right to self-determination.[176]

4.6.6.1 Relativity of title

In making a territorial claim, a state must demonstrate two elements: the intention and will to exercise sovereignty, and the manifestation of state activity.[177]

The manifestation of state activity is relative in two ways. First, title is relative to the claims made by other parties. There is no minimum threshold level of state activity. It must simply be shown that one state's claim

---

[175] See Shaw, above note 56, 501. See also D. P. O'Connell, *International Law* (1965), 497; Jennings and Watts, above note 13, 702–5, Jennings above note 121, 55–62; cf. Stephen M. Schwebel, 'What Weight to Conquest?' (1970) 64 *American Journal of International Law* 344.

[176] Martin Griffiths, 'Self Determination, International Society and World Order' (2003) 3 *Macquarie Law Journal* 29; W. Michael Reisman, 'Sovereignty and Human Rights in Contemporary International Law' (1990) 84 *American Journal of International Law* 866; Thomas Fleier-Gerster and Michael A. Meyer, 'New Developments in Humanitarian Law: A Challenge to the Concept of Sovereignty' (1985) 34 *International and Comparative Law Quarterly* 267; Rupert Emerson, 'Self-Determination' (1971) 65 *American Journal of International Law* 459.

[177] *Island of Palmas* case, above note 17; *Legal Status of Eastern Greenland*, above note 150.

is stronger than that of another.[178] Secondly, the type of territory is relevant to determining the kind of effective control required. For example, regarding uninhabited and remote territory, 'very little in the way of actual exercise of sovereign rights might be sufficient in the absence of competing claim'.[179]

4.6.6.2 Inter-temporal law and critical dates

Judge Huber, in the *Island of Palmas* case, stated that the principle of inter-temporal law requires that '[a] juridical fact must be appreciated in the light of the law contemporary with it, and not of the law in force at the time such a dispute in regard of it arises or falls to be settled'.[180] It is a relatively well-established principle of law, and is tied to concepts of stability and certainty.

However, in many cases there will be a so-called critical date: the period when 'the material facts of a dispute are said to have occurred . . . [and] after which the actions of the parties to a dispute can no longer affect the issue'.[181] For example, if the territorial dispute centres upon an alleged cession by treaty, the date of the treaty may be the critical date for that is the moment at which the rights of the states have crystallized. Critical dates are particularly important in the context of *uti possidetis* whereby a new state will inherit the boundaries of its predecessor.[182] In such a situation the moment of independence is normally the critical date, though this does not preclude the possibility that some situation or act had crystallized state rights earlier. Of course, some cases may have multiple dates of importance, and in some cases there may be no critical date at all.[183] The importance of the concept of a critical date depends on the circumstances, and it is open to a tribunal to relegate little weight to it, as was done in the *Argentine-Chile Frontier* case[184] and *Frontier Dispute* case.[185]

---

178 *Minquiers and Ecrehos* case, above note 150; Clipperton Island Arbitration (1930) 26 *American Journal of International Law* 390, 394; *Legal Status of Eastern Greenland*, above note 150, 45–6.

179 *Legal Status of Eastern Greenland*, above note 150.

180 *Island of Palmas* case, above note 17, 845.

181 L.F.E. Goldie, 'The Critical Date' (1963) 12 *International and Comparative Law Quarterly* 1251, 1251.

182 *Case Concerning the Frontier Dispute* (*Burkina Faso/Mali*), above note 119. The *uti possidetis* principle is discussed below at section 4.9.2.

183 Shaw, above note 121, xxii.

184 *Argentine–Chile Frontier* case (*Argentina v Chile*) (1969) 38 ILR 20.

185 *Frontier Dispute* (*Burkina Faso and Republic of Mali*), above note 119.

4.6.6.3 Continued and effective occupation and administration

A vital element common to all modes of acquisition, aside from cession and accretion, is the effective occupation and administration of territory. As put by Judge Huber in the *Island of Palmas* case, 'the actual continuous and peaceful display of State functions is in case of dispute the sound and natural criterion of territorial sovereignty'.[186] The principle owes its importance in the area of acquisition of territory to the nature of the international system and the need for stability. In a system of law horizontally structured with no overarching authority with the power of compulsory jurisdiction, greater emphasis must be given to concrete manifestations of possession of territory, rather than upon abstract rights of possession, in order to substantiate claims.[187]

The law in this area was developed by three pivotal cases. In the *Island of Palmas* case,[188] Judge Huber's determination in favour of the Netherlands was decided on the basis of that state's peaceful and continuous displays of state authority over the island. The subsequent *Clipperton Island* arbitration[189] and the *Eastern Greenland* case[190] similarly used the criterion of continued and effective occupation and administration as a central criterion of territorial sovereignty.

4.6.6.4 Changing values in the international community and the principle of stability

International law has always been caught between competing needs to move with changing political realities and social norms, and to uphold a sense of stability and certainty in international relations. This is even more apparent in the area of territorial sovereignty as territorial delineations are one of the most important anchors for stability in human communities. The strong emphasis on possession in occupation and prescription may be seen as a result of the need to recognize the realities of territorial situations and maintain border stability. And yet, as the international community gives increasing weight to concepts such as self-determination and human rights, accordingly international law is re-imagining the rela-

---

[186] *Island of Palmas* case, above note 17, 840.

[187] As put by Judge Huber, 'International law, the structure of which is not based on any super-state organization, cannot be presumed to reduce a right such as territorial sovereignty, with which almost all international relations are bound up, to the category of an abstract right, without concrete manifestations': *Island of Palmas* case, above note 17, 839.

[188] Ibid.

[189] (1931) 2 RIAA 1105.

[190] *Legal Status of Eastern Greenland*, above note 150.

tionship between people and their territory. For example, in *Cameroon v Nigeria* the ICJ noted that the territorial rights of the state consisted not only of its territorial integrity, but of considerations with regard to the killing of people and the serious risk of further harm to others, indicating a strong link between the interests of individuals and the territorial rights of the state.[191]

4.7 SCOPE OF TERRITORIAL SOVEREIGNTY

It is to state the obvious to say that sovereignty cannot be exercised over an area that does not comprise the territory of the state, and for that reason it is worth briefly looking at what constitutes a state's territory.

A state's territory first and foremost comprises its land, which includes its subsoil. It also includes its national (internal) waters and, if it is a coastal state, its territorial sea. Further, a state may possess limited rights to areas of water beyond the territorial sea. The United Nations Convention on the Law of the Sea (UNCLOS)[192] delineates the state's contiguous zone, exclusive economic zone and continental shelf, and what rights attach to each. A state's territory also includes its territorial airspace, which comprises the airspace above its territorial land, national waters and territorial sea, extending upwards towards outer space.[193] However, there is currently no international agreement on the point at which the legal regime of airspace ends and outer space begins. Any airspace not within a state's territorial limits is, like the high seas, a *res communis*.

Interestingly, the latter half of the twentieth century saw the emergence of special treaty regimes to protect the 'common heritage of mankind', a recognition that particular territorial areas should remain open to all humanity as a *res communis*, and should not be subject to the territorial claims of individual states. This principle was first articulated in the Outer Space Treaty, which recognizes 'the common interest of all mankind in the progress of the exploration and use of outer space for peaceful purposes'.[194] As a result, outer space and celestial bodies cannot be subject

---

[191] *Cameroon v Nigeria* (Provisional Measures) [1996] ICJ Rep 13, [39], [42].

[192] United Nations Convention on the Law of the Sea (adopted 10 December 1982, entered into force 14 November 1994) 450 UNTS 11.

[193] See generally Blewett Lee, 'Sovereignty of the Air' (1913) 7 *American Journal of International Law* 470.

[194] The Treaty on Principles Governing the Activities of States in the Exploration and Use of Outer Space, including the Moon and Other Celestial Bodies (opened for signature 27 January 1966, entered into force 10 October 1967).

to any territorial sovereignty claims. In contrast, the Antarctic Treaty and subsequent agreements effectively 'froze' the territorial claims of states at the time it entered into force, such that sovereignty claims were not recognized, renounced or prejudiced.[195] With the issue of sovereignty suspended, Antarctica has become a scientific preserve with established freedom of scientific research.[196]

4.8 FUTURE DIRECTIONS IN TERRITORIAL SOVEREIGNTY

As the law governing territorial sovereignty, its acquisition and scope continue to evolve slowly in reflection of changing international community values, scholars have speculated on a move away from the dominant statist order. Notably, Allot proposes an international order in which sovereignty over territory no longer exists.[197] Similarly, Gottmann notes that the dominance of the territorially based view of the twentieth century appears to be simply one more stage in the evolution of international law, and the 'sovereign state, based on exclusive territorial jurisdiction, may have been the evolution's purpose from the sixteenth to the mid-twentieth century. By 1970 sovereignty has been by-passed, and a new fluidity has infiltrated the recently shaped map of multiple national states.'[198]

Recent developments in the areas of self-determination and human rights, the rise of non-territorial actors and the revival of natural law philosophy have prompted some conjecture on the possible demise of the territorially defined statist order.[199] This speculation

---

Similarly, the Moon was declared to be 'the common heritage of mankind' in the Agreement Governing Activities of States on the Moon and Other Celestial Bodies (opened for signature 18 December 1979, entered into force 11 July 1984), Art. 1.

[195] Final Act of the Agreement between the Government of Australia and the Governments of Argentina, Chile, the French Republic, Japan, New Zealand, Norway, the Union of South Africa, the Union of the Soviet Socialist Republics, the United Kingdom of Great Britain and Northern Ireland and the United States of America concerning the Peaceful Uses of Antarctica ('Antarctic Treaty') (adopted 1 December 1959, entered into force 1961) [1961] ATS 12, Art. 4

[196] Ibid., Art. 2.

[197] Phillip Allott, *Eunomia: New Order for a New World* (Oxford: Oxford University Press, 1990).

[198] Gottmann, above note 138, 26–7.

[199] See generally John A. Agnew, *Globalization and Sovereignty* (Lanham, MD: Rowman and Littlefield, 2009); Christopher Rudolph, 'Sovereignty and Territorial Borders in a Global Age' (2005) 7 *International Studies Review* 1; Hans

has particular resonance in the context of the Charter of the United Nations which entrenches concepts of self-determination, the rights of individuals, and international social, economic and cultural cooperation.[200] Nonetheless, this trend against sovereignty – what Koskenniemi refers to as a 'reduction to purpose'[201] – can easily be overstated and there is little evidence to suggest that the importance of sovereignty, bound up as it is in the concept of controlled territory, has meaningfully diminished. To be sure, it has gone through change and been affected by the modernization of international law, but it remains the physical framework around which international law and relations are understood and practised.

4.9 PEOPLES AND SELF-DETERMINATION

The development of statehood, particularly in the second half of the twentieth century, is profoundly tied to the principle of self-determination, which has seen numerous colonized territories restored to statehood and self-control. It is hardly possible to talk now about the development of states and their role and status in the international legal regime without considering the concept of peoples and self-determination.

Self-determination has been defined as 'the right of cohesive national groups ("peoples") to choose for themselves a form of political organization and their relation to other groups'.[202] The United Nations General Assembly (UNGA) has stated that the right to self-determination gives 'peoples' the right to 'freely determine their political status and freely pursue their economic, social and cultural development'.[203]

While it is a right recognized as being a principle of customary law,[204] and accepted as being a right with *erga omnes* status,[205] the precise content of the rule and the circumstances in which it is to be applied are elusive. For example, there is a popular assumption that the exer-

---

J. Morgenthau, 'The Problem of Sovereignty Reconsidered' (1948) 48 *Columbia Law Review* 341.

[200] Shaw, above note 121, 11.

[201] See Martti Koskenniemi, 'What Use for Sovereignty Today?' (2011) 1 *Asian Journal of International Law* 61, 68.

[202] Brownlie, above note 2, 580.

[203] Declaration on the Granting of Independence to Colonial Countries and People, GA Res. 1514(XV) UN GAOR, 15th sess., 947th plen. mtg, UN Doc. A/RES/1514 (1960) ('Declaration on the Granting of Independence').

[204] *Western Sahara* (Advisory Opinion) above note 36, 32.

[205] *East Timor* (*Portugal v Australia*) (Judgment) [1995] ICJ Rep 90, 102.

cise of the right to self-determination will always result in the right of a people to achieve independence. However, while the realization of self-determination may involve independence, it may also involve free association with an independent state or integration with an independent state.[206] Additionally, while for a long time it has been, both theoretically and in practice, confined to colonial situations, the break-up of Yugoslavia has indicated that the principle may be extended to other, non-colonial circumstances.

4.9.1 Development of the Principle of Self-determination

4.9.1.1 Self-determination up to the Second World War

The idea of self-determination is new. Some attribute the first recognition of its legal relevance to the American Declaration of Independence of 1776.[207] Others refer to the Bolshevik Revolution and Soviet treaties concluded in the period 1920 to 1921,[208] or even the French Revolution.[209] During the First World War, the notion of self-determination was actively pushed by President Wilson and implicitly included in his speech known as 'Wilson's Fourteen Points'.[210] However, he did not succeed in having the principle included in the League of Nations Covenant, and it was clearly not yet accepted as a legal principle.[211] Indeed, in the *Aaland Islands* case (heard before the first session of the League of Nations), both the report of the International Commission of Jurists[212] and the report of the Committee of

---

206 Principles which Should Guide Members in Determining whether or not an Obligation Exists to Transmit the Information Called for under Article 73e of the Charter, GA Res. 1541(XV) UN GAOR, 15th sess., 948th plen. mtg, Supp. No. 16, 29, UN Doc. A/RES/1541(1961), Principle VI ('Principles which should Guide Members'). *Erga omnes* refers to the procedural scope of application of the relevant rule (whether a right or obligation) being towards all (see Shaw, above note 56, 133–4).

207 See, e.g., Karl Doehring, 'Self-Determination', in Bruno Simma (ed.), (2002, 2nd edn) Vol. 1, 50; Daniel Thürer and Thomas Burri, 'Self-determination', in Rüdiger Wolfrum (ed.), *Max Planck Encyclopedia of Public International Law* (Heidelberg: Max-Planck-Institut, 2010), [1], online edition available at http://www.mpepil.com .

208 See, e.g., Crawford, above note 10, 108; Brownlie, above note 2, 580; Cassese, above note 39, 60 [3.7.1].

209 Ibid.

210 President Wilson's Message to Congress, 8 January 1918 (Record Group 46, Records of the United States Senate, National Archives).

211 Shaw, above note 56, 269; Thürer and Burri, above note 207.

212 Report of Commission of Jurists (Larnaude, Huberm Struycken), LNOJ Sp. Supp. No. 3 (October 1920).

Rapporteurs[213] explicitly accepted that the principle of self-determination was a political concept but not a legal rule of international law.

The facts of that case concerned the question of whether at the time Finland did possess the relevant qualities of statehood and whether the Islanders might have a right to claim self-determination. As Crawford notes, it is important to qualify the findings of the reports by the League of Nations by considering the specific circumstances in which they were made. He points out that, under current international law, the principle of self-determination would not apply to cases such as the Aaland Islands as it is not applicable to separate minorities within a state.[214] In addition, both reports specifically accepted the possibility that where territories are misgoverned to the point that they are effectively separated from the ruling state, the principle may apply.[215] The report of the Rapporteurs also pointed out that the population of the islands did not consist of a 'people', as opposed to the population of Finland, who formed a distinct 'people'. Even if Finland had not been separate from the Russian Empire before 1917 (as the report found it had), its secession would have been acceptable.[216] Therefore, while the reports expressly held that self-determination was not at the time a rule of international law, they did presage its post-Second World War development as a principle of international law. Interestingly, the report of the Rapporteurs (which was adopted) found that, although Finnish sovereignty over the Islands was established, some minority guarantees were recommended,[217] further demonstrating the political relevance of self-determination at the time.[218]

The principle of self-determination was next invoked during the Second World War,[219] and declared as a right belonging to all people as one of the eight points in the Atlantic Charter – an agreement made in 1941 between British Prime Minister Winston Churchill and United States President Franklin D. Roosevelt. The Atlantic Charter was influential on the United Nations Conference on International Organizations which was held in San Francisco between 25 April and 26 June 1945 ('San Francisco Conference'). This was a convention of 50 delegates which finalized the

---

213 Report of the Committee of Rapporteurs (Beyens, Calonder, Elkens), 16 April 1921: LN Council Doct. B7/21/68/106 [VII].

214 Crawford, above note 10, 111.

215 Ibid.

216 Ibid.

217 Resolution of 24 June 1921, LNOJ Sp. Supp. No. 5, 24; Convention relating to the Status of the Aaland Islands, 20 October 1921, 9 LNTS 212.

218 Crawford, above note 10, 111.

219 Shaw, above note 56, 270; Thürer and Burri, above note 207.

creation of the UN Charter, and influenced the incorporation of the principle of self-determination into the Charter.[220]

4.9.1.2 The UN Charter and Resolutions

The UN Charter uses the term 'self-determination' twice – in Articles 1(2) and 55. Article 1(2) refers to the need to respect the principle of self-determination '[t]o develop friendly relations among states'.[221] Article 55 states the conditions that the UN will promote in order to achieve 'the creation of conditions of stability and well-being which are necessary for peaceful and friendly relations among nations based on respect for the principle of equal rights and self-determination of peoples'.[222] In addition, Chapters XI (dealing with non-self-governing territories) and XII (dealing with trusteeship systems) implicitly refer to the principle. Chapter XI concerns the process of decolonization, and encourages all Member States 'which have or assume responsibilities for the administration of territories whose peoples have not yet attained a full measure of self-government'[223] to promote the interests of the inhabitants to achieve self-government.[224] Chapter XII created the International Trusteeship system, by which Trust Territories were placed under supervision by individual agreements with the states administering them.[225]

Again, the objective of the system was to promote self-government and independence of the territories, amongst other things.[226] There were three categories of territory which could be placed under the system:

(a) territories held under mandate at the time;
(b) territories which may be detached from enemy states as a result of the Second World War; and
(c) territories voluntarily placed under the system by states responsible for their administration.[227]

Self-determination can mean two things: first, 'the sovereign equality of existing States, and in particular the right of the people of a State to

220 Thürer and Burri, above note 207.
221 Charter of the United Nations, above note 14, Art. 1(2).
222 Ibid., Art. 55.
223 Ibid., Art. 73.
224 Ibid., Art. 73.
225 Ibid., Art. 75.
226 Ibid., Art. 76.
227 Ibid., Art. 77.

choose its own form of government without external intervention';[228] and, secondly, 'the right of a specific territory (or more correctly its 'people') to choose its own form of government irrespective of the wishes of the rest of the state of which that territory is a part'.[229] Crawford suggests that the explicit references to self-determination in Articles 1(2) and 55 most likely refer to the first of these meanings, while the implicit references in Chapters XI and XII appear to refer to the second meaning.

Several UN General Assembly resolutions have interpreted these sections and developed the status of the principle of self-determination. The 1960 Declaration of Granting Independence to Colonial Countries and Peoples states that all people have a right to self-determination, and that '[i]mmediate steps shall be taken, in Trust and Non-Self-Governing Territories or all other territories which have not yet attained independence, to transfer all powers to the peoples of those territories, without any conditions or reservations, in accordance with their freely expressed will and desire, without any distinction as to race, creed or colour, in order to enable them to enjoy complete independence and freedom'.[230] Brownlie argues that this declaration is not a 'recommendation' but rather an authoritative interpretation of the Charter.[231]

The 1961 Principles which should Guide Members in Determining whether or not an Obligation Exists to Transmit the Information Called for under Article 73e of the Charter,[232] as its title suggests, details a list of principles which were to guide members in deciding whether certain territories qualified as territories to which Chapter XI of the UN Charter applied. It also explicitly states that a 'Non-Self-Governing Territory can be said to have reached a full measure of self-government' where one of three circumstances (referred to above) exists: (i) independence, (ii) free association with an independent State, or (iii) integration with an independent state.[233] These three circumstances were confirmed as applying in general to self-determination in the 1970 Declaration on Principles of International Law,[234] which pro-

---

[228] Crawford, above note 10, 114.

[229] Ibid.

[230] GA Res. 1514(XV) UN GAOR, 15th sess., 947th plen. mtg, UN Doc. A/RES/1514 (1960).

[231] Brownlie, above note 2, 581.

[232] GA Res. 1541(XV) UN GAOR, 15th sess., 948th plen. mtg, Supp. No. 16, 29, UN Doc. A/RES/1541(1961).

[233] Principles which should Guide Members, ibid.

[234] GA Res. 2625(XXV) UN GAOR, 25th sess., 1883rd plen. mtg, UN Doc. A/RES/2625 (1970) ('Declaration on Principles of International Law').

vides the most detailed and authoritative articulation of the principle of self-determination.

The 1970 Declaration restates the right of self-determination and reaffirms the earlier resolutions that '[e]very state has a duty to promote, through joint and separate action, realization of the principle of equal rights and self-determination of peoples'.[235] It goes on to state that every state has a duty to 'refrain from forcible action which deprives peoples referred to above in the elaboration of the present principle of the right to self-determination and freedom and independence'.[236] It also makes clear that nothing in the preceding paragraphs should be interpreted as 'authorizing or encouraging any action which would dismember or impair, totally or in part, the territorial integrity or political unity of sovereign and independent states'.[237]

The principle of self-determination, as reaffirmed in the 1966 Declaration of Granting Independence[238] was also adopted in the identical Article 1 of the International Covenant on Civil and Political Rights[239] and the International Covenant on Economic, Social and Cultural Rights.[240] Inclusion in both of these covenants further bolstered the fundamental human right nature of the principle of self-determination,[241] particularly once the Covenants came into force in 1976, thereby binding parties that were signatory to them.[242] Indeed, inclusion of the principle of self-determination in the covenants created a new and independent legal basis for that right under international law.[243] Further, these multilateral treaties were created by UN organs and impose binding obligations between all parties, providing important and authoritative interpretations of the Charter.[244]

4.9.2 Decolonization and *Uti Possidetis*

Self-determination has traditionally been confined to the decolonization process. *Uti possidetis juris* expresses the principle that colonial boundaries

---

[235] Declaration on Principles of International Law, ibid.
[236] Ibid.
[237] Ibid.
[238] Declaration of Granting Independence, above note 230.
[239] International Covenant on Civil and Political Rights (adopted 16 December 1966, entered into force 23 March 1976), 999 UNTS 171.
[240] International Covenant on Economic, Social and Cultural Rights (adopted 16 December 1966, entered into force 3 November 1976) 993 UNTS 3.
[241] Thürer and Burri, above note 207.
[242] Doehring, above note 207, 53.
[243] Ibid., 53.
[244] Ibid., 53.

cannot be challenged upon the independence of new states without consent.[245] As noted in the *Frontier Dispute* case, this is to promote stability and peace, and has the effect of confining self-determination to existing colonial territories, such that minorities have not been able to secede from pre-existing frontiers.[246] The modern principle[247] of *uti possidetis* was first, and mainly, used in Latin America, where the new independent states adopted administrative borders that existed from Spanish and Portuguese colonization.[248] This principle was also accepted by the Organization of African Unity and applied in Africa.[249]

Furthermore, the concerns for territorial integrity and peace and stability have continually been emphasized by the UN.[250] For example, in the case of Gibraltar, the UN General Assembly clearly applied the principle of territorial sovereignty in its adoption of Resolution 2353 (XXII),[251] determining that a colonial situation which even partially breaches the principles of national unity and territorial integrity is incompatible with the purposes and principles of the UN Charter. Nevertheless, the principle of self-determination and the application of *uti possidetis* have evolved in recent practice, such that *uti possidetis* may no longer operate as the constraint it once was.

4.9.3 Recent Developments

Since 1945 the legal consequences of the principle of self-determination for particular territories have evolved. Not surprisingly, it has been argued

---

[245] *Frontier Dispute* (*Burkina Faso and Republic of Mali*), above note 119, 565; Higgins, above note 5, 122; Shaw, above note 56, 311.

[246] *Frontier Dispute* (*Burkina Faso and Republic of Mali*), above note 119, 565.

[247] The principle has ancient roots, dating back to Roman Law and has been used throughout history in relation to territorial conquests.

[248] Higgins, above note 5, 122.

[249] *Frontier Dispute* (*Burkina Faso and Republic of Mali*), above note 119, 565–6.

[250] See, e.g., Declaration on the Granting of Independence, above note 230; Declaration on Principles of International Law, above note 234; Question of Gibraltar, GA Res. 2353(XXII) UN GAOR, 22nd sess., 1641st plen. mtg, UN Doc. A/RES/2353 (1967). However, although *uti possidetis* is concerned with the stability of borders, it is not the same as the principle of territorial integrity. As David Raič explains, *uti possidetis* is only applicable temporarily, during the transition of sovereignty, while the principle of territorial integrity only applies after the transition has occurred and the territorial entity has been established as a state: David Raič, *Statehood and the Law of Self-Determination* (The Hague: Kluwer Law International, 2002), 303.

[251] Question of Gibraltar, ibid.

that how and where self-determination applies has 'remained as much a matter of politics as law'.[252]

The clearest example of this is the break-up of the Socialist Federal Republic of Yugoslavia (SFRY) and the independence of several territories within it. The SFRY was formed in 1946 and comprised six republics: Croatia, Serbia, Slovenia, Montenegro, Bosnia-Herzegovina and Macedonia, and two autonomous entities which were both included in Serbia – the Autonomous Region of Kosovo-Metohija and the Autonomous Province of Vojvodina.[253] From the 1960s, tensions arose in different regions of the Republic, which contained separate groups with distinct cultures, languages and histories, and during the 1980s economic problems fuelled the tensions and anti-federalist sentiments.[254] A combination of events in the late 1980s and early 1990s led to the break-up of the SFRY.

In 1991 both Slovenia and Croatia proclaimed independence, which was declared illegitimate by the Yugoslav legislature, and which called for the federal army to prevent any changes or divisions to Yugoslavia and its borders. This led to the federal army occupying areas of Slovenia. The European community offered their good offices to the parties in order to mediate the conflict. However, there was no international recognition of the proclamations of independence. In July 1991, the Brioni Accord was reached between the federal, Croat and Slovene authorities; this reaffirmed the hold on the declarations of independence in order to complete negotiations on their future relations. The Brioni Accord stated that the negotiations should be based on the human rights principles of the Helsinki Final Act and the Paris Charter for a New Europe, and the right to self-determination should form this basis.[255]

However, in August 1991 tensions escalated and war broke out in Croatia, during which many Croats who lived in areas where Serbs formed the majority were killed, and towns and cultural and religious objects were destroyed, as Serb paramilitary forces took over more disputed Croatian territory. On 8 October 1991, Croatia once again proclaimed independence, and was recognized by the international community in the beginning of 1992.[256]

The Badinter Commission provided 15 opinions on the break-up of the

---

[252] Crawford, above note 10, 115; Dickinson, above note 119, 558.

[253] Yugoslav Constitution 1946, Art. 2.

[254] Raič, above note 250, 344, 346.

[255] Brioni Accord, Europe Documents, No. 1725, 16 July 1991, 17.

[256] Raič, above note 250, 350–4. See also *Prosecutor v Milošević* (Decision on Motion for Judgment of Acquittal) IT-02-54-T (16 June 2004).

SFRY. Importantly, it held in Opinion 2 that 'the Republics must afford the members of those minorities and ethnic groups all the human rights and fundamental freedoms recognized in international law, including, where appropriate, the right to choose their nationality'.[257]

Although the Badinter Commission found that Croatia did not satisfy all the conditions needed for recognition,[258] Croatia issued a formal statement that these deficiencies would be resolved; it was recognized as an independent state and admitted into the European Union and United Nations in January 2002. An important factor in Croatia's successful secession was the considerable political support for independence it received in the international community. Despite Croatia clearly not being an instance of decolonization, the international community (or significant members of it) still viewed the right of self-determination as being applicable to Croatia, as well as other territorial units in the SFRY.[259]

The European Community declared in 1991 that it would not accept any outcome of the Yugoslav conflict that would violate the principle that all established borders cannot be changed by the use of force.[260] Opinion 3 of the Badinter Commission expressly recognized the applicability of *uti possidetis* to the SFRY, and stated that this principle was not confined to situations of decolonization.[261] In this way, both the principles of self-determination and *uti possidetis* were adapted to a non-colonial situation in ways that, as we shall see, raise more questions than they answer.

The most recent example of the principle of self-determination being invoked in the context of secession is the agreement by the Republic of Sudan to secede South Sudan. In January 2011, a referendum on independence for southern Sudan was held: 98.83 per cent of the electorate opted for secession.[262] The referendum was held in compliance with the Machakos Protocol, adopted in 2002. Although the government of Sudan enshrined the principle of self-determination in the national constitution in 1997, it was in 2002 that the government of Sudan agreed to hold a

---

[257] Arbitration Commission of the International Conference on Yugoslavia, Opinion 2, 11 January 1992, 92 ILR 167.

[258] Arbitration Commission of the International Conference on Yugoslavia, Opinion 5, 11 January 1992, 92 ILR 173.

[259] See, e.g., Arbitration Commission of the International Conference on Yugoslavia, Opinion 5, ibid.; Raič, above note 250, 356.

[260] EC/US/USSR Declaration on Yugoslavia, The Hague, 18 October 1991.

[261] Arbitration Commission of the International Conference on Yugoslavia, Opinion 3, 11 January 1992, 92 ILR 170.

[262] 'South Sudan backs Independence – Results', *BBC News*, 7 February 2011, available at http://www.bbc.co.uk/news/world-africa-12379431

referendum on the self-determination of southern Sudan.[263] The government's commitment to hold a referendum was granted in exchange for the Sudan Peoples' Liberation Movement/Army (SPLM/A) giving up its demand for a secular Sudan.[264] Importantly, the referendum posed a choice between a united Sudan and an independent South Sudan. This choice was considered to be the mechanism for giving effect to the agreement to hold a referendum on the self-determination of southern Sudan.

4.9.4 Self-determination and Recognition in the Current Climate

It is clear that self-determination is a legal principle well established at international law. As seen, there appears to be a strong link between self-determination and statehood. However, whether self-determination has become a criterion of statehood,[265] or whether self-determination may compensate for a lesser standard of effective and independent government, or other requirements, is, in the contemporary environment, difficult to determine.

The effect of acknowledgement by the Badinter Commission of the right of groups within a territory to self-determination may be significant. Alain Pellet put it in this way:

> It is not insignificant that the Court[sic], without an express statement to that effect, appeared to link the rights of minorities to the rights of peoples. This shows that the notion of 'people' is no longer homogeneous and should not be seen as encompassing the whole population of any State. Instead of this, one must recognize that within one State, various ethnic, religious or linguistic communities might exist. These communities similarly would have, according to Opinion No. 2, the right to see their identity recognized and to benefit from 'all the human rights and fundamental freedoms recognized in international law, including, where appropriate, the right to choose their national identity'.[266]

The creation of Slovenia and Croatia as new states formed out of the dissolution of Yugoslavia was highly contentious – it was certainly not freely agreed to by (what is now) Serbia. At the same time, the minorities within these new states were accorded rights as 'peoples' – so that, for example,

---

[263] 'In-depth: Sudan Peace Process', 2002, IRIN, available at http://www.irinnews.org/InDepthMain.aspx?InDepthId=32&&ReportId=70709

[264] Ibid.

[265] Crawford, above note 10, 107; Brownlie, above note 2, 582.

[266] Alain Pellet, 'The Opinions of the Badinter Arbitration Committee: A Second Breath for the Self-Determination of Peoples' (1992) 3 *European Journal of International Law* 173, 179.

members of the Serbian population in Bosnia and Croatia were 'to be recognized under agreements between the Republics as having the nationality of their choice, with all the rights and obligations which that entails with respect to the states concerned'.[267]

What meaning does this carry in the context of post-colonial modern Europe, or elsewhere? Concerns expressed by certain countries upon the declaration of independence by Kosovo give some clue to the potential ramifications of this view. Spain and China[268] were two obvious concerned members of the international community, but they were far from alone. While the Badinter Commission reaffirmed the application of the principles of self-determination and *uti possidetis* to post-colonial Europe – to the extent that the echo of its opinions impacted upon Kosovo's declaration of independence (ostensibly sponsored by the US and Europe and made possible by the UN) – one is left to consider the potentially broad circumstances in which a group not subject to colonial rule might successfully seek not just a right to some form of self-determination, but perhaps to exclusive statehood.

4.10 CONCLUSIONS

At the beginning of this chapter I posed several questions. The first of these related to the subjects of international law. States are clearly the primary subjects of international law. They possess full capacity as participants in the international legal system that carries a vast array of rights and responsibilities. Nothing in this proposition, true now for close to 400 years, is really open to challenge. Of much less certainty is how precisely in the modern context statehood is to be attained. The traditional criteria, seemingly clear and rational, will not suffice to guarantee a privileged place at the table of world affairs. The differing practices of recognition, the potential relevance of factors beyond those required by the Montevideo Convention, and the preparedness of the international community of states to adjust the bar make certainty as to the creation of statehood extremely difficult to articulate.

Making this process more complex is the evolving position of self-determination. Created to effectuate a process of decolonization following

---

[267] Arbitration Commission of the International Conference on Yugoslavia, Opinion 2, above note 257, [3].

[268] See, e.g., Bing Bing Jia, 'The Independence of Kosovo: A Unique Case of Secession?' (2009) 8 *Chinese Journal of International Law* 27, 28.

the Second World War, self-determination following the break-up of the former Yugoslavia may operate to create a far broader set of rights to groups within existing state boundaries – even to the extent that statehood may, in certain circumstances, be a valid expression of the right of these groups to self-determination. The comments of the Badinter Commission and the ascertainment of independence by Kosovo are an insufficient basis to conclude – let alone articulate the content of – evolving rights to statehood in international law. They do suggest that self-determination applies outside the traditional colonial context. They also suggest that, while the declaratory theory may be the express preference of the Badinter Commission, the actions of the international community and the Commission itself – in accepting Slovenia and Croatia, not to mention Bosnia-Herzegovina, well before they had established critical elements required for statehood as articulated in the Montevideo Convention – suggest that states will be constituted when powerful states say they are (the constitutive theory of recognition).

Kosovo further confounds the position. Created by the waging of armed aggression by powerful states of the international community against Milošević's pariah state of Serbia, Kosovo was given autonomy and the means to self-govern and control its territory only by virtue of a massive and expensive United Nations mission. Seen positively, it is an example of the power of humanitarian intervention[269] to rescue persecuted groups within an oppressive state regime. Seen negatively, Kosovo is like a sophisticated slow-motion version of the discredited US foreign policy of intervening in the political affairs of Latin American (and other) countries during the Cold War.

The development of events since the 1990s in the Balkans – particularly in light of recent events relating to South Ossetia and Abkhazia – reveal certain developments in world politics. They also raise the very real potential of changes in international law relating to the development and existence of statehood and the place of states in international law.

Other and related developments may even suggest that the status of sovereignty itself in international law is today under something of a threat. A demise of formalism and the growing idea of international law as a normative system, capable of rising to the great moral challenges of our times, suggest something of a trend towards cosmopolitanism, in the sense of a system of international governance based on shared

[269] The use of force for purposes of 'humanitarian intervention', and other developing aspects of the use of force in international law, will be discussed in Chapter 8.

morality.[270] The increasing importance of non-state subjects of international law (considered in the following chapter) and a growing expression of normativism in the form of action (often UN-led or -sanctioned) on behalf of the international community (including armed interventions such as in Libya), suggest a movement away from the traditional profound respect for statehood by international law.[271] Koskenniemi, in a recent defence of the value of sovereignty, calls this move toward 'objectives' and 'values' a kind of international 'managerialism', threatening sovereignty itself and its inherent value as a system of rules.[272]

While it is, and is likely for some time to be, premature to talk of a system in which states are not the primary power brokers, there is something meaningful in the debate about a reduction of the unquestioned position of states in international law. After all, if sovereignty 'did not arise as a philosophical invention but out of Europe's exhaustion from religious conflict',[273] then it is not entirely out of the question that a post-modern world might arise from exhaustion over the failure of states to adequately reflect and regulate an increasingly global world.

---

[270] See Carsten Stahn, *The Law and Practice of International Territorial Administration – Versailles to Iraq and Beyond* (Cambridge: Cambridge University Press, 2008), 762.

[271] For a discussion of the nature of international law itself in these terms, see discussion in Chapter 1, section 1.6.

[272] Koskenniemi, above note 201, 65.

[273] Quote from Koskenniemi, above note, 201 65. This reference is to the Peace of Westphalia (see Chapter 1, section 1.3.2).

5. Other subjects of international law: non-state actors and international law's evolution

This chapter focuses on the 'other' participants in international law – in other words, non-state actors who have, to a greater or lesser degree, rights and responsibilities as legal persons. These other subjects – international organizations, non-governmental organizations, individuals, groups, corporations and certain other anomalous entities – are, in a real sense, derivative subjects of international law. By definition, the phrase 'non-state actor' connotes a presumption in the relationship of power within the international community. As Philip Alston has said, defining actors in terms of what they are not combines 'impeccable purism in terms of traditional international legal analysis' and with it comes the capacity to marginalize other actors.[1] Indeed, if the history of international law teaches us anything, it is that states are infinitely jealous of their real or imagined claims to sovereignty and their usually conservative attitudes are the main drivers in the development or stagnation of the global normative order. International law then is still very much state-centric.[2] States still hold the keys to the international system and in this respect not much has changed since the time when scholars spoke of a *jus gentium* ('the law of nations').

Nonetheless, it is impossible to speak of international law today as though states are the only stakeholders within the international system. International law has evolved over the last century at a frenetic rate, such that the traditional owners of the modern system can hardly claim an exclusive domain. The recognition – by courts, international organs and,

---

[1] Philip Alston, 'The "Not-a-Cat" Syndrome: Can the International Human Rights Regime Accommodate Non-State Actors?', in Philip Alston (ed.), *Non-State Actors and Human Rights* (Oxford; New York: Oxford University Press, 2005) 3, 3.

[2] Zoe Pearson suggests this state-centrism is a form of hierarchy, belying the much lamented horizontal nature of international law: Zoe Pearson, 'Non-Governmental Organisations and International Law: Mapping New Mechanisms for Governance' (2004) 23 *Australian Yearbook of International Law* 73, 75.

of course, states themselves – of the ever increasing and expanding role of non-state actors in international law speaks to a period of great diversity, renewal and progress in the international system. The trend of non-state participation has been accelerating since the establishment of the United Nations in 1945 and whole special areas have developed around other subjects – the law of international organizations, international administrative law and international criminal law being prominent examples.

A healthy and progressive international system will seek to harmonize the interests of states and non-state actors. Of course, this transformation of international law has been made possible in part by the preparedness of states to cede some of their authority. Indeed, the creation of the United Nations, with its expressed aims relating to international peace and security and respect for human rights, presaged such a development. Failures in the international system caused two world wars in the first half of the twentieth century. A genuine endeavour to avoid a third was always going to require an extraordinary shift toward pluralism and a meaningful and mostly – if not always – respected international legal system.

This chapter will begin with a consideration of international organizations, which are now so critical an aspect of the international system that it would doubtless collapse without them. The pre-eminent international organization is the United Nations, which will be considered, as will the nature of its international personality. The growing role of civil society in international law, expressed through the place of non-governmental organizations, will then be considered. The chapter will then examine the non-state actor that has impacted most upon the international legal system over the past half century or so – if not practically, then certainly morally. Individuals have developed a set of profound rights and duties within the international system, such that scholars have at times enthusiastically sounded the death knell of states as the primary actor of international law. While this is clearly an overstatement, the individual – after all, the real subject for whom all laws are made to serve – has caused something of a rupture in the statist conception of international law, such that it requires close attention. Corporations – entities wielding enormous economic power and yet still inadequately regulated as active bodies in the realm of international law – have played an important role as actors within the international legal system, at different times and in different ways, and warrant consideration. Finally, some miscellaneous non-state actors, including insurgents, terrorists and national liberation movements, will be considered briefly before conclusions are drawn about the contemporary place of the participants of international law and what the future may hold in this area.

5.1 INTERNATIONAL ORGANIZATIONS

International (or intergovernmental) organizations are a modern phenomenon linked to the maturing of the international legal system. The first international organizations were established in the late nineteenth century to coordinate mainly logistical matters. For example, the Universal Postal Union (UPU) was established in 1874 to coordinate the process of international mail handling and delivery. With 191 members, the UPU is now responsible for setting worldwide rules for international mail exchanges and constitutes a forum for discussing matters affecting the industry. The trend that started with international organizations like the UPU snowballed into a veritable 'move to institutions',[3] as the international community realized the utility of permanent collective bodies in many, if not most, aspects of their international relations.

Perhaps the greatest of all expressions of this tendency is the League of Nations and the United Nations (UN), set up after the First and Second World Wars respectively. Indeed, the institutionalization of international diplomacy was a product of an 'internationalist sensibility' and was gradually extended and reinforced, emphasizing collective interests. Even the extreme polarization of the Cold War did not reverse this trend; it only made progress in certain areas, such as the creation of a permanent international criminal court, more difficult to ascertain. José Alvarez summarizes the trend as:

> a move from utopian aspirations to institutional accomplishment; that is, a move to replace empire with institutions that would promote the economic development of the colonized, end war through international dispute settlement, affirm human rights and other 'community' goals through discourse, advance 'democratic' governance at both the national and international levels, and codify and progressively develop . . . international rules – all by turning to the construction of proceduralist rules, mechanisms for administrative regulation, and forums for institutionalized dispute settlement.[4]

The fall of the Soviet bloc in 1991 and the advent of increasing economic, social and political integration – the phenomenon of globalization – have accelerated the institutionalization of international society. For example, the international legal framework on international trade is near

---

[3] David Kennedy, 'The Move to Institutions' (1987) 8 *Cardozo Law Review* 841; Martii Koskenniemi, *The Gentle Civilizer of Nations: The Rise and Fall of International Law, 1870–1960* (Cambridge: Cambridge University Press, 2002).

[4] José Alvarez, 'International Organizations: Then and Now' (2006) 100 *American Journal of International Law* 324, 325.

comprehensive, as a result largely of the existence and work of organizations such as the World Trade Organization (WTO).[5] While initially it was largely idle, the International Court of Justice (ICJ) is now extremely busy and has been complemented by an increasingly important patchwork of international courts and tribunals. New international organizations are constantly being created or morphed so as to regulate the myriad of *sui generis* legal issues on the international plane.

From a legal perspective, international organizations are entities created by states as a vehicle to further their common interests. They are constituted by treaty and are usually composed of three organs: (1) a plenary assembly of all Member States, (2) an executive organ with limited participation, and (3) a secretariat, or administrative body.[6] The fact that international organizations have a personality distinct from their Member States distinguishes them from these states merely acting in concert.[7] Diplomatic conferences such as the G8, institutions lacking organs such as the Commonwealth, and treaties such as the former General Agreement on Tariffs and Trade (GATT) (now superseded by the WTO) are not international organizations. International organizations are analogous to corporations in domestic law and fulfil a similar function as an efficient network of contracts harmonizing the interests of their members.[8] Prominent international organizations include the UN, its specialized agencies such as the World Health Organization (WHO) and the International Labour Organization (ILO), and regional organizations such as the European Union (EU).[9]

---

[5] Vaughan Lowe, *International Law* (Oxford: Oxford University Press, 2007) 12.

[6] Alvarez, above note 4, 324. Note that international organizations (IOs) can become members of other IOs. This does not affect the 'intergovernmental' nature of IOs, as member IOs are themselves ultimately traceable to states.

[7] Rosalyn Higgins, *Problems and Processes: International Law and How We Use It* (Oxford: Clarendon Press, 1994) 46–7.

[8] P.R. Menon, 'The Legal Personality of International Organizations' (1992) 4 *Sri Lanka Journal of International Law* 79, 93; Lowe, above note 5, 123.

[9] Note that until 2009 it was generally accepted that the EU did not have international personality: House of Commons Library Research Paper 07/80, 22 November 2007: 'The EU Reform Treaty: Amendments to the Treaty on European Union', 72, available at http://www.parliament.uk/commons/lib/research/rp2007/rp07-080.pdf (accessed 5 December 2010). Rather, international personality belonged to the European Community (EC), a separate organization. Recently, the Treaty of Lisbon 2009 amended the Treaty of Rome (which constituted the European Community) and the Treaty of Maastricht (which constituted the EU) so as to transfer the international personality of the EC to the EU. The Treaty of Lisbon was another step towards greater European integration.

As with states, international organizations can possess international personality, but while every state possesses full personality, international organizations only possess personality granted in either their constituent treaty or arising by necessary implication from their functions.[10] Being associations of states, their existence depends on the consent of Member States. States theoretically retain the power to close even the most prominent of international organizations; even though it is a separate legal person, the continued existence of an international organization depends on its members not winding it up, as is the case with corporations at domestic law. In this sense, international organizations possess a personality derived from grants by Member States, which are the 'original' persons of international law.[11] Although the long-standing and entrenched nature of some of these institutions, such as the UN, indicates that states are very unlikely to revoke the international personality conferred, this does not affect their derivative foundations.

It is generally accepted that an international organization must possess three core features before it can be said to have international personality: (1) a permanent association of states, made up of organs, (2) being legally distinct from its members and (3) possessing international rights and duties (for example, the capacity to enter into treaties with other international actors), not merely duties exercisable in domestic legal systems.[12] The following section examines the international organization that has come to dwarf all others on the international scene: the United Nations.

5.1.1 The United Nations

5.1.1.1 Organs and functions of the United Nations

After the Second World War claimed over 50 million lives, more than half of which were civilian,[13] the international community resolved to found a new world order to promote a gentler international society. At the San

[10] *Reparation for Injuries Suffered in the Service of the United Nations* (Advisory Opinion) [1949] ICJ Rep 174, 178, 182; *Legality of the Use by a State of Nuclear Weapons in Armed Conflict* (Request by the World Health Organization) [1996] ICJ Rep 66, 79.

[11] Antonio Cassese, *International Law in a Divided World* (Oxford: Clarendon Press, 1988) 76–7.

[12] Ian Brownlie, *Principles of Public International Law* (Oxford: Oxford University Press, 2008, 7th edn) 677; Lowe, above note 5, 60.

[13] See, e.g., John Keegan, *The Second World War* (London; New York: Penguin, 1990), 590.

Francisco Conference in 1945, the overwhelming majority of states[14] concluded the United Nations Charter, which established the United Nations Organization. Its stated purpose was to 'save succeeding generations from the scourge of war', to 'reaffirm faith in fundamental human rights', to 'establish conditions under which justice and respect for the obligations arising from . . . international law can be maintained' and to 'promote social progress and better standards of life'.[15]

The UN was to be the successor organization to the League of Nations set up after the First World War and in many respects the drafters learned from the mistakes of the old order. Chapter II of the UN Charter provides for 'open' membership – 'all peace-loving states' that are willing and able to carry out the obligations under the Charter may join the Organization.[16] The organs of the United Nations are established by Chapter III; their compositions, functions and powers are laid out in following Chapters. The principal organs are:

- the General Assembly;
- the Security Council;
- the Economic and Social Council;
- the Trusteeship Council;
- the International Court of Justice; and
- the Secretariat.

Subsidiary organs may be established when deemed necessary, [17] as was the case when the Security Council controversially created the International Criminal Tribunal for the former Yugoslavia (ICTY) through SC Resolution 827 (1993), to try the major war criminals in the violent break-up of the former Yugoslavia.[18] The UN Human Rights Council (UNHRC, formerly the UN Commission on Human Rights (UNCHR)) is a subsidiary organ of the General Assembly.

---

[14] *Reparation for Injuries Suffered in the Service of the United Nations*, above note 10, 185. Fifty states participated in drafting the UN Charter at the San Francisco Conference.

[15] Charter of the United Nations, Preamble.

[16] Ibid., Art. 4(1).

[17] Ibid., Arts 7, 22, 29.

[18] See, e.g., V. Gowlland-Debbas, 'Security Council Enforcement Action and Issues of State Responsibility' (1994) 43 *International Criminal Law Quarterly* 55; Gabriël H. Oosthuizen, 'Playing Devil's Advocate: the United Nations Security Council is Unbound by Law' (1999) 12 *Leiden Journal of International Law* 549.

5.1.1.1.1 The General Assembly The General Assembly is the plenary body of the UN, consisting of representatives of all Members.[19] It is the forum *par excellence* for international debate, producing non-binding recommendations (by way of resolutions) to Members or the Security Council.[20] Resolutions on specified 'important' matters, such as the maintenance of international peace and security, are determined by a two-thirds majority, in contrast to a simple majority vote required for other matters.[21] Given the virtually universal membership of the United Nations, resolutions adopted by large majorities of the General Assembly may amount to very strong *opinio juris* as an element of customary international law. As discussed in Chapter 2, General Assembly resolutions have had a great influence on the development of customary law, so much so that the ICJ has at times engaged in the dubious practice of basing its findings on customary law entirely on such resolutions.[22]

The General Assembly may initiate studies for, among other things, 'promoting international co-operation' and 'encouraging the progressive development of international law and its codification'.[23] In accordance with this power, the General Assembly created the International Law Commission (ILC) in 1947, a permanent body of independent experts tasked with promoting the codification and progressive development of international law. The opinions of this knowledgeable body are highly persuasive in the interpretation of international law in numerous fora.[24] The General Assembly also controls the apportionment among Members of the Organization's expenses.[25]

5.1.1.1.2 The Security Council The Security Council is the executive arm of the UN Organization. The real power of the new world order is embodied by the endowment of the Security Council with primary responsibility for the maintenance of international peace and security. In addition to powers for overseeing the peaceful settlement of disputes,[26] the Security Council can take enforcement action against threats to the peace,

---

19 Charter of the United Nations, Art. 9(1).
20 Ibid., Art. 10.
21 Ibid., Art. 18.
22 See discussion in Chapter 2, section 2.2.2.5.
23 Charter of the United Nations, Art. 13.
24 The considerable influence of the Commission on the making of important treaties such as the Vienna Convention on the Law of Treaties 1969 is discussed in Chapter 2.
25 Charter of the United Nations, Art. 17.
26 Ibid., Ch. VI.

breaches of the peace and acts of aggression.[27] Enforcement can consist of sanctions falling short of armed force, such as economic sanctions or the severance of diplomatic relations.[28] However, where such sanctions prove inadequate, the Security Council may deploy armed forces supplied by its Members, to forcibly maintain or restore international peace and security.[29] This power is the centrepiece of an international order based around the prevention of global war.

As discussed in Chapter 8, Article 2(4) of the UN Charter establishes the now customary law prohibition against the use of force other than in individual or collective self-defence. The UN has deployed 'peacekeepers' in areas such as Kosovo (UN Interim Administration Mission in Kosovo (UNMIK)), as well as forces more properly termed 'peacemakers' in enforcement actions, such as the intervention in the Congo during the Katanga secession crisis of the 1960s (UN Operation in the Congo (ONUC)).[30] At times the UN has put itself in an untenable position by deploying UN peacekeepers on the ground without extending their mandate to include the use of force other than in self-defence. This occurred most infamously during the Rwandan genocide in 1994, where the UN peacekeeping force (UNAMIR) was not authorized, nor provided with adequate resources, to do anything more than evacuate Westerners and watch while hundreds of thousands of Tutsis were massacred.[31] In 1995, the UN failed to prevent the Srebrenica genocide in Bosnia under similar circumstances.[32] These tragic incidents represent a clear failure of political will at the international level; the states with the means to intervene were not prepared to do so. The circumstances in which the Security Council has been prepared to take adequate – or any – measures has sometimes led to mission confusion (or 'creep')[33] as well as allegations of selectivity, based on the geopolitical interests of the permanent five members of the Council and their allies.[34]

---

[27] Ibid., Ch. VII.

[28] Ibid., Art. 41.

[29] Ibid., Art. 42.

[30] UNSC Resolution 169 (1961); Georges Abi-Saab, *The United Nations Operations in the Congo 1960–1964* (Oxford: Oxford University Press, 1978).

[31] Christine Gray, *International Law and the Use of Force* (Oxford: Oxford University Press, 2008, 3rd edn) 292.

[32] Manuel Fröhlich, 'Keeping Track of UN Peace-keeping – Suez, Srebrenica, Rwanda and the Brahimi Report' (2001) 5 *Max Planck Yearbook of United Nations Law* 185, 187–8.

[33] Gray, above note 31, 150–75. See Chapter 8.

[34] A recent example of this might be the preparedness of the Security Council to authorize military action in Libya but not in other trouble-afflicted states of the Middle East (such as Bahrain, Yemen and Syria).

The UN has also set up interim administrations and otherwise offered its services after other states have unilaterally and without UN authorization deployed force, ostensibly justified by humanitarian intervention (as with the NATO bombing of Serbia)[35] or pre-emptive self-defence (as with the invasion of Iraq by the Coalition of the Willing).[36] The role of UN peacekeepers and their responsibilities under the laws on the use of force are very complex issues and the subject of much debate.[37] Various factors may hamper their performance on the ground: resourcing and mandate confusion, rapidly changing circumstances on the ground and the fact that the UN's role is in considerable part subject to global power politics.[38] The UN administration in Kosovo, UNMIK, even engaged in 'state building', providing Kosovo with the means necessary to function as an independent state and thus facilitating its declaration of independence from Serbia on 20 February 2008.[39] Another example of the enormous power open to the Security Council's authority to take measures to maintain and restore international peace and security is the creation of entire derivative international organizations, such as the war crimes tribunals for the former Yugoslavia and Rwanda – binding all states to cooperate with the exercise by these courts of their mandates and costing the international community over 200 million US dollars each year.[40]

Members of the UN undertake to implement the decisions of the Security Council, which includes providing troops for peacekeeping or enforcement missions.[41] Although the Security Council is composed of 15

---

[35] Security Council, 3988th meeting, UN Doc. S/PV.3988, 24 March 1999.

[36] Gray, above note 31, 216ff. See Chapter 8, section 8.2.2. The infamous 'Bush Doctrine' asserts the right of the US to take 'pre-emptive action' against potentially belligerent states: see 'The National Security Strategy of the United States of America', White House, Washington, 15 September 2002.

[37] Christopher Greenwood, 'International Humanitarian Law and United Nations Military Operations' (1998) 1 *Yearbook of International Humanitarian Law* 3.

[38] For a general discussion of these issues, see Bruce Oswald, 'The Law on Military Occupation: Answering the Challenges of Detention during Contemporary Peace Operations' (2007) 8 *Melbourne Journal of International Law* 311–26. See also Secretary-General's Bulletin, 'Observance by United Nations Forces of International Humanitarian Law', 6 August 1999 ST/SGB/1999/13, available at http://www1.umn.edu/humanrts/instree/unobservance1999.pdf.

[39] See *Accordance with International Law of the Unilateral Declaration of Independence in Respect of Kosovo* (Advisory Opinion) 22 July 2010, ICJ General List No. 141. See also Chapter 4, section 4.5.1.

[40] For a discussion of the controversial creation of these Tribunals, see Gowlland-Debbas, above note 18; Oosthuizen, above note 18.

[41] Charter of the United Nations, Arts 25, 43–9.

Members, only five (China, France, Russia, the United Kingdom and the United States of America) are permanent members that have the power of veto over all non-procedural decisions. In practice, the stipulation that the veto does not apply to procedural decisions is not absolute, as a preliminary decision on whether a decision is procedural is considered itself to be non-procedural.[42] The power of veto entrenches the hegemony of the permanent members by effectively preventing action contrary to their interests. The veto must, however, be actually cast; an abstention will not constitute a veto, as the USSR discovered after its abstention from certain resolutions in 1950 – recommending that Members assist South Korea during the Korean War – proved to be ineffective in paralyzing the Security Council.[43]

5.1.1.1.3 The Economic and Social Council Economic and social cooperation is a major aspect of the UN's work, as the Charter considers this necessary for peaceful and friendly relations between nations.[44] The task of promoting solutions for international economic, social, health and related problems, and universal respect for human rights is bestowed specifically on the Economic and Social Council (ECOSOC).[45] Composed of 54 Members, ECOSOC may initiate studies and reports, make recommendations, draft conventions and convene international conferences on these issues.[46]

One of ECOSOC's primary functions is to coordinate the activities of the UN 'specialized agencies' that have been 'brought into relationship' with the UN.[47] This means that organizations that become specialized agencies of the UN shed their previous international personality and come under the umbrella of the international personality of the UN; however, they retain much of their previous autonomy.[48] The specialized agencies include the International Labor Organization (ILO), the World Health Organization (WHO), the World Bank,[49] the International Monetary Fund (IMF) and the United Nations Children's Fund (UNICEF).

---

42 Hans Kelsen, *Principles of International Law* (New York: Holt, Rinehart and Winston, 1966, 2nd edn), 276.

43 Ibid., 277.

44 Charter of the United Nations, Art. 55.

45 Ibid.

46 Ibid., Arts 61–2.

47 Ibid., Arts 57, 59–60, 63–4.

48 See discussion below at section 5.1.1.2.

49 The World Bank is composed of the International Bank for Reconstruction and Development (IBRD), the International Finance Corporation (IFC), the International Center for Settlement of Investment Disputes (ICSID), the

A current example of work produced by ECOSOC with the aid of many of these specialized agencies is the Millennium Development Goals Report issued on 23 June 2010. The Report details the progress taken towards ending world poverty as well as providing information on other issues such as fighting the spread of AIDS and ensuring universal access to clean water. Through this Report and similar activities, ECOSOC conducts a leadership role in monitoring and coordinating advances in economic and social development.

5.1.1.1.4 The Trusteeship Council The Trusteeship Council was established to oversee the trusteeship system, whereby former colonies (mainly of defeated states) were administered by trustee states with a view to maintaining domestic peace and fostering the conditions for the trust territories' eventual independence.[50] Trustee states would conclude individual agreements for this purpose.[51] The principal objectives of the trusteeship system were, among other things, to further international peace and security by ensuring that former colonies would not fall into chaos and to promote the political, economic, social, and educational advancement of the inhabitants of the trust territories, and their progressive development towards self-government or independence.[52] The trusteeship system had replaced the system of mandates under the League of Nations. Although the trusteeship system was suspended in 1994 when the last trust territory, Palau, attained independence, it has historically been a potent mechanism for promoting the efficient transition of former colonies to independence.

5.1.1.1.5 The International Court of Justice The International Court of Justice (ICJ), commonly known as the 'World Court', is the principal judicial organ of the UN.[53] Its functions and powers are primarily determined by the ICJ Statute annexed to the UN Charter. The ICJ has power to determine cases referred to it by states that are parties to a dispute, or on the initiative of a state if the other state party has made a declaration that the jurisdiction of the Court is compulsory.[54] Advisory Opinions on legal questions can be requested by the General Assembly and other organs and

---

International Development Association (IDA) and the Multilateral Investment Guarantee Agency (MIGA).

[50] Charter of the United Nations, Chs XII, XIII. See Chapter 4, section 4.9.1.2.
[51] Ibid., Art. 75.
[52] Ibid., Art. 76.
[53] Ibid., Art. 92.
[54] Statute of the International Court of Justice, Art. 36.

specialized agencies of the UN arising within the scope of their activities.[55] The bench is composed of 15 judges, representing the main forms of civilization and the principal legal systems of the world.[56]

The ICJ is the successor to the Permanent Court of International Justice (PCIJ). Operating from 1920 until the breakdown of the League of Nations system with the outbreak of the Second World War in 1939, the PCIJ was highly respected, no state daring to refuse implementation of its decisions.[57] The PCIJ was itself the result of a process that began at the Hague Peace Conferences of 1899 and 1907, where voices extolling the desirability of a truly international court succeeded in persuading states to establish the Permanent Court of Arbitration.[58] The PCIJ was the next logical step, made all the more imperative by the League of Nations' goal of preventing the recurrence of the First World War.

The ICJ Statute borrowed heavily from the PCIJ Statute, including replicating almost verbatim its Article 38(1) which sets out the now universally accepted sources of international law.[59] However, the ICJ, especially in its earlier years, was not as successful as the PCIJ. The denial of standing by the ICJ to Liberia and Ethiopia in the *South West Africa* cases[60] to review whether South Africa was fulfilling its obligations under the mandate for South-West Africa (now Namibia), sparked a furor in the UN General Assembly by the majority of states as being based on a Western conception of world order.[61] This led to a protracted period where defendants would refuse to appear before the Court and the ICJ generally had little work to do.[62] However, with the largely applauded decision in the *Nicaragua* case[63] – given the judgment's compelling analysis of principles such as those concerning the use of force, and its ostensibly unbiased finding against a major Western state (the United States) in favour of

---

55 Charter of the United Nations, Art. 96.

56 Statute of the International Court of Justice, Art. 9.

57 D.J. Harris, *Cases and Materials on International Law* (London: Sweet & Maxwell, 2004, 6th edn), 1027.

58 Mohammed Bedjaoui, 'Preface', in Sam Muller, D. Raič and J.M. Thuránszky (eds), *The International Court of Justice: Its Future Role after Fifty Years* (The Hague; Boston: Martinus Nijhoff, 1997), xxvi.

59 See Chapter 2.

60 *South West Africa* cases (*Ethiopia v South Africa; Liberia v South Africa*) [1966] ICJ Rep 6.

61 Harris, above note 57, 1027, fn 29.

62 See, e.g., Hugh Thirlway, *Non-Appearance before the International Court of Justice* (Cambridge: Cambridge University Press, 1985).

63 *Military and Paramilitary Activities in and against Nicaragua* (Merits) [1986] ICJ Rep 14.

Nicaragua – the World Court regained a general level of confidence within the international community.

The Court has been criticized as being of limited legal utility.[64] As discussed in Chapter 2, it has sometimes let its judicial function be superseded by political considerations, as its (non) opinion in the *Nuclear Weapons* case[65] indicates. Also, its judgments at times lack the rigour and poise appropriate to a Court of its stature, as evidenced by the slackening of its judicial method in relation to the discovery of customary international law and its over-reliance on its own prior decisions. However, the Court has rendered many important decisions and its rulings have, since the Court's revival in the late 1980s, been largely implemented and enforced, although the United States' veto of a draft General Assembly resolution insisting on 'full compliance' with the *Nicaragua* judgment is a disappointing exception.[66] That said, any assessment of the performance of the World Court must take into consideration the horizontal system of international law, which is not easily susceptible to enforcement by judicial pronouncements.

5.1.1.1.6 The Secretariat The final principal organ is the Secretariat, the administrative staff of the Organization. Its chief administrative officer and the UN's most prominent figure is the Secretary-General. The Secretariat is loyal only to the Organization and may not receive instructions from any external government or authority, or act inconsistently with its position as a body of international officials.[67] Article 101(3) of the UN Charter states:

> [T]he paramount consideration in the employment of staff and in the determination of the conditions of service shall be the necessity of securing the highest standards of efficiency, competence and integrity.

---

64 See, e.g., Eric Posner and Miguel de Figueiredo, 'Is the International Court of Justice Biased?' (2005) 34 *Journal of Legal Studies* 599; Andrew Coleman, 'The International Court of Justice and Highly Political Matters' (2003) 4(1) *Melbourne Journal of International Law* 29.

65 *Legality of the Threat or Use of Nuclear Weapons (*Advisory Opinion) [1996] ICJ Rep 226.

66 Noam Chomsky, 'The New War against Terror', in Nancy Scheper-Hughes and Philippe Bourgois (eds), *Violence in War and Peace: An Anthology* (Malden, MA; Oxford, UK: Blackwell Publishing, 2004) 217, 218; UN Information Centre London, *Newsletter*, 6 November 1986. See also Geoffrey DeWeese, 'The Failure of the International Court of Justice to Effectively Enforce the Genocide Convention' (1998) 26(4) *Denver Journal of International Law and Policy* 265.

67 Charter of the United Nations, Art. 100(1).

This provision was the basis from which the ICJ considered that the General Assembly had implied power to create the UN Administrative Tribunal, which functions as an employment law court for the Secretariat.[68]

5.1.1.2 International personality of the United Nations

The seminal case on the international personality of the United Nations, and international organizations generally, is the ICJ decision in the *Reparations* case.[69] This case arose out of the death in September 1948 of Count Bernadotte in the state of Israel, which was not yet a Member of the UN. Bernadotte was a Swedish national performing functions as Chief UN Truce Negotiator in Palestine. Although he was allegedly killed by a group of private terrorists, Israel admitted international responsibility for failing to protect him. The General Assembly requested the Court provide an Advisory Opinion on two questions. The first question was whether the UN had the capacity to bring an international claim against a responsible state, for injury suffered by one of its agents in the performance of his duties and for damage caused to the UN, or to the victim or his estate.[70] The Court began by establishing that international persons are 'not necessarily identical in their nature or in the extent of their rights' and their nature 'depends on the needs of the community'.[71] The Court was laying down a functional test, rather than one grounded in principle. It found that, as a general proposition, the UN was an international person with broad powers.

The Court pointed to the fact that the UN Charter granted the UN 'political tasks of an important character', including the maintenance of international peace and security, and that Articles 104 and 105 granted the UN legal capacity, privileges and immunities in the territories of its Members. The Organization had also concluded a number of agreements with states, such as the Convention on the Privileges and Immunities of the United Nations 1946, indicating that it was an entity distinct from its Members. The UN was thus an international person.[72] More specifically, the Court had to consider whether, in the absence of an express Charter provision, the functions of the Organization implied the power to bring an international claim for damage caused to UN agents. It considered

---

[68] *Effect of Awards of Compensation Made by the United Nations Administrative Tribunal* (Advisory Opinion) [1954] ICJ Rep 47.

[69] *Reparation for Injuries Suffered in the Service of the United Nations*, above note 10.

[70] Ibid., 175.

[71] Ibid., 178.

[72] Ibid., 178–9.

that the rights and duties of an international organization 'must depend upon its purposes and functions as specified or implied in its constituent documents and developed in practice'.[73] Thus, specific powers to operate on the international plane may be granted by states in the organization's constitution or 'by necessary implication as being essential to the performance of its duties'.[74]

The Court concluded that the UN had found it necessary to entrust its agents with 'important missions to be performed in disturbed parts of the world', which may involve 'unusual dangers'.[75] These duties could not be properly performed without the UN providing effective support for its agents, including the ability to bring a claim for damage caused to the victim and the UN itself in such circumstances. The fact that the victim's national state may also have a claim for diplomatic protection of its national, did not affect the necessity for the UN to possess this implied power, as the concerned state may not be entitled or inclined to sue in a particular case.[76] Having established that the UN had personality to bring such a claim, the Court concluded that the UN's personality was opposable even to states that were not Members of the Organization.[77]

The second question put by the General Assembly was how an action by the UN could be reconciled with rights possessed by the national state of the victim. The Court acknowledged that the death of a national in the territory of another state can give rise to a right of diplomatic protection leading to a claim by the national state for reparation, and that circumstances may occur where the UN might have a concurrent claim. The Court held that, as an international tribunal would not allow double recovery arising from the same wrong, it was up to the UN and national states to conclude agreements 'inspired by goodwill and common sense' to manage this overlap.[78]

The Court's Advisory Opinion involved a two-step process. First, it established that the UN was an international person, relying on an objective analysis[79] in view of the powers in the Charter and the actions already taken by the UN. But that was insufficient by itself to point to the specific power claimed. The right to bring a claim for damage to the UN's agents had to be expressed in the constitution or necessarily implied as 'essential'

---

[73] Ibid., 180.
[74] Ibid., 182.
[75] Ibid., 183.
[76] Ibid.
[77] Ibid., 185.
[78] Ibid., 185–6.
[79] Higgins, above note 7, 46.

for the performance of its functions.[80] It appears that the Court was laying down a broad test of essentiality. The question is not whether the UN can function without the implied power claimed, but whether possession of the power would promote the functioning of the UN at its full capacity.[81]

The general principle outlined in the *Reparations* case does, however, have its limits. In 1996, the WHO, a specialized agency of the UN, asked the ICJ to render an Advisory Opinion on the legality of the threat or use of nuclear weapons. In a controversial decision, the ICJ held that the WHO did not have power to request an Advisory Opinion on that issue.[82] Under Article 96(2) of the UN Charter, a specialized agency may request an Advisory Opinion from the Court on legal questions arising within the scope of its activities. However, the Court held that the WHO was only authorized to deal with the *effects* on health of hazardous activities such as the use of nuclear weapons, and to take preventive measures to protect populations at risk.[83] The WHO request, in reality, related to the *legality* of the use of nuclear weapons *in view of* their health and environmental effects. The WHO's mandate to deal with human health, however, is not affected by whether health matters have been caused by legal or illegal acts.[84] Further, the Court opined that 'due account' should be taken 'of the logic of the overall system contemplated by the Charter'.[85] The WHO, as a specialized agency of the UN, possesses functions limited to public health and cannot encroach on the functions of other UN organs.[86] Accordingly, the Court held that:

> questions concerning the use of force, the regulation of armaments and disarmament are within the competence of the United Nations and lie outside that

[80] See also *Effect of Awards of Compensation Made by the United Nations Administrative Tribunal*, above note 68, 56.

[81] Dapo Akande, 'The Competence of International Organizations and the Advisory Jurisdiction of the International Court of Justice' (1998) 9 *European Journal of International Law* 437, 444; Elihu Lauterpacht, 'The Development of the Law of International Organizations by the Decision of International Tribunals' (1976, IV) 152 *Recueil de Cours* 387,430–32. For a discussion of the unprecedented nature of this ruling, see Catherine Brölmann, 'The International Court of Justice and International Organisations' (2007) 9 *International Community Law Review* 181, 184–5.

[82] *Legality of the Use by a State of Nuclear Weapons in Armed Conflict*, above note 10.

[83] Ibid., 76.

[84] Ibid.

[85] Ibid., 79–81.

[86] Ibid., 80.

> of the specialized agencies. Besides, any other conclusion would render virtually meaningless the notion of a specialized agency.[87]

Hence, a power to take steps to promote the unlawfulness of nuclear weapons was not an implied power of the WHO. Soon after the Court's ruling, the UN General Assembly submitted a similar request, which successfully extracted the Advisory Opinion. The Court's decision in the WHO *Nuclear Weapons* case is difficult to reconcile with the broad view espoused in the *Reparations* case and other ICJ decisions.[88] Despite acknowledging the preventive role of the WHO, the Court denied it the power to take steps calculated to make the use of nuclear weapons less likely. This finding is the more bizarre given that Article 2(k) of the WHO Constitution empowers the WHO to 'propose conventions, agreements and regulations' relating to health matters. Equally dubious is the principle that the notion of 'specialized agency' connotes exclusivity of functions. Legitimate overlap already exists: for example, the ILO has been the agency that proposes conventions and recommendations dealing with the health of workers, even though the WHO has concurrent power to regulate the health area.[89]

The extensive powers bestowed on the UN in its Charter, and the broad formulation of implied powers sanctioned by the ICJ, has led some to conclude that the UN is a 'world government' and the Charter is effectively a 'world constitution'.[90] Factors in support of this include the near universal membership of the UN[91] and the fact that the Charter establishes a regime

---

[87] Ibid., 80–81.

[88] *Effect of Awards of Compensation Made by the United Nations Administrative Tribunal*, above note 68; *Certain Expenses of the United Nations* (Advisory Opinion) [1962] ICJ Rep 157.

[89] Akande, above note 81, 450. It is also important to note that the specialized agencies of the UN are not intended to possess international personality distinct from the UN. For example, the headquarters agreement for the ICTY was concluded between the Netherlands and the UN: see Christian Walter, 'Subjects of International Law', in *Max Planck Encyclopedia of Public International Law* (Heidelberg: Max-Planck-Institut, 2010) 4.

[90] Erika de Wet, 'The International Constitutional Order' (2006) *International and Comparative Law Quarterly* 51; Blaine Sloan, 'The United Nations Charter as a Constitution' (1989) *Pace Year Book of International Law* 61; N. White, 'The United Nations System: Conference, Contract, or Constitutional Order?' (2000) 4 *Singapore Journal of International and Comparative Law* 281.

[91] The UN currently has 192 Members out of the 195 states of the world. The three non-members are Taiwan (excluded from membership given the dissonance between Taiwan's claim to being the legitimate government of China and China's claim that Taiwan is part of its territory), Kosovo (a state that had only declared

for the non-use of force other than in self-defence *except* when the UN is undertaking enforcement under Chapter VII to maintain or restore 'international peace and security'. The Charter therefore envisages that the UN has greater international personality to use force than any state[92] and, according to Article 103, the Charter prevails over any inconsistent treaty between Members or between a Member and a non-Member. It may seem to follow that the Charter recalibrates the world order by placing the UN at the top of the hierarchy, making it a 'supranational' organization.

Although it is in some ways enticing to conceive of the UN in this way, it is more accurate to say that the UN possesses some elements consistent with world government, but ultimately falls short of such a characterization. The UN does possess a strong executive arm – the Security Council. However, it is entirely dependent on states to enforce its directives. The possibility in Article 43 of the Charter for states to enter into special agreements with the UN to provide a permanent UN allied army has never been acted on.[93] Further, the General Assembly is not a 'legislature' by any stretch of the imagination, since its resolutions are not binding and are often fragmented. Finally, the ICJ has no mechanism for judicial review to keep the UN within constitutional limits and it can only settle a dispute when states that are parties to a dispute have accepted its jurisdiction.[94] Any decisions of the ICJ must be implemented by states: if a state fails to comply with an order of the Court, all that the claimant state can do is apply to the Security Council, which may recommend action by states individually or collectively.[95] All of this comports with the intention of the drafters of the Charter to avoid all implications that the UN was a 'superstate'.[96]

---

independence in February 2008) and the Holy See (which does not wish to become a Member).

92 White, above note 90, 35, 47.

93 Jean E. Krasno, *The United Nations: Confronting the Challenges of a Global Society* (Boulder, CO: Lynne Rienner Publishers, 2004), 225. For the legal basis of the creation of peacekeeping forces, see Gray, above note 31, 261–2.

94 See discussion above at section 5.1.1.1.

95 Charter of the United Nations, Art. 94(2).

96 Menon, above note 8, 83; Hersch Lauterpacht, 'The Subjects of the Law of Nations' (1947) 63 *Law Quarterly Review* 438, 447.

5.2 NON-GOVERNMENTAL ORGANIZATIONS: THE GROWING PLACE OF CIVIL SOCIETY IN INTERNATIONAL LAW

Non-governmental organizations (NGOs) are entities created under national law, with voluntary, private membership, to pursue a particular cause that may transcend national boundaries.[97] Familiar examples include Human Rights Watch, Amnesty International, the International Committee of the Red Cross (ICRC), and the International Campaign to Ban Landmines (ICBL). NGOs possess little if any international personality and often appear as a mere afterthought in studies of international law. In reality, they can have a profound impact on the practice and development of international law. The ICBL, a conglomeration of NGOs, is a Nobel Peace Prize Co-Laureate for its efforts in pushing for the drafting of the Ottawa Convention on the Prohibition of the Use, Stockpiling, Production and Transfer of Anti-Personnel Mines and on their Destruction 1997.

The ICRC has worked since 1863 to develop the law and practice of international humanitarian law and, unusually for an NGO, has been granted a mandate under the Geneva Conventions and their Additional Protocols for the protection of war victims and the amelioration of the effects of armed conflict.[98]

Indeed, the ICRC and the International Federation of Red Cross and Red Crescent Societies can be said to possess rights commonly granted to international organizations, such as headquarters and agreements concluded with states providing for privileges and immunities.[99] In fact, the work of the ICRC is considered so important that the ICTY Trial Chamber has held that there exists a customary international law norm that ICRC employees are immune from testifying about what they witnessed during their employment.[100] The structure of the Red Cross and Red Crescent Movement also points to the unique nature of this organization: the

---

[97] Steve Charnovitz, 'Nongovernmental Organizations and International Law' (2006) 100 *American Journal of International Law* 348, 350.

[98] The ICRC received the Nobel Peace Prize in 1917, 1944 and 1963.

[99] Menno Kamminga, 'The Evolving Status of NGOs under International Law: A Threat to the Inter-State System?', in Philip Alston (ed.), *Non-State Actors and Human Rights*, above note 1, 93, 98–9; Menon, above note 8, 82.

[100] *Prosecutor v Simić* (Trial Chamber Decision on the Prosecution Motion under Rule 73 for a Ruling Concerning the Testimony of a Witness) IT-95-9-PT (27 July 1999), [74]. But see Chapter 2 for criticism of the Chamber's methodology in finding the necessary *opinio juris*.

membership of the International Conference of the Red Cross and Red Crescent, its 'supreme deliberative body', is drawn from the National Societies of the Red Cross/Red Crescent, the ICRC, the Federation and the States Parties to the Geneva Conventions.[101] Nevertheless, what differentiates the Conference from the deliberative body of an international organization is that the Movement's Fundamental Principles stipulate its political independence as a private organization.[102]

NGOs have been instrumental in the drafting process of the new International Criminal Court (ICC).[103] They also have a powerful influence on the development and content of international law in the nascent area of climate change law. A group of NGOs, including Greenpeace and the World Wildlife Foundation, presented 'A Copenhagen Climate Treaty: Version 1.0' at the Copenhagen Climate Conference of 2009, amounting to a proposal for an amended Kyoto Protocol and a new Copenhagen Protocol by members of the NGO community. Although the Conference ultimately terminated without significant agreement between states, it exemplifies how NGOs with resources and determination can play an influential role on the world stage. Indeed, it is not only at international summits that NGOs can apply pressure to governments – even when state representatives return home from an international summit they will be confronted by intensive, and often highly effective, lobbying by NGOs in the domestic sphere.[104]

The oft-held misconception that NGOs are a relatively new phenomenon is belied by the longevity of the ICRC and early work of other private organizations pursuing international ends. In 1905, the Convention creating the International Institute of Agriculture (an international organization later superseded by the Food and Agriculture Organization) was the

---

[101] Statutes of the International Red Cross and Red Crescent Movement, Art. 9(1) (adopted by the 25th International Conference of the Red Cross at Geneva in 1986, as amended). See also Michael Meyer, 'The Importance of the International Conference of the Red Cross and Red Crescent to National Societies: Fundamental in Theory and in Practice' (2009) 91 (876) *International Review of the Red Cross* 713.

[102] Preamble to the International Red Cross and Red Crescent Movement Statutes, ibid.

[103] See Mahnoush Arsanjani, 'The Rome Statute of the International Criminal Court' (1999) 93 *American Journal of International Law* 22, 23.

[104] See Nina Hall and Ros Taplin, 'Room for Climate Advocates in a Coal-focused Economy? NGO Influence on Australian Climate Policy' (2008) 43(3) *Australian Journal of Social Issues* 359; M. Guigni, D. McAdam and C. Tilly (eds), *How Social Movements Matter* (Minneapolis, MN; London: University of Minnesota Press, 1999).

first treaty to formally provide for NGO consultation.[105] As early as 1910, the Institut de Droit International and the International Law Association, pre-eminent NGOs dedicated to the development of international law, suggested that states should conclude a convention to grant legal personality to NGOs.[106] The modern foundations for the institutionalized participation of NGOs were laid when Article 71 was included in the UN Charter:

> The Economic and Social Council may make suitable arrangements for consultation with nongovernmental organizations which are concerned with matters within its competence. Such arrangements may be made with international organizations and, where appropriate, with national organizations after consultation with the Member of the United Nations concerned.

There are currently over 3000 NGOs in consultative status with ECOSOC that regularly advocate for particular causes by bringing a diverse and progressive voice to debates.[107] NGOs also possess consultative status in other international organizations, such as the International Labour Organization, in which governments and representatives of employers and workers are equal participants.[108] They are also permitted to make submissions on an ad hoc basis at international conferences. Certain controls are in place to ensure that NGOs meet minimum standards: for instance, ECOSOC requires that, for an NGO to be granted consultative status, it must 'be of recognized standing within the particular field of its competence or of a representative character'.[109] From 1997, NGOs have also briefed representatives to the UN Security Council and, from 2004, have made direct submissions.[110]

---

[105] Article 9(f) of the Convention on the International Institute of Agriculture 1905 compels the Institute to 'submit to the approval of the governments . . . measures for the protection of the common interests of farmers and for the improvement of their condition, after having utilized all the necessary sources of information, such as the wishes expressed by *international or other agricultural congresses or congresses of sciences applied to agriculture, agricultural societies*, [etc]' (emphasis added).

[106] Charnovitz, above note 97, 356.

[107] United Nations, 'NGO-related Frequently Asked Questions', available at http://www.un.org/esa/coordination/ngo/faq.htm (accessed 5 December 2010).

[108] Constitution of the International Labour Organisation, Art. 3(1).

[109] 'Consultative Relationship between the United Nations and Non-governmental Organizations', ESC Res. 1996/31 (1996), available at http://www.un.org/esa/coordination/ngo/Resolution_1996_31/index.htm (accessed 5 December 2010).

[110] Charnovitz, above note 97, 368.

Another function of NGOs on the international plane is their delivery of submissions to international courts and tribunals as *amici curiae*, or 'friends of the court'. Tribunals such as the ICTY and ICTR, and the ICC, have occasionally asked NGOs to make submissions,[111] but the World Court has been less open to their participation.[112] In 2004, the ICJ promulgated Practice Direction XII, permitting NGOs in advisory proceedings to make submissions on their own initiative.[113] Such submissions would not be part of the case file, but would be kept available for use by the parties in the same manner as publications in the public domain. Although this allows for greater NGO participation at the ICJ, it is not an ideal procedure. During the *Israeli Wall* case,[114] an NGO invoked Practice Direction XII of the Court to place a submission in the case file. However, as it was not part of the case file and no record of it was kept at the Registry of the Court, neither the contents of the document nor whether it was used by the parties will ever be known.[115] The WTO dispute settlement panels employ a more open process. In the *US – Shrimp* case,[116] the Appellate Body of the WTO allowed three groups of NGOs to submit *amicus curiae* briefs without a prior request by the panel.[117] However, under pressure from several Member States who considered that giving NGOs the right to make submissions was inconsistent with the nature of the WTO Agreement as a multilateral treaty, the Appellate Body has imposed stringent requirements for NGO submissions in subsequent cases.[118]

---

111 For a detailed discussion of this, see Gideon Boas, James L. Bischoff, Natalie L. Reid and B. Don Taylor III, *International Criminal Procedure* (Cambridge: Cambridge University Press, 2011), Chapter 5, section 5.6.

112 Dinah Shelton, 'The Participation of Nongovernmental Organizations in International Judicial Proceedings' (1994) 88 *American Journal of International Law* 611.

113 The ICJ has the power to invite NGOs to make submissions under Article 96 of the ICJ Statute, but invitations have been only infrequently extended.

114 *Legal Consequences of the Construction of a Wall in the Occupied Palestinian Territory* (Advisory Opinion) [2004] ICJ Rep 136.

115 Shelton, above note 112, 152.

116 *United States – Import Prohibition of Certain Shrimp and Shrimp Products* 1998, Report of the Appellate Body, WTO Doc. WT/DS58/AB/R, adopted November 1998, [186].

117 Ibid., Part IIIA. Note that under Article 13 of the Understanding on Rules and Procedures Governing the Settlement of Disputes (Annex 2 to the WTO Agreement), the dispute resolution panels have the right to request information from 'any individual or body which it deems appropriate'.

118 *EC – Asbestos*, Report of the Appellate Body, WTO Doc. WT/DS135/AB/R, adopted 5 April 2001, [51]–[57]; Gillian Triggs, *International Law: Contemporary Principles and Practices* (Sydney: LexisNexis Butterworths, 2011, 2nd edn) 758.

Given their transnational mobility and access to the most recent information, NGOs such as Human Rights Watch perform an important monitoring role to help compel state compliance with international law.[119] In very exceptional cases, NGOs have even been able to initiate claims in international fora, such as via Article 44 of the American Convention on Human Rights 1978, which provides:

> Any person or group of persons, or any nongovernmental entity legally recognized in one or more Member States of the Organization, may lodge petitions with the Commission containing denunciations or complaints of violation of this Convention by a State Party.

Although NGOs have participated in the international system since the mid-nineteenth century, their influence and status is accelerating. The trend is very much for greater NGO participation and a growing acknowledgement of their importance in promoting the development and enforcement of international law. Zoe Pearson has suggested that the existing state-centric structures and processes of international law are inadequate to accommodate the 'diversity and fluidity' of emerging global civil society actors.[120] Currently, the very limited ability of NGOs to participate in international law depends on the willingness of states – mainly through international organizations – to allow such participation. If Pearson's suggestion for formal integration of NGOs into the fabric of international law eventually becomes reality, processes should be introduced (preferably by multilateral treaty) to further regulate what could become a potentially chaotic and congested international scene.[121]

5.3 INDIVIDUALS: THE RUPTURE OF STATE-CENTRIC INTERNATIONAL LAW?

It has been said that the debate over the position of the individual in international law goes to the heart of legal philosophy.[122] If law is ultimately for the benefit of human beings, it would seem a strange way to attain that end by conferring rights and duties solely on states, relegating the place of the individual to near invisibility. Yet this is precisely how the Westphalian system of international law, which continues to constitute

---

119 Charnovitz, above note 97, 362.

120 Pearson, above note 2.

121 Ibid., 99–103; Charnovitz, above note 97, 364, 372.

122 D.P. O'Connell, *International Law* (London: Stevens, 1965), 116.

the basic foundation of modern international law, developed.[123] It is often overlooked that, prior to the emergence of the state-centric approach with its nineteenth-century positivist overlay, scholars such as Plutarch, Vitoria and Grotius considered international law to be grounded in natural law concepts of the common good, which included the recognition of individual rights.[124]

There is nothing inherent in international law that denies legal personality to individuals. The fact that states are empowered to develop international law as its primary participants, does not exclude the presence of other powerful forces on the international playing field. Indeed, if international organizations and other collectivities can develop a significant presence, then why not also those stakeholders for whom all laws are created and enforced – individuals? Indeed, such a consciousness has grown out of the post-Second World War United Nations model. The increased international personality of individuals in the second half of the twentieth century has seen something of a rupturing of the state-centric conception that has endured since the Peace of Westphalia. Even so, despite very significant developments in the rights (and obligations) of individuals as subjects and subject to international law, their participation remains very much dependent on the will of states. International law remains state-created law and what has been created can also be taken away. This section will explore just how significant the individual in international law has become and in what ways these developments reflect the future of the international legal system.

5.3.1 International Duties of Individuals

It has long been recognized that an individual caught engaging in piracy is punishable in the national courts of any state. This was the first international crime, in the sense that states had recognized extraterritorial jurisdiction under international law to try private individuals for committing robbery on the high seas. By definition, piracy could only be committed by private individuals and their capture and trial was an established exception to the freedom of the high seas, where no state could perform acts of

---

[123] For a discussion of the historical development of international law, see Chapter 1, section 1.2.

[124] Hugo Grotius, *De Jure Praedae Commentarius* (1604), cited in Erica-Irene Daes, *The Individual's Duties to the Community and the Limitations on Human Rights and Freedoms under Article 29 of the Universal Declaration of Human Rights: A Contribution to the Freedom of the Individual under International Law: A Study* (New York, NY: United Nations, 1983), 44.

sovereignty over foreign ships.[125] Slavery and violations of the laws and customs of war also entailed the extraterritorial application of national law, although today punishment is based on what has sometimes been referred to as 'universal jurisdiction' – that is, a state is under an obligation to prosecute or extradite an individual who has committed these most heinous of international crimes.[126] Hans Kelsen points out that, although it is an organ of the state that is bringing the pirate, the slave trafficker or war criminal to justice, the sanction is also being applied in the execution of a norm of international law.[127] In this way, individuals possess international duties and are thus cognizable under international law, even as long ago as the eighteenth and nineteenth centuries.

5.3.1.1 Individual criminal responsibility

The purpose of individual responsibility in international criminal law is to capture all of the methods and means by which an individual may contribute to the commission of a crime, or be held responsible for a crime under international law.[128] It is interesting that the idea of the individual's *responsibility* (duty) developed within the international law system before any structured protection of his or her human rights was to appear after the Second World War. One of the earlier and normatively important examples of the international community's consciousness of the responsibility of individuals for atrocity came in 1915, in the form of a joint declaration issued by the French, British and Russian governments, condemning the massive and widespread deportation and extermination of over one million Christian Armenians by the Ottoman government:

> In view of these new crimes of Turkey against humanity and civilization, the Allied governments announce publicly to the *Sublime Porte* that they will hold personally responsible [for] these crimes all members of the

---

[125] *In re Piracy Jure Gentium* [1933–34] Ann Dig 7 (No. 89).

[126] *Arrest Warrant of 11 April 2000* (*Democratic Republic of Congo v Belgium*) [2002] ICJ Rep 3 (Separate Opinion of Judges Higgins, Kooijmans and Buergenthal) 75. For a discussion of jurisdiction, including universal jurisdiction, see Chapter 6.

[127] See Antonio Cassese, *International Criminal Law* (Oxford; New York: Oxford University Press, 2003), 12.

[128] See Gideon Boas, James L. Bischoff and Natalie L. Reid, *Forms of Responsibility in International Criminal Law* (Cambridge: Cambridge University Press, 2007), Chapter 1. See examples of this expressed in case law: *Prosecutor v Muvunyi*, Case No. ICTR-00-55A-T, Judgment, 11 September 2006, [459]–[460]; *Prosecutor v Gacumbitsi*, Case No. ICTR-2001-64-T, Judgment, 14 June 2004, [267]; *Prosecutor v Delalić, Mucić, Delić and Landžo* (Judgment) IT-96-21-T (16 November 1998), [321], [331].

Ottoman Government and those of their agents who are implicated in such massacres.[129]

Largely failed attempts at holding individuals criminally responsible after the First World War[130] were followed by the Nuremberg, Tokyo and other post-Second World War tribunals that, along with national trials held by Allied countries, tried many thousands of war criminals stretching over decades.[131]

Developments in international criminal law slowed during the Cold War and early plans for a code of crimes against the peace and security of mankind and an international criminal court were, for a long time, unattainable.[132] In 1993 the ICTY was established, under the Security Council's Chapter VII powers to maintain international peace and security, to try persons who had committed serious violations of international humanitarian law in the territory of the former Yugoslavia.[133] Similarly, the Security Council established the ICTR in 1994 to try perpetrators of the Rwandan genocide.[134] These ad hoc Tribunals have tried a number of war criminals,

---

129 United Nations War Crimes Commission, *History of the United Nations War Crimes Commission and the Developments of the Laws of War* (London: HMSO, 1948), 35. See also Robert Cryer, Håkan Friman, Darryl Robinson and Elizabeth Wilmshurst, *An Introduction to International Criminal Law and Procedure* (Cambridge: Cambridge University Press, 2007), 187–8; Cassese, above note 127, 67; Machteld Boot, *Genocide, Crimes Against Humanity, War Crimes: Nullum Crimen Sine Lege and the Subject Matter Jurisdiction of the International Criminal Court* (Antwerp; New York: Intersentia, 2002), 458; Roger S. Clark, 'Crimes against Humanity at Nuremberg', in George Ginsburgs and V.N. Kudriavtzev (eds), *The Nuremberg Trials and International Law* (Dordrecht; Boston: M. Nijhoff, 1990); Egon Schwelb, 'Crimes Against Humanity' (1946) 23 *British Yearbook of International Law* 181.

130 See Treaty of Versailles, Art. 228; C. Mullins, *The Leipzig Trials* (London: H.F. & G. Witherby, 1921). For a discussion of the abortive war crimes trials following the First World War, see Gideon Boas, James L. Bischoff and Natalie L. Reid, *Elements of Crimes in International Law* (Cambridge: Cambridge University Press, 2008), Chapter 2, section 2.1.1; Timothy L.H. McCormack, 'From Sun Tzu to the Sixth Committee: The Evolution of an International Criminal Law Regime', in Timothy L.H. McCormack and Gerry J. Simpson (eds), *The Law of War Crimes: National and International Approaches* (The Hague; London: Kluwer Law International, 1997).

131 Gillian Triggs, 'Australia's War Crimes Trials: All Pity Choked', in McCormack and Simpson, ibid., 123.

132 See William Schabas, *An Introduction to the International Criminal Court* (Cambridge: Cambridge University Press, 2007, 3rd edn), 8–11.

133 SC Resolution 827 (1993).

134 SC Resolution 955 (1994).

including the former President of Serbia, Slobodan Milošević, and the former Prime Minister of Rwanda, Jean Kambanda, and have laid down volumes of jurisprudence developing international criminal justice.[135] In 1998, the international community (but with the notable absence of Security Council members, the USA, China and Russia) finally concluded the Rome Statute of the International Criminal Court (ICC), establishing the world's first permanent international criminal tribunal. Sitting in The Hague, the ICC is tasked with delivering international justice in respect of the 'most serious crimes of concern to the international community as a whole': genocide, crimes against humanity, war crimes and (possibly) aggression.[136]

Finally, a number of 'hybrid' or 'internationalized' criminal tribunals have been established to apply a mixture of international and domestic law, the benches of which reflect this hybridity:

- the Special Court for Sierra Leone – to try war crimes and crimes against humanity committed since 1996;
- the Extraordinary Chambers in the Courts of Cambodia – to try senior leaders of the Khmer Rouge for genocide, war crimes and crimes against humanity and Cambodian criminal law, committed during 1975–79;
- the Special Tribunal for Lebanon – to prosecute those responsible for the assassination in 2005 of Rafik Hariri, President of Lebanon; and
- the Special Panels of the Dili District Court – created by the UN Transitional Administration in East Timor (UNTAET) to try crimes such as murder, rape and torture perpetrated during 1999.

The idea of individual criminal responsibility for the core international crimes (war crimes, crimes against humanity and genocide) is now indisputably accepted in international law.

---

[135] Gideon Boas, *The Milošević Trial: Lessons for the Conduct of Complex International Criminal Proceedings* (Cambridge: Cambridge University Press, 2007).

[136] Rome Statute of the International Criminal Court, Art. 5. See further Antonio Cassese, *The Rome Statute of the International Criminal Court: A Commentary* (Oxford; New York: Oxford University Press, 2002).

5.3.2 International Rights of Individuals

While the duties of individuals under international law have developed considerably in some areas in recent years, so too have certain rights. However, despite the extraordinary growth of instruments and customary law, particularly in the area of international human rights, the character of such rights and the capacity of individuals to exercise them vis-à-vis states remains attenuated.

The traditional reticence to acknowledge that international law can bestow rights on individuals was expressed in the 1928 PCIJ decision in the *Danzig Railway Officials* case.[137] This early case involved consideration of the terms of a treaty between Germany and Poland providing for pecuniary claims to be made against the Polish Railways Administration by railway officials who had passed from German to Polish service. Although the Court confirmed that a treaty could provide for claims under the domestic law of the parties, a treaty, 'being an international agreement, cannot as such create direct rights and obligations for private individuals'.[138]

International law has since moved beyond this extreme state-centric interpretation of treaties that on their face confer individual rights. The *LaGrand* case[139] involved Germany's claim before the ICJ against the United States for an alleged breach of Article 36(1) of the Vienna Convention on Consular Relations. Germany claimed that the United States had denied a German national his rights under this sub-paragraph and had executed him despite provisional measures of protection ordered by the ICJ. In finding the United States in breach, the Court observed that Article 36, paragraph 1, *creates individual rights*, which, by virtue of Article 1 of the Optional Protocol, may be invoked in this Court by the national state of the detained person. These rights were violated in the present case.[140]

According to the Court, the debate is no longer about whether a norm of international law can confer individual rights, but whether the correct interpretation of a particular norm compels this conclusion.[141] As the *LaGrand* case implies, however, the fact that an individual has rights under international law does not necessarily mean that he or she has the capacity to enforce those rights.[142] Indeed, under the ICJ Statute, only states may

---

[137] *Danzig Railway Officials* (Advisory Opinion) [1928] PCIJ (Ser. B) No. 15).
[138] Ibid., 17, 287.
[139] *LaGrand* (*Germany v United States*) [2001] ICJ Rep 466.
[140] Ibid., 494 (emphasis added).
[141] Walter, above note 89, 5.
[142] See also *Appeal from a Judgment of the Hungaro-Czechoslovak Mixed Arbitral Tribunal* (*The Peter Pázmány University v The State of Czechoslovakia*)

bring claims before the ICJ.[143] Some hold the view that a right without a remedy is no right at all.[144] However, besides being contrary to modern jurisprudence, this view would be destabilizing in a decentralized system like international law, where enforcement normally occurs through voluntary compliance rather than through what nineteenth-century positivists called an 'effective sanction'.[145]

To deny recognition of the individual's substantive right would hamstring the later development of an individual enforcement mechanism. Historically, the fear of a slippery slope leading to the enforcement of human rights is what caused oppressive regimes, such as the former Soviet Union, to oppose the development of human rights jurisprudence, especially in its early years.[146] As a prominent Soviet jurist explained in 1990:

> [T]he reserved attitude of the Soviet Union in the past towards control mechanisms in the area of human rights protection, the neurotic reaction to the slightest criticism . . . was not only the result of ideological dogmatism but also testified to the fact that in the area of human rights there are things to hide in our country.[147]

5.3.2.1 Human rights

Although individual rights have developed in other areas, such as consular relations and diplomatic protection, it is in the field of human rights that the most far-reaching development of individual rights in international law has taken place. The UN Charter calls upon states to 'reaffirm faith in fundamental human rights, in the dignity and worth of the human person, equal rights for men and women . . . and to promote social progress and better standards of life in larger freedom'.[148] The broad statements in the Charter were not intended to be a source of rights

(1933) PCIJ (Ser. A/B) No. 61, 231, in which the PCIJ stated: 'It is scarcely necessary to point out that the capacity to possess civil rights does not necessarily imply the capacity to exercise those rights oneself.'

[143] Statute of the International Court of Justice, Art. 34(1).

[144] See, e.g., Kelsen, above note 42, 234.

[145] Higgins, above note 7, 53.

[146] Cassese, above note 11, 75.

[147] Rein Mullerson, 'Human Rights and the Individual as Subject of International Law: A Soviet View' (1990) 1 *European Journal of International Law* 33, 43.

[148] Preamble, Charter of the United Nations. Note that the guarantee of human rights became a major war aim of the Allies: see the *Atlantic Charter* (21 August 1941) as adopted by most of the Allies by 1 January 1942 (1942) 36 *American Journal of International Law*, Supp. 191.

and obligations,[149] but they changed the spirit of international discourse. The Universal Declaration of Human Rights 1948 – the touchstone for later developments – was similarly non-binding, being in the nature of a General Assembly recommendation. It was with the numerous subsequently concluded human rights treaties that states undertook direct obligations to guarantee fundamental rights. The major treaties include the International Covenant on Civil and Political Rights 1966 (ICCPR), the International Convention on the Elimination of All Forms of Racial Discrimination 1966 (ICERD), the Convention on the Elimination of Discrimination against Women 1979 (CEDAW) and the Convention on the Rights of the Child 1989 (CRC). It has been subsequently recognized that if a state engages in a consistent pattern of gross violations of human rights, or if a violation amounts to one of the core crimes under international law (such as crimes against humanity or genocide), the state will have breached customary international law independent of these treaties.[150]

Usually, an individual does not have procedural capacity to initiate a claim to vindicate his or her human rights. The protection afforded by human rights law is therefore quite narrow, given that it is often the individual's own state that is violating his or her rights and that governments on good terms with the state concerned are unlikely to bring such an international claim against it. It is also unlikely that the domestic law of the state directly incorporates the international law of human rights – even in monist countries human rights law may be declared by the courts to be non-self-executing.[151] In practice, a right of individual petition to an international body is the best way of maximizing vigilance over state action.[152] Thus, under Optional Protocol 1 to the ICCPR:

> a State Party to the Covenant that becomes a Party to the present Protocol recognizes the competence of the [Human Rights] Committee to receive and consider communications from individuals subject to its jurisdiction who claim to be victims of a violation by that State Party of any of the rights set forth in the Covenant.[153]

---

[149] Kelsen, above note 42, 226.

[150] *Restatement (Third) of the Foreign Relations Law of the United States* (American Law Institute, 1987) Vol. 2, 165. Note that serious violations of such human rights give rise to obligations *erga omnes* – i.e. any state may sue: ibid.; see Chapter 2.

[151] Mullerson, above note 147, 37. See Chapter 3.

[152] Lowe, above note 5, 16.

[153] Optional Protocol to the International Covenant on Civil and Political Rights, Art. 1.

However, before this provision becomes operational in respect of a particular state, that state must have ratified Optional Protocol 1 and the individual must have first exhausted all available domestic remedies.[154] Furthermore, decisions of the Human Rights Committee are in the nature of non-binding 'views' rather than judgments proper. An example of such a communication was *A v Australia*,[155] a case in which a Cambodian refugee claimed that his continuing four-year immigration detention amounted to arbitrary detention under Article 9(1) of the ICCPR and that his right to judicial review was denied by a clause in the Migration Act 1958 (Cth), contrary to Article 9(4) of the ICCPR. Australia, having ratified Optional Protocol 1, enabled the complaint to be brought directly to the HRC. Although the Human Rights Committee found for the author, its view was not implemented by Australia (in contrast to a previous communication in *Toonen v Australia*[156]).

The individual complaints processes in other human rights treaties follow a similar pattern. A notable exception is the European Convention on Human Rights (1950), where the obligation to allow individual petition is not dependent on the state accepting a further optional protocol, and decisions of the European Court of Human Rights are legally binding at international law.[157] Although human rights law offers only limited practical protection to individuals and its enforcement relies on the goodwill and political interests of states, it is not necessarily less effective than many other modes of compliance with international law.[158]

5.4 CORPORATIONS

Although transnational or multinational corporations (those operating across state boundaries) have had precursors dating back at least to the Hanseatic League of trading cities in the late Middle Ages, it is in the past half century that private corporations have started to play an enormously influential role in world affairs. They were the major drivers of the

---

[154] International Covenant on Civil and Political Rights, Art. 41(1).

[155] *A v Australia*, UN Human Rights Committee, Communication No. 560/1993 (adopted 3 April 1997).

[156] *Toonen v Australia*, UN Human Rights Committee, Communication No. 488/1992 (adopted 4 April 1994). See also Chapter 3, section 3.3.

[157] European Convention on Human Rights, Arts 34 and 46; Lowe, above note 5, 17; Cassese, above note 11, 101–2. The African Court on Human and Peoples' Rights now has similar powers.

[158] Cassese, ibid., 103.

phenomenon of 'globalization', whereby the planet is becoming increasingly interconnected economically and socially. The economic power of many multinational corporations has come to eclipse that of some smaller states.[159] This ability to make a significant difference to the economies of developing states means that economic power often entails political power – that is, sufficient leverage to effect political change. However, the practical importance of corporations in world affairs has not been matched by a commensurate articulation of international rights and duties. Although there is much scholarly debate around the desirability of enlisting corporations in the service of international law to promote and protect global public goods, such as human rights and the environment,[160] corporations remain mostly unregulated on the international scene. Furthermore, they are, by definition, primarily self-interested – with any apparent altruism reflecting more a marketing objective than anything like a *raison d'être*. In this important way, corporations are quite different from international organizations and other non-state actors.

The international personality of corporations derives from two sources. First, states have concluded treaties among themselves, such as the ICSID Convention, which gives corporations the ability to bring claims in international fora, in this case the International Centre for Settlement of Investment Disputes. Secondly, corporations have been ever active in protecting their overseas interests by concluding long-term concession contracts with foreign governments for the construction and exploitation of mines, oil wells and other resources. These are a fusion of treaty and domestic commercial contracts, in that they may be subject to international law.[161] Whether international law is applicable depends on the intention of the parties to the international commercial contract – that is whether, 'for the purposes of interpretation and performance of the con-

---

[159] Karsten Nowrot, 'New Approaches to the International Legal Personality of Multinational Corporations towards a Rebuttable Presumption of Normative Responsibilities', Paper presented to the ESIL Research Forum on International Law: Contemporary Issues Graduate Institute of International Studies, May 2005; 1–3; available at http://www.esil-sedi.eu/fichiers/en/Nowrot_513.pdf (accessed 9 December 2010).

[160] David Kinley and Junko Tadaki, 'From Talk to Walk: The Emergence of Human Rights Responsibilities for Corporations at International Law' (2004) 44(4) *Virginia Journal of International Law* 931; Rebecca Wallace and Olga Martin-Ortega, *International Law* (London: Sweet & Maxwell, 2009, 6th edn) 98; Nowrot, ibid.

[161] Lowe, above note 5, 16; *Amoco International Finance Corp v Iran* (1987) 15 Iran-US CTR 189. See also George Aldrich, *The Jurisprudence of the Iran-US Claims Tribunal* (Oxford: Clarendon Press, 1996), 188ff.

tract, it should be recognized that a private contracting party has specific international capacities'.[162] Multinational corporations have promised to adhere to certain codes of conduct, such as the UN Global Compact of 26 July 2000, through which corporations undertake, among other things, to support and respect human rights and take a precautionary approach to environmental challenges. These codes are not binding and may be freely revoked by the corporations that have accepted them. They are more in the nature of 'soft law'.[163]

There have been some suggestions that corporations may be accountable under international criminal law for complicity in international crimes.[164] The recent controversial United States Court of Appeals for the Second Circuit judgment in *Khulumani v Barclay National Bank*[165] found that the dozens of defendant corporations were complicit in aiding and abetting the apartheid regime in South Africa.[166] Only Judge Katzmann decided so on the basis of customary international law, via the gateway of the US Alien Tort Claims Act.[167] Judge Korman dissented, stating the orthodox view that an 'artificial entity' cannot be vicariously liable for international crimes, 'because the relevant norms of international law at issue plainly do not recognize such liability'.[168] He also raised the issue of non-retrospectivity, finding that '[t]he only sources of customary law that suggest some movement toward the recognition of corporate liability post-date the collapse of the apartheid regime'.[169] Judge Korman's dissent is strong, given that Judge Katzmann based his conclusion on the customary law basis of corporate criminal liability in international criminal tribunal statutes (the ICC Statute, for example), which contemplate only individual

---

162 *Texaco Overseas Petroleum Company and California Asiatic Oil Company v Libya* (1977) 53 ILR 389, 457.

163 Triggs, above note 118, 244.

164 Andrew Clapham, 'Extending International Criminal Law beyond the Individual to Corporations and Armed Opposition Groups' (2008) 6(5) *Journal of International Criminal Justice* 899.

165 *Khulumani v Barclay National Bank Ltd; Ntsebeza v Daimler Chrysler Corp*, 504 F.3d 254 (2d Cir 2007).

166 See Chapter 2 for discussion on the *jus cogens* nature of the international crime of apartheid. See also Kristen Hutchens, 'International Law in American Courts – Khulumani v Barclay National Bank Ltd: The Decision Heard "Round the Corporate World"' (2008) 9(5) *German Law Journal* 639.

167 The other majority judge, Judge Hall, thought that domestic law was applicable under the Alien Tort Claims Act in that case.

168 *Khulumani v Barclay National Bank Ltd; Ntsebeza v Daimler Chrysler Corp*, above note 165, Dissenting Opinion of Korman J.

169 *Khulumani v Barclay National Bank Ltd; Ntsebeza v Daimler Chrysler Corp*, ibid., Dissenting Opinion of Korman J.

complicity in international crimes. The issue appears unsettled at present, although the advantages to holding companies liable for facilitating the most heinous of crimes would seem to be appropriate.

Although corporations do not as yet possess significant international duties, the devastating Deepwater Horizon oil spill of 2010, which flowed for three months and caused untold damage to the Gulf of Mexico and the human economy dependent on it, is likely to strengthen the argument that corporations should be made more internationally accountable. Similarly, recent years have seen the rise of the privatized military industry, where states increasingly turn to a market of mercenaries supplied by private military companies.[170] Although little used since the Napoleonic Wars,[171] mercenaries are making a comeback, with potentially destabilizing consequences to regional and international public order.[172] The few, and often poorly ratified, international conventions prohibiting mercenary use define 'mercenaries' too narrowly to be of much practical use against modern private military firms.[173] Not being accountable under international law as legal persons means private military companies can potentially commit abuses without fear of being hurt other than via their hip pockets. A recent example is the fatal shooting of seventeen Iraqis by Blackwater (now Xe Services) operatives in 2007.[174] There is also a need to regulate the flipside to mercenary use: the protection of the interests of mercenaries themselves, as indicated by the beating, killing and subsequent public burning of four Blackwater employees in March 2004 by Fallujah insurgents.

Of course, if corporations undertake international law obligations, this may signal another shift in the state-centric conception of international law, in the sense that other subjects within the milieu of international law will play a role in the application and possibly the development of international human rights in practical and important global contexts.

---

[170] Peter Singer, 'Corporate Warriors: The Rise of the Private Military Industry and its Ramifications for International Security' (2001) 26(3) *International Security* 186; Deborah Avant, 'Mercenaries' (Jul/Aug 2004) Issue 143 *Foreign Policy*.

[171] Deborah Avant, 'From Mercenary to Citizen Armies: Explaining Change in the Practice of War' (2000) 54(1) *International Organization* 41.

[172] Anna Leander, 'The Market for Force and Public Security: The Destabilizing Consequences of Private Military Companies' (2005) 42(5) *Journal of Peace Research* 605.

[173] See Additional Protocol I; International Convention against the Recruitment, Use, Financing and Training of Mercenaries (1989), Art. 47; Sabelo Gumedze, 'Towards the Revision of the 1977 OAU/AU Convention on the Elimination of Mercenarism in Africa' (2007) 16(4) *African Security Review* 22.

[174] See, e.g., 'Testimony of Jeremy Scahill before the Senate Democratic Policy Committee' *The Nation*, 21 September 2007.

5.5 SOME OTHER NON-STATE ACTORS

Some significant 'others' in international law include insurgents, terrorists and national liberation movements.[175] These groups have challenged and continue to challenge the statist legal order of international law. Since liberation movements like the Palestinian Liberation Organization have gained prominence in the international community, participating in the United Nations and other international fora, complexities as to their ultimate status and effect on the international legal order have arisen, and persist. Terrorism after 11 September 2001 has changed the international political and legal landscape, spawning Security Council Resolutions, radical national legislative activity and war.[176] Even so, the international community has been unable to agree on a definition of what terrorism in international law might be.

There are also some atypical subjects of international law.[177] The Sovereign Order of Malta[178] is an entity that has controlled no territory since the British occupation of Malta, yet maintains diplomatic relations with over 93 states.[179] In confirming the continuing international personality of this mainly humanitarian entity, the Italian Court of Cassation stated: 'The modern theory of the subjects of international law recognizes a number of collective units whose composition is independent of the nationality of their constituent members and whose scope transcends by virtue of their universal character the territorial confines of any single State.'[180]

---

[175] See Cassese, above note 11, 94–5; Robert Fisher, 'Following in Another's Footsteps: The Acquisition of International Legal Standing by the Palestine Liberation Organization' (1975) 3 *Syracuse Journal of International Law & Commerce* 221, 228–32, 251–2; *Applicability of the Obligation to Arbitrate under Section 21 of the United Nations Headquarters Agreement of 26 June 1947* (Advisory Opinion) [1988] ICJ Rep 12; W. Michael Reisman, 'An International Farce: The Sad Case of the PLO Mission' (1989) 14 *Yale Journal of International Law* 412.

[176] See, e.g., Michael Bothe, 'Terrorism and the Legality of Pre-emptive Force' (2003) 14(2) *European Journal of International Law* 227; Miriam Sapiro, 'Iraq: The Shifting Sands of Pre-emptive Self-Defense' (2003) 97 *American Journal of International Law* 599.

[177] Walter, above note 89, 3.

[178] The Order's official title is the Sovereign Military Order of St John of Jerusalem, of Rhodes and of Malta.

[179] Harris, above note 57, 143.

[180] *Nanni v Pace and the Sovereign Order of Malta* (1935–37) 8 AD 2 (Italian Court of Cassation); see also Brownlie, above note 12, 64.

5.6 CONCLUSIONS

The explosion of non-state actors in international law has brought its own challenges to the international order. With the growth in influence of international organizations, corporations and non-governmental organizations, the international stage is becoming increasingly cluttered with voices seeking to make claims across state boundaries. These voices also have a tendency to rise in volume independently of any specific legitimation, as the 'mission creep' of many international organizations has indicated.[181] International courts and tribunals have often pronounced on the extremely broad potential for non-state actors to have a say on the international stage. There is even a sense that individual states are losing control of the momentum of change, given the expectations created by an increasingly pluralistic and connected world order. The recent Wikileaks scandal, where thousands of US diplomatic cables were leaked and posted on the internet without states having the capability to stem the tide, is a graphic illustration of the modern clash between the traditional state-centric system and the rise in importance of global civil society. The scandal is a sharp reminder that, while states still ultimately hold the keys to international law-making, they themselves need to evolve and adapt towards sharing the international system with other actors with different interests.

The participation of NGOs at the Copenhagen Climate Conference – to the extent of drafting a proposed convention on this cutting-edge area of international law – further indicates the insistent way in which non-state actors have sought to influence international power relations. To the extent that these global changes have redirected the focus on what was, until the second half of the twentieth century, considered the 'internal affairs of states', it has given international law unprecedented reach. M.L. Schweitz has argued:

> We need to find some intelligent way to deal with these challenges, to discover principles upon which to found claims of legitimacy or illegitimacy. . . . This is the story of humanity assuming responsibility for its own future, through increasingly representative forms of political organisation and through a fully engaged civil society. From the perspective of world order, it is about finding the proper level (local through supranational) at which to make different sorts of decisions, and who (among government, business and the so-called 'third

---

[181] David Malone (ed.), *The UN Security Council: From the Cold War to the 21st Century* (Boulder, CO: Lynne Reinner Publishers, 2004), 1–115; Jessica Einhorn, 'The World Bank's Mission Creep' (Sept/Oct 2001) *Foreign Affairs*.

> sector') should make them. It is the story of promoting the unity of humankind while at the same time cherishing its diversity.[182]

The more non-state actors, and especially individuals, gain rights and obligations under international law, the more the system resembles a domestic legal system. Indeed, international law already has criminal courts for the punishment of individuals and civil courts where companies and individuals can bring international claims. In the context of human rights, Hans Kelsen has identified an inherent paradox that may produce a destabilizing effect on the international order. The international human rights of individuals in a particular state depend on that state for their implementation and observance, yet if the state refuses to do so, current international enforcement measures are of a collective character, which may result in severe economic sanctions and war – measures which are themselves immensely destructive of human rights.[183] If, however, the international order develops a centralized legal authority with comprehensive mechanisms for enforcement within a state, without ultimate recourse to war, we have not 'the transformation of international law but the disappearance of this law through the replacement of the present system of states by a world state' – it would be 'indistinguishable from the structure and technique of municipal law'.[184] Whether or not the international order is in the process of developing into an integrated supranational empire, presumably with a world government such as a significantly enhanced and democratized UN, the trend is certainly towards increasing participation of non-state actors in international affairs and the governance challenges that this new reality brings.

---

182 M.L. Schweitz, 'NGO Participation in International Governance: The Question of Legitimacy' (1995) *American Society of International Law Proceedings* 413, 417.

183 Kelsen, above note 42, 241.

184 Ibid., 242.

6. Jurisdiction privileges and immunities

State sovereignty and equality are the foundational principles of international law and protect each state's jurisdictional powers from interference by other states.[1] To what extent, however, does international law recognize and protect the exercise of jurisdiction by states, and to what extent are limitations imposed on the power of states by virtue of their interaction and participation in the international system? It is a logical corollary of the nature of a system of sovereign equals that the legally recognized jurisdiction of one state cannot be superior to that of another. Hence, only in very particular circumstances may states exercise power within the territory of another state.[2] Further, state agents and senior government officials are generally considered to be personally immune from the exercise of jurisdiction by foreign powers, at least while acting in an official capacity. Failure to accord such immunities may amount to an internationally wrongful act.[3] The breadth and nature of the exercise of power by states through their domestic law and the limits imposed upon them by international law form the subject of this chapter.

The International Court of Justice in the *Arrest Warrant* case considered the ability of a Belgian judge to exercise criminal jurisdiction by issuing an international arrest warrant against the then Minister for Foreign Affairs of the Democratic Republic of the Congo (DRC) for alleged war crimes and crimes against humanity.[4] The acts in question did not occur in Belgium, nor was any Belgian national a victim. The DRC argued that Belgium had no jurisdiction to issue the warrant, as there was no connection between the alleged acts and that state, and that even if

---

[1] Ian Brownlie, *Principles of Public International Law* (Oxford: Oxford University Press, 2008, 7th edn), 289.

[2] Malcolm N. Shaw, *International Law* (Cambridge; New York: Cambridge University Press, 2008, 6th edn), 647.

[3] Gillian D. Triggs, *International Law: Contemporary Principles and Practices* (Sydney: LexisNexis Butterworths, 2011, 2nd edn), 469.

[4] *Arrest Warrant of 11 April 2000* (*Democratic Republic of the Congo v Belgium*) (Judgment) [2002] ICJ Rep 3.

there were jurisdiction Foreign Minister Yerodia was protected by diplomatic immunity. This case has become something of a modern symbol of the tension between the limits on jurisdiction designed to protect a sovereign state from external interference (what might be considered the 'old' international law) on the one hand, and the extent to which jurisdiction might extend across sovereign borders to punish heinous international crimes by state agents and officials (the 'new' international law) on the other.[5]

This chapter considers the traditionally accepted grounds for the exercise of jurisdiction by states, both internally and internationally. This requires consideration of the prescriptive and enforcement forms of jurisdiction asserted by states, and the grounds on which they are permitted in international law to exercise their authority. The territorial and nationality principles are undisputed as grounds for the exercise of power, while others are more contentious. Protective jurisdiction, relating to the state's right to impose jurisdiction where its security is threatened, is exercised particularly by Western countries, but is the subject of dispute. Passive personality, which purports to grant a state jurisdiction where its nationals are victims of acts outside of its territory, has been exercised (most notably by the US), but is also considered to be controversial. Universal jurisdiction especially has been challenged, partly owing to the authority it gives states to extend their jurisdiction far beyond control of their territory and nationals, and partly because there is much dispute and misunderstanding as to what falls within the meaning of this form of jurisdiction. The process usually associated with extradition and extraterritorial enforcement mechanisms are also addressed.

The classical exceptions to those rules in the form of immunities from jurisdiction will then be considered. While it may seem obvious that immunities can only be understood by reference to the jurisdictional power of states, because they are immune from the exercise of jurisdiction, this goes precisely to one of the criticisms of the International Court of Justice in the *Arrest Warrant* case. This area of law remains unsettled with regard to the acceptance of a test for determining the nature of acts as acts *jure imperii* (acts done in a public capacity) which attract immunity both for states and their officials, and acts *jure gestionis* (acts done in a private or commercial capacity) which do not attract immunity. These issues will be considered in light of contemporary practice and possible future development.

---

[5] Triggs, above note 3, 467.

6.1 TYPES OF JURISDICTION: PRESCRIPTION AND ENFORCEMENT

There are two key aspects of state jurisdiction: jurisdiction to prescribe and jurisdiction to enforce. It is also possible to talk of a subsidiary form of prescriptive jurisdiction, being the jurisdiction to adjudicate, although in truth adjudication does not form – and is not usefully spoken of – as a distinct head of jurisdiction. Prescriptive and enforcement jurisdiction reflect the legislative, judicial and executive branches of government.

6.1.1 Prescriptive Jurisdiction

Prescriptive, or legislative, jurisdiction describes the competence of states to create norms, recognized as valid by international law. This power is binding within a state's territory and, under certain circumstances, beyond. National law may cover any subject matter, but in certain areas a state has exclusive jurisdiction that may not be interfered with by other states. A state may not attempt to alter the legislative, judicial or administrative framework of a foreign state by so legislating.[6] While this would be ineffective, as the legislating state would have no way to enforce its 'reforms', the mere act of legislating would amount to an interference with the subject state's sovereignty.[7]

This principle extends to other sovereign prerogatives, being those rights available only to the state and not private individuals, such as the levying of taxes. These powers are validly recognized by international law when exercised in relation to local and foreign nationals, where there is a 'real link' to the territorial state. This link could be the nationality or state of domicile of the taxpayer, or the location or subject of the transaction. However, in other contexts, what suffices to establish this connection may differ.[8] For example, the mere presence of tourists within the state's territory for a few days might represent a sufficient connection to support a requirement to register with police, but not to allow them to be conscripted

---

[6] *The Island of Palmas* case (*or Miangas*) (*United States of America v Netherlands*) (1928) 2 RIAA 829 (hereafter '*Island of Palmas* case'); *Imperial Tobacco Co. of India v Commissioner of Income Tax* (1958) 27 ILR 103 (hereafter '*Imperial Tobacco* case').

[7] Michael Akehurst, 'Jurisdiction in International Law' (1972–3) 46 *British Yearbook of International Law* 145, 179.

[8] F.A. Mann, 'Jurisdiction in International Law' (1964) 111 *Hague Recueil des Cours*, 109.

for military service.[9] Equally, an Indian company, domiciled in India may not be taxed by Pakistan for profits from transactions occurring in India, as there is no connection with the prescribing state.[10] Further, states may legislate to nationalize property within their territory or held by nationals abroad. In the latter case enforcement will depend on the willingness of the foreign court to enforce the prescribing state's law, but this does not alter that state's prescriptive jurisdictional competence.[11]

Legislation may provide for criminal sanctions to be imposed on people with a sufficient connection with the legislating state. This requires the exercise of the jurisdiction to adjudicate to determine guilt, and enforcement jurisdiction to impose the penalty. The prescriptive jurisdiction, in this case, is used to define the offence, penalty, procedure for trial, and so on. While exercised most frequently within the state's territory, it can also be used to bind a state with regard to acts committed abroad.[12] Foreign nationals, outside the jurisdiction, who commit acts damaging to the regulating state, may also be subjected to this jurisdiction under the protective principle.[13]

6.1.2 Enforcement Jurisdiction

Enforcement, or executive, jurisdiction describes a state's authority to act coercively to enforce its law.[14] This form of jurisdiction may be freely exercised only on the territory of the enforcing state because of its coercive nature. Employment of enforcement jurisdiction on the territory of another state without consent or under some other 'permissive rule' of international law is prohibited as interference in the sovereignty of another state.[15]

A classic example of this is the abduction by Israeli agents of Adolf Eichmann from Argentina in 1960. While this clearly overreached Israel's enforcement jurisdiction, being undertaken in secret and without Argentina's consent, the Supreme Court of Israel ruled that the invalidity

---

9 Ibid.; *Polites v Cth* [1945] 70 CLR 60, 208.

10 *Imperial Tobacco* case, above note 6.

11 Akehurst, above note 7, 251–2.

12 See, e.g., the Australian Criminal Code (Cth), Division 272, Subdivision B, which prohibits certain sexual offences committed by Australian citizens or residents in other states.

13 See below, section 6.3.3.

14 Akehurst, above note 7, 147.

15 *SS 'Lotus' (France v Turkey)* (1927) PCIJ (Ser. A) No.10, 18 (hereafter 'the *Lotus* case').

of the arrest under international law did not vitiate its jurisdiction to try him under Israeli law[16] (a position consistently maintained in contemporary national and international law).[17] However, the UN Security Council considered the interference with Argentinian sovereignty a danger to international peace and security, and ordered Israel to pay reparations.[18] The prohibition on such interference with the 'domestic jurisdiction by any state' is implicit in the principle of the sovereign equality of states and is reflected in Article 2(7) of the Charter of the United Nations.

6.2 CIVIL AND CRIMINAL JURISDICTION

The question of whether international law treats civil as opposed to criminal jurisdiction differently, in cases involving an international element, is a matter of dispute.[19] It is clear that diplomatic protest is more frequently raised with regard to the excessive exercise of criminal jurisdiction.[20] Civil jurisdiction, on the other hand, is frequently exercised in cases that have limited connection with the forum state, and only limited diplomatic objections are raised. Indeed, where objection is taken, it almost always relates not to the exercise of jurisdiction but to some ancillary issue. If the absence of protest is taken to reflect the permissive nature of international law in the area, then significant limitations on the exercise of civil jurisdiction are not apparent.[21] Yet state practice also discloses a number of limitations based on the practicalities of enforcing judgments against people and property outside the jurisdiction.

Common law courts premise civil jurisdiction on the proper service of legal process, which necessitates either the defendant's presence in the territory of the forum, or the defendant's voluntary submission to the court's jurisdiction.[22] The duration of stay in the territory is not relevant, so long as service is affected within that period.[23] While courts may stay proceedings where their continuation would be unjust, the fact that a defendant

---

16 *A-G of the Govt. of Israel v Adolf Eichmann* (1961) 36 ILR 5 (hereafter 'the *Eichmann* case').

17 See discussion below in section 6.3.5.4.

18 SC Res. 138, UN SCOR, 15th sess., 868th mtg, UN Doc. S/4349.

19 Akehurst, above note 7, 170.

20 *LaGrand* (*Germany v United States of America*) [2001] ICJ 466.

21 But see Brownlie, above note 1, 300.

22 See, e.g., Rules of the High Court (Hong Kong), Cap 4A, s. 10; Supreme Court (General Civil Procedure) Rules 2005 (Vic), Orders 6 and 7; Federal Rules of Civil Procedure 2010 (USA) rl 4.

23 Akehurst, above note 7, 171.

is a foreign national only temporarily within the jurisdiction is not per se a source of injustice.[24] In the United States, this has been extended to include use of the notion of 'transaction of business' within the forum territory, such that a person sending a letter through the jurisdiction, flying over it, or having previously held a meeting in it, may be subject to a US court's jurisdiction.[25]

In contrast, courts in civil law systems often base their jurisdiction on the place of habitual domicile of the defendant. Other states base jurisdiction on the defendant's ownership of property located within the territory, with some (such as the Netherlands and South Africa) limiting jurisdiction to the value of those assets.[26] In spite of these differences, diplomatic protest is rarely raised at the exercise of civil jurisdiction against foreign nationals, even when the link to the forum jurisdiction is tenuous. This is in contrast to the strong reaction to the exercise of criminal jurisdiction in the same context, and the attendant infrequency and caution with which it is exercised.[27]

Criminal, like civil, jurisdiction is primarily based on territory. It may be exercised over foreign nationals who are within the forum territory with regard to acts committed there. Nationals of the forum state may be subject to adjudicatory jurisdiction while within the territory for acts done, both at home and abroad.[28] However, unilateral enforcement may only be conducted when the offender returns home. Any exercise of official jurisdiction on the territory of another sovereign state, without its consent, amounts to interference with that state's sovereignty and is prohibited by international law.[29] Exercising enforcement and adjudication jurisdiction over foreign nationals for acts committed abroad is permitted only

---

24 *Baroda (Maharaneee of) v Wildenstein* [1972] 2 QB 283.

25 Foreign Sovereign Immunities Act, 28 USC §§ 1330, 1332(a)(2)–(4), 1391(f), 1441(d), 1602–1611; *Louis Marx & Co Inc v Fuji Seiko Co. Ltd*, 453 F Supp 385 (SDNY 1978); *Unidex Systems Corp. v Butz Engineering Corp.*, 406 F Supp 899 (DDC 1976).

26 Akehurst, above note 7, 171; David F. Cavers, 'Contemporary Conflicts Law in American Perspective' (1970) 131 *The Hague Recueil des Courses* 75, 295.

27 Akehurst, above note 7, 170; Brownlie, above note 1, 300–301; But see *LaGrand*, above note 20.

28 See, e.g., Commonwealth Criminal Code 1995 (Cth), ss 273.5 and 273.6 for child pornography offences committed outside Australia; Sexual Offences Act 2003 (UK), s. 72; *Strafgesetzbuch* ('*StGB*') [Penal Code] (Germany), § 5.

29 Declaration on Principles of International Law Friendly Relations and Co-Operation among States in Accordance with the Charter of the United Nations, GA Res. 2625(XXV), UN GAOR, 25th sess., 1883rd plen. mtg, Agenda Item 85, UN Doc. A/RES/2625(XXV) (24 October 1970); *Lotus* case, above note 15.

in certain limited circumstances, as will be seen in the following section. The variety of such limitations demonstrates that even if in principle, as Brownlie argues, there is 'no great difference between the problems presented by the assertion of civil and criminal jurisdiction over aliens'[30] or anyone else for that matter, in practice the consequences are very different and the circumstances in which criminal jurisdiction may be exercised are severely limited in comparison to civil jurisdiction.

6.3 BASES OF JURISDICTION

The sovereign equality of states presumes a more or less plenary power within the confines of state borders. As such, jurisdiction has traditionally been founded on territory. However, several issues have arisen in international law rendering the exercise of jurisdiction across borders increasingly complex. This can in part be explained by the increase in international exchange and organization, the growing instance of transnational crime (notably terrorism, people and drug trafficking, as well as war) and the development of responsibility relating to certain international crimes (such as crimes against humanity and genocide), necessitating cross-border regulation and truly international enforcement mechanisms.

The development of international human rights, international criminal law and, to an ever growing extent, international environmental law has led to some states taking a bolder view of the extension of jurisdiction across state boundaries. In this way, states have been increasingly willing to exercise jurisdiction on the grounds of nationality, national protection, passive personality and, in some cases, universal jurisdiction.[31] Some of these developments are highly controversial, giving rise to reactions and counter-reactions in international law that make traditional conceptions of jurisdiction more tenuous. The progressive Separate Opinions of Judges Higgins, Buergenthal and Kooijmans in the *Arrest Warrant* case before the International Court of Justice capture this sentiment of a developing law of jurisdiction:

> The contemporary trends, reflecting international relations as they stand at the beginning of the new century, are striking. The movement is towards bases of jurisdiction other than territoriality. 'Effects' or 'impact' jurisdiction

---

[30] Brownlie, above note 1, 302; see also F.A. Mann, *Doctrine of Jurisdiction in International Law* (Leiden: A.W. Sijthoff, 1964), 49–51; Bartin, *Principes de droit international privé* (Paris: Editions Domat-Montchrestien, 1930), Vol. I, 113.

[31] *Arrest Warrant* case, above note 4.

> is embraced both by the United States and, with certain qualifications, by the European Union. Passive personality jurisdiction, for so long regarded as controversial, is now reflected not only in the legislation of various countries (the United States; France), and today meets with relatively little opposition, at least so far as a particular category of offences is concerned.[32]

There are generally considered to be five bases for the exercise of state jurisdiction in international law: territorial principle, nationality principle, protective principle, passive personality principle and the universality principle. These jurisdictional principles were considered in the impressive work of the Harvard Research into jurisdiction with respect to crime in 1935,[33] and are still considered to be influential despite obvious developments in the content and expression of them in state practice since.[34]

6.3.1 Territorial Principle

The principle that the domestic courts of the state in which a crime is committed have jurisdiction over that crime is universally accepted, even where the accused may be a foreign national.[35] This reflects the exclusivity of sovereignty within the state's territorial limits (land, sea and air), and its responsibility for maintaining order. As such, there is a clear presumption in favour of the jurisdiction of the territorial state,[36] which also reflects the fact that in the great majority of cases the territorial state is the most convenient forum, given that the accused, witnesses, evidence and victims will almost always be located there.[37]

There are two possible applications of territorial jurisdiction, referred to as 'subjective' and 'objective'. The 'subjective' application of territorial

---

[32] Ibid. (Judges Higgins, Buergenthal and Kooijmans) [47].

[33] See Edwin D. Dickinson, 'Introductory Comment to the Harvard Convention Research Draft Convention on Jurisdiction with respect to Crime' (1935) 29 *American Journal of International Law Sup.* 443.

[34] See, e.g., Mitsue Inazumi, *Universal Jurisdiction in Modern International Law: Expansion of National Jurisdiction for Prosecuting Serious Crimes under International Law* (Antwerp: Intersentia, 2005); D.J. Harris, *Cases and Materials on International Law* (London: Sweet & Maxwell, 2004, 6th edn), 265ff.

[35] *Holmes v Bangladesh Binani Corporation* [1989] 1 AC 1112, 1137; *R v Bow Street Metropolitan Stipendiary Magistrate, ex parte Pinochet Ugarte (No. 3)* [2000] 1 AC 147, 188.

[36] *R v West Yorkshire Coroner, ex parte Smith* [1983] QB 335, 358. See also *Bankovic v Belgium et al.* 41 ILM 517, [59] – a reductive human rights ruling in which the European Court of Human Rights characterizes state jurisdiction as 'primarily territorial'.

[37] *Arrest Warrant* case, above note 4, Guillaume J, [4].

jurisdiction grants jurisdiction, where a crime is commenced within the territorial state but completed in another, to the state in which the conduct was initiated. For example, crimes like drug trafficking frequently occur across national frontiers, and many preparatory acts (such as conspiracy) may be carried out in one state before the principal offence (sale or supply) is committed in another state. Under this principle, the first state has jurisdiction notwithstanding the fact that the offence is completed or consummated abroad. Of course, the second state would also be able to validly prosecute, and which state ultimately does so will (usually) depend on the location of the defendant. While there is no obligation in such a scenario for the first state to exercise its jurisdiction (at least in customary international law), where the exercise of such jurisdiction by it is necessary to combat transnational or international crime, a number of treaties (and possibly customary international law) might give rise to an obligation on its part to either prosecute, or to extradite the accused to another state to do so.[38]

The 'objective' application of territorial sovereignty refers to the exercise of jurisdiction by a state where the effects of a crime are felt, even though the crime (or at least its initiation or substantial elements of it) is committed outside its territory. For example, a fraudulent letter posted by the defendant in England, to the victim in Germany, may be tried in Germany.[39] This application of territorial sovereignty was considered by the Permanent Court of International Justice in the landmark *Lotus* case.[40] In that case, a French steamer (the *SS Lotus*) collided with a Turkish collier (the *Boz-Kourt*), sinking and killing eight people. When the *Lotus* reached port, in Turkey, the French officer of the watch was arrested and charged with manslaughter. France protested that Turkey had no jurisdiction to try its national in this way. The majority judgment considered that it was axiomatic to an international system of independent states that 'failing the existence of some permissive rule to the contrary [a state]

---

[38] See, e.g., Convention for the Suppression of Counterfeited Currency and Protocol (adopted 20 April 1929, entered into force 22 February 1931) 112 LNTS 371; Convention for Suppression of the Illicit Traffic in Dangerous Drugs (adopted 26 June 1936, entered into force 10 October 1947) 198 LNTS 301. A range of multilateral anti-terrorism treaties also contain such obligations as between states parties, e.g., International Convention for the Suppression of Terrorist Bombings (adopted 15 December 1997, entered into force 23 May 2001) A/RES/52/164; International Convention for the Suppression of Acts of Nuclear Terrorism (adopted 13 April 2005, not yet entered into force) A/RES/59/766.

[39] *Board of Trade v Owen* [1957] 602, 634 (CA); *R v Cox* [1968] 1 ER 410, 414; *DPP v Doot* [1973] AC 807.

[40] The *Lotus* case, above note 15.

may not exercise its power in any form in the territory of another state'.[41] The court considered, however, that it did not follow that 'international law prevents a state from exercising jurisdiction in its own territory, in respect of any case which relates to acts which have taken place abroad, and in which it cannot rely on some permissive rule of international law'.[42]

Having once stated this principle, however, the majority went on to determine that the offence took place on board a Turkish ship which, for the purposes of determining jurisdiction, was to be considered Turkish territory.[43] Turkey did have jurisdiction to try the French officer of the watch once he was in Turkey, on the basis of the objective territoriality principle. The crime originated in France, or rather on board the French vessel, but because a 'constituent element [of the crime], and more especially its effects' occurred on the Turkish collier, which amounted to Turkish territory, the crime was 'nevertheless to be regarded as having been committed in the national territory' of the forum state.[44] This statement of the law has been criticized as permitting too broad an exercise of jurisdiction. Some states 'stretch' this doctrine by means of the legal fiction of the continuing offence, to permit prosecution – for example, for theft when a thief, having stolen goods in one state, crosses a border while still in possession of the stolen goods, a constituent element of the crime supposedly continuing while the goods are in his or her possession.[45] Other states prosecute where effects only are felt in that state. Akehurst argues that as state practice is so inconsistent in the application of the constituent element rule, the effects doctrine must be preferred, but is in itself too broad. He proposes limiting it to only effects felt 'directly' or most 'substantially' by the state seeking to exercise jurisdiction.[46] This, he suggests, is the only rule compatible with decided cases, and prevents excessive claims of jurisdiction.

Since the *Lotus* case, the subjective and objective territoriality principles have permitted states to exercise jurisdiction over people, property and events, where a constituent element of the cause of action occurs within their territory or the direct or substantial effects of the events are felt there. Where there may be competing claims by states over jurisdiction, regard will be had to the degree of connection a state has in relation to

---

41 Ibid., 18.
42 Ibid., 19.
43 Ibid., 23.
44 Ibid.
45 *R v von Elling* [1945] AD 234; for stowaways see *Robey v Vladinier* (1936) 154 LT 87; for procuring see *R v Mackenzie and Higginson* (1911) 6 Cr. App. Rep. 64.
46 *Akehurst*, above note 7, 154.

the matter,[47] although it seems obvious that the exercise of enforcement jurisdiction will depend largely on having custody of the accused.[48]

With the exception of the territorial principle, all other bases of jurisdiction are extraterritorial in that they permit states to legislate with respect to persons, property and events occurring outside of their territory. This is true even where they must wait for the presence of the defendant within their territory to exercise enforcement jurisdiction. While the nationality principle in this context is relatively uncontroversial, contention can arise in determining nationality, especially with regard to corporations and subsidiary companies. The United States has exercised enforcement jurisdiction over banks based in the US and their subsidiaries abroad, requiring them to freeze all Iranian assets in dollar-denominated accounts.[49] Similar instances of extraterritorial enforcement are justified on the basis of the 'effects doctrine'.

6.3.1.1 The effects doctrine

US courts consider that when foreign activity causes effects that are felt in the US and are in breach of US law, they are competent to make orders including those for the disposition of property, restructuring of industry and production of documents, subject to another state's exclusive sovereign jurisdiction. Judgments of this nature may be executed against property held by the foreign entity in the US.[50] The UK has objected to the exercise of this jurisdiction on the ground that the only positive principle of jurisdiction recognized in international law is the territorial principle, with all other jurisdictional bases being exceptions to it, and as there is no rule permitting the exercise of enforcement jurisdiction in this way, it is illegal. However, the European Community exercises extraterritorial jurisdiction in a similar fashion with regard to anti-competitive practices. Article 101 of the Consolidated Version of the Treaty on the Functioning of the European Union[51] permits the European Court of Justice to exercise jurisdiction over overseas corporations for cartel behaviour, even where these corporations have never traded within the European Community,

---

[47] Ibid.

[48] See Harris, above note 34, 266.

[49] 44 Fed Reg 65, 956, 1979.

[50] *US v Aluminum Co. of America*, 148 F 2d 416 (1945); *US v Watchmakers of Switzerland Information Centre Inc.*, 133 F. Supp. 40 (1955); 134 F. Supp. 710 (1955).

[51] European Union, Consolidated Version of the Treaty on the Functioning of the European Union (adopted 13 December 2007, entered into force 1 December 2009) 2008/C 115/01.

so long as the effect of the cartel activity was intended to be felt and was actually felt within the European Community.[52]

The US has tempered its expansive approach, partly in response to the wave of diplomatic protest and 'blocking legislation' generated in response to the *Westinghouse* case,[53] in which a US court ordered discovery of documents located in a number of overseas jurisdictions. The subsidence of the UK objections in the face of the European position appears to indicate that the effects doctrine has gained acceptance at least in these jurisdictions. As such, states may be considered to have the extraterritorial jurisdiction necessary to enforce their valid legislative jurisdiction, which seems to depend on a substantial or effective connection, keeping the effects doctrine alive in substance, if not in name.[54]

6.3.2 Nationality Principle

The nationality principle allows states to exercise jurisdiction over their nationals for acts done within or outside the state's territory. This principle stems from the recognition that sovereign states may legitimately impose obligations on their subjects.

Nationality is, in international law, the legal link between a state and its people. The rights and obligations of nationals vis-à-vis their states include such things as the right to a passport and the obligation to perform military service and pay taxes. The authority to provide and oblige these things to and of nationals is an exercise of state jurisdiction based solely on the person's nationality. This authority extends to the civil and criminal jurisdiction of the state's courts.

It is for states to make their own laws regarding nationality.[55] However, the recognition of those laws in international law depends on whether they are 'consistent with international conventions, international custom and the principles of law generally recognized with regard to nationality'.[56] The International Court of Justice has held that nationality is 'a legal bond

---

[52] *Ahlström Oy and Others v Commission of the European Communities* (*Wood Pulp*) [1988] ECR 5193.

[53] *Re Uranium Antitrust Litigation*, 480 F Supp 1138, 1148 (9th Cir, 1979); *Re Uranium Antitrust Litigation*, [1980] USCA7 143; 617 F 2d 1248, 1255 (7th Cir, 1980).

[54] Brownlie, above note 1, 311.

[55] *Nationality Decrees in Tunis and Morocco* (1923) PCIJ (Ser. B) No. 4; 2 AD 349.

[56] Hague Convention on the Conflict of Nationality Laws (adopted 12 April 1930, entered into force 1 July 1937) 179 LNTS 89, Art. 1.

having as its basis a social fact of attachment, a genuine connection of existence, interests and sentiments, together with the existence of reciprocal rights and duties'.[57] Without such a genuine connection, international law will not recognize the grant of nationality.

Corporations have the nationality of the state of registration or incorporation, or that of their main place of business. Daughter companies do not automatically have any connection via nationality with their parents. Ships and aircraft carry the nationality of the state of registration, but here too there must be a genuine connection with the state of registration. Variation exists in the law ascribing nationality to children born on board ships and aircraft depending on their location and state of registration, as for nationality laws generally.

States with civil law traditions are more likely than common law states to exercise jurisdiction based on nationality, although states across all legal traditions practise this form of jurisdiction.[58] Jurisdiction with respect to civil and especially family law matters often depends solely on the nationality of the parties. In common law states, this jurisdiction is generally only exercised with regard to very serious criminal offences, or where the territorial principle is not appropriate.[59] In some cases this has led to the creation of obscure offences, such as leaving the state with intent to commit a crime, in order to prevent nationals travelling to another jurisdiction to commit proscribed conduct (such as duelling) where it is not prohibited.[60]

6.3.3 Protective Principle

States frequently prosecute foreign nationals under the protective principle for acts done abroad, the effects of which are prejudicial to the forum state. While this often encompasses political acts, it also extends to acts compromising the state's economic, immigration, currency and national security interests.

---

[57] *Nottebohm* case (*Lichtenstein v Guatemala*) [1955] ICJ Rep 4, 23.

[58] See Dickinson, above note 33, 519.

[59] See, e.g., Australian Criminal Code (Cth), Division 272, Subdivision B, which prohibits certain sexual offences committed by Australian citizens or residents in other states; similarly, Antarctica Act 1994 (UK), s. 21 (offences by British nationals in Antarctica), and offences under the Official Secrets Act 1989 (UK), s. 15.

[60] Donnedieu de Vabres, *Les principes modernes du droit penal international* (Paris: Sirey, 1928) 391; Akehurst, above note 7, 157.

In *Liangsiriprasert v Government of the United States of America*,[61] the House of Lords considered an appeal against an extradition order against a Thai national from Hong Kong to the US. Liangsiriprasert was found to have conspired to import heroin into the US from Thailand, but as the US had no extradition agreement covering drug trafficking, US and Thai authorities tricked Liangsiriprasert into going to Hong Kong, where he thought he would collect payment for the shipment, but was instead arrested. On appeal the question was whether a court in Hong Kong had jurisdiction to try a conspiracy entered into in Thailand to import drugs into Hong Kong, whether or not any overt acts had been done in Hong Kong. This was necessary for the extradition order, under the principle of double criminality.[62] The court held that an inchoate crime, such as conspiracy, which is intended to have an effect in Hong Kong, would be triable in Hong Kong even if no overt element of the plan was carried out in Hong Kong.[63] This decision reflects the protective principle in allowing states to exercise jurisdiction over acts done outside their territory having, or even intending to have, a prejudicial impact within that state.

In *Nusselein v Belgium*[64] a Dutch soldier was convicted of aiding the enemy on the basis of acts done both inside and outside Belgium. The Belgian Court of Cassation held that it had jurisdiction over the soldier irrespective of where the events occurred, as they constituted 'crimes against the external safety of the state'.[65] Similarly in *Joyce v DPP*,[66] a foreign national who left England fraudulently using an English passport and subsequently broadcasted propaganda for the enemy in wartime, was found guilty by the House of Lords of treason. It was held that as he travelled on a British passport he owed allegiance to the Crown. Hence, even though Joyce committed the acts in another state and was not in fact a British national, the prejudice to British interests was sufficient to ground jurisdiction under this principle.[67]

6.3.4 Passive Personality Principle

The controversial passive personality principle has been accepted by different states at different times. The principle allows states to exercise their

---

61 [1991] 1 AC 225.
62 See the discussion on extradition at section 6.4 below.
63 *Liangsiriprasert* case, above note 61, 251.
64 (1950) 17 ILR 136.
65 Ibid.
66 [1946] AC 347.
67 Ibid.

jurisdiction over foreign nationals for actions done outside their territory, but which affect the forum state's nationals. The case of *Cutting* is often cited to illustrate the principle. The case concerned an American who published material defaming a Mexican in Texas. Cutting was later arrested while in Mexico and charged on the basis that defamation was criminal in Mexico at the time, the prosecution seeking to exercise jurisdiction based on the passive personality principle.[68] The controversial nature of the principle is evident in the fact that Cutting did an act which was not criminal in the jurisdiction in which the act was done. Nevertheless, he was subject to the criminal jurisdiction of another state by reason only of the nationality of the victim. The principle was also one of several jurisdictional bases evoked to justify prosecution of a terrorist by a US court.[69]

The passive personality principle was, as far back as 1935, considered so controversial, and its practice so incomplete, that it was left out of the Harvard Draft Convention.[70] Nonetheless, it is and has been applied and is broadly accepted as a form of jurisdiction in international law, having been applied in a recent case before the International Court of Justice.[71]

6.3.5 Universal Jurisdiction

Universal jurisdiction is a broad concept that is often used without specificity as to what precisely is meant. The term has been employed to describe the right of – and often obligation upon – states to prosecute or extradite in respect of certain categories of crime (*aut dedere aut judicare*).[72] This form of universal jurisdiction, if that is what it is, is referred to by President Guillaume in the *Arrest Warrant* case as a 'subsidiary' form.[73] It tends to arise out of treaty obligation, rather than recognition that there is a rule of customary international law obliging the exercise of jurisdiction by states. 'Voluntary' universal jurisdiction refers to the true form, whereby a state with no territorial, nationality or other connection with a crime may

---

[68] J.B. Moore, *Digest of International Law* (Washington, DC: GPO, 1906), Vol. II, 228.

[69] *Yunis*, 924 F 2d 1086, 1090–3 (CADC, 1991).

[70] See Dickinson, above note 33, 579. The Harvard Draft Convention was an important early work undertaken by scholars to explain and rationalize the forms of jurisdiction relating to crimes in international law.

[71] See *Arrest Warrant* case, above note 4, [47] (Judges Higgins, Kooijmans and Buergenthal), [44] and [16] (President Guillaume).

[72] See above, section 6.3.

[73] *Arrest Warrant* case, above note 4, [7] (President Guillaume).

nonetheless assert jurisdiction over that crime and those responsible.[74] The question over whether a state in such circumstances is obliged to do so is far less clear. Although such jurisdiction is said to arise out of the nature of the criminality as offending the 'laws of humanity', state practice certainly does not support the view that international law obliges states to exercise such jurisdiction.

Crimes attracting universal jurisdiction are those considered to be offensive to the international community as a whole, and are generally described as offending humanity itself or the laws of nations. The crimes generally referred to as giving rise to universal jurisdiction include piracy, genocide, crimes against humanity and war crimes, torture and slavery. Neither customary nor conventional international law providing for universal jurisdiction permits interference in another state's sovereignty in apprehending an accused. This fact demonstrates the limits of universal jurisdiction; while jurisdiction may be prescribed, enforcement may be very much another matter. The different forms of universal jurisdiction will now be examined, as will some practical implications of its application (the illegal apprehension of suspects and its consequences and the United States under the Alien Tort Claims Act of 1789).[75]

6.3.5.1 Crimes at customary international law

It is often said that customary international law empowers states to try individuals accused of certain crimes that are considered particularly opprobrious by the international community. The crime of piracy on the high seas was the first of such crimes, and is seen as the classical example.[76] Piracy itself includes illegal acts of violence, detention or depredation committed for private ends by the crew or passengers of a private ship or private aircraft and directed against another ship or aircraft (or persons or property therein) on the high seas of *terra nullius*.[77]

---

[74] Ibid., [51] (Judges Higgins, Kooijmans and Buergenthal). See distinction between subsidiary and voluntary universal jurisdiction in Harris, above note 34, 303.

[75] See generally the 'Princeton Principles on Universal Jurisdiction', Program in Law and Public Affairs, Princeton University (2001), available at http://lapa.princeton.edu/hosteddocs/unive_jur.pdf.

[76] *In re Piracy Iure Gentium* [1934] AC 586; see President Guillaume's reference in the *Arrest Warrant* case, above note 4, [4]; see also M. Cherif Bassiouni, 'Universal Jurisdiction for International Crimes: Historical Perspectives and Contemporary Practice' (2001) 42 *Virginia Journal of International Law* 1.

[77] United Nations Convention on the Law of the Sea (adopted 10 December 1982, entered into force 16 November 1994) 1833 UNTS 397 (hereinafter UNCLOS), Art. 101.

Interestingly, the Genocide Convention of 1948 (the substantive content of which has been applied in the statutes of all the relevant international criminal tribunals and many states' domestic legislation) did not prescribe universal jurisdiction for this crime.[78] Although the UN Secretary-General's preliminary draft Article VII provided for a primary obligatory universal jurisdiction, states' suspicion of the courts of other jurisdictions led to its omission.[79] The prohibition against genocide is now widely considered a *jus cogens* norm. Judge Elihu Lauterpacht has stated that 'genocide has long been regarded as one of the few undoubted examples of *jus cogens*'.[80] Such norms sit at the top of the hierarchy of international law sources and cannot therefore be derogated from by states, either by international agreement or national legislative action.[81] All crimes prohibited under *jus cogens* norms have been said to entail universal jurisdiction; courts and international law scholars have overwhelmingly accepted this position both as a general proposition, and particularly in respect of genocide.[82] The prohibition of genocide also constitutes an obligation *erga omnes* binding on all states in their dealings with the international community, whether with other states or with individuals.[83]

It is less clear whether crimes against humanity qualify for similar treatment. On one hand, there is considerable scholarly argument – and some jurisprudence of the post-Second World War tribunals, domestic courts, and the ad hoc Tribunals – supporting the view that crimes against human-

---

[78] Convention on the Prevention and Punishment of the Crime of Genocide (adopted 9 December 1948, entered into force 12 January 1951) 78 UNTS 277, Art. VI.

[79] For a discussion of this process, see Inazumi, above note 34, 59–60.

[80] *Application of the Convention on the Prevention and Punishment of the Crime of Genocide* (*Bosnia and Herzegovina v Yugoslavia*) [1993] ICJ Rep 325, 440 (Separate Opinion of Judge ad hoc Elihu Lauterpacht).

[81] See Michael Akehurst, 'The Hierarchy of the Sources of International Law' (1974–75) 47 *British Yearbook of International Law* 273; Shaw, above note 2, 123–8.

[82] See, e.g., M. Cherif Bassiouni, 'International Crimes: *Jus Cogens* and *Obligatio Erga Omnes*' (1996) 59 *Law and Contemporary Problems* 63. See also *Application of the Convention on the Prevention and Punishment of the Crime of Genocide* (*Bosnia-Herzegovina v Yugoslavia*) (Preliminary Objections) [1996] ICJ Rep 565, [31] (hereafter '*Bosnia v Yugoslavia* Preliminary Objections Judgment').

[83] *Reservations to the Convention on the Prevention and Punishment of the Crime of Genocide* (Advisory Opinion) ('*Reservations* Opinion') [1951] ICJ Rep 15, 23. See also *Bosnia v Yugoslavia* Preliminary Objections Judgment, above note 82, [31]; *Barcelona Traction, Light and Power Co. Ltd* (*Belgium v Spain*) [1970] ICJ Rep 3, [33]–[34].

ity violate *jus cogens* norms and give rise to universal jurisdiction.[84] On the other hand, the International Court of Justice in the *Arrest Warrant* case suggested (rather unconvincingly) that, while crimes against humanity are no doubt prohibited under customary international law, the notion that they violate *jus cogens* norms and give rise to universal jurisdiction may at this stage be more aspirational.[85] The preponderance of scholarly and preferable juridical writings suggests that crimes against humanity may give rise to universal jurisdiction; indeed, if the justification for application of this jurisdictional principle is that certain crimes contravene some notion of the laws of humanity it is difficult to see how crimes against humanity fail to reach this threshold.

One category of war crimes (grave breaches of the Geneva Convention) certainly gives rise to universal jurisdiction, at least the expression of this form of jurisdiction in terms of the so-called *aut dedere aut judicare* obligation.[86] Despite reductive arguments about the jurisdictional scope of the Geneva Conventions,[87] the preferable view is that the Conventions create an obligation on each state (and these Conventions are now universally ratified) to search for and try suspects in their own courts for alleged breaches of the grave breaches regime.[88]

Torture is another crime giving rise to such an expression of universal jurisdiction. In *Ex parte Pinochet (No. 3)*, torture was referred to by several judges as a crime giving rise to universal jurisdiction, general state

---

[84] See, e.g., Larry May, *Crimes against Humanity: A Normative Account* (Cambridge; New York: Cambridge University Press, 2005), 24–39; M. Cherif Bassiouni, *Crimes Against Humanity in International Criminal Law* (1998, 2nd edn), 210–17, 227–42; Tristan Gilbertson, 'War Crimes' (1995) 25 *Victoria University Wellington Law Review* 315, 327–8.

[85] See *Arrest Warrant* case, above note 4, [71] and [42]–[51] Joint Separate Opinion of Judges Higgins, Kooijmans and Buergenthal (carefully considered analysis of whether universal jurisdiction attaches to crimes against humanity). See also Robert Jennings and Arthur Watts, *Oppenheim's International Law* (London: Longman, 1996, 9th edn), 998 (noting that 'there are clear indications pointing to the gradual evolution' of the principle that crimes against humanity give rise to universal jurisdiction). According to the ICJ, at least, this point has not yet been reached.

[86] Grave breaches of the Geneva Conventions include a range of serious crimes committed in an international armed conflict. For a detailed discussion, see Gideon Boas, James L. Bischoff and Natalie L. Reid, *Elements of Crimes in International Criminal Law* (Cambridge: Cambridge University Press, 2008), Chapter 4.

[87] See, e.g., D.W. Bowett, 'Jurisdiction: Changing Patterns of Authority over Activities and Resources' (1982) 53 *British Yearbook of International Law* 12.

[88] See Inazumi, above note 34, 57–8.

practice and support for the UN Convention against Torture reinforcing this view.[89]

6.3.5.2 Treaties providing for 'universal jurisdiction': *aut dedere aut judicare*

Some multilateral treaties confer a form of jurisdiction upon states that is often described as 'universal'. These treaties generally require States Parties to create in their domestic law provisions proscribing the relevant conduct and allowing prosecution in certain circumstances, and to prosecute or extradite accused persons – the *aut dedere aut judicare* principle. The Hague Convention for the Suppression of the Unlawful Seizure of Aircraft, for example, requires States Parties to provide for prosecutions for certain crimes committed on board any aircraft which lands in that state's territory with the offender still on board, and where the offender is present in the jurisdiction and is not extradited.[90]

This is an exercise of what might be termed 'quasi', or 'subsidiary', universal jurisdiction and is distinguishable from true (or 'voluntary') universal jurisdiction. The accused must have a territorial link with the forum state – here, physical presence within the state. The Convention against Torture and Other Cruel, Inhuman or Degrading Treatment or Punishment[91] contains such provisions and provides that States Parties shall include torture in extradition agreements with other States Parties.[92] The Convention was considered in *Ex parte Pinochet (No. 3)*.[93] A majority of the House of Lords found that English courts had no jurisdiction to try acts of torture committed outside the UK before the implementation of the Convention into English municipal law by way of section 134 of the Criminal Justice Act 1988.[94] After that date they were obliged to exercise 'quasi-universal jurisdiction' to prosecute accused persons in their territory, or to extradite them. This meant only a small proportion of the charges brought could be considered in the extradition request.

---

89 *Ex parte Pinochet (No. 3)*, above note 35. See discussion of the *Pinochet* case in 6.3.5.2. See also analysis of the Trial Chamber in the ICTY case, *Prosecutor v Furundžija* (Judgment) ('*Furundžija* Trial Judgment') IT-95-17/1-T (10 December 1998), [147]ff.

90 Convention for the Suppression of Unlawful Seizure of Aircraft (adopted 16 December 1970, entered into force 14 October 1971), 1973 UNTS 105.

91 Convention against Torture and Other Cruel, Inhuman or Degrading Treatment or Punishment (adopted 10 December 1984, entered into force 26 June 1987) 1465 UNTS 85.

92 Ibid., Art. 4.

93 *Ex parte Pinochet Ugarte (No. 3)* above note 35, 275.

94 Ibid., 195–7.

Lord Millet, dissenting, considered torture to be a crime at customary international law attracting universal jurisdiction and hence held that, as custom is incorporated into English common law, English courts had jurisdiction at the necessary time before the implementation of the Torture Convention.[95] Extradition to Spain was ultimately refused by the Home Secretary on medical grounds.

A proliferation of counter-terrorist and other treaties also reflect the *aut dedere aut judicare* principle.[96] Indeed, following the 11 September 2001 terrorist attacks in the US, the Security Council issued a Resolution requiring all states to:

> Ensure that any person who participates in the financing, planning, preparation or perpetration of terrorist acts or in supporting terrorist acts is brought to justice and ensure that, in addition to any other measures against them, such terrorist acts are established as serious criminal offences in domestic laws and regulations and that the punishment duly reflects the seriousness of such terrorist acts'.[97]

6.3.5.3 True universal jurisdiction

The crimes to which universal jurisdiction is said to attach include piracy, genocide, crimes against humanity, war crimes, torture and slavery. Other offences, including hijacking, apartheid and even drug trafficking, have also been considered to give rise to universal jurisdiction,[98] although evidence does not appear to support the extension under customary international law of the universality principle to these broader categories of crime.

A case of potentially great importance in the area of universal jurisdiction was the *Arrest Warrant* case before the International Court of Justice in 2002.[99] In 1993, Belgian courts were given jurisdiction by national legislation to exercise universal jurisdiction in trying charges of war crimes, crimes against humanity and genocide. Pursuant to this legislation, in 2000, a warrant was issued by Belgian authorities for the arrest of Abdoulaye Yerodia Ndombasi, the then Minister of Foreign Affairs of the Democratic People's Republic of the Congo (DRC). The Court was initially asked by the DRC to consider (1) whether Belgium acted unlawfully by legislating and issuing an arrest warrant for another state's incumbent Foreign Minister, for crimes committed by him within his country

---

95 Ibid., 276; 119 ILR 135.
96 See, e.g., the multilateral treaties referred to above at note 38.
97 S/Res/1373 (2001), [2(e)].
98 See *DPP v Doot and Others*, above note 39 (per Lord Wilberforce).
99 *Arrest Warrant* case, above note 4.

and with no connection whatever with Belgium's territory, its nationals (as perpetrator or victim), and (2) whether Foreign Minister Yerodia was protected by the doctrine of sovereign immunity. Unfortunately, the parties and the Court agreed to resolve the matter on the question of immunity alone, rejecting the opportunity to clarify the position of universal jurisdiction in international law. As rightly noted in a joint Separate Opinion, the resolution of the question of immunity cannot properly be resolved without also addressing jurisdiction – it is after all immunity *from* jurisdiction.[100]

The story of Belgium's endeavours to extend application of the universality principle in its jurisdiction is perhaps indicative of the current state of the principle, and its complex interrelationship with international power politics.[101] Having boldly amended its laws to enable the prosecution of war crimes, crimes against humanity and genocide exercising universal jurisdiction, and having a system that allowed victims to initiate criminal complaints before an investigating judge, Belgium tried and convicted four Rwandans for the genocide in Rwanda and accepted complaints against an extraordinary range of potential defendants, including Israeli Prime Minister Ariel Sharon, Cuban President Fidel Castro and Iraqi President Saddam Hussein, among others. The diplomatic response from affected states to this increased litigation was far from favourable, and included Israel withdrawing its ambassador in protest.

As challenging as this was, the wheels only really fell off the Belgian universal jurisdiction machine when Iraqi victims sought to bring an action against US President George H.W. Bush, Vice-President Dick Cheney and others for committing war crimes in the 1991 Gulf war. Overt threats by US Secretaries of State Colin Powell and later Donald Rumsfeld, including the refusal to fund a new NATO headquarters in Belgium, led to a series of amendments brought by the Belgian Prime Minister that significantly emasculated the Belgian law, including the removal of the *partie civile* component and recognizing a wide range of immunities under international law.[102]

It is fair to say that Belgium's domestic experience, as well as the ruling of the International Court of Justice in the *Arrest Warrant* case, has delivered something of a blow to the trajectory of a true universal jurisdiction.

---

[100] Ibid., 64, [3] (Judges Higgins, Kooijmans and Buergenthal).

[101] For a detailed account of these events, see Steven Ratner, 'Belgium's War Crimes Statute: A Postmortem' (2003) 97 *American Journal of International Law* 888.

[102] Ibid.

6.3.5.4 Illegal apprehension of accused

Any exercise by a state outside of its own territory raises difficult questions about potentially competing sovereign rights. The apprehension of a pirate on the high seas is a less controversial application of the principle. A more difficult ramification of the exercise of universal jurisdiction can occur where states seek to exercise their jurisdiction in violation of another state's sovereignty. For example, can states exercise jurisdiction over an accused when they have been abducted from another country? The Israeli District and Supreme Courts considered this issue in the Eichmann trial and (not surprisingly) held that the fact of the accused's abduction in violation of international law did not prevent it from trying Eichmann for war crimes.[103] While the Security Council considered the abduction to be a potential threat to international peace and security and ordered reparations be paid,[104] it stopped short of suggesting or requiring Eichmann's release from Israeli custody.

Courts in the United Kingdom, Australia, France, South Africa, Israel and the United States have historically held that the manner in which a person is brought before the court does not affect its jurisdiction (*male captus bene detentus*).[105] This is still the position of the United States Supreme Court, where the so-called *Ker-Frisbie* doctrine operates,[106] with the exception that, where an extradition treaty is in force between the abducting state and the former host state, and the abduction was contrary to the treaty, jurisdiction may not be exercised.[107] Another recognized exception to this rule is where US officials have been involved in inflicting torture on an apprehended person in the course of that person's abduction and transfer to US territory.[108]

Other common law states – including New Zealand, Australia, South Africa, Canada and the United Kingdom – have, in recent times, distanced themselves from the robust position operating in the US.[109]

---

103 *Eichmann* case, above note 16, 5, 277.

104 UNSC Res. 138 (1960).

105 See generally Susan Lamb, 'The Powers of Arrest of the International Criminal Tribunal for the Former Yugoslavia' (1999) 70 *British Yearbook of International Law* 165, 230–31.

106 Based on two US Supreme Court cases (*Ker v Illinois*, 119 US 436, 444 (1886), and *Frisbie v Collins*, 342 US 519 (1952)).

107 *Sosa v Alvarez-Machain*, 542 US 692 (2004).

108 See *United States v Toscanino*, 500 F 2d 267, 275 (2d Cir.1974).

109 See Paul Michell, 'English-speaking Justice: Evolving Responses to Transnational Forcible Abduction after Alvarez-Machain' (1996) 29 *Cornell International Law Journal* 383. See also *R v Horseferry Road Magistrate's Court, ex parte Bennett* [1994] 1 AC 42, 62 (HL); *R v Bow Street Magistrates, ex parte*

6.3.6 The Alien Tort Claims Statute

An unusual application of extraterritorial jurisdiction is found in the United States. The Alien Tort Claims Act of 1789 provides for the original jurisdiction of the District Court of the United States to hear and determine claims brought by aliens in 'tort only, committed in violation of the law of nations or a treaty of the United States'.[110] This was interpreted in as late as 1980 as permitting a tort action by a Paraguayan national, against a Paraguayan police officer for acts of torture committed in Paraguay, to be heard in the United States.[111] Since then, *Tel-Oren v Libyan Arab Republic*[112] and *Sanchez-Espinoza v Reagan*[113] have made it clear respectively that a cause of action in international law was necessary, that political crimes will not be considered by the court, and that state immunities prevent judgment against people acting in an official capacity.[114]

6.4 EXTRADITION

Extradition refers to the practice of surrendering an accused person to the authorities of another state for prosecution. It is commonly organized by way of bilateral treaties, which are reflected in the domestic legislation of each state. There is no obligation to extradite at customary international law, nor is there any customary law obligation to prosecute if extradition is refused. However, as discussed above, many multilateral treaty regimes add particular offences, such as hijacking and terrorist bombing, to the offences for which extradition is required unless the forum state is prepared and able to prosecute.

The two key principles reflected in many extradition treaties are the requirements for double criminality and speciality of the prosecution. The double criminality principle requires the offence in question to be criminal in both the sending and receiving states. In *Ex parte Pinochet (No. 3)* the operation of this principle prevented extradition for offences committed before 1988, when the Convention Against Torture was implemented in the UK. Prior to that date the offences were not part of UK law and

---

Mackeson (1981) 75 Crim. App. R. 24; *State v Ebrahim* [1991] 2 SALR 553(q), 31 ILM 442 (South Africa Supreme Court, Appellate Division).

[110] Title 28, United States Code, §1350.

[111] *Filartiga v Peña-Irala*, 630 F. 2d 876 (2d Cir. 1980); 77 ILR 169.

[112] 726 F. 2d 774 (DC Cir. 1984).

[113] 770 F. 2d 202 (DC Cir 1985).

[114] See *Alvarez-Machain v United States*, 41 ILM 2002, 130.

could not form the basis of an extradition order.[115] The speciality principle requires that the accused be tried and punished in the receiving state only for the crime for which he or she is surrendered. An interesting example of a contest relating to this latter principle can be seen in the extradition proceedings brought by Sweden against Julian Assange, who is residing in the United Kingdom. One of the defence arguments in this case is that Sweden, upon receipt of custody of Assange, will send him to the US upon a request from the US relating to violation of its state secrets (an entirely different crime from that for which he is sought by Sweden).[116]

Political offences are generally excluded from the list of extraditable crimes, with the exception of terrorist offences. In particular, the European Convention for the Suppression of Terrorism 1977[117] lists in Article 1 a number of offences not to be considered political. Many states also do not allow the extradition of their own nationals, especially where they have the capability of prosecuting domestically for crimes committed by nationals abroad,[118] although this approach is by no means universal.[119] Finally, some multilateral extradition arrangements prohibit extradition on the principle of *non refoulement* or where the subject will be put in danger,[120] or is likely to suffer human rights violations,[121] which includes the risk that the accused will not receive a fair trial in the requesting state.[122]

Other forms of extradition not undertaken on the basis of formal arrangements (bilateral treaty and domestic implementing legislation) have recently become notorious in the so-called 'war on terror' era. The use of informal and extraordinary rendition techniques, particularly by

---

[115] *Ex parte Pinochet (No. 3)*, above note 35.

[116] *The Judicial Authority in Sweden v Julian Paul Assange* [2011] EW Misc 5 (MC).

[117] European Convention on the Suppression of Terrorism (adopted 27 January 1977, entered into force 4 August 1978) ETS 90.

[118] See, e.g., French Extradition Law of 1927, Art. 3(1); Basic Law of the Federal Republic of Germany, Art. 16.

[119] For example, in Australia extradition of Australian nationals may be ordered in response to requests by other states: *Vasiljkovic v Cth* (2006) 227 CLR 614.

[120] Convention relating to the Status of Refugees (adopted 28 July 1951, entered into force 22 April 1954) 189 UNTS 150.

[121] Convention for the Protection of Human Rights and Fundamental Freedoms (adopted 4 November 1950, entered into force 3 September 1953) CETS 194 ('ECHR'), Arts 2, 3, 5, 6; Extradition Act 1988 (Cth), s. 7(b); Extradition Act 2003 (UK) c.41, s. 21.

[122] ECHR, Art. 6; Extradition Act 1988 (Cth), s. 7(b); Extradition Act 2003 (UK) c.41, s. 21.

the United States with the aid of a number of allies, has raised serious human rights – as well as international law – questions.[123]

6.5 IMMUNITY FROM JURISDICTION

The remainder of this chapter will consider limitations upon a state's exercise of its otherwise lawful jurisdiction. The preceding discussion has examined the areas in which international law recognizes the valid exercise of state authority. The complexities arising in this area are largely because of the interface between equal sovereign powers, and the need to allocate competence for the exercise of authority. This final section will examine the extent to which international law provides protection to the person, agents or property of a sovereign state while it is present within the territory or otherwise subject to the jurisdiction of another state. An important preliminary point is worth raising. As Judges Higgins, Kooijmans and Buergenthal explained in their joint Separate Opinion in the *Arrest Warrant* case: "Immunity" is the common shorthand phrase for "immunity from jurisdiction". If there is no jurisdiction *en principe*, then the question of an immunity from a jurisdiction which would otherwise exist simply does not arise'.[124] It is therefore important to understand the concept of immunity within international law in relation to the existence of jurisdictional authority open to a state.

6.5.1 Origins: The Doctrine of Absolute Sovereign Immunity

State sovereignty, until relatively recently, was seen as vesting in the person of the head of state. As an individual from whom all the power and authority of the state emanated, the head of state could not be subject to the authority of his or her own courts, nor – on the principle of sovereign equality – the courts of a foreign state. Over time, the personality of the sovereign was replaced by the abstraction of the state, yet the principle of

---

[123] See Leila Nadya Sadat and Henry H. Oberschelp, 'Extraordinary Rendition, Torture and Other Nightmares from the War on Terror' (2007) 75 *George Washington Law Review* 1200; David Weissbrodt and Amy Bergquist, 'Extraordinary Rendition and the Torture Convention' (2006) 46:4 *Virginia Journal of International Law* 585; Jane Mayer, 'Outsourcing Torture', *The New Yorker* (New York) 14 February 2005, available at http://www.newyorker.com/archive/2005/02/14/050214fa_fact6.

[124] *Arrest Warrant* case, above note 4, Separate Opinion of Judges Higgins, Kooijmans, Buergenthal, [3].

sovereign equality remained and the immunity afforded was preserved. Chief Justice Marshall in *The Schooner Exchange v McFadden*, considered that the principle of sovereign immunity means that 'every sovereign is understood to waive the exercise of part of [their] complete exclusive territorial jurisdiction'.[125] This principle was confirmed more recently by Lord Browne-Wilkinson in *Ex parte Pinochet (No. 3)*, when he explained that 'the foreign state is entitled to a procedural immunity from the processes of the forum state', which embraces both criminal and civil process.[126] Sovereign immunity has its foundation in customary international law and the fundamental principle of sovereign equality,[127] and has ancient roots in international law.[128]

Sovereign immunity is based on the status of an individual. Once it is determined that the person is entitled to immunity, he or she cannot be subjected to the legal system of the host state except in a few limited exceptions. The traditional doctrine of sovereign immunity meant that an agent of a foreign state could never be brought before the courts of another state. The principle was explained in *The Parlement Belge*,[129] in which Brett LJ considered that states had a 'duty to respect the independence and dignity of every other sovereign state', and therefore each

> declines to exercise by means of its courts any of its territorial jurisdiction over the person of any sovereign or ambassador of any other state, or over the public property of any state which is destined to public use . . . though such sovereign, ambassador or property be within its jurisdiction.[130]

In applying this statement of principle, it was necessary to determine which entities were to be considered sovereign states and what interests in property would fall within the protective scope of the immunity.

Two factors are relevant in determining the status of entities claiming immunity. The first is that state organs need not conform to a particular mode of organization to qualify as such. The way in which state agencies are incorporated or otherwise organized is a matter for the state and courts need not examine these in determining claims of immunity.[131]

---

[125] 11 US (7 Cranch) 116 (1812).

[126] *Ex parte Pinochet (No. 3)*, above note 35, 201.

[127] Lord Millett in *Holland v Lampen-Wolfe* [2000] 1 WLR 1573, 1588; 119 ILR 367.

[128] See discussion in Chapter 1, section 1.3.1.

[129] (1880) 5 PD 197.

[130] Ibid., 214–15 (Brett LJ).

[131] *Krajina v Tass Agency* [1949] 2 All ER 274, 281 (Cohen LJ); 16 AD 129; and *Baccus SRL v Servicio Nacional del Trigo* [1957] 1 QB 438; 23 ILR 160.

Secondly, the issue of a certificate by the executive, showing recognition of the statehood of the claimant is sufficient to allow a court to determine its status as such. English courts will not look beyond such a certificate.[132]

As states began to engage in commerce, nationalize industry and employ people, on a large scale in public agencies and in private capacities, outside their territory, the reasons for immunity based solely on status began to be questioned. It no longer made sense for foreign states to be protected from liability when engaging in the same conduct as private entities, which carried the full responsibility for their delicts.

6.5.2 The Restrictive or Qualified Sovereign Immunity Doctrine

These developments, which have occurred particularly and increasingly since the end of the Second World War, led in many jurisdictions to the development of the restrictive (or qualified) doctrine of immunity to replace the absolute approach to sovereign immunity. The restrictive doctrine differentiates between acts done in the capacity of a state for which immunity attaches (*jure imperii*), and those acts done in a private capacity (*jure gestionis*).

This conception of state immunity is based around the nature of the transaction rather than the status of the person transacting. The status of the person is still important in determining who may claim immunity, but it will be extended to cover only *acta jure imperii*, acts in the nature of public authority. This distinction has formed the basis of immunities legislation enacted in the 1970s and 1980s in many common law jurisdictions.[133] In the United States, the principle was applied in *Victory Transport Inc. v Comisaria Generalde Abasteciementosy Transportes*, a case concerning the charter of a ship by an arm of the Spanish Ministry of Commerce, to transport grain. The court in this case held that transporting grain was neither particularly political nor public, and hence did not give rise to a claim of immunity.[134] In the UK, the absolute principle set out in *The Parlement Belge*[135] was definitively overturned by the Privy Council in the *Philippine Admiral*[136] case, in which a foreign state was con-

---

[132] *Duff Development Company v Kelantan* [1924] AC 797; 2 AD 124; and State Immunity Act 1978 (UK), s. 21.

[133] See, e.g., Foreign Sovereign Immunity Act 1976 (USA); State Immunity Act 1978 (UK); State Immunity Act 1981 (Canada); Foreign State Immunities Act 1981 (South Africa); Australian Foreign States Immunities Act 1985.

[134] 35 ILR 1, 110.

[135] *The Parlement Belge*, above note 129.

[136] [1977] AC 373.

sidered not to be immune from the jurisdiction of local courts in admiralty actions *in rem* with respect to state-owned commercial vessels or cargoes. *Trendtex Trading Corporation Ltd v Central Bank of Nigeria*,[137] in which the Court of Appeal unanimously accepted the restrictive approach as reflecting international practice, is now the settled position in UK law and is often cited in international and national courts as reflecting the contemporary doctrine of sovereign immunity.[138] The restrictive approach is now enshrined in the national legislation of numerous common and civil law countries, and is also reflected in certain multilateral treaties.[139]

6.5.3 The Nature Test

The restrictive approach requires courts to determine whether the sovereign was acting in its public or private capacity in the relevant transaction, in order to ascertain whether jurisdiction is to be affirmed or not. Initially, a number of methods were employed to make this determination. Courts in different jurisdictions considered the nature of the relationship encompassed by the transaction (a private contract for example), whether private entities are capable of engaging in the conduct, and the purpose of the conduct in their determinations on this point.

It seems now to be generally accepted that the purpose of the transaction is not relevant as to its characterization as an act *jure imperii* or an act *jure gestionis*. The purposive approach presents difficulties as it inevitably involves a political judgment as to what is a public purpose and what is not[140] and, as Mitchell and Beard point out, 'almost any act of a sovereign can be said to have a public purpose of some sort'.[141] This is reflected in Lord Denning's ruling in the *Trendtex Trading* case, in which he stated that the purpose of a contract is irrelevant to the question of immunity.[142] That case concerned the supply of concrete from a Swiss company to the

---

137 [1977] QB 529; [1977] 2 WLR 356; 64 ILR 122.

138 *Reid v Republic of Nauru* [1993] 1 VR 251, 252; *Reef Shipping Co. v The Fua Kavenga* [1987] 1 NZLR 550, 571; *Prosecutor v Blaškić* (Judgment on the Request of the Republic of Croatia for Review of the Decision of Trial Chamber II of 18 July 1997) (Judgment) IT-95-14 (29 October 1997).

139 See states and instruments referred to in Triggs, above note 3, [8.57].

140 G. Fitzmaurice, 'State Immunity from Proceedings in Foreign Courts', 14 *British Yearbook of International Law* (1933), 101 at 121.

141 Andrew Mitchell and Jennifer Beard, *International Law: In Principle* (Pyrmont, NSW: Thomson Lawbook Co., 2009), 127.

142 *Trendtex Trading Corporation v Central Bank of Nigeria*, above note 137. The statutory position was subsequently altered by the State Immunity Act 1978 (UK).

Nigerian government for the purpose of constructing an army barracks. The dispute arose when the Nigerian government refused to pay and claimed that the transaction was subject to sovereign immunity. The Court held that, while the purpose of the contract was related to a public purpose (the building of army barracks), the transaction was clearly in the nature of a commercial transaction, to which immunity did not attach. So, too, the German Constitutional Court, in the *Empire of Iran* case, stated that 'one should rather refer to the nature of the state transaction or the resulting legal relationships, and not to the motive or purpose of the state activity'.[143]

The sources of international law governing this area are generally limited to domestic judgments, with the exception of the European Convention on State Immunity 1972[144] and the UN Convention on Jurisdictional Immunities of States and their Property 2004.[145] The latter incorporates the restrictive doctrine, denying immunity in relation to commercial transactions.[146] While not yet in force, the Convention reflects a general trend in the acceptance of the restrictive doctrine in international law.[147]

6.5.4 Functional Immunity

Functional immunity prevents a state from exercising jurisdiction over foreign officials for acts carried out in the conduct of their official duties. Such acts are attributable to the state rather than the individual. Lord McNair, considering the *McLeod* incident, stated the following principle:

> [A]n individual doing a hostile act authorized and ratified by the government of which he is a member cannot be held individually answerable as a private trespasser or malefactor, but that the Act becomes one for which the State to which he belongs is in such a case alone responsible.[148]

More recently, the International Criminal Tribunal for the former Yugoslavia explained functional immunity in terms of the authority of states to determine their internal structure and, in particular, to designate

---

[143] *Claims against the Empire of Iran* (1963) BVerfGE 16; 45 ILR 57.

[144] European Convention on State Immunity (adopted 16 May 1972, entered into force 11 June 1976) ETS 74.

[145] UN Convention on Jurisdictional Immunities of States and their Property 2004 (adopted 2 December 2004, not yet in force) GA Res. 59/38, Annex, Supplement No. 49 (A/59/49).

[146] Ibid., Arts 2 and 10.

[147] See Triggs, above note 3, 471–4.

[148] Lord McNair, *International Law Opinions: Selected and Annotated* (Cambridge: Cambridge University Press, 1956), ii, 230.

the individuals acting as state agents or organs, as well as a state's right to issue instructions to those organs, whether operating internally or abroad, and to provide sanctions for non-compliance. The necessary implication of this authority is that 'each state is entitled to claim that acts or transactions performed by one of its organs in its official capacity be attributed to the state, so that the individual organ may not be held accountable for those acts or transactions'.[149] This protection shares the same rational foundation as the foreign state immunity doctrine discussed above. Indeed, it is a corollary of the equality of sovereign states that individuals do not incur responsibility for actions carried out in performance of their function as state agents. Accordingly, the immunity is held by the state, not the individual. It merely extends to embrace their conduct. As such, waiver of the immunity may be done by the state, not the individual, and nothing prevents individual agents being tried if the sending state waives its immunity, irrespective of the wishes of the individual representative.[150]

Exactly who is likely to be protected by this immunity and the extent of it are considered below.

6.5.4.1 The scope of functional immunity

Functional immunity prevents the exercise of jurisdiction over agents and organs of foreign states with regard to conduct in the execution of their official duties. Conduct outside the scope of those acts attributable to the state is not, however, subject to immunity and may form the subject of a legal claim.[151]

A further limitation on immunity applies where the official act is in breach of the sending state's international legal obligations and includes the commission of a serious crime under the law of the host state. In such circumstances, the individual may be prosecuted or subject to punitive measures in addition to international legal responsibility attaching to the sending state. This exception is illustrated by the *Rainbow Warrior* incident and subsequent arbitral award.[152] This incident concerned the blowing up of a Greenpeace ship (the *Rainbow Warrior*) by French intelligence agents during a period of protest against French nuclear testing in the South

149 *Prosecutor v Blaškić, Decision on the Objections of the Republic of Croatia to the Issuance of Subpoena Duces Tecum* (Judgment) IT-95-14-PT (18 July 1997), [41]–[42]

150 Antonio Cassese, *International Law* (Oxford: Oxford University Press, 2005, 2nd edn) 113.

151 See Chapter 7, section 7.3.

152 *'Rainbow Warrior'* case (*New Zealand v France*) (1990) 20 RIAA 217; see UN Secretary-General's Ruling of 1986, Rainbow Warrior, 74 ILR 241, 212–14.

Pacific. The ship was at the time docked in Auckland Harbour and a Greenpeace photographer was killed in the attack, leading to the finding by a New Zealand court that France had interfered with New Zealand's sovereignty and its agents were guilty of, among other offences, manslaughter.[153] The sinking of the ship was an interference with New Zealand sovereignty in breach of international law, occurring on the territory of the forum state, which involved a very serious criminal offence. While the actions of the French agents were performed in the course of their duty as agents of France, because the acts were a breach of France's international legal obligations the agents were not protected by functional immunity.

A second exception involves international crimes. In the *Blaškić* case before the ICTY, the Appeals Chamber considered that immunity does not extend to conduct disclosing international crimes, such as genocide, war crimes and crimes against humanity.[154] The norms prohibiting such crimes preclude the availability of immunity. As in the *Rainbow Warrior* case, international responsibility for international crimes will attach to the state as well as criminal liability attaching to the individual responsible for the commission of, or contribution to, these crimes.[155] Just as extraterritorial (including universal) jurisdiction may attach to crimes that violate the 'laws of humanity', so too are such crimes exempt from claims of immunity. This sentiment can be traced at least back to the diplomatic protest by the French, British and Russian governments condemning the massive and widespread deportation and extermination of over one million Christian Armenians by the Ottoman government in 1915:

> In view of these new crimes of Turkey against humanity and civilisation, the Allied governments announce publicly to the *Sublime Porte* that they will hold personally responsible [for] these crimes all members of the Ottoman Government and those of their agents who are implicated in such massacres.[156]

As we shall see, however, the personal or status immunities, particularly in relation to heads of state and sitting foreign ministers, in some circum-

---

[153] Two of the agents, Major Mafart and Captain Prieur, were subsequently arrested in New Zealand and, having pleaded guilty to charges of manslaughter and criminal damage, were sentenced by a New Zealand court to ten years' imprisonment: *R v Mafart and Prieur*, 74 ILR 241, 243.

[154] *Prosecutor v Blaškić*, above note 149.

[155] Similar issues concerning state immunity will be considered by the ICJ in *Jurisdictional Immunities of the State* (*Germany v Italy*), pending.

[156] United Nations War Crimes Commission, *History of the United Nations War Crimes Commission and the Developments of the Laws of War* (London: HMSO, 1948), 35.

stances extend even to the protection of these offices from prosecution in relation to such heinous offences.

The specific immunities of heads of state, other senior officials and diplomats are personal and will depend on their status. These are discussed below.

6.5.4.2 Personal status immunity

Heads of states and governments, and senior government officials such as foreign ministers and diplomatic staff, are immune from the exercise of state jurisdiction with regard to the conduct of their official functions as agents of their state, as discussed above. In addition, certain officials enjoy limited immunity with respect to private conduct, the premises where they carry out their official functions and their private residences. The immunity here is based on the need to prevent interference with the official's functions – *ne impediatur officium*.[157] Hence it is necessary to protect the official's private life by rendering private acts and property immune or inviolable. In this way, as the International Court of Justice has unequivocally stated, certain officials of a state (at least heads of state, heads of government and foreign affairs ministers) enjoy complete and inviolable immunity from all acts, public or private, while they are in office:

> The Court accordingly concludes that the functions of a Minister for Foreign Affairs are such that, throughout the duration of his or her office, he or she when abroad enjoys full immunity from criminal jurisdiction and inviolability. That immunity and that inviolability protect the individual concerned against any act of authority of another State which would hinder him or her in the performance of his or her duties. . . .
>
> In this respect, no distinction can be drawn between acts performed by a Minister for Foreign Affairs in an 'official' capacity, and those claimed to have been performed in a 'private capacity'.[158]

This immunity attaches to the person even for acts committed prior to the taking of office, as the purpose of the immunity is to enable a state to exercise its official functions (through the person of the senior government agent) unfettered by the exercise of jurisdiction of foreign courts.[159]

Unlike functional immunities, personal immunities extend even to protection from prosecution for crimes under national and international law. In the *Arrest Warrant* case, the majority of the International Court of Justice held that there was no exception to the personal immunity of a

[157] *Arrest Warrant* case, above note 4, [51].
[158] Ibid., [53] and [54].
[159] Ibid., [54].

serving foreign minister that would permit a foreign state to prosecute even international crimes, such as crimes against humanity or war crimes.[160] The decision drew considerable criticism (from scholars as well as from judges of the Court who dissented or provided Separate Opinions), both for its lack of legal coherence and for the message that it sent about the impunity of state leaders who commit the most heinous crimes against their own people.[161] The majority considered that immunity did not amount to impunity, as various jurisdictional possibilities existed for his prosecution:

- Yerodia (like others in his position) could still be subject to prosecution at any time by courts in his own state;
- his immunity might be waived by the Congolese government;
- while after leaving office his functional immunity would continue, his personal immunity would lapse permitting prosecution for acts done before or after his term in office; and
- international courts may not be affected by the immunity.[162]

Despite this, as Judges Higgins, Buergenthal and Kooijmans point out, the likelihood of any of these conditions being met was rather remote, and would not prevent impunity in practice.

6.5.4.2.1 Diplomatic and consular immunity The importance of diplomatic relations in international law cannot be overstated. The role of diplomats as representatives of their state is critical to the functioning of international law and relations, whether between friendly or hostile states, in times of peace and in armed conflict.[163] Diplomatic immunities, necessary to ensure the integrity of the foreign state's agents and property, have

---

160 The facts of the case and the story of the Belgian legislation are set out above in the text accompanying notes 100–102.

161 *Arrest Warrant* case, above note 4, 97–9 [5]–[8] (Judge Al Khasawneh), 87 [78] (Judges Higgins, Buergenthal and Kooijmans); Lorna McGregor, 'Torture and State Immunity: Deflecting Impunity, Distorting Sovereignty' (2007) 18(5) *European Journal of International Law* 903; Lee M. Caplan, 'State Immunity, Human Rights, and Jus Cogens: A Critique of the Normative Hierarchy Theory' (2003) 97 *American Journal of International Law* 741; Phillippe Sands, 'After Pinochet: the Role for National Courts', in Phillippe Sands (ed.), *From Nuremberg to The Hague: The Future of International Criminal Justice* (Cambridge: Cambridge University Press, 2003) 68, 95–108.

162 *Arrest Warrant* case, above note 4, [48].

163 See generally Eileen Denza, *Diplomatic Law: Commentary on the Vienna Convention on Diplomatic Relations* (Oxford: Oxford University Press, 2008, 3rd

been codified in the Vienna Convention on Diplomatic Relations 1961.[164] Diplomatic immunity for the most part covers the functions, property and conduct of a state's diplomatic agents. These prevent interference with the private as well as public life of diplomatic staff and so ensure they are able to carry out their mission – *ne impediatur legatio*. As such, the immunities are extended to family members forming part of the household, who are not nationals of the host state.

As in the case of the other forms of immunity discussed, it does not attach to the individual but is rather an extension of the sovereignty of the sending state. That state has the power to waive or maintain that immunity, as it is for that state's benefit, not that of the individual to whom it attaches. Diplomatic personnel are immune, subject to exceptions identified in the Vienna Convention, from criminal jurisdiction and powers of arrest and detention. The host state can, of course, declare a diplomat *persona non grata* and require the sending state remove him or her. This reflects the fact that there is no right of legation and all diplomatic relations are based on consent.[165] If the sending state does not remove its representative within a reasonable time, the host state may cease to recognize the diplomat as part of the mission, and act as though diplomatic immunity has lapsed.[166]

Civil jurisdiction may be exercised over diplomatic staff only to the extent that it is relevant to their private activities. Specifically, jurisdiction may be exercised in matters relating to real property in the host state, not held for an official purpose, succession, and any professional or commercial activities beyond their official role.[167] Also, personnel have the ability to waive their immunity by voluntarily submitting to the jurisdiction by, for example, filing a claim in a court of the host state. The immunity could not then be raised to have a counterclaim struck out.

The premises of foreign diplomatic missions are inviolable. They remain part of the territory of the host state, but the authorities of the host state may not exercise jurisdiction on the premises of a foreign diplomatic mission without the express consent of the head of the mission. Further, Article 22(2) makes it incumbent on the host state to prevent any disturbance of the peace or impairment of the dignity of the

---

edn); *United States Diplomatic and Consular Staff in Tehran* (*United States of America v Iran*) [1980] ICJ Rep 3, 43.

164 Vienna Convention on Diplomatic Relations (adopted 18 April 1961, entered into force 24 April 1964) 500 UNTS 95 ('VCDR').

165 Brownlie, above note 1, 342.

166 VCDR, above note 164, Art. 9.

167 Ibid., Art. 31.

mission.[168] Similarly, the private residences of individual diplomatic personnel are inviolable, as are any records, papers and correspondence. The property of the foreign mission may not be subject to search, requisition, attachment or execution; the diplomatic bag, courier, coded messages and cipher may not be 'violated'. Finally, diplomatic agents are immune from any requirements to pay taxes, subject to listed exception in Article 34.[169]

Where a diplomat is a permanent resident or national of the receiving state, a number of these immunities do not apply. This is in the interest of ensuring accountability in at least one jurisdiction. The functional immunity element will remain as the official remains an agent of the sending state, but Article 38(1) provides that 'except insofar as privileges and immunities may be granted by the receiving state, a diplomatic agent who is a national of or permanently resident in that state shall enjoy only immunity from jurisdiction and inviolability, in respect of official acts performed in the exercise of his functions'.[170]

6.6 CONCLUSIONS

To what extent does international law preserve or limit the expression of the power and authority of sovereign states? There is inherent tension in the need to protect the sovereign authority of states, yet simultaneously prevent any single state from interfering in the functions of another. The *Arrest Warrant* case is a recent example of these principles coming into conflict. The majority decision in that case has been criticized and seems not to be in line with the trend towards increased accountability for government officials, at least with regard to serious human rights abuses, war crimes and crimes against humanity.

Historically, changes in the immunities enjoyed by sovereigns have been forced by the necessities of trade. While the absolute approach to sovereign immunities required the primacy of sovereignty, the growth of state interest and capacity in commerce brought state actors into contact with individuals in pursuit of private and commercial interests. The need for subjects to have the same confidence in transactions with state commercial entities led to the abandonment of absolute sovereign immunity, permitting subject and sovereign to engage, while enjoying confidence in equal legal protection, in their private or commercial capacities. This shift

---

168 Ibid., Art. 22(2).
169 Ibid., Art. 34.
170 Ibid., Art. 38(1).

became necessary to protect the rights and interests of subjects from the vast asymmetry of state power.

The current trend towards limiting sovereign immunity with regard to serious international crimes such as genocide, war crimes and crimes against humanity, reflects a similar – although arguably more profound – change in the conception of the role of the state in the international system. The spectrum of competence allocated to states is narrowing, and individuals acting in the state's name beyond that narrowing scope are more frequently being held to account. Similarly, individual responsibility is being imposed on individuals who traditionally would have been shielded by sovereign immunity in cases of serious crimes. States and their rulers are decreasingly able to rely on their sovereign equality for protection.

The mechanism for this change is primarily treaty-driven. Customary international law, as a relatively conservative force, allows governments to cling to the absolutist immunities doctrine, a point reflected in the reductive reasoning of the majority in the *Arrest Warrant* case. However, cases like *Pinochet* (where conventional international law permitted the prosecution of a head of state for very serious crimes), radical legislative and judicial activity like that seen in Belgium around the turn of the century, and an increasingly broad framework of human rights and international criminal law accountability all suggest a potential trend away from strict rules of sovereign protection. The continuing development of international human rights and humanitarian law standards is narrowing the scope of legitimate state behaviour, though the gradual shift towards accountability for senior government officials and heads of state, particularly with respect to serious international crimes, remains contentious. This external restriction on state sovereignty, and a ceding of absolute sovereign control of what goes on within a state's own borders, reflects a broader theme of change in the international legal and political landscape, and is consistent with other areas of international law.

7. State responsibility

A member of the International Law Commission (ILC) recently remarked: 'Responsibility is the corollary of international law, the best proof of its existence and the most credible measure of its effectiveness.'[1] Every legal system allocates responsibility. Norms, or 'secondary rules', operate to hold a person accountable for contravening a 'primary' legal obligation. For example, a primary rule in domestic law might be the obligation not to interfere with another person's property. Whether the interference is attributable to a particular person and, if so, what remedies the victim can seek are determined by the secondary rules. State responsibility for internationally wrongful acts follows the same logic.[2] Secondary rules in international law are no different from primary rules in that they must be shown to derive from a treaty, custom or general principles.[3] As the term suggests, however, secondary rules are the rights and obligations that apply after a primary rule has been violated.

The leading source in this area is the International Law Commission's Articles on Responsibility of States for Internationally Wrongful Acts (2001) ('ILC Articles' or 'Articles').[4] The Articles have undergone a long gestation period and they exert a powerful influence on the development of the law.

---

[1] Alain Pellet, 'The Definition of Responsibility in International Law', in James Crawford, Alain Pellet and Simon Olleson (eds), *The Law of International Responsibility* (Oxford: Oxford University Press, 2010), 3.

[2] The international responsibility of non-state actors is discussed in Chapter 5.

[3] See Chapter 2.

[4] Articles on Responsibility of States for Internationally Wrongful Acts, with Commentaries (2001), Report of the ILC, 53rd sess., [2001] II(2) *Yearbook of the ILC* 26, UN Doc. A/56/10 (2001) ('ILC Articles').

7.1 THE ILC ARTICLES AND THE CHANGING DISCOURSE OF STATE RESPONSIBILITY

7.1.1 The Long Road to Codification

Although initially plagued by a fixation with the law on the treatment of aliens, driven by the third special Rapporteur, Roberto Ago, the ILC moved in the 1960s towards a measure of political acceptance of the Articles by introducing the distinction between 'primary' and 'secondary' rules.[5] Rather than codifying all rules on responsibility, the ILC decided to confine itself to the rules of general application. The ILC Commentaries accompanying the Articles ('Commentaries') describe the work as being concerned with:

> the general conditions under international law for the state to be considered responsible for wrongful actions or omissions, and the legal consequences which flow therefrom. The Articles do not attempt to define the content of the international obligations, breach of which gives rise to responsibility.[6]

The high level of abstraction and political neutrality of the Articles was a weakness, but, given the ILC's propensity to postpone the project over time, it was also a strength.[7]

Two topics did not survive to codification as they were considered to be too progressive. First, a dispute settlement mechanism for claims arising out of the Articles was suggested.[8] The mechanism was ultimately dropped given its unpopularity with states and the belief that a state in breach could invoke the (necessarily lengthy) procedures to frustrate genuine countermeasures.[9]

Secondly, Draft Article 19 of the 1996 Draft Articles defined an 'international crime of state' as breach of an obligation 'so essential for the protection of fundamental interests of the international community that its breach is recognized as a crime by the community as a

---

[5] Roberto Ago, 'Report of the Sub-Committee on State Responsibility' [1963] 2 *Yearbook of the ILC* 227, 228 [5], UN Doc. A/CN.4/SER.A/1963/Add.1.

[6] ILC Articles, above note 4, 31; General Commentary, [1].

[7] Robert Rosenstock, 'The ILC and State Responsibility' (2002) 96 *American Journal of International Law* 792, 793.

[8] Willem Riphagen, 'Seventh Report on State Responsibility' [1986] 2 *Yearbook of the ILC* 1, UN Doc. A/CN.4/SER.A/1986/Add.1 (Part 1).

[9] David Bederman, 'Counterintuiting Countermeasures' (2002) 96 *American Journal of International Law* 817, 824; Rosenstock, above note 7, 796. See also section 7.6.4.

whole'.[10] The proposal's validity was strongly contested by scholars and states, which is not surprising given that no state practice existed for state criminal responsibility.[11] Also, unlike the area of individual criminal responsibility, the Draft Articles lacked any defined mechanisms for the attribution of responsibility – that is, proper definition of crimes, an investigative process, the right to a fair trial, punitive sanctions and a system of rehabilitation.[12] Indeed, some of these concepts simply do not align with the idea of the responsibility of an entity such as a state. In 2000, Draft Article 19 was deleted and replaced with the concept of *jus cogens*, which is significantly less controversial.[13]

Supporting the logic of the ILC's approach, the International Court of Justice in the *Bosnian Genocide* case[14] considered whether Serbia (successor state to the Federal Republic of Yugoslavia (FRY)) was responsible for the Srebrenica genocide committed by the Bosnian Serb insurrectional movement, Republika Srpska (RS). The Court held that the Genocide Convention impliedly imposed state responsibility for genocide, including complicity in genocide. In its judgment, the Court referred to the ILC's rejection of state crimes and expressly denied that 'obligations and responsibilities under international law' can be 'of a criminal nature'.[15]

7.1.2 Significance of the Articles

There is no overarching multilateral treaty and most responsibility rules are customary in nature. Although the Articles are in the form of a draft convention, the ILC decided not to subject them to a diplomatic conference. At the same time, previous drafts had already been cited

---

[10] Draft Articles on the Responsibility of States for Internationally Wrongful Acts adopted on first reading, Report of the ILC, 48th sess., [1996] II(2) *Yearbook of the ILC* 58.

[11] See, e.g., Alain Pellet, 'Can a State Commit a Crime? Definitely, Yes!' (1999) 10(2) *European Journal of International Law* 425; Christian Dominicé, 'The International Responsibility of States for Breach of Multilateral Obligations' (1999) 10(2) *European Journal of International Law* 353.

[12] James Crawford, *The International Law Commission's Articles on State Responsibility: Introduction, Text and Commentaries* (Cambridge; New York: Cambridge University Press, 2002) 18–19, 36; Pellet, above note 11.

[13] ILC Articles, Arts 40 and 41: see further below at section 7.6.2.

[14] *Application of the Convention on the Prevention and Punishment of the Crime of Genocide* (*Bosnia and Herzegovina v Serbia and Montenegro*) (Judgment) [2007] ICJ Rep 91 ('*Bosnian Genocide* case'). See generally Antonio Cassese, 'On the Use of Criminal Law Notions in Determining State Responsibility for Genocide' (2007) 5 *Journal of International Criminal Justice* 875.

[15] Ibid., [170].

with approval by the ICJ and various international tribunals[16] and the ILC felt they could exert an influence on the crystallization of custom.[17] Accordingly, the General Assembly did nothing more than 'take note' of the Articles.[18] Since then the Articles have been cited as a key source by courts and tribunals.[19]

While the Articles may, and often are, relied upon to determine the content of rules of state responsibility, there is an argument to be made that this is less than satisfactory. In international law – devoid as it is of a constitution, legislature and a compelling enforcement regime – it is axiomatic that 'subsidiary' sources like the Articles (or the judicial decisions on which the Articles are primarily based) are not interpreted and applied as formal sources of international law. Care must be taken to ensure that the Articles do not become a substitute for an examination of state practice and *opinio juris* in the determination of the content of rules of custom or general principles of international law.[20]

7.2 INTERNATIONALLY WRONGFUL ACTS

An important principle grounded in sovereign equality is that every internationally wrongful act of a state entails the international responsibility of that state (Article 1 of the Articles).[21]

An internationally wrongful act is defined in Article 2 as an action or omission that (1) is attributable to the state, and (2) constitutes a breach

---

16 See, e.g., *Gobčikovo-Nagymaros Project* (*Hungary v Slovakia*) [1997] ICJ Rep 7, 38–41, 46, 54, 55–6 ('*Hungarian Dams* case'); *Loewen Group v United States* (Competence and Jurisdiction), ICSID Case No. ARB(AF)/98/3 (5 January 2001), [46]–[47]; *Turkey – Restrictions on Imports of Textile and Clothing Products*, Report of 31 May 1999, WT/DS344/R, [9.42]–[9.43].

17 James Crawford and Simon Olleson, 'The Continuing Debate on a UN Convention on State Responsibility' (2005) 54 *International and Comparative Law Quarterly* 959, 960.

18 GA Res. 56/83 (12 December 2001).

19 See, e.g., *Bosnian Genocide* case, above note 14, [170]; *United States – Definitive Safeguard Measures on Imports of Circular Welded Carbon Quality Line Pipe from Korea*, Report of 15 February 2002, WT/DS202/AB/R, [259] (WTO); *Ilaşcu and Others v Moldova and Russia* (Merits and Just Satisfaction), Application No. 48787/99, Grand Chamber Judgment, 8 July 2004, [319], [320]–[321] (European Court of Human Rights).

20 See detailed discussion on the sources of international law in Chapter 2.

21 *Factory at Chorzów* (*Claim for Indemnity*) (Merits) (1927) PCIJ Rep (Ser. A) No. 9, 4, 29; *Corfu Channel* (*United Kingdom v Albania*) (Merits) [1949] ICJ Rep 4, 23.

of an international obligation of the state. There is no requirement that damage be caused to another state.[22] The Articles also reaffirm the now generally accepted principle of objective responsibility. For example, in the *Caire* case[23] the question arose as to whether Mexico was responsible for the actions of Mexican soldiers who shot a French national after trying to extort money from him. In finding Mexico responsible, the French–Mexican Claims Commission applied the principle of objective responsibility, defining it as 'the responsibility for the acts of the officials or organs of a state, which may devolve upon it even in the absence of any "fault" of its own'.[24] In its Commentary, the ILC considers that fault may form part of the primary obligation, but there is no general (secondary) rule to that effect.[25]

Article 3 of the Articles further provides that the characterization of an act as internationally wrongful is not affected by its characterization in internal law. This reflects the basic principle discussed in Chapter 3 that a state may not legislate away its international obligations or plead insufficiency of its internal law.[26]

7.3 THE RULES OF ATTRIBUTION

A state is internationally responsible if a breach of a primary obligation is attributed it. Attribution, or imputing an act to a state, is thus a necessary prerequisite for responsibility to accrue to that state.

7.3.1 State Organs

The conduct of any state organ shall be considered an act of the state, whether the organ exercises legislative, executive, judicial or any other function, whatever position it holds in the organization of the state, and whatever its character as an organ of the central government or of a territorial unit of the state (Article 4 of the Articles).[27] An organ includes

---

22 ILC Commentary to Article 2, [9]. See also Pellet, above note 1, 9–10.

23 *Caire (France) v Mexico* (1929) 5 RIAA 516.

24 Ibid., 529–31. See also *Union Bridge Company (United States) v Great Britain* (1924) 4 RIAA 138, 141.

25 ILC Commentary to Article 2, [3], [10].

26 See, e.g., *Exchange of Greek and Turkish Populations* case (Advisory Opinion) (1925) PCIJ Rep (Ser. B) No. 10, 20; Draft Declaration on Rights and Duties of States 1949, Art. 13, [1949] *Yearbook of the ILC*, 286. See also ILC Articles, above note 4, Art. 32.

27 See, e.g., *Difference relating to Immunity from Legal Process of a Special Rapporteur of the Commission on Human Rights* [1999] ICJ Rep 62, 87.

any person or entity which has that status in accordance with the internal law of the state,[28] although this definition is not exhaustive. An international court will consider all the circumstances to determine whether a person not classified as an organ under internal law is, in truth, part of the state apparatus.[29]

The fact that an organ of an autonomous government in a federation commits the wrongful act does not absolve the state of responsibility.[30] An example of breach by the judiciary is where it commits a denial of justice in relation to a foreign national.[31] Further, a breach by the legislature may occur if it fails to honour the state's treaty commitment to pass certain legislation. In the absence of a specific commitment, legislation must typically be acted upon for state responsibility to arise.[32] However, in *Prosecutor v Furundžija*, the ICTY stated:

> In the case of torture, the mere fact of keeping in force or passing legislation contrary to the international prohibition of torture generates international State responsibility. The value of freedom from torture is so great that it becomes imperative to preclude any national legislative act authorizing or condoning torture.[33]

Whether legislation gives rise to state responsibility will therefore depend upon the object and purpose of the primary rule in question.

7.3.2 Governmental Authority

Actions of persons who are not state organs will be attributed to the state if they are empowered to exercise elements of governmental authority

28 ILC Articles, above note 4, Art. 4(2).

29 ILC Commentary to Article 4, [11]; *Church of Scientology* case, Bundesgerichtshof Judgment of 26 September 1978, VI ZR 267/76, NJW 1979, 1101.

30 *Heirs of the Duc de Guise* (1951) 8 RIAA 150, 161. See ILC Commentary to Article 4, [8]–[10].

31 See, e.g., *Massey* (*United States*) *v Mexico* (1927) 4 RIAA 155. A non-denial of justice example is the *Special Rapporteur* case, above note 27. Denial of justice will be discussed in more detail at section 7.6.1.

32 *Mariposa Development Company and Others* (*United States*) *v Panama* (1933) 4 RIAA 338, 340–41. See Ian Brownlie, *Principles of Public International Law* (Oxford: Oxford University Press, 2008, 7th edn), 451.

33 *Prosecutor v Furundžija* (Trial Chamber Judgment) IT-95-17/1-T (10 December 1998), [150] (footnote omitted). Torture is a *jus cogens* norm: see discussion in Chapter 2.

and they act in that capacity in the particular instance (Article 5 of the Articles).

Two elements must be satisfied: that the power exercised is of a governmental nature, and that the entity was empowered to exercise it. As to the former, international case law suggests that two enquiries again are relevant.[34] The first enquiry is whether there is a high level of government control of the entity. In the case of a company, a rebuttable presumption of governmental authority arises where the state controls the voting power of the company.[35] The second enquiry is whether the functions being exercised are 'typically' or 'essentially' state functions.[36] In *Oil Field of Texas, Inc. v Iran*,[37] the Iran-United States Claims Tribunal had to decide whether the National Iranian Oil Company (NIOC) was exercising governmental functions in the context of breaches by an associated company of agreements with an American company for the lease of petroleum exploration and drilling equipment. The Tribunal found NIOC's breaches attributable to Iran as Iran was the company's sole shareholder and NIOC was established in order to exercise the ownership right of the Iranian nation in the oil and gas resources.[38]

The second element of Article 5 is that the entity was 'empowered by law' to exercise those functions. This requirement shields the state from responsibility where it has not appointed the entity to the functions it is purportedly exercising.

Acts of an organ or an entity empowered to exercise governmental authority that exceed their authority or contravene their instructions will still be considered an act of the state if the entity acts in the capacity of a state entity (Article 7). In the *Union Bridge Company* case[39] a British railway official confiscated neutral property believing it to belong to a belligerent. The Tribunal held that:

> liability is not affected either by the fact that he did so under a mistake as to the character and ownership of the material or that it was a time of pressure and confusion caused by war, or by the fact . . . that there was no intention on the part of the British authorities to appropriate the material in question.[40]

---

34 See, e.g., *Maffezini v Spain* (2000) 16 ICSID (W. Bank) 212.

35 Ibid., 239.

36 Ibid., 241; *Ceskoslovenska Obchodni Banka, AS v Slovakia* (1999) 14 ICSID Rev 251, 257.

37 *Oil Field of Texas, Inc. v Iran* (1982) 1 Iran-US Cl Trib Rep 347.

38 Ibid., 351. The fact that a company is for profit does not preclude it from exercising governmental functions: *Maffezini v Spain* (2000), above note 34, 241.

39 *Union Bridge Company* (*United States*) *v Great Britain*, above note 24.

40 Ibid., 141.

A fine distinction is, however, drawn as to when an entity acts in a governmental or private capacity.[41] A person may still act in a governmental capacity if acting within the apparent limits of his or her functions.[42] Thus, in the *Caire* case discussed above, Mexico could not escape responsibility for the actions of uniformed Mexican police officers who extorted and shot a French national, even though they were acting in excess of their authority under Mexican law. The Commission held that the officers 'acted at least to all appearances as competent officials or organs'.[43] Conversely, the 2011 incident involving allegations of sexual assault by the then leader of the International Monetary Fund would have occurred in an exclusively private setting and thus would not be attributable to that international organization.[44]

Exceptionally, in the context of international humanitarian law, acts of members of the armed forces during an armed conflict are always attributable to the state, even though they may not have been acting in that capacity.[45]

Article 9 of the Articles restates the rare situation where a person or group of persons is in fact exercising governmental authority in the absence or default of the official authorities and in circumstances that call for its exercise. This has relevance to failed states or the situation immediately after a successful revolution.[46]

7.3.3 Instructions, Direction or Control

The conduct of a person or group of persons who are neither an organ of the state nor an entity vested with governmental authority may still be attributed to the state where they are in fact acting on the instructions, or under the direction or control of, the state (Article 8). This restates what under customary international law are two distinct elements: (1) persons

---

41 This distinction also bedevils the area of state immunity *ratione materiae*: see Chapter 6.

42 *Mossé* case (1953) 13 RIAA 494.

43 *Caire (France) v Mexico*, above note 23, 530.

44 Note that the responsibility of international organizations and states on this issue are the same under international law: Article 7 of the ILC Draft Articles on Responsibility of International Organisations adopted on first reading, Report of the ILC, 61st sess., 2009, UN Doc. A/64/10, 23.

45 Recently applied in *Armed Activities on the Territory of the Congo (Democratic Republic of the Congo v Uganda)* [2005] ICJ Rep 168, 242.

46 *Yeager v Iran* (1987) 17 Iran-US Cl Trib Rep 92, 104 [43]; ILC Commentary to Article 9.

acting on the instructions of the state; or (2) under the direction or control of the state.

The leading ICJ decision is the *Nicaragua* case,[47] in which Nicaragua alleged that the United States had violated the prohibition against the use of force by mining Nicaraguan waters and providing vital assistance to an insurrectional movement against the Nicaraguan government. Although the mine laying was clearly attributable to the United States as acts of state organs (that state's armed forces), the ICJ found that breaches of international humanitarian law by the rebel *contras* were not attributable. First, despite finding that the United States largely financed, trained, equipped, armed and organized the *contras*, the Court found that the *contras* were not in fact organs of the United States[48] or acting under the instructions of the United States.[49] The Court then considered direction and control. What would have to be proved is that the United States had 'effective control' of the military and paramilitary operations 'in the course of which the alleged violations occurred' and that it 'directed and enforced' those violations.[50]

This test for direction and control was subsequently challenged by the ICTY Appeals Chamber in *Prosecutor v Tadić*,[51] which concerned an appeal against conviction for breaches of international humanitarian law committed during the Bosnian War. The ICTY had to decide whether the 'grave breaches' regime in the Geneva Conventions applied – that is, whether the Bosnian Serb insurrection movement, RS, 'belonged to' the Federal Republic of Yugoslavia.[52] Instead of applying the 'effective control' test, the Tribunal considered that the test was at variance with judicial and state practice[53] and was not consonant with the logic of state responsibility.[54] The Tribunal formulated its own test. Where unorganized individuals are concerned, the 'effective control' test would apply, but where individuals make up an organized and hierarchically structured group, such as a military unit or armed bands of rebels, the test is one of 'overall control'.[55] Mere financing, training, equipping or providing

---

[47] *Military and Paramilitary Activities in and against Nicaragua* (*Nicaragua v United States*) (Merits) [1986] ICJ Rep 14.

[48] See also the *Bosnian Genocide* case, supra note 14, 140 [391]–[392], discussed above at section 7.1.1.

[49] *Nicaragua* case, above note 47 [109]–[112].

[50] Ibid., [115].

[51] *Prosecutor v Tadić* (Appeals Chamber Judgment) IT-94-1-A (15 July 1999).

[52] Ibid., [93].

[53] Ibid., [124]–[145].

[54] Ibid., [116]–[123].

[55] Ibid., [120].

operational support to the group would not suffice, but the conduct will be attributable if the state 'has a role in organizing, coordinating or planning the military actions of the military group'.[56]

The ILC in its Commentary to the Articles took the view that *Tadić* should be confined to the threshold question in international humanitarian law of whether an international armed conflict exists.[57] This view was vindicated, as far as the ICJ is concerned, by the *Bosnian Genocide* case, which expressly reaffirmed the *Nicaragua* test.[58] However, the *Bosnian Genocide* case failed to grapple convincingly with the issue of direction or control. The ICJ made no effort to engage with the considerable state practice and judicial decisions cited by the ICTY.[59] It also arguably turned the clock back to Cold War-era international law. *Nicaragua* was, as Travalio and Altenburg put it:

> decided in the context of a largely bipolar world, in which the United States and the former Soviet Union had fought and were fighting 'proxy wars' of varying intensities throughout the world. To hold that both the United States and the Soviet Union had engaged in armed attacks whenever groups that they supported did so would have obviously created a far more dangerous world.[60]

One of the contemporary implications of the ICJ's 'effective control' test is to make it much more difficult to hold states accountable for the use of mercenaries and private military firms.[61]

7.3.4 Adoption and Insurrection Movements

Another avenue of attribution is where a state acknowledges and adopts conduct as its own (Article 11 of the Articles). In the *Tehran Hostages* case,[62] Iranian militants seized the United States Embassy in Tehran and held the consular and diplomatic staff hostage. The Iranian government's failure to protect the United States mission, and its passive acceptance of the situation after the attack, violated diplomatic law.[63] It was only

---

[56] Ibid., [137]. This would apply *mutatis mutandis* to non-military groups.
[57] ILC Commentary to Article 8, [5].
[58] *Bosnian Genocide* case, above note 14, [396]–[407].
[59] See Cassese, above note 14.
[60] Greg Travalio and John Altenburg, 'Terrorism, State Responsibility, and the Use of Military Force' (2003) 4 *Chicago Journal of International Law* 97, 105.
[61] See Chapter 5.
[62] *United States Diplomatic and Consular Staff in Tehran* (*United States v Iran*) (Judgment) [1980] ICJ Rep 3.
[63] Ibid., [63], [66]–[67].

after the Iranian government eventually publicly adopted the militants' activities as official policy that this 'translated continuing occupation of the Embassy and detention of the hostages into acts of that State', as the militants 'had now become agents of the Iranian State for whose acts the State itself was internationally responsible'.[64] It should be noted that mere support or endorsement will not suffice – the conduct must be adopted as the state's own.[65]

The situation of insurrection movements is more complicated. The conduct of rebels, for example in destroying alien property, is not attributed to the state if the state is not negligent in suppressing the rebellion.[66] This amounts to a kind of *force majeure*.[67] However, if the insurrection is successful and the group eventually becomes the government of the state (or a new breakaway state), actions of members of that group carried out in that capacity during the insurrection will be attributed to the state (Article 10).[68]

7.3.5 Derived Responsibility

Under Article 16 of the Articles, conduct will be attributed to a state where it 'aids or assists' another state in the commission of an internationally wrongful act and where the former knew of the circumstances of the internationally wrongful act.[69] The physical element of 'aid or assist' is broad and would include conduct that makes it materially easier for another state to commit a wrongful act. The mental element of 'knowledge' is, however, narrow and often difficult to prove.[70] What is required is knowledge of the 'specific intent' of the other state.[71] For example, a state must not supply arms to another state where the supplying state knows that the receiving state will use them to commit acts of aggression.

Less common is the scenario where one state 'directs and controls'

---

64 Ibid., [72]–[74].

65 ILC Commentary to Article 11, [6].

66 *Solis* (1951) 4 RIAA 358, 361; ILC Commentary to Article 10, [3].

67 Brownlie, above note 32, 455.

68 *Short v Iran* (1987) 16 Iran-US Cl Trib Rep 76; *Yeager v Iran* (1987), above note 46; *Rankin v Iran* (1987) 17 Iran-US Cl Trib Rep 135; Commentary to Article 10, [4].

69 *Bosnian Genocide* case, supra note 14, [420].

70 Jessica Howard, 'Invoking State Responsibility for Aiding the Commission of International Crimes – Australia, the United States and the Question of East Timor' (2001) 2 *Melbourne Journal of International Law* 1.

71 *Bosnian Genocide* case, supra note 14, [421]–[422].

another state in the commission of an internationally wrongful act. This may occur, for instance, during belligerent occupation.[72] Here, the dominant state is responsible not because it has power to direct and control, but because of direction and control actually exercised, with knowledge of the circumstances of the wrongful act (Article 17 of the Articles).[73] Similarly, a state is responsible where it coerces another state to commit a wrongful act, with knowledge of the circumstances of the wrongful act (Article 18).[74] Coercion amounts to *force majeure* for the coerced state as a result of the use of force, severe economic pressure or other measures forcing the coerced state to commit the wrongful act.[75]

7.3.6 *Lex Specialis*

These general rules of attribution can be displaced by *lex specialis*.[76] Currently a very topical issue is whether a new norm of customary *lex specialis* has emerged that engages state responsibility for 'harbouring' or 'supporting' terrorists.[77] The attitude of the international community has become extremely assertive, culminating in a series of unanimous General Assembly and Security Council resolutions following the 11 September 2001 attacks on the United States, condemning those who provide 'active or passive' support to terrorists.[78] Of course, one of the major stumbling blocks to such a categorization is the fact that the international community has still, after decades of negotiation, failed to agree on a definition of terrorism that excludes (legitimate) freedom fighters.[79]

---

72 ILC Commentary to Article 17, [5].

73 *Brown (United States) v Great Britain* (1923) 6 RIAA 120; ILC Commentary to Article 17, [6]–[7].

74 See Dominicé, above note 11, 288–9.

75 ILC Commentary to Article 18, [3].

76 ILC Articles, above note 4, Art. 55.

77 See, e.g., Scott Malzahn, 'State Sponsorship and Support of International Terrorism: Customary Norms of State Responsibility' (2002) 26 *Hastings International and Comparative Law Review* 83.

78 See, e.g., 'Declaration on Principles of International Law concerning Friendly Relations and Co-operation among States', GA Res. 2625, UN GAOR, 25th sess., Supp. No. 28, UN Doc. A/8028 (1970), 123. For a complete list of resolutions, see Malzahn, above note 78, 88, fnn 18 and 19.

79 See Ben Saul, *Defining Terrorism in International Law* (Oxford; New York: Oxford University Press, 2006); John Murphy, 'Defining International Terrorism: A Way out of the Quagmire' (1989) 19 *Israel Year Book of Human Rights* 13, 14. On the continuing struggle with the distinction, see Chapter 5.

7.4 CIRCUMSTANCES PRECLUDING WRONGFULNESS

Chapter V of Part 1 of the Articles sets out general rules for circumstances that preclude responsibility for what would otherwise be an internationally wrongful act. There is some doctrinal dispute about whether the circumstances precluding wrongfulness are primary or secondary rules, although their status as generally applicable rules is settled.[80] The circumstances precluding wrongfulness are, by their nature, temporary – when the circumstance ceases to operate, the obligation to perform the primary rule is restored.[81]

Article 26 states that nothing in Chapter V precludes the wrongfulness of an act that is not in conformity with a *jus cogens* norm. This carefully worded savings clause avoids the doctrinal anomaly presented by the fact that a state can consent to the use of force by, for example, allowing another state to station troops on its territory.[82] The law on the use of force is discussed in Chapter 8.

7.4.1 Consent

Valid consent by a state to the commission of an act by another state precludes the wrongfulness of that act in relation to the former state to the extent that the act remains within the limits of that consent (Article 20). Consent can be express or implied. The *Russian Indemnity* case[83] concerned a claim by Russia against Turkey for interest on a long-standing indemnity. The Permanent Court of Arbitration held:

> In the relations between the Imperial Russian Government and [Turkey], Russia therefore renounced its right to interest, since its Embassy repeatedly accepted without discussion or reservation and mentioned again and again in its own diplomatic correspondence the amount of the balance of the indemnity as identical with the amount of the balance of the principal.[84]

---

[80] See discussion above at section 7.1.

[81] ILC Articles, above note 4, Art. 27(a).

[82] ILC Commentary to Article 26, [6]; Ademola Abass, 'Consent Precluding State Responsibility: A Critical Analysis' (2004) 53 *International and Comparative Law Quarterly* 211, 211–13, 223–4.

[83] *Russian Claim for Interest on Indemnities* (*Damages Claimed by Russia for Delay in Payment of Compensation Owed to Russians Injured during the War of 1877–78*) (1912) 11 RIAA 421.

[84] Ibid., [9]. See also *Armed Activities on the Territory of the Congo* (*Democratic Republic of the Congo v Uganda*) , above note 45, 211 [99]; *Savarkar* (*Great Britain v France*) (1911) 11 RIAA 243.

Consent should emanate from authorities competent to give such consent under the internal law of the state, although ostensible authority might suffice in an appropriate case.[85]

The *Savarkar* arbitration[86] illustrates the flexibility of this rule. The case concerned the transportation of a prisoner by ship to British India where he was to face trial. While the ship was docked in Marseilles harbour, the prisoner escaped and swam ashore, where he was seized by a French *gendarme* who, with the assistance of members of the British crew, brought the fugitive back. The Permanent Court of Arbitration held that French sovereignty had not been violated, as all parties had acted in good faith and the British officials were entitled to regard the behaviour of the *gendarme* as valid consent to their actions in the circumstances.[87]

7.4.2 Self-defence

The wrongfulness of an act of a state is precluded if the act constitutes a lawful measure of self-defence taken in conformity with the UN Charter (Article 21). Self-defence is discussed in Chapter 8.

7.4.3 *Force majeure*

Force majeure applies when an act is carried out in response to the occurrence of irresistible force or of an unforeseen event, beyond the control of the state, making it materially impossible in the circumstances to perform the obligation. A state cannot invoke *force majeure* if the situation was caused, either alone or in combination with other factors, by the conduct of the state or if it has assumed the risk (Article 23 of the Articles).

Force majeure can arise from purely natural causes, such as bad weather forcing the diversion of an aircraft onto another state's territory, or from human causes outside the state's control, such as the conduct of insurrection movements.[88] Similar to the cognate concept of supervening

---

[85] Abass, above note 82, 215; ILC Commentary to Article 20, [4]–[8]; Affef Mansour, 'Circumstances Precluding Wrongfulness in the ILC Articles on State Responsibility: Consent', in Crawford et al., above note 1, 439, 443.

[86] *Savarkar* arbitration, above note 84.

[87] Ibid., 254.

[88] ILC Commentary to Article 23, [3]; *Gould Marketing, Inc. v Ministry of National Defense of Iran,* Interlocutory Award No. ITL 24-49-2, (1983) 3 Iran-US Cl Trib Rep 147, 153; *Ottoman Empire Lighthouses Concession* (1956) 7 RIAA 155, 219–20.

impossibility of performance in the law of treaties, the fact that performance is rendered more difficult – because of an economic crisis, for example – does not excuse non-performance.[89]

7.4.4 Distress

The wrongfulness of an act of a state is precluded if the author of the act has no other reasonable way, in a situation of distress, of saving the author's life or the lives of those entrusted to the author's care. Distress cannot be invoked if the situation is caused, either alone or in combination with other factors, by the conduct of the invoking state, or if the act is likely to create a comparable or greater peril (Article 24). It is sufficient that the author reasonably believed that the danger existed.[90]

In the *Rainbow Warrior* incident,[91] two French agents had destroyed a ship in the port of Auckland. By treaty, France agreed to make the prisoners serve out their sentences on the island of Hao. However, before their sentences had expired, France repatriated them to their homeland in contravention of its undertakings to New Zealand. The Permanent Court of Arbitration accepted France's argument of distress in relation to one of the agents, who had to be repatriated to receive treatment for a serious medical condition that could threaten his life. The Court held that France had demonstrated an 'extreme urgency involving medical or other considerations of an elementary nature'.[92] By requiring a threat to life, the ILC deliberately departed from the arbitral body's formulation in the *Rainbow Warrior* case that distress had to be tightly circumscribed to avoid abuse.[93] It thus remains unclear whether distress is available for situations falling short of threat to life.

7.4.5 Necessity

Necessity is an exceptional excuse for non-performance.[94] Necessity cannot be invoked unless it is the only means to safeguard an essential

---

89 *Russian Indemnity* case, above note 83, [6].

90 James Crawford, 'Second Report on State Responsibility' (1999), UN Doc. A/CN.4/498, [271].

91 *Difference between New Zealand and France concerning the Interpretation or Application of Two Agreements, concluded on 9 July 1986 between the Two States and which related to the Problems Arising from the Rainbow Warrior Affair* (1990) 20 RIAA 215.

92 Ibid., 255 [79].

93 ILC Commentary to Article 24, [6].

94 *Hungarian Dams* case, above note 16, [51]–[52]; ILC Commentary to Article 25, [2], [14].

interest of the state against a grave and imminent peril, and it does not impair an essential interest of the state towards which the obligation exists, or of the international community as a whole.

It is only interests of a similar gravity to preservation of the natural environment, economic survival or the subsistence of the population that would be 'essential'.[95] For example, when the Liberian supertanker Torrey Canyon ran onto submerged rocks, Britain was justified in bombing the ship to burn up the oil that would otherwise have threatened the British coastline.[96] What is 'essential' and whether a 'grave and imminent peril' existed is judged objectively, rather than from the subjective intent of the invoking state,[97] and breaching the primary obligation must be the only means of preventing that peril.[98]

Furthermore, necessity may not be invoked if the primary rule excludes the possibility of its invocation, even if implicitly.[99] For example, in the *Israeli Wall* case,[100] the ICJ held that the course chosen by Israel for the wall was 'necessary to obtain its security objectives'.[101] However, in doing so Israel would be 'gravely infringing' international human rights and humanitarian law, and those infringements 'cannot be justified by military exigencies or by the requirements of national security or public order'.[102]

Necessity cannot be invoked if the state has contributed to the situation of necessity. In the *Hungarian Dams* case,[103] necessity was closed to Hungary as it had 'helped' to bring about any situation of necessity.[104] However, on the point of 'grave and imminent peril', *Hungarian Dams*

---

[95] *Hungarian Dams* case, ibid., [53]; Roberto Ago, 'Addendum to the Eighth Report on State Responsibility' [1980] II(1) *Yearbook of the ILC* 12, [78]; *CMS Gas Transmission Company v Argentina*, ICSID Case No. ARB/01/08), award of 12 May 2005, 14 ICSID Rep 152, [322]–[329] (economic crisis where other means, albeit more onerous, could be used and the state contributed to the crisis).

[96] *The 'Torrey Canyon'*, Cmnd 3246 (1967).

[97] *Hungarian Dams* case, above note 16 [51]; ILC Commentary to Article 25, [15]–[16].

[98] *The M/V Saiga (No. 2)* (*Saint Vincent and the Grenadines v Guinea*) (1999) 38 ILM 1323, [135]–[136]; *Hungarian Dams* case, above note 16, [54].

[99] ILC Articles, above note 4, Art. 25(2)(a); ILC Commentary to Article 25, [19].

[100] *Legal Consequences of the Construction of a Wall in the Occupied Palestinian Territory* [2004] ICJ Rep 136.

[101] Ibid., [136].

[102] Ibid., [135]–[136].

[103] *Hungarian Dams* case, above note 16.

[104] Ibid., [57].

considered that a peril appearing in the long term might be 'imminent' if its occurrence was nevertheless inevitable.[105]

7.5 CONSEQUENCES OF BREACH

Once it is established that an international obligation has been breached and that the breach is attributable to a state that cannot avail itself of any circumstances precluding wrongfulness, new secondary obligations descend upon that state to make good the injury caused to the injured state or the international community as a whole.[106]

7.5.1 Cessation

The obligation of cessation is crucial to the international rule of law and the underlying principle of *pacta sunt servanda*.[107] As a wrongful act does not affect the state's continued duty to perform the obligation,[108] a state is under a duty to cease its act, if it is continuing (Article 30(a) of the Articles). In practice, cessation is often the primary remedy sought.[109] In some cases cessation can be indistinguishable from restitution, especially where the wrongful conduct is an omission,[110] such as the obligation on Iran to free the hostages in *Tehran Hostages* case.[111] Cessation was inapplicable in *Rainbow Warrior*[112] as the violated treaty obligation was no longer in force.[113]

---

[105] Ibid., [55].

[106] ILC Articles, above note 4, Art. 28. See *LaGrand* (*Germany v United States*) [2001] ICJ Rep 466, [48].

[107] Dinah Shelton, 'Righting Wrongs: Reparations in the Articles on State Responsibility' (2002) 96 *American Journal of International Law* 833, 839. On efficient breach, see, e.g., Lewis Kornhauser, 'An Introduction to the Economic Analysis of Contract Remedies' (1986) 57 *University of Colorado Law Review* 683, 686; cf Charles Fried, *Contract as Promise: A Theory of Contractual Obligation* (Cambridge, MA; London: Harvard University Press, 1981), 9.

[108] ILC Articles, above note 4, Art. 29.

[109] ILC Commentary to Article 30, [4].

[110] ILC Articles, above note 4, Art. 2.

[111] *Tehran Hostages* case, above note 62.

[112] *Rainbow Warrior* case, supra note 91.

[113] Ibid., [114].

7.5.2 Assurances and Guarantees of Non-repetition

A state is also under an obligation to offer appropriate assurances and guarantees of non-repetition, if the circumstances so require (Article 30(b)). In *LaGrand*,[114] the ICJ found the United States to be in breach of diplomatic law in its failure to inform two condemned German prisoners of their right to communicate with the German consulate.[115] The Court considered that the apology by the United States did not suffice in the circumstances.[116] The Court noted that the United States' commitment to implement a 'vast and detailed programme' to ensure future compliance was met with 'Germany's request for a *general* assurance of non-repetition'.[117] As to *specific* assurances, the ICJ intimated that if the United States again breached the rule to the detriment of German nationals, and if the individuals concerned were subjected to prolonged detention or sentenced to severe penalties, 'it would be incumbent upon the United States to allow the review and reconsideration of the conviction and sentence'.[118]

The circumstances in which a state should offer guarantees or assurances are exceptional, and the area is still developing.[119] The rule is likely to apply only if there is a real risk that a serious breach causing substantial injury to another state may be repeated.[120] The choice of means of compliance will usually be left to the discretion of the responsible state.[121]

7.5.3 Reparations

In *Chorzów Factory*,[122] the Permanent Court of International Justice ordered Poland to pay reparations to Germany for wrongfully appropriating land owned by German companies in Polish Upper Silesia. Under treaty, Poland could only apply state, and not private, property in payment of German war reparations. The following statement is

---

114 *LaGrand* case, above note 106.

115 Vienna Convention on Consular Relations 1963, Art. 36(1)(b).

116 *LaGrand* case, above note 106, [123].

117 Ibid., [123]–[124] (emphasis added).

118 Ibid., [125]. See also *Land and Maritime Boundary between Cameroon and Nigeria* (*Cameroon v Nigeria: Equatorial Guinea Intervening*) [2002] ICJ Rep 303, [318].

119 ILC Commentary to Article 30, [13].

120 James R. Crawford, 'State Responsibility', in *Max Planck Encyclopedia of Public International Law* (Heidelberg: Max-Planck-Institut, 2010), [26]

121 *LaGrand* case, above note 106, [125].

122 *Chorzów Factory* case, above note 21.

canonical:[123] 'Reparation must, as far as possible, wipe out all the consequences of the illegal act and re-establish the situation which would, in all probability, have existed if that act had not been committed'.[124]

This is reflected in Article 31 of the Articles, which provides for an obligation of full reparation for the injury caused by the internationally wrongful act.[125] The concept of 'injury' is broad and includes any damage, material or moral. Insults to a state and pain and suffering are the main examples of 'moral' damage. In the *I'm Alone* case,[126] the US-Canadian Claims Commission held that the sinking of a Canadian registered private vessel by the United States did not cause any material damage to Canada as it was owned and operated by American citizens. Nevertheless, the act caused moral damage to Canada, for which the Commission recommended that the United States apologise and pay $25,000 compensation.[127]

The Articles only partly elaborate on the principle of causation. The Commentary takes the view that questions of 'directness' and 'remoteness of damage' are too flexible to be reduced to a 'single verbal formula'.[128] However, under the mitigation rule in Article 39, account shall be taken of the contribution to the injury by wilful or negligent conduct of the injured state or person (for example, a national) in relation to whom the injured state seeks reparation.[129] The Articles do not address the situation where the injury is partly caused by a lawful act of a third party, or questions of contribution as between two responsible states.[130] The way in which these general principles apply in international law is largely unexplored.[131]

Reparation takes the form of, singly or in combination, restitution, compensation and satisfaction.[132]

---

[123] See, e.g., *Hungarian Dams* case, above note 16, [149]–[150].

[124] *Chorzów Factory* case, above note 21, 47.

[125] See also *'Lusitania'* case (*United States, Germany*) (1923) 7 RIAA 32, 39.

[126] *SS 'I'm Alone'* case (*Canada, United States*) (1935) 3 RIAA 1609.

[127] Ibid., 1618.

[128] ILC Commentary to Article 31, [10], quoting with approval Patrick Atiyah, *An Introduction to the Law of Contract* (Oxford: Clarendon Press, 1995, 5th edn), 466.

[129] See also *Hungarian Dams* case, above note 16, [80].

[130] ILC Articles, above note 4, Art. 47(2)(b); ILC Commentary to Article 47, [10].

[131] See Shelton, above note 107, 846–7.

[132] ILC Articles, above note 4, Art. 34.

7.5.4 Restitution

Article 35 of the Articles restates the orthodoxy that restitution is the primary remedy for injury caused by an internationally wrongful act.[133] Restitution can take the form of restoration of territory, persons or property or reversal of a juridical act.[134] For example, in the *Temple of Preah Vihear* case,[135] the ICJ required Thailand to withdraw its detachment of armed forces and restore any objects it removed from a Cambodian temple.[136] In the *Arrest Warrant* case,[137] Belgium was obliged to cancel an arrest warrant in breach of state immunity.

Restitution is not available to the extent that it is materially impossible (for example, if appropriated property has been destroyed or sold to a third party), or if it involves a burden out of all proportion to the benefit being sought from restitution, especially if compensation would be a sufficient remedy.[138] These limitations mean that in some areas, such as trade or investment, restitution is rarely ordered.[139] Despite these reservations, retaining restitution as a primary remedy is justified to discourage rich states from paying for illegally obtained advantages that cannot be so obtained by poorer states.[140]

7.5.5 Compensation

To the extent that damage is not made good by restitution, the responsible state must pay compensation for any financially assessable damage, including loss of profits (Article 36 of the Articles).

A common and flexible remedy, compensation usually comprises the 'fair market value' of property (appropriately valued), an award of lost profits if not too speculative, and incidental expenses

---

[133] *Chorzów Factory* case, above note 21, 47; ILC Commentary to Article 35, [3].

[134] ILC Commentary to Article 35, [5].

[135] *Case concerning the Temple of Preah Vihear* (*Cambodia v Thailand*) (Merits) [1962] ICJ Rep 6.

[136] Ibid., 36.

[137] *Arrest Warrant of 11 April 2000* (*Democratic Republic of Congo v Belgium*) [2002] ICJ Rep 3.

[138] ILC Articles, above note 4, Arts 35(a) and (b); ILC Commentary to Article 35, [9]; *Chorzów Factory* case, above note 21, 47; *Forests of Central Rhodope* (1933) 3 RIAA 1405, 1432.

[139] See, e.g., Bruno Simma and Dirk Pulkowski, '*Leges Speciales* and Self-Contained Regimes', in Crawford, above note 12, 139, 156.

[140] Brownlie, above note 32, 463; Shelton, above note 108, 844.

incurred.[141] For personal injury to a national, compensation lies for medical expenses, loss of earnings and moral damage.[142] These statements are very general and the measure of damages very much depends on the primary obligation breached and the circumstances of the case.[143] Equitable considerations and proportionality also play a role.[144]

The flexibility of compensation is demonstrated by the jurisprudence on nationalizations. Where a state expropriates the property of a foreign national, there is no general customary rule of 'prompt, adequate and effective' compensation (the so-called 'Hull formula'), as developing states have long considered that expropriation during non-discriminatory large-scale nationalizations for a public purpose do not oblige states to pay full compensation. Appropriate compensation must take into account the state's right to permanent sovereignty over its resources.[145]

7.5.6 Satisfaction

The third remedy is satisfaction (Article 37 of the Articles). Satisfaction may consist of an acknowledgement of the breach, a formal apology or another appropriate modality, such as an inquiry into the causes of an incident or the prosecution of individuals.[146] Assurances and guarantees of non-repetition may also have the effect of producing satisfaction. Sometimes the ICJ has considered that its condemnation of the responsible state is adequate satisfaction.[147] Satisfaction may not be out of proportion to the injury or be humiliating.[148] Importantly, satisfaction may not amount to punitive damages, a remedy of deterrence not known to international law.[149]

---

[141] ILC Commentary to Article 36, [2], [21]. See, e.g., *Amoco International Finance Corp. v Iran* (1987) 15 Iran-US Cl Trib 189.

[142] ILC Commentary to Article 36, [16].

[143] Ibid., [7]ff.

[144] Shelton, above note 107, 838; ILC Commentary to Article 36, [7].

[145] Resolution on Permanent Sovereignty over Natural Resources 1962, GA Res. 1803 (XVII), GAOR, 17th sess., Supp. 17, 15, [4]; Charter of Economic Rights and Duties of States 1974, GA Res. 3281 (XXIX), (1975) 14 ILM 251, Art. 2(c). The 'Hull formula' is stated in *Anglo-Iranian Oil Co* (*United Kingdom v Iran*) (*United Kingdom v Iran*) [1952] ICJ Rep 93, Memorial submitted by the United Kingdom, 105–6.

[146] ILC Articles, above note 4, Art. 37(2); ILC Commentary to Article 37, [5].

[147] See, e.g., *Corfu Channel* case, above note 21, 35.

[148] ILC Articles, above note 4, Art. 37(3).

[149] *Velásquez Rodriguéz v Honduras*, Judgment of 21 July 1989, Inter-Am Ct H R (Ser. C) No. 7 (1989), [38].

Satisfaction is particularly suited to remedy moral damage that is not financially assessable, as demonstrated by the *I'm Alone* case discussed above.[150]

7.6 INVOCATION OF STATE RESPONSIBILITY

Central to international law is the mechanism for holding states accountable for their internationally wrongful acts. The Articles rightly define 'invocation' narrowly – that is, as the commencement of proceedings before an international court or tribunal.[151] This ensures that states do not have to show standing for protests or similar expressions of *opinio juris*.

7.6.1 The Injured State

A state is entitled as an 'injured state' to invoke the responsibility of another state if the obligation breached is owed to

(a) that state individually; or
(b) a group of states including that state and the breach
  (i) specially affects that state; or
  (ii) radically changes the position of all the other states to which the obligation is owed with respect to the further performance of the obligation (Article 42 of the Articles).

This formulation follows Article 60 of the Vienna Convention on the Law of Treaties, and similar considerations apply.[152] An example of sub-paragraph (b)(ii) would be one state claiming sovereignty over an unclaimed area of Antarctica contrary to the Antarctic Treaty. The position of all parties to the Treaty would be radically changed.[153]

An injured state loses the right to invoke responsibility if it has explicitly waived the claim or, by reason of its delay, it can be inferred that it validly acquiesced in the claim's lapse (Article 45).[154] In the *Boeing*

---

150 See discussion above at section 7.5.3.
151 ILC Commentary to Article 42, [2].
152 ILC Commentary, Article 42, [4]. See Chapter 2 for more detailed treatment of these concepts in the context of the law of treaties.
153 ILC Commentary to Article 42, [14].
154 *Certain Phosphate Lands in Nauru* (*Nauru v Australia*) (Preliminary Objections) [1992] ICJ Rep 240, [32]. The considerations for waiver are similar to those for consent: see discussion above at 7.4.1.

case,[155] the Iran-United States Claims Tribunal imputed acquiescence to Iran for its three-year delay in bringing a claim against Boeing, given that it had 'ample opportunity' to bring such a claim if it had so desired.[156] Conversely, in *LaGrand*[157] Germany brought its claim on the eve of execution of its second national on death row, more than 15 years after the United States' breaches commenced. Thus, both humanitarian considerations and the behaviour of the parties have a bearing on acquiescence.[158]

7.6.2 The Non-injured State

A 'non-injured state' may invoke responsibility where the obligation breached is owed to

(a) a group of states including that state, and is established for a collective interest of the group (such as collective defence), or
(b) the international community as a whole (Article 48(1) of the Articles).

Article 48(1)(b) reflects the principle that *erga omnes* obligations, including but not limited to *jus cogens* norms, can be invoked by any state.[159] In such a case, a non-injured state can seek cessation and assurances and guarantees of non-repetition.[160]

Under the Articles, where a state commits a serious (that is gross or systematic) breach of *jus cogens*, all states have a duty to cooperate to end the breach through lawful means.[161] This duty is admittedly a progressive development.[162] The other consequence is that states shall not recognize as lawful a situation created by such a breach, nor render aid or assistance in maintaining that situation.[163] In the *Israeli Wall* case,[164] the ICJ declared:

---

155 *The Boeing Company et al. v Iran et al.* (1986) 6 Iran-US Cl Trib Rep 43.
156 Ibid., 50.
157 *LaGrand* case, above note 106.
158 Abass, above note 82, 222.
159 See Chapter 2 on the definition and nature of *erga omnes* obligations and *jus cogens* norms.
160 ILC Articles, above note 4, Art. 48(2)(a).
161 Ibid., Art. 41(1).
162 ILC Commentary to Article 41, [3]; but see *Israeli Wall* case, supra note 101, [159]. This is similar to the emerging 'responsibility to protect' principle discussed at section 7.8.
163 ILC Articles, above note 4, Art. 41(2).
164 *Israeli Wall* case, above note 100.

> Given the character and the importance of the rights and obligations involved, the Court is of the view that all States are under an obligation not to recognize the illegal situation resulting from the construction of the wall . . . They are also under an obligation not to render aid or assistance in maintaining the situation created by such construction.[165]

7.6.3 Plurality of Injured or Responsible States

Where several states are injured by the same wrongful act, each may separately invoke responsibility.[166] Similarly, where several states are responsible for the same internationally wrongful act, the responsibility of each may be invoked.[167] This rule does not apply where states commit different wrongful acts causing the injury, such as where one state aids or assists another to commit a wrongful act.[168]

An important procedural rule is that responsibility cannot be invoked if a *necessary* step in the claim is a finding of a wrongful act by a non-party to the proceedings. In the *East Timor* case,[169] Australia acquired certain East Timorese submarine resources under a treaty with Indonesia. Portugal claimed that Australia had breached its *erga omnes* obligation not to infringe the East Timorese people's right to self-determination. The Court dismissed the claim, as it would have had to pronounce on the lawfulness of Indonesia's claim to East Timor.[170]

7.6.4 Countermeasures

International law distinguishes between reprisals (forcible unlawful responses), countermeasures (non-forcible unlawful responses) and retorsions (unfriendly but lawful responses). Reprisals are prohibited. However, in a decentralized system such as international law countermeasures are tolerated as a self-help mechanism provided strict requirements are observed.

An injured state may take countermeasures that comprise non-performance of obligations it owes to the responsible state, provided

---

165 Ibid., [159].

166 ILC Articles, above note 4, Art. 46; *SS 'Wimbledon'* case [1923] PCIJ (Ser. A) No. 1, 4, 20.

167 ILC Articles, above note 4, Art. 47; ILC Commentary to Article 47, [2].

168 ILC Articles, above note 4, Art. 16; see discussion above at section 7.3.5.

169 *East Timor* case (*Portugal v Australia*) [1995] ICJ Rep 90.

170 Ibid., [37]. See also *Monetary Gold Removed from Rome in 1943* (Judgment) [1954] ICJ Rep 19, 32.

resumption of the obligation is possible.[171] Thus, in the *Hungarian Dams* case[172] Czechoslovakia's irreversible step of diverting the Danube, taken in response to Hungary's treaty breaches, was not a lawful countermeasure.[173] As the object of countermeasures is to induce the responsible state to cease its wrongful conduct,[174] they must be terminated as soon as the responsible state has complied or if the dispute is pending before a competent court or tribunal.[175]

Secondly, Article 51 of the Articles requires countermeasures to be 'commensurate with the injury suffered', in view of the gravity of the wrongful act and the importance of the rights in question.[176] Couched in the positive, this requirement is harder for an injured state to satisfy than the formulation in the *Air Services* case,[177] in which France wrongfully refused to allow a change of gauge in London on Pan Am flights from the US west coast. The Arbitral Tribunal held that the United States' suspension of all Air France flights to Los Angeles was 'not clearly disproportionate' as it had 'some degree of equivalence with the alleged breach'.[178] Hence, proportionality remains an unsettled area.[179]

Before taking countermeasures, the injured state must notify the responsible state of its decision and offer to negotiate, but it can dispense with this requirement if urgent countermeasures are necessary to preserve its rights.[180]

7.7 THE STATE'S DIPLOMATIC PROTECTION OVER ITS NATURAL AND JURISTIC PERSONS

Following the jurisprudence of Vattel[181] the Permanent Court of International Justice stated in *Mavromattis*:

---

171 ILC Articles, above note 4, Art. 49.

172 *Hungarian Dams* case, above note 16.

173 Ibid., [87].

174 ILC Commentary to Chapter II of Part Three, [4].

175 ILC Articles, above note 4, Arts 52(3) and 53.

176 *Hungarian Dams* case, above note 16, [85].

177 *Air Service Agreement of 27 March 1946* (*United States v France*) (1978) 18 RIAA 417.

178 Ibid., [83].

179 Bederman, above note 9, 821–2.

180 ILC Articles, above note 4, Art. 52(1); ILC Commentary to Article 52, [3].

181 Emerich Vattel, *Le droit des gens, ou principes de la loi naturelle, appliqués a la conduite et aux affaires des Nations et Souverains* (Washington, DC: Carnegie Institution of Washington, 1916), Bk II, Ch. vi. See generally C. Amerasinghe,

> a State is entitled to protect its subjects, when injured by acts contrary to international law committed by another State, from whom they have been unable to obtain satisfaction through the ordinary channels.[182]

Following decolonization, disagreements between states paralyzed legal development in this area. Developed states considered there was an international minimum standard for the treatment of aliens, while developing states denied that aliens could be treated more favourably than nationals.[183] Equally divisive was the question of permanent sovereignty over natural resources[184] and whether to jettison the fiction that the state sues on account of injury to itself.[185] Therefore it was only in 2006 that the ILC produced, and the General Assembly took note of, its Draft Articles on Diplomatic Protection.[186] However, the Draft Articles deal only with the procedural rules relating to nationality of claims and exhaustion of local remedies.[187]

Some substantive rules have developed. Generally, a state can freely choose to refuse entry to an alien or set conditions on entry, including refusing them civil rights such as the right to vote.[188] Expulsion, however, must not be arbitrary, discriminatory or in breach of the expelling state's obligations.[189] A state may also sue for a denial of justice committed against its national – the action here is founded on the malfunctioning of the state's judicial system.[190]

Diplomatic Protection (Oxford: Oxford University Press, 2009) Oxford Scholarship Online.

182 *Mavromattis Palestine Concession* case (*Greece v United Kingdom*) (Jurisdiction) (1924) PCIJ Rep (Ser. A) No. 2, 12. See also *Administrative Decision No. V* (*United States v Germany*) (1924) 7 RIAA 119.

183 See *Neer Claim* (*United States v Mexico*) (1926) 4 RIAA 60.

184 See discussion above at section 7.5.5.

185 Mohamed Bennouna, 'Preliminary Report on Diplomatic Protection' [1998] II(1) *Yearbook of the ILC* 309 [2]; John Dugard, 'First Report on Diplomatic Protection', UN Doc. A/CN.4/506 (2000), [17].

186 GA Res. A/Res/61/35 (4 December 2006).

187 See Chapter 9.

188 See, e.g., Brownlie, above note 32, 520 (and the cases cited therein). This may not be true in the specialized field of refugee law.

189 *Rankin v Iran* (1987), above note 68, [22]; cf Malcolm Shaw, *International Law* (Cambridge; New York: Cambridge University Press, 2008, 6th edn), 826. This includes constructive expulsion: *International Technical Products Corp. v Iran* (1985) 9 Iran-US Cl Trib Rep 18.

190 *Azinian v Mexico* (1999) ILR 121, 1, 23–4. For the rules on expropriation of foreign property, see above at section 7.5.5.

7.8 CONCLUSIONS

In one sense, when the ILC Articles were finalized in 2001, their relevance was already in question as a result of the burgeoning of the personality of non-state actors. That very year, the Al Qaeda attacks on the US set in motion a chain of events that seem to be changing the face of international law. Concepts such as state responsibility for harbouring or supporting terrorists, the (non-)consequences of a 'legal black hole' in Guantánamo Bay and atrocities by private military contractors in Iraq all post-dated this area's most influential text.

Now, world leaders and scholars are talking of states as having a 'responsibility to protect' the populations of other states where their own state is unable or unwilling to do so.[191] This is partly the old wine of the aspirational concept of humanitarian intervention in new bottles.[192] However, when the President of the United States speaks of the coalition against Libya as those 'who have chosen to meet their responsibilities to defend the Libyan people', this is more than idle rhetoric – it constitutes emerging *opinio juris*.[193]

Attribution is one area where the Articles (and the ICJ) appear to be bogged down in Cold War thinking. Although excessively liberal attribution could result in oppressive supervision by states of their nationals, the current 'effective control' test allows states to support insurrection movements and terrorists in full knowledge of human rights and humanitarian law violations, as long as the state does not specifically direct them to commit such violations.

Some may say that the fragmentation of international law and the proliferation of self-contained regimes have relegated the general rules on state responsibility to the status of gap filler.[194] However, the existence of a web of overarching rules undoubtedly brings stability to the international system; the Articles are and continue to be relied upon as authority for the role of state responsibility, and they no doubt set a useful foundation for the development of this important area of international law.

---

[191] See discussion in Chapter 8, section 8.6.1.

[192] See Chapter 8, section 8.4.

[193] Barack Obama, Remarks by the President in Address to the Nation on Libya, Speech of 28 March 2011 at National Defense University, Washington, DC, available at http://www.whitehouse.gov/the-press-office/2011/03/28/remarks-president-address-nation-libya (accessed 30 May 2011).

[194] Daniel Bodansky and John Crook, 'Symposium: The ILC's Responsibility Articles: Introduction and Overview' (2002) 96 *American Journal of International Law* 773, 774.

8. International law and the use of force

For much of history, a state could generally resort to warfare as a legitimate method of pursuing its international agenda against other states.[1] In this environment, it was widely accepted that the conquest of territory by an aggressive state could bestow title.[2] Whilst some diplomatic constraints might have operated on a decision to resort to war, the use of force was considered to be an essential element of statehood.[3]

Since the end of the First World War, the right of a state to use armed force has been extensively curtailed. International organizations – most notably the League of Nations and the United Nations – thereafter have sought to prohibit the use of force, without limiting the right of states to act in their own or collective self-defence.[4] Despite some extraordinary success in developing an almost universal system of collective security under the United Nations, the use of force in a variety of expressions remains a profound presence both within and between states. Indeed, from the end of the Second World War, there have been over 300 internal and international armed conflicts. Because of its devastating impact on people and international relations, the use of force remains one of the most important areas of international law.

This chapter will explore the development of the prohibition on the threat or use of armed force by states, its different applications and exceptions. It will start by examining the meaning and content of force and developments in its prohibition – in custom and under the UN Charter. The use of force in circumstances involving invitation and intervention will then be considered, including peacekeeping and enforcement actions

1 Stanimir Alexandrov, *Self-Defense against the Use of Force in International Law* (The Hague; London: Kluwer Law International, 1996), 19.

2 Ian Brownlie, *International Law and the Use of Force by States* (Oxford: Clarendon Press, 1963), 729.

3 Yoram Dinstein, *War, Aggression and Self-Defence* (Cambridge: Cambridge University Press, 2005, 4th edn), 73.

4 Judith Gardam, *Necessity, Proportionality and the Use of Force by States* (Cambridge: Cambridge University Press, 2004), 10–11, 138.

and the authority of regional organizations. This chapter will also consider the authority of the UN Security Council to authorize the use of force in response to an act of aggression or threat to the peace, and the complex and developing doctrines of humanitarian intervention and the responsibility to protect. There are several traditional exceptions to the use of force in the post-UN Charter era. With the unlikely but possible exception of the doctrine of humanitarian intervention, only self-defence and action sanctioned by the Security Council remain as genuine exceptions, and these will be explored. As with all topics considered in this book, the use of force in international law will also be examined in the context of contemporary developments and events.

8.1 DEVELOPMENT OF THE LAW ON THE USE OF FORCE IN INTERNATIONAL LAW

8.1.1 Early Attempts to Regulate the Use of Force

In relative terms, the prohibition on the use of force as a viable tool of international relations is a very modern concept. Whilst there have been numerous attempts to regulate the use of force, the notion of a global approach to prohibiting unprovoked military aggression is unique to the twentieth century.

Ancient civilizations were often prepared to resort to war against rival groups or societies to settle disputes or to pursue strategic interests.[5] This often included access to resources or the conquest of territory under the control of another group. The consequences of warfare between societies were often brutal; survivors on the losing side would often be enslaved as part of the victor's attempts to destroy the vanquished society.[6]

The Romans had several requirements that needed to be satisfied before they would commit to warfare. Before engaging in a military campaign, Roman leaders would often seek the approval of the college of fetiales. This religious body would then assess whether the proposed war was in accordance with the implied commands of the gods. The Roman scholar, Cicero, wrote that, until a formal declaration of war had been made, no war could be considered just.[7]

---

[5] Brownlie, above note 2, 5.

[6] Michael Morgan, *Classics of Moral and Political Theory* (Indianapolis, IN: Hackett, 2005), 835.

[7] Elizabeth Asmis, 'A New Kind of Model: Cicero's Roman Constitution in De Republica' (2005) 126(3) *American Journal of Philology* 377, 387.

8.1.2 Early Religious Doctrines

The early Christian Church initially refused to accept that war could, in any circumstances, be morally sanctioned. Because of this belief, Christians were forbidden from joining any army until 170 AD.[8] The Christian scholar, St Augustine, was vehemently opposed to wars of conquest, and defined the concept of just war in the following vague terms:

> Just wars are usually defined as those which avenge injuries, when the nation or city against which warlike action is to be directed has neglected either to punish wrongs committed by its own citizens or to restore what has been unjustly taken by it. Further that kind of war is undoubtedly just which God himself ordains.[9]

Of course, what 'God himself ordains' was and is invariably a matter of human contrivance and the prescription of a just war theory clearly opened a floodgate of aggressive wars waged by churches and their leaders.[10] Such 'just war' notions would come to plague moral and legal debate about the right to use force and in what circumstances – evidenced by its vague content being hijacked by all sides in the so-called 'war on terror' and even in currently developing conceptions of a responsibility to protect.[11] Early scholars of Islam also wrote of religious doctrines which contained guidance on acceptable reasons to resort to war.[12] These reasons included punishment for apostasy, defence of land or self, and authorized warfare against societies not of the Islamic faith.[13]

8.1.3 The Age of Enlightenment

Historically, the most progressive attempt to regulate the use of military force occurred during the Age of Enlightenment, also known as the Age of

---

[8] C. John Cadoux, *The Early Christian Attitude to War* (London: Hedley Bros. Publishers Ltd, 1919), 96.

[9] St Augustine, cited in Brownlie, above note 2, 5.

[10] For a discussion of St Augustine's development of the just war doctrine and its implications on the laws of war, see Christopher Greenwood, 'Historical Development and Legal Basis', in Dieter Fleck (ed.), *The Handbook of Humanitarian Law in Armed Conflicts* (Oxford; New York: Oxford University Press, 1995); Leslie C. Green, *Essays on the Modern Law of War* (Dobbs Ferry, NY: Transnational Publishers, 1985).

[11] For a discussion of the 'Responsibility to Protect' doctrine, see below section 8.6.1.

[12] Youssef Aboul-Enein and Sherifa Zuhur, *Islamic Rulings on Warfare* (Carlisle Barracks, PA: Strategic Studies Institute, US Army War College, 2004), 2.

[13] Ibid., 5.

Reason. In an intellectual and philosophical movement that spread across Europe in the eighteenth century, the Enlightenment questioned religious and traditional values, including the validity of powerful European nations resorting to warfare to resolve disputes with rival states.

One of the most prominent philosophers during the Age of Enlightenment on the prevalent use of warfare was Jean-Jacques Rousseau. The Age of Enlightenment is particularly significant, as the concepts espoused by Rousseau and other influential philosophers eventually formed the basis of customary international law on the use of force. Whilst not seeking to prohibit the use of force outright, the Age of Enlightenment cast doubt over the validity of European powers declaring war to advance strategic interests or obtain territory.

After the French Revolution of 1789, the National Assembly drafted a new French Constitution, which was reluctantly approved by King Louis XVI. Despite its very short operation, this document was a progressive statement about the legality of unprovoked warfare. Title VI of the 1791 Constitution contained a significant statement: 'The French nation renounces the undertaking of any war with a view of making conquests, and it will never use its forces against the liberty of any people.'[14] Chapter III of the Constitution outlined a process which had to be followed before the King of France could declare war on another nation, and severely restricted the King's ability to conduct a declared war without the approval of the National Assembly.[15]

8.1.4 Early Twentieth Century

Numerous endeavours were made to regulate the use of force before the outbreak of the First World War. Beginning with the Hague Conventions of 1899 and 1907, states attempted to develop laws to govern the resolution of disputes and to prohibit aggressive nations from resorting to force as an integral aspect of diplomatic relations.[16] Despite the vague wording of the Conventions, the treaties represented an extraordinary multilateral approach to the regulation of armed force.[17] These early international

---

[14] The Constitution of 1791 (entered into force 3 September 1791), Title VI.

[15] Ibid., Chapter III, Section 1, Art. 2.

[16] Robert Kolb and Richard Hyde, *An Introduction to the International Law of Armed Conflicts* (Oxford: Hart Publishing, 2008), 63; Corneliu Bjola, *Legitimising the Use of Force in International Politics: Kosovo, Iraq and the Ethics of Intervention* (London; New York: Routledge, 2009), 45, 47.

[17] Donald Anton, Penelope Mathew and Wayne Morgan, *International Law: Cases and Materials* (Oxford: Oxford University Press, 2005), 485.

agreements encouraged states to denounce warfare as a readily available tool of diplomatic relations and established an international consensus – first enunciated in the Hague Conventions, and later enshrined in the Geneva Conventions of 1949 – that the use of force should be both restricted and regulated. Whilst a prohibition on resorting to war in all circumstances was not outlined, the notion of reducing the reliance of states on the use of force is not a concept that is unique to the United Nations system.

8.1.5 The League of Nations

In the aftermath of the First World War, the newly established League of Nations made a concerted attempt to restrict the use of force in international relations. The Covenant of the League of Nations (1919) imposed procedural constraints on states in order to reduce the possibility of resorting to war.[18] Whilst the Covenant sought to reduce the likelihood of warfare, the use of force remained permissible if certain prescribed conditions were exhausted.[19] The clear intention of the drafters was to reduce the reliance of states on force as a method of dispute resolution.[20] As Article X dictates, states had an obligation to respect the territorial integrity and political independence of other states. Most importantly, however, is Article XVI, which specifies that a state will have committed an act of war if it resorts to force without satisfying the preconditions contained in the Covenant.[21]

Despite the clear attempt to reduce the reliance on armed force, the Covenant fell far short of prohibiting states from resorting to war in all circumstances.[22] To address this issue, the Sixth Assembly of the League of Nations on 25 September 1925 passed a resolution stating that a war of aggression constitutes 'an international crime'.[23] While the provisions of the Covenant of the League of Nations represented an important

---

[18] Bjola, above note 16, 45–7.

[19] Rosalyn Higgins, 'The Legal Limits to the Use of Force by States: United Nations Practice' (1962) 37 *British Yearbook of International Law* 269, 272.

[20] J.L. Brierly, *The Law of Nations* (Oxford: Clarendon Press, 1963, 6th edn), 408.

[21] Covenant of the League of Nations (opened for signature 28 April 1919, entered into force 10 January 1920) LNTS, Art. X.

[22] Sam Blay, Ryszard Piotrowicz and Martin Tsamenyi, *Public International Law: An Australian Perspective* (Oxford: Oxford University Press, 2005, 2nd edn), 226.

[23] Resolution of the Sixth Assembly of the League of Nations, 25 September 1925.

development in the endeavour to proscribe the use of force by states, a more significant regime concerning the use of force emerged in this period. The General Treaty for the Renunciation of War (1928) (commonly referred to as the Kellogg-Briand Pact)[24] is a multilateral treaty that remains in force to the present day.[25] When it first entered into operation in 1928, the Pact applied almost universally, as only four states had not ratified or assented to it before the outbreak of the Second World War.[26]

The Kellogg-Briand Pact has been recognized as the background to customary international law regarding the prohibition on the use of force.[27] Its key provisions are contained in Articles I and II, which contain two critical elements for prohibiting the use of force. First, states are not to have recourse to war to resolve international disputes.[28] Second, states have an obligation to settle disputes exclusively by peaceful means.[29] When combined with the provisions of the League of Nations Covenant, the Kellogg-Briand Pact operated as the predominant set of regulations concerning the prohibition on the use of force between 1928 and the outbreak of the Second World War in 1939. Far from being simply an aspirational document, the Kellogg-Briand Pact was invoked on several occasions between 1928 and 1939.[30] In 1929, the United States of America cited it to condemn the hostilities between China and the Soviet Union, and again in 1931 when referring to the conflict between China and Japan.[31] The League of Nations also referred to the Pact when condemning the Soviet operations in Finland, beginning in November 1939.[32]

Despite widespread support for the Pact, the treaty clearly did not have the desired impact of dramatically reducing the use of armed force by states; it was not effective in preventing conflicts such as the Japanese invasion of Manchuria in 1931 or other events leading to the outbreak of

---

[24] General Treaty for the Renunciation of War as an Instrument of National Policy (opened for signature 27 August 1928, entered into force 4 September 1929) LNTS.

[25] Brierly, above note 20, 409.

[26] Ian Brownlie, 'International Law and the Use of Force by States Revisited' (2001) 21 *Australian Yearbook of International Law* 21, 23.

[27] Brownlie, above note 2, 730.

[28] Brierly, above note 20, 409.

[29] Antonio Cassese, *International Law* (Oxford: Oxford University Press, 2005, 2nd edn), 300–301.

[30] Brownlie, above note 2, 731.

[31] Ibid.

[32] Ibid.

the Second World War.[33] It is, however, recognized as forming the basis for the international norm that the threat or use of military force, and resulting territorial acquisitions, are unlawful. Importantly, the Pact was essential for the establishment of the crime of aggression and was the basis of the International Military Tribunals in Nuremberg and Tokyo.[34]

8.2 THE UNITED NATIONS AND THE POST-WAR SYSTEM OF COLLECTIVE SECURITY

The prohibition on the use of force underpins the United Nations system.[35] In the aftermath of the Second World War, the drafters of the UN Charter sought to restrict the use of force to very limited circumstances, and exclude any right to take unprovoked and aggressive action against a foreign state.[36] Brownlie describes the rationale for the prohibition on the use of force under the UN system:

> The security scheme based upon the primary role of the Security Council is not an abstract scheme but reflects the international consensus that individual States, or a group of States, cannot resort to force (for purposes other than self-defence) except with the express authorization of the United Nations.[37]

8.2.1 The Meaning of 'Force' and 'Threat of Force'

The UN Charter refers to the concept of 'force', as opposed to 'war'.[38] This is significant because force encompasses a much broader range of conduct, and there is no requirement for a state to make a formal declaration of war for it to be in breach of the prohibitions on the use of force. Article 2(4) of the UN Charter prohibits the use and threat of force, except in specifically designated circumstances, and emphasizes the requirement for states to settle their differences by peaceful means:

---

[33] Ibid.

[34] See Justice Robert Jackson, 'Opening Statement for the Prosecution', Nuremberg Trials Proceedings, 21 November 1945, 144–5; available at http://avalon.law.yale.edu/imt/11-21-45.asp.

[35] Louis Henkin, *How Nations Behave: Law and Foreign Policy* (New York: Columbia University Press for the Council on Foreign Relations, 1979, 2nd edn), 135.

[36] Oscar Schachter, *International Law and Theory in Practice* (Dordrecht; London: Martinus Nijhofff, 1991), 106–7.

[37] Brownlie, above note 2, 746.

[38] Charter of the United Nations, Art. 2(4).

> 3. All Members shall settle their international disputes by peaceful means in such a manner that international peace and security, and justice, are not endangered.
> 4. All Members shall refrain in their international relations from the threat or use of force against the territorial integrity or political independence of any state, or in any other manner inconsistent with the Purposes of the United Nations.

The most blatant use of force is an invasion or attack by the armed forces of a state upon the territory of another state.[39] This includes any military occupation, however temporary, and any attempt to forcibly annex the territory. States are prohibited from bombarding the territory of other states with any form of weaponry and this extends to targeting assets of a foreign state, such as ships or aircraft outside territorial borders. The concept of force applies to the practice of blocking access to ports or attempting to prohibit passage to and from airfields, and incorporates conduct such as preventing supplies, such as food and medical supplies, from reaching another state, whether by land, sea or air.

A state can be in breach of the general prohibition on the use of force even if the territorial sovereignty of another state is not breached.[40] The International Court of Justice in the seminal *Nicaragua* case, held that a state is not permitted to place its own territory at the disposal of another for the purpose of preparing for an attack against a third state, nor to provide weapons, funding or training to opposition groups or mercenaries in a foreign state.[41] In that case, the US had provided assistance to the Nicaraguan rebel forces (the *contras*) with the apparent intent of destabilizing the Nicaraguan government – actions deemed by the Court to constitute a use of force, even though the US had not committed any ground troops or large-scale military resources.[42]

A state that threatens the use of force will also have violated the prohibition on the use of force. This was confirmed by the International Court of Justice in its Advisory Opinion on the threat or use of nuclear weapons.[43]

---

[39] Definition of Aggression, GA Res 3314 (XXIX), UN GAOR, 29th sess (1974) Art. 3.

[40] Gabriella Venturini, 'Necessity in the Law of Armed Conflict and in International Criminal Law' (2010) 41 *Netherlands Yearbook of International Law* 45, 47.

[41] *Military and Paramilitary Activities in and against Nicaragua* (*Nicaragua v USA*) [1986] ICJ Rep 14, 93 ('*Nicaragua* case').

[42] Ibid., 135.

[43] *Legality of the Threat or Use of Nuclear Weapons* (Advisory Opinion) [1996] ICJ Rep 226 ('*Nuclear Weapons* (Advisory Opinion)'). For a discussion of the facts of this case and its relevance to self-defence, see discussion below at 8.5.2.

In that case, the Court was called upon to determine whether 'the threat or use of nuclear weapons in any circumstance is permitted under international law'.[44] In determining this issue, the Court stated:

> If the envisaged use of force is itself unlawful, the stated readiness to use it would be a threat prohibited under Article 2, paragraph 4. Thus it would be illegal for a State to threaten force to secure territory from another State, or to cause it to follow or not follow certain political or economic paths. The notions of 'threat' and 'use' of force under Article 2, paragraph 4, of the Charter stand together in the sense that if the use of force itself in a given case is illegal – for whatever reason – the threat to use such force will likewise be illegal. In short, if it is to be lawful, the declared readiness of a State to use force must be a use of force that is in conformity with the Charter.[45]

8.2.2 The Meaning of 'Against the Territorial Integrity or Political Independence'

At times it has been argued that a particular use of force by a state has not violated the territorial integrity or political independence of another state, and therefore was not in breach of Article 2(4) of the UN Charter. An often cited example of this was Israel's armed incursion on the territory of Uganda for the purpose of rescuing its nationals from an Air France plane that had been hijacked by two Palestinian and two German nationals and rerouted to Entebbe. Uganda reacted angrily, forwarding a letter to the President of the Security Council seeking Israel's condemnation for its act of aggression.[46] Although the matter was debated vigorously before the Security Council, no agreement could be reached and no resolution passed.

There was considerable support, including from the US and UK, for the proposition that, in circumstances where the nationals of a state are at risk, a state may intervene militarily to rescue them and that such an incursion would not be a violation of the territorial integrity or political independence of that state. This was rejected by a number of other states in debates before the Security Council who viewed the actions of Israel, whatever justification it might have, as a clear violation of Article 2(4). As Thomas M. Franck has noted:

---

[44] Ibid., [20].

[45] Ibid., [47].

[46] Letter dated 5 July 1976 from the *Chargé d'Affaires* of the Permanent Mission of Uganda to the United Nations, addressed to the President of the Security Council (S/12124).

> The opposition of so many states, in this instance, thus illustrates the depth of fear of opening the door, however narrowly, to unilateral use of force, even where the justification for intervention is strong. But the considerable support Israel aroused also demonstrates the persuasive power of a well-presented and demonstrated case.[47]

Examples of conduct that challenges the meaning of territorial integrity or political independence in the use of force by states can be cited, much depending on the balance of power in the Security Council and the political realities of the day.[48] Interesting contemporary examples revolve around justifications for the use of force by powerful states that engage natural law conceptions of international law; humanitarian intervention and the evolving doctrine of the responsibility to protect have recently been evoked to justify the use of force in non-traditional contexts. The NATO bombing of Serbia in 1999 and the war on Iraq were justified, more or less convincingly, on these grounds. Just where the line in respect of a state's territorial integrity or political independence is to be drawn is increasingly difficult to determine. The fact that the US would not even acknowledge any incursion on Pakistan's territorial sovereignty when it sent in forces to attack and kill Osama bin Laden in 2011 further entrenches confusion about the limits of international law to regulate strongly supported political objectives, particularly where force is being employed by one of the 'Great Powers'.[49]

8.3 INVITATION AND INTERVENTION

8.3.1 Non-international Armed Conflicts

The UN Charter clearly contemplates an international system that is primarily concerned with diplomatic relations between states.[50] States can be held accountable for their actions and subjected to punitive measures if they do not comply with the rules of international law.[51] Examples include

---

47 Thomas M. Franck, *Recourse to Force: State Action against Threats and Armed Attacks* (Cambridge: Cambridge University Press, 2002), 85.

48 Ibid., see Chapter 6 generally.

49 For a discussion of humanitarian intervention, see below section 8.4. For a discussion of the responsibility to protect doctrine, see below section 8.6.1.

50 Fernando Tesón, 'Collective Humanitarian Intervention' (1996) 17 *Michigan Journal of International Law* 323, 324.

51 Richard Falk, 'Humanitarian Intervention after Kosovo', in Aleksandar Jokic (ed.), *Lessons of Kosovo: The Dangers of Humanitarian Intervention* (Peterborough, ON: Broadview Press, 2003), 43.

condemnation resolutions, economic sanctions and the use of force as a last resort to alleviate a threat to international peace and security.

However, the UN Charter does not contain an explicit procedure for the resolution of conflicts that are wholly contained within a single state, for the simple reason that (traditionally, at any rate) what occurs within a state's borders are its internal concerns and not a matter of international law. Unless a situation involves two or more states, Article 2(7) of the Charter appears to prevent the UN, outside of Security Council enforcement action under Chapter VII, from taking any coercive action:

> Nothing contained in the present Charter shall authorize the United Nations to intervene in matters which are essentially within the domestic jurisdiction of any state . . . but this principle shall not prejudice the application of enforcement measures under Chapter VII.

For example, the international community cannot forcibly intervene to mitigate the effects of a widespread famine or cholera epidemic if the crisis is confined to a single state.[52] Whilst there may be a moral imperative to intervene, the concept of state sovereignty prevents collective action without the consent of the affected state.

This prohibition on international action when a crisis or conflict is contained within a single state can cause widespread frustration. The failure of the UN to intervene to prevent the Rwanda genocide stands as the modern example *par excellence*. To overcome this prohibition without expressly encroaching on a state's sovereignty, states have at times – and selectively – developed legal justifications to intervene in, and to mitigate the impact of, humanitarian crises. Examples include the doctrine of humanitarian intervention (and possibly, more recently, the doctrine of the responsibility to protect), delivery of humanitarian aid and the role of regional organizations.

8.3.2 Delivery of Humanitarian Aid

The provision of humanitarian aid is an integral function performed by various actors in the international community. Traditionally the domain of powerful states, the task of providing vital aid to war-torn and devastated civilian populations is now shared between a number of bodies, including the UN, individual states and non-government organizations. The importance of delivering humanitarian aid is enshrined in Article

---

52 John Kabia, *Humanitarian Intervention and Conflict Resolution in West Africa* (Farnham, UK; Burlington, VT: Ashgate Publishing, 2009), 9.

1(3) of the UN Charter as one of the fundamental purposes of the UN – namely 'to achieve international co-operation in solving international problems of an economic, social, cultural, or humanitarian character'.[53]

A useful definition of humanitarian aid is provided by the Principles and Good Practice of Humanitarian Assistance ('Stockholm Principles'). The following definition was endorsed in 2003 by a group of 17 major donors of humanitarian aid, including the US:

> The objectives of humanitarian action are to save lives, alleviate suffering and maintain human dignity during and in the aftermath of man-made crises and natural disasters as well as to prevent and strengthen preparedness for the occurrence of such situations.[54]

Humanitarian aid can include a wide variety of measures for the purpose of providing assistance to an affected population. In addition to the provision of emergency food and water supplies, humanitarian aid can include medical supplies, temporary shelters and sanitation equipment.[55] The stated aim of humanitarian assistance is to ensure a return to sustainable livelihoods and to strengthen the capacity of affected communities to prevent and mitigate future crises.[56] The Stockholm Principles explain that humanitarian aid must focus on long-term development, in addition to short-term emergency relief.[57] These Principles have guided national policies on the provision of aid since their inception in 2003. The Principles declare that aid must be provided impartially and solely on the basis of need, without discrimination between affected populations. In addition, humanitarian aid must be provided without the impression of favouring one side in a conflict, and cannot be compromised by political or military objectives.[58]

The provision of humanitarian assistance to a civilian population is

---

[53] Charter of the United Nations, Art. 1(3).

[54] Principles and Good Practice of Humanitarian Donorship (endorsed in Stockholm on 17 June 2003) ('Stockholm Principles'), Art. 1.

[55] United Nations Peacekeeping Operations: Principles and Guidelines, available at http://www.peacekeepingbestpractices.unlb.org/pbps/library/capstone_doctrine_eng.pdf

[56] Stockholm Principles, above note 54, Art. 9.

[57] Ibid.

[58] One example of how the Stockholm Principles have influenced the domestic practices of states can be found in the Australian Humanitarian Action Policy of January 2005, based on the principles of neutrality, impartiality and independence: see 'Humanitarian Action Policy of Australia' (AusAID) (January 2005) 4; available at http://www.ausaid.gov.au/publications/pdf/humanitarian_policy.pdf.

such a vital function that it is often exempt from UN sanctions regimes. The international community is often reluctant to deny assistance to desperate citizens when it is considering imposing restrictions on the ruling regime of a state. A contemporary example of humanitarian assistance being exempt from a sanctions regime is the no-fly zone imposed on Libya in March 2011. Paragraph 7 of UN Security Council Resolution 1973 contains a relevant exemption, and states as follows:

> 6. *Decides* to establish a ban on all flights in the airspace of the Libyan Arab Jamahiriya in order to help protect civilians;
> 7. *Decides further* that the ban imposed by paragraph 6 shall not apply to flights whose sole purpose is humanitarian, such as delivering or facilitating the delivery of assistance, including medical supplies, food, humanitarian workers and related assistance.[59]

UN Security Council Resolution 1973 illustrates the clear intention of the international community to allow humanitarian assistance to continue to flow to the civilians of Libya, despite the imposition of sanctions on the regime of Muammar Gaddafi. Other examples, including the long-standing sanctions regime against Iraq before the 2003 war, reveal a lack of genuine concern on the part of the international community for the effect of sanctions on innocent civilians of a rogue regime.[60]

8.3.3 Regional Peacekeeping and Enforcement Actions

The UN Charter explicitly allows for the operation of regional peacekeeping and enforcement organizations.[61] Rather than simply relying on the Chapter VII authority of the Security Council, regional organizations can be granted a specific mandate to respond to an emerging threat to international peace and security.[62]

---

[59] 'The Situation in Libya', SC Res. 1973, UN SCOR, 66th sess., 6498th mtg, UN Doc. S/RES/1973 (17 March 2011).

[60] 'Iraq-Kuwait', SC Res. 661, UN SCOR, 45th sess., 2933rd mtg, UN Doc. S/RES/661 (6 August 1990), and 'Iraq-Kuwait', SC Res. 687, UN SCOR, 46th sess., 2981st mtg, UN Doc. S/RES/687 (3 April 1991). These sanctions were not lifted until 15 December 2010 in a series of three resolutions: 'The Situation concerning Iraq', SC Res. 1956, UN SCOR, 65th sess., 6450th mtg, UN Doc. S/RES/1956 (15 December 2010); 'The Situation concerning Iraq', SC Res. 1957, UN SCOR, 65th sess., 6450th mtg, UN Doc. S/RES/1957 (15 December 2010); 'The Situation concerning Iraq', SC Res. 1958, UN SCOR, 65th sess., 6450th mtg, UN Doc. S/RES/1958 (15 December 2010).

[61] Charter of the United Nations, Arts 52, 53 and 54.

[62] Brownlie, above note 2, 737–8.

Examples of these regional organizations are the North Atlantic Treaty Organization (NATO) and the ANZUS Alliance (Australia, New Zealand and USA).[63] These organizations require their members to commit to take varying degrees of collective action should a fellow member be subjected to an armed attack.[64] As part of this commitment Member States often share intelligence resources and information, participate in joint military exercises and collaborate to establish regional security objectives.[65]

Article 52 of the UN Charter allows regional agencies to deal with 'matters relating to the maintenance of international peace and security as are appropriate for regional action', on condition that they act in accordance with UN purposes and principles and 'make every effort to achieve pacific settlement of local disputes' (with the encouragement of the Security Council) before referring them to the Security Council. Article 53 of the UN Charter enables regional agencies, where appropriate and with the authorization of the Security Council, to undertake enforcement action on behalf of the UN. In all activities undertaken or contemplated by regional agencies for the maintenance of international peace and security, the Security Council must be at all times kept fully informed.

8.4 HUMANITARIAN INTERVENTION

For an increasingly interventionist community of states, difficulties arise where a conflict or emerging crisis is contained within the borders of a single state. The prohibition contained in Article 2(4) of the UN Charter focuses on the threat or use of force against the territorial integrity of a foreign state.[66] The wording clearly contemplates a situation of conflict as and between states. This is because the framework of collective security envisioned under the UN Charter maintains a clear deference for the sovereignty of all states. No matter how big or small, superpower or rogue regime, each state's sovereign 'privacy' is, at least in principle, to be protected. However, there has developed in recent years something of a normative shift towards intervention by a powerful part of the international community in the internal affairs of a state, particularly where that state is engaged in or subjected to an internal upheaval that gives rise to a massive humanitarian crisis.

---

63 Security Treaty between Australia, New Zealand and the United States of America (ANZUS) [1952] ATS, No. 2, 131 UNTS 84, Arts IV and V.

64 Anton, Mathew and Morgan, above note 17, 529.

65 Ibid.

66 Tesón, above note 50, 324.

Of primary significance to understanding the doctrine of humanitarian intervention is that it is military action taken by a collective of states *outside* a Security Council mandate, usually because one or more permanent members of the Security Council have threatened to veto any attempt to achieve Chapter VII authority for the use of force. The justification for such use of force has a ring of natural law to it, suggesting that the strictly positivist model of a sovereign equality of states is inadequate to protect a greater moral imperative to protect innocent civilians from the tyranny of its own leaders.

8.4.1 Sovereignty and Humanitarian Intervention

Humanitarian intervention concerns the forcible intervention within the sovereign territory of a state to prevent or mitigate the impact of a conflict or massive human rights violations. This course of action is mostly considered where a domestic government is an active participant (including mass arbitrary killings, forced expulsions and the deliberate targeting of ethnic groups[67]), but can also arise where a state is simply unable to protect its own citizens from gross violations of human rights.[68]

A permissive definition of the practice of humanitarian intervention is:

> The justifiable use of force for the purpose of protecting the inhabitants of another state from treatment so arbitrary and persistently abusive as to exceed the limits which the sovereign is presumed to act with reason and justice.[69]

The concept of humanitarian intervention in response to gross and systematic breaches of human rights is fraught with legal and moral complexity. As examples like the crises in Somalia, Rwanda and Serbia/Kosovo illustrate, direct intervention in the domestic affairs of another state without consent is a controversial course of action, and no binding guidelines have yet been developed by the international community.[70] This is no doubt in part because such action is so demonstrably political, rather than based on legal doctrine.

Humanitarian concerns as the justification for the use of force are not a

[67] Secretary-General Ban Ki-moon, 'Report of the Secretary-General: Implementing the Responsibility to Protect', UN GAOR, 63rd sess., UN Doc. A/63/677 (12 January 2009), [61].

[68] International Commission on Intervention and State Sovereignty, 'The Responsibility to Protect' (Final Report, December 2001) ('ICISS Report'), [6.11].

[69] Anton, Mathew and Morgan, above note 17, 541.

[70] See 8.3.1–8.3.3 above for specific examples.

new idea. From the Russian, British and French involvement in the Greek War of Independence in 1824 to Vietnamese intervention in Cambodia in 1978 and the NATO bombing of Yugoslavia in 1999, humanitarian concerns for the internal population of a state have long been used as excuses for the application of armed force against the sovereign territory of a state. As Brownlie has noted, any historical application of such a doctrine was 'inherently vague',[71] and often 'appeared as a cloak for episodes of imperialism, including the invasion of Cuba by the United States in 1898'.[72] The development of this practice into something of a coherent doctrine, if it is that, is a recent development.

Humanitarian intervention highlights a clash of two fundamental principles of international law – namely the protection of innocent people reflected in the human rights and international humanitarian law regimes, and the foundational concept of state sovereignty. The independent authority of a state within its own domestic jurisdiction is reflected in Article 2(7) of the UN Charter.[73] On one level, the principle of sovereignty operates to protect weaker states from any undue influence that may be exercised by stronger states within the international community.[74] To this extent, each state has the right to determine its own economic, social and foreign policies without any uninvited interference from an external force. To protect this right, no state is permitted to aggressively breach territorial borders to forcibly alter the domestic practices of a sovereign nation.[75]

Practice in this area, however, seems to suggest an emerging view of sovereignty as no longer absolute.[76] Guided most recently by the repeated statements of former UN Secretary-General Kofi Annan, state sovereignty may be viewed as being affected by a demonstrable lack of respect for basic principles of human dignity.[77] A tempting argument might be

---

[71] Brownlie, above note 2, 338.

[72] Ian Brownlie, *Principles of Public International Law* (Oxford: Oxford University Press, 2008, 7th edn), 742.

[73] Thomas Weiss, *Humanitarian Intervention* (Cambridge, UK: Polity Press, 2007), 19.

[74] Susan Breau, *Humanitarian Intervention: The United Nations and Collective Responsibility* (London: Cameron May, 2005), 225. This seems also to be the tenor of Koskenniemi's argument: Martti Koskenniemi, 'What Use for Sovereignty Today?' (2011) 1 *Asian Journal of International Law* 61.

[75] Kabia, above note 52, 9.

[76] John Janzekovic, *The Use of Force in Humanitarian Intervention: Morality and Practicalities* (Aldershot, UK; Burlington, VT: Ashgate, 2006) 143–4.

[77] Secretary-General Kofi Annan, 'Sovereignty and Responsibility', Speech delivered to the Ditchley Foundation, United Kingdom, 26 June 1998; Secretary-General Kofi Annan, 'In Larger Freedom: Towards Security, Development and

that a balance now exists between sovereignty and an obligation to respect human rights.[78]

This tendency toward eroding the traditional place of state sovereignty has not been accepted lightly.[79] Opposition to the practice of humanitarian intervention focuses on Article 2(7) of the UN Charter, which precludes interference by states in the internal affairs of another state, except where the Security Council is taking enforcement measures under Chapter VII of the UN Charter to ensure international peace and security. The central premise of Article 2(7) is that the UN does not have the authority to force a change or impose its will on the domestic affairs of any state.[80] This may include a prohibition on compelling a change of government or demanding amendments to budgetary spending. Article 2(7) is intended to protect states from undue external influence and to ensure that the functions of executive government can be performed effectively. It is premised on the foundational principle of the sovereign equality of all states that underpins modern international law, and is preserved under the United Nations system.

Opponents of humanitarian intervention argue that Article 2(7) constitutes an absolute prohibition on international interference in domestic matters, including a ruling regime's treatment of its own citizens.[81] On this view, an uninvited use of force within territorial borders would be an unacceptable breach of each state's unfettered domestic authority, and amount to an unprovoked act of aggression.[82] To this extent, a stringent interpretation of Article 2(7) must be maintained to prevent stronger states from violating the sovereignty of weaker states. Regarded in this way, any legal recognition of a right to humanitarian intervention may be open to abuse – what Franck refers to as the 'slippery slope' argument.[83]

Human Rights for All', UN GAOR, 59th sess., UN Doc. A/59/2005 (21 March 2005), [132].

[78] Janzekovic, above note 76, 143.

[79] Opponents of humanitarian intervention include Alan Kuperman, *The Limits of Humanitarian Intervention* (Washington, DC: Brookings Institution Press, 2001). A summary of arguments opposing humanitarian intervention is contained in Thomas Franck, 'Legality and Legitimacy in Humanitarian Intervention', in Terry Nardin and Melissa Williams (eds), *Humanitarian Intervention* (New York; London: New York University Press, 2006), 145; Aidan Hehir, *Humanitarian Intervention After Kosovo: Iraq, Darfur and the Record of Global Civil Society* (Basingstoke, UK: Palgrave MacMillan, 2008), 65.

[80] Weiss, above note 73, 19.

[81] Franck, above note 79, 145.

[82] Hehir, above note 79, 65.

[83] Franck, above note 47, 185.

On the other hand, as William Schabas has noted, genocidal atrocities and widespread killings have often been committed under the direction or with the benign complicity of the ruling regime of the state in question.[84] When considered in this light, the absolute opposition to external intervention may be short-sighted. At any rate, as history shows, if Article 2(7) does represent an absolute prohibition, then the principles of non-intervention and state sovereignty can be subject to abuse by oppressive domestic regimes.[85] Free from any fear of invasion, authoritarian governments can manipulate domestic policies to commit systematic human rights abuses against political opponents and the civilian population.[86]

If support for a broader doctrine of humanitarian intervention is to operate outside the rubric of ad hoc political responses generated by the Great Powers against rogue states,[87] then a compelling legal justification for humanitarian intervention should be made. One obvious response is to focus on the explicit exception contained within Article 2(7), that the protective domain of state sovereignty 'shall not prejudice the application of enforcement measures under Chapter VII'.[88] This means that the Security Council's authority to identify and respond to emerging threats to international peace and security is not curtailed by Article 2(7).[89] To this extent, Chapter VII contains the most relevant provisions when considering humanitarian intervention, rather than the 'chameleon'[90] Article 2(7). The role of the Security Council in responding to abuses of sovereignty certainly has greater legal merit than non-Council sanctioned humanitarian intervention. In this way, operationalization of ideas such as the responsibility to protect (as seen in the Security Council sanctioned intervention in Libya in 2011[91]) can be tested and developed within the

---

[84] William A. Schabas, *Genocide in International Law: The Crime of Crimes* (Cambridge; New York: Cambridge University Press, 2009, 2nd edn), 1.

[85] Fernando Tesón, *Humanitarian Intervention: An Inquiry into Law and Morality* (Ardsley, NY: Transnational Publishers, 2005), 193.

[86] Kabia, above note 52, 9; Secretary-General Kofi Annan, 'We the Peoples: The Role of the United Nations in the 21st Century', UN GAOR, 54th sess., UN Doc. A/54/2000 (3 April 2000), 48.

[87] See generally Gerry Simpson, *Great Powers and Outlaw States: Unequal Sovereigns in the International Legal Order* (Cambridge; New York: Cambridge University Press, 2004).

[88] Charter of the United Nations. Art. 2(7).

[89] Tesón, above note 85, 280.

[90] Ibid., 287.

[91] 'The Situation in Libya', SC Res 1973, UN SCOR, 66th sess., 6498th mtg, UN Doc. S/RES/1973 (17 March 2011). The use of force against Libya is discussed in sections 8.3.2 and 8.6.1.

UN system of collective security. This approach will be discussed further below in the context of Chapter VII as an exception to the prohibition on the use of force.[92]

8.4.2 Legitimacy and the Future of Humanitarian Intervention

Humanitarian intervention as a doctrine of international law might be looked at as a struggle between law and legitimacy. In 1991, Oscar Schachter viewed this idea of using force based on a humanitarian intention outside of Security Council approval as potentially pardonable.[93] While Schachter's motivation might be understood in the context of the time (looking back at Security Council inertia during the Cold War years), the idea has only recently gained in popularity, notably peaking in UK politics and legal scholarship around the time of the NATO bombing of Serbia.[94] Viewed as a struggle between law and legitimacy,[95] humanitarian intervention makes sense, and may act as a 'plea in mitigation' where a state or coalition of states that use force for stated humanitarian purposes later seek absolution and political and technical assistance from the UN to implement transitional governance.

Such was the case following the NATO bombing in Serbia, where the UN set up a massive post-conflict administration in Kosovo (UNIMIK) that led to the ultimate insult to Serbia – Kosovo's declaration of independence – which was made possible only by the NATO bombing and UN infrastructure. Indeed, the 'Goldstone Commission' set up to investigate these issues concluded that the actions of NATO were not legal but they were legitimate.[96] As tempting as it is to accept such a rationalization, the

---

[92] Chapter VII authority of the UN Security Council is discussed below at section 8.6.

[93] Schachter, above note 36.

[94] See arguments by then Foreign Minister Robin Cook (cited in Franck, above note 47, 183, note 27) and then Prime Minister Tony Blair for a reinvigorated doctrine of humanitarian intervention (Tony Blair, Speech delivered at Sedgefield, justifying military action in Iraq, Friday 5 March 2004, cited in Gerry Simpson, 'International Law in Diplomatic History', in James Crawford and Martti Koskenniemi (eds), *The Cambridge Companion to International Law* (Cambridge: Cambridge University Press, 2011)).

[95] Franck, above note 47, Chapter 10.

[96] Independent International Commission on Kosovo, *Kosovo Report: Conflict, International Response, Lessons Learned* (Oxford: Oxford University Press, 2000), 163–98, cited in Franck, above note 47, 181–2. For a discussion of Kosovo's passage to independence and the legal implications, see Chapter 4, sections 4.4 and 4.5.1.

fact remains that, on a legal assessment, humanitarian intervention as a *legal* doctrine is not a part of international law. It may in time become a principle of international law, but there is insufficient state practice and *opinio juris* to yet say that it is.[97]

8.5 EXCEPTION TO THE RULE: SELF-DEFENCE AND COLLECTIVE SELF-DEFENCE

The most significant exception to the prohibition on the use of force is the right to self-defence. It has long been recognized under international law that if an armed attack occurs against a state, it is the inherent right of that state to use force to defend itself.[98]

8.5.1 Development of Self-defence

The concept of self-defence was first addressed in the *Caroline* dispute of 1837.[99] In this landmark case, British forces attacked a ship moored on the Niagara River, which was suspected of supporting an armed rebellion against the British.[100] Without warning, British forces boarded the ship and attacked 33 American occupants.[101] The British forces sent the *Caroline* adrift over the Niagara Falls, killing twelve Americans.[102] The British forces claimed that they acted in self-defence, as they were responding to the impending threat of an armed rebellion.[103] In a diplomatic exchange, US Secretary of State, Daniel Webster, outlined his interpretation of the requirements for a valid act of self-defence:

> It will be for that Government to show a necessity of self-defence, instant, overwhelming, leaving no choice of means, and no moment for deliberation . . . (and) did nothing unreasonable or excessive; since the act, justified by the necessity of self-defence, must be limited by that necessity and kept clearly within it.[104]

---

[97] See Brownlie, above note 72, 745.
[98] See, e.g., Brownlie, above note 72, 732; Gillian Triggs, *International Law: Contemporary Principles and Practices* (Sydney: LexisNexis Butterworths, 2011, 2nd edn), 613–14; Franck, above note 47, Chapter 3.
[99] Malcolm Shaw, *International Law* (Cambridge: Cambridge University Press, 2008, 6th edn), 1131.
[100] *Caroline* case 29 BFSP 1137–8.
[101] Ibid.
[102] Ibid.
[103] Ibid.
[104] US Secretary of State Daniel Webster, Letter to British Ambassador Lord Ashburton (24 April 1841), cited in Kenneth Shewmaker (ed.), *The Papers of*

The principles expressed by Webster have been recognized as the basic foundation of the principle of self-defence in international law.[105] This statement introduced the twin requirements of necessity and proportionality, which still operate under the UN system today.[106] Jurisprudence following the *Caroline* dispute regarded the practice of self-defence as an act of self-preservation, which could only be permitted in dire circumstances.[107]

The right to self-defence was expressly recognized in the Kellogg-Briand Pact,[108] and, in reservations to the treaty, signatory states make reference to 'the reservation of the right of self-defence and also of collective self-defence'.[109]

8.5.2 Self-defence under the UN Charter

Article 51 of the UN Charter reserves the right of states to engage in individual or collective self-defence. Article 51 represents the only explicit exception to the prohibition on the use of force that is available to states, and is outlined as follows:

> Nothing in the present Charter shall impair the inherent right of individual or collective self-defence if an armed attack occurs against a Member of the United Nations, until the Security Council has taken measures necessary to maintain international peace and security. Measures taken by Members in the exercise of this right of self-defence shall be immediately reported to the Security Council and shall not in any way affect the authority and responsibility of the Security Council under the present Charter to take at any time such action as it deems necessary in order to maintain or restore international peace and security.[110]

There are several important issues of interpretation that arise from the wording of Article 51. The use of the term 'inherent right of individual or collective self-defence' indicates that Article 51 is not the only source of the principle. The use of this language implies that customary international law and previous state practice on the issue of self-defence are relevant

---

Daniel Webster: Diplomatic Papers, Vol. 1, 1841–43 (Hanover, NJ: University Press of New England, 1983) 42.

[105] Triggs, above note 98, 613–14.

[106] *Nicaragua* case, above note 41, 93 and 112, and *Nuclear Weapons* (Advisory Opinion), above note 43, 245.

[107] Brownlie, above note 2, 734.

[108] See discussion above in section 8.1.5.

[109] Brownlie, above note 2, 734.

[110] Charter of the United Nations, Art. 51.

considerations, a view supported by the International Court of Justice in the *Nicaragua* case:

> [T]he United Nations Charter . . . by no means covers the whole area of the regulation of the use of force in international relations . . . Article 51 of the Charter is only meaningful on the basis that there is a 'natural' or 'inherent' right of self-defence, and it is hard to see how this can be other than of a customary nature, even if its present content has been confirmed and influenced by the Charter.[111]

The language used in Article 51 is significantly different from the terminology in Article 2(4), which contains the general prohibition on the use of force. Whilst Article 2(4) refers to the 'threat or use of force',[112] Article 51 uses the term 'armed attack'.[113] This means that Article 51 has a more restricted application, and requires a state-sponsored strike to be carried out against a UN Member State before the right to self-defence can be invoked. Accordingly, not every threat or use of force that breaches Article 2(4) will invoke a state's right to self-defence under Article 51.

Despite the apparent distinction between Articles 2(4) and 51, there is some uncertainty about what activities will constitute an 'armed attack'. The majority of the ICJ in the *Nicaragua* case attempted to define an 'armed attack' for the purposes of Article 51 as follows:

> [A]n armed attack must be understood as including not merely action by regular armed forces across an international border, but also 'the sending by or on behalf of a State of armed bands, groups, irregulars or mercenaries, which carry out acts of armed force against another State of such gravity as to amount to' (*inter alia*) an actual armed attack conducted by regular forces, 'or its substantial involvement therein.'

This description, contained in Article 3, paragraph (g), of the Definition of Aggression annexed to General Assembly Resolution 3314 (XXIX), may be taken to reflect customary international law.[114]

This definition is supplemented by the ICJ in the *Oil Platforms* case, in which the Court held that the right of self-defence can only be invoked in response to 'the most grave forms of the use of force'.[115] However, an armed attack may also consist of a series of attacks which, when

---

[111] *Nicaragua* case, above note 41, 176.
[112] Charter of the United Nations, Art. 2(4).
[113] Ibid., Art. 51.
[114] *Nicaragua* case, above note 41, 195.
[115] *Oil Platforms* case (*Islamic Republic of Iran v USA*) [2003] ICJ Reports 161, 51.

considered individually, would not justify a response in self-defence.[116] If an armed attack has occurred against a state, that state's response in self-defence is limited to actions that are necessary and proportionate,[117] requirements that were subsequently supported by the ICJ in the *Oil Platforms* case[118] and the *Legality of the Threat or Use of Nuclear Weapons* (Advisory Opinion).[119]

An important requirement of Article 51 is that any measure taken in self-defence must be 'immediately reported' to the Security Council.[120] This requirement exists so that the international community can assess whether an armed attack has occurred, and whether actions taken by the victim state in self-defence are necessary and proportionate to the original aggression. This is a clear break from customary international law, which contained no such reporting requirement to a multilateral authority. As explained by the ICJ in the *Nicaragua* case, this requirement to report to the Security Council is vital to assess objectively whether the victim state can legitimately claim that it has acted in self-defence.[121]

Article 51 also contains explicit protection of the Security Council's authority under Chapter VII, regardless of any measures taken in self-defence by a victim state.[122] Therefore, a state's right to take action in self-defence supplements measures that may be taken by the Security Council, which expressly retains its authority and responsibility under Article 39 to undertake its own assessment of a potential threat to international peace and security, and to take such action as it deems necessary to maintain or restore it. The Security Council is also able to utilize measures under Articles 41 and 42 to resolve any threat that has been identified. This authority can be exercised independently of, and at any time before, during or after, any self-defence measures that may be validly adopted by the victim state.

The application of the principle of the right to self-defence has been tested in a number of cases before the International Court of Justice. In the first case decided by the Court, it considered the issue of self-defence in a dispute between Albania and the United Kingdom. In May 1946, Royal Navy ships were fired upon by Albanian fortifications when attempting to

116 Ibid.
117 *Nicaragua* case, above note 41, 94 [176].
118 *Oil Platforms* case, above note 115, 196 [74].
119 *Nuclear Weapons* (Advisory Opinion), above note 43, 245 [41] and [42]. These decisions are discussed below.
120 Charter of the United Nations, Art. 51.
121 *Nicaragua* case, above note 41, 200.
122 Charter of the United Nations, Art. 51.

cross the Corfu Channel. In October, the British destroyers *Saumarez* and *Volage* struck mines in the Corfu Channel and were extensively damaged, causing the death of 44 sailors. In response to this incident, the Royal Navy engaged in mine sweeping missions on 12 and 13 November 1946. Importantly, these operations were carried out in Albanian territorial waters, without the permission of the Albanian government.

The United Kingdom argued that the minesweeping operation was an act of self-defence to protect British ships and the lives of sailors. The UK denied that its actions were designed to threaten the territorial integrity and political independence of Albania. This position was rejected by the Court, which stated that an intervention such as the minesweeping operation of the UK 'cannot . . . find a place in international law'.[123] This is because such a policy could be subject to 'most serious abuses' and 'might easily lead to perverting the administration of justice itself'.[124] Accordingly, the UK was found not to have validly acted in self-defence when sweeping for mines in Albanian territorial waters.

The content of the right to self-defence was tested in the *Oil Platforms* case between Iran and the United States. Between 1980 and 1988, Iran and Iraq were engaged in a civil war. In 1984, Iraqi ships began to attack oil tankers in the Persian Gulf on their way to and from Iran. Iran then began to attack Iraqi ships in retaliation in an escalation which became known as the Tanker War. Iranian retaliatory strikes often focused on neutral ships that were sailing towards ports in Kuwait or Saudi Arabia. In October 1987, a US-flagged oil tanker was struck by a missile in the vicinity of a Kuwaiti harbour. The US assumed that the attack was launched from a nearby Iranian oil platform. In response to the strike on the oil tanker, the US attacked and destroyed two offshore Iranian oil stations. When another US vessel struck a mine in waters near Bahrain in April 1988, the US destroyed another two nearby Iranian oil platforms.

In 1992, Iran brought an application before the International Court of Justice complaining of the US attacks on the oil platforms in the Persian Gulf.[125] The Court held that the US had not acted validly in self-defence. In view of all the circumstances, it could not be shown that the attacks on the Iranian oil platforms were a justifiable response to an armed attack on US ships. This is because the attacks on the Iranian platforms

---

[123] *Corfu Channel* (*United Kingdom v Albania*) (Judgment) [1949] ICJ Reports 4.

[124] Ibid., 35.

[125] *Oil Platforms* case, above note 115.

were not *necessary* to respond to the strikes on the US ships. The attacks were conducted as part of an extensive military operation. By considering the attacks on all four oil platforms, the actions of the US could not be considered *proportionate* to the threat posed by the strikes on the oil tankers. As the attacks on the oil platforms were neither necessary nor proportionate, the US did not validly act in self-defence.

This approach was reinforced by the Court in its Advisory Opinion on the threat or use of nuclear weapons: 'The submission of the exercise of the right to self-defence to the conditions of necessity and proportionality is a rule of customary international law.'[126] In that opinion, the Court held that the principle of proportionality would not automatically prohibit the use of nuclear weapons in all circumstances. Both the threatened use and deployment of nuclear weapons would only be permissible in response to proportionate threat. Because of the inherently destructive nature of nuclear weapons and the high possibility of a retaliatory exchange, their use would be confined to the most extreme circumstances. However, the possession of nuclear weapons was held not to be a threat of force prohibited by Article 2(4) of the UN Charter. To be a prohibited threat, the possessor state would need to direct a threat against the territorial integrity of another state. Despite the fact that the threat or use of nuclear weapons could not definitively be said to be contrary to international law, the Court noted that the use of such weapons would be 'scarcely reconcilable' with the 'overriding consideration of humanity'.[127] Not surprisingly, the Court's reasoning on self-defence has been heavily criticized.[128]

8.5.3 Collective Self-defence

An important aspect of Article 51 is the explicit reference to 'collective self-defence'. It is clear from this reference that a victim state can seek assistance from other states to repel an 'armed attack'.

However, an issue can arise as to when other states can legitimately assist a victim state under Article 51. An assisting state or coalition of states cannot unilaterally decide to intervene and repel a perceived armed

---

[126] *Nuclear Weapons* (Advisory Opinion), above note 43, 245.

[127] Ibid., 262.

[128] See, e.g., Timothy McCormack, 'A *Non Liquet* on Nuclear Weapons – The ICJ avoids the Application of General Principles of International Humanitarian Law' (1997) 37 *International Review of the Red Cross* 1; Theo Farrell and Hélène Lambert, 'Courting Controversy: International Law, National Norms and American Nuclear Use' (2001) 27 *Review of International Studies* 309.

attack. In the *Nicaragua* case, the ICJ emphasizes this principle: 'There is no rule permitting the exercise of collective self-defence in the absence of a request by the State which regards itself as the victim of an armed attack.'[129] To permit other states to assist in a collective self-defence action, the state for whose benefit the action is taken must consider itself to be the victim of an armed attack.

Nicaragua applied to the ICJ, alleging that the United States had laid mines in Nicaraguan waters and engaged in unprovoked attacks on ports. Nicaragua also alleged that the US trained, funded and supported a group of anti-government rebels in their struggle against the incumbent ruling regime of Nicaragua. It was argued that the US had violated the sovereignty of Nicaragua, thereby violating the principle of non-intervention contained in Article 2(7) of the UN Charter, and engaged in an unlawful use of force. The US argued that it acted in collective self-defence for the benefit of El Salvador because of Nicaragua's practice of harbouring Communist opponents of the government of El Salvador.

The Court stated that there is 'a specific rule whereby self-defence would warrant only measures which are proportional to the armed attack and necessary to respond to it, a rule well established in customary international law'.[130] It held that Nicaragua's conduct in relation to El Salvador did not constitute an armed attack. Whilst an armed attack could include 'assistance to rebels in the form of the provision of weapons or logistical or other support',[131] there was insufficient evidence to conclude that Nicaragua had been engaged in an armed attack against El Salvador. A state cannot engage in acts of collective self-defence until the target of an armed attack requests assistance. If this assistance is requested, the intervening state must notify the Security Council in accordance with Article 51 of the UN Charter. In this case, there was no evidence to support a finding that El Salvador had requested assistance, and the USA had not notified the Security Council of its actions. Therefore, even if El Salvador had been the victim of an armed attack, the USA could not engage in acts of collective self-defence against the territory of Nicaragua, because such assistance had not been requested and the Security Council was not notified.

---

[129] *Nicaragua* case, above note 41, 199.

[130] Ibid., 94. The same phrase is cited by the Court in its *Nuclear Weapons* (Advisory Opinion), above note 43, 245.

[131] Affirming General Assembly Resolution 3314 (XXIX) Art. 3(g).

8.5.4 Status of Anticipatory Self-defence

The most controversial aspect of Article 51 concerns whether a state's right to self-defence against an armed attack includes the right to anticipatory self-defence. This concept arises when a state believes that an armed attack is imminent, but there has not yet been an act of aggression. Advocates of anticipatory self-defence argue that a state should have the right to use necessary and proportionate force to prevent an armed attack on its territory, without having to wait for such an attack to be imminent or inevitable.[132]

Article 51 of the UN Charter explains that a state has the right to act in self-defence 'if an armed attack occurs'. A literal interpretation of the wording of Article 51 suggests that an armed attack must already be in progress before a state can legitimately act in self-defence. This appears to exclude any right to engage in acts of anticipatory self-defence.

During the drafting discussions at the San Francisco Conference, no recorded discussion exists about the intended meaning of the term 'if an armed attack occurs'.[133] Timothy McCormack argues that this lack of discussion means that the words were included without a limitation as to their meaning,[134] which is significant when compared to the extensive discussion of the language to be used in other provisions. One possible interpretation is that the drafters of the UN Charter did not intend to prohibit acts of anticipatory self-defence under Article 51.[135]

Because of the wording of Article 51, supporters of anticipatory self-defence are forced to cite customary international law to support their position.[136] Advocates refer to the opinion of US Secretary of State Webster in the *Caroline* case, namely that a state can take anticipatory steps in self-defence, provided that the need for the adopted measures

---

[132] Timothy McCormack, 'Anticipatory Self-Defence in the Legislative History of the United Nations Charter' (1991) 25 *Israel Law Review* 1, 35–7. See also Donald Rothwell, 'Anticipatory Self Defence' (2005) 24(2) *University of Queensland Law Review* 337; Dinstein, above note 3, 168.

[133] McCormack, above note 132, 35.

[134] Ibid., 35–40. See also Natolino Ronzitti, 'The Expanding Law of Self-Defence' (2006) 11(3) *Journal of Conflict and Security Law* 343.

[135] Michael Glennon, 'The Fog of Law: Self-Defense, Inherence, and Incoherence in Article 51 of the United Nations Charter' (2002) 25 *Harvard Journal of Law and Public Policy* 539.

[136] Brownlie, above note 2, 734–5. See also Terry Gill, 'The Temporal Dimension of Self-Defence: Anticipation, Pre-emption, Prevention and Immediacy' (2006) 11(3) *Journal of Conflict and Security Law* 361.

is instant, overwhelming and there is no moment for deliberation.[137] However, as Brownlie suggests, relying on Webster's 1837 formulation may also be viewed as 'anachronistic and indefensible'.[138]

The concept of anticipatory self-defence was supported by the UN High-Level Panel on Threats, Challenges and Change. In its December 2004 report, the Panel outlined the following position:

> [A] threatened state, according to long established international law, can take military action as long as the attack is *imminent*, no other means would deflect it and the action is proportionate. The problem arises where the threat in question is not imminent but still claimed to be real; for example the acquisition, with allegedly hostile intent, of nuclear weapons making capability.[139]

This report appears to give support to the position that a state can use force to prevent an imminent attack on its own territory. For example, if a state is amassing troops, positioning weapons and publicly declares its intent to invade, the victim state may be permitted to use a necessary and proportionate amount of force to nullify the imminent threat.

In 1981, Israel bombed an Iraqi nuclear reactor that was under construction in Osirak on the basis of anticipatory self-defence. Israel argued that the construction of a nuclear reactor in a hostile state posed a direct threat to its sovereignty and political independence. Notwithstanding any future hostility that may ensue, Israel was not under an imminent threat of nuclear or other armed attack from Iraq. The actions of Israel were unanimously condemned in Security Council Resolution 487 as a 'clear violation of the Charter of the United Nations', as there was no imminent threat of armed attack posed by Iraq.[140]

8.5.5 Self-defence and Pre-emption

The notion of pre-emption allows a state the right to use military force to nullify a perceived threat to its sovereignty or territorial integrity. Pre-emption can be distinguished from anticipatory self-defence, because an attack does not have to be imminent to invoke

---

137 Brownlie, above note 2, 735.

138 Ibid., 734. See also Leo van den Hole, 'Anticipatory Self-Defence Under International Law' (2004) 19 *American University International Law Review* 69.

139 UN Doc. A/59/565, 2 December 2004, 54.

140 'Iraq-Israel', SC Res. 487, UN SCOR, 36th sess., 2288th mtg, UN Doc. S/RES/487 (19 June 1981), [1].

the justification of a pre-emptive strike.[141] To this extent, the state acting in pre-emption does not have to be expecting an armed attack, and can simply be responding to a perceived military threat.[142] This can lead to a military strike against a state before there is any evidence that an attack has been planned or even contemplated.

Pre-emption was included in the very controversial 2002 National Security Strategy of the United States of America, commonly known as the 'Bush Doctrine'.[143] In response to the attacks of 11 September 2001, President Bush argued that the United States has the right to eliminate the threat posed by a 'rogue state and their terrorist clients'.[144] Significantly, this policy targeted non-state actors as well as states, and extended far beyond the concept of anticipatory self-defence.[145]

The Bush Doctrine is an aggressive policy that overtly threatens the sovereignty of adversaries of the US. The concept of pre-emption operates far beyond the scope of Article 51 of the UN Charter, as a perceived threat does not have to be imminent or even planned to be used as the justification for retaliation. By its very nature, a pre-emptive strike cannot be a defensive action, as there is no current threat to which a target state is responding. This indicates that the doctrine of pre-emption is not an act of self-defence, but rather a policy of threat and aggression.

8.6 EXCEPTION TO THE RULE: CHAPTER VII AUTHORITY OF THE SECURITY COUNCIL

The prohibition on the use of force is subject to the unique authority of the Security Council. Chapter VII of the UN Charter bestows on the Security Council a responsibility to identify and investigate any emerging threat to

---

141 Christopher Greenwood, 'International Law and the Pre-emptive Use of Force: Afghanistan, Al-Qaida, and Iraq' (2004) 4 *San Diego International Law Journal* 7, 8. See also Gill, above note 136.

142 Michael Bothe, 'Terrorism and the Legality of Pre-emptive Force' (2003) 14(2) *European Journal of International Law* 227, 235. See also Sanjay Gupta, 'The Doctrine of Pre-emptive Strike: Application and Implications during the Administration of President George W. Bush' (2008) 29(2) *International Political Science Review* 181.

143 'The National Security Strategy of the United States of America' (September 2002), available at http://www.au.af.mil/au/awc/awcgate/nss/nss_sep2002.pdf

144 Ibid. See also Miriam Sapiro, 'Iraq: The Shifting Sands of Preemptive Self-Defense' (2003) 97 *American Journal of International Law* 599.

145 Anton, Mathew and Morgan, above note 17, 545. See 'The National Security Strategy of the United States of America', above note 143.

international peace and security. Most importantly, Chapter VII provides the Security Council with the power to authorize the use of collective force in response to a wide variety of crises. The primary reason for bestowing this authority on the Security Council is explained by Brownlie:

> In spite of the weakness involved in multilateral decision-making, the assumption is that the Organization (UN) has a monopoly on the use of force, and a primary responsibility for enforcement action to deal with breaches of the peace, threats to the peace or acts of aggression.[146]

Article 39 of the UN Charter allows the Security Council to identify emerging issues and crises within the international community. This authority is often the basis for UN Security Council resolutions, particularly on issues involving potential border disputes or armed hostilities. It is a broad authority that allows the Council to explore many avenues to resolve a crisis. If armed hostilities have not commenced, the Security Council may first pass a condemnation resolution to attempt to 'shame' a state into complying with its obligations under international law. An example is UN Security Council Resolution 660 in 1990, which stated that the international community '(c)ondemns the Iraqi invasion of Kuwait'[147] and '(d)emands that Iraq withdraw immediately and unconditionally all of its forces'.[148]

If these measures prove ineffective, the Security Council can then utilize its authority under Article 41 of the UN Charter, which enables it to call upon states to take certain measures, including 'complete or partial interruption of economic relations and of rail, sea, air, postal, telegraphic, radio, and other means of communication, and the severance of diplomatic relations'. Examples of targeted sanctions include freezing an individual's assets,[149] restrictions on diplomatic representation,[150] ending

---

[146] Brownlie, above note 2, 738.

[147] 'Iraq-Kuwait', SC Res. 660, UN SCOR, 45th sess., 2933rd mtg, UN Doc. S/RES/660 (2 August 1990), [1]; 'Non-proliferation/Democratic People's Republic of Korea', SC Res. 1874, UN SCOR, 64th sess., 6141st mtg, UN Doc. S/RES/1874 (12 June 2009), [1]; 'The Situation in Côte d'Ivoire, SC Res. 1975, UN SCOR, 66th sess., 6508th mtg, UN Doc. S/RES/1975 (30 March 2011), [3], [4], [5] and [9].

[148] 'Iraq-Kuwait', SC Res. 660, ibid, [2].

[149] 'Peace and Security in Africa', SC Res. 1970, UN SCOR, 66th sess., 6491st mtg, UN Doc. S/RES/1970 (26 February 2011) and 'The Situation in Libya', SC Res. 1973, UN SCOR, 66th sess., 6498th mtg, UN Doc. S/RES/1973 (17 March 2011). See also the targeted asset freezing measures in 'The Situation in Côte d'Ivoire', SC Res. 1975, UN SCOR, 66th sess., 6508th mtg, UN Doc. S/RES/1975 (30 March 2011).

[150] See, e.g., the restrictions on Libyan diplomats abroad after Libya refused to extradite suspects for the Lockerbie bombing in 'Libyan Arab Jamahiriya',

military cooperation[151] and imposing aviation bans.[152] These measures are not designed to adversely affect the general population, but rather to compel the ruling elite of a state to comply with the demands of the international community. However, sanctions can have a devastating impact on the civilian population,[153] exacerbating an already dire situation in the target state.[154]

Importantly, the Security Council must exhaust all viable diplomatic measures before the use of force can be considered to resolve an emerging crisis. This requirement clearly indicates that military force authorized by the UN Security Council is only to be used as the last resort after all other avenues have proved to be ineffective.

If all viable diplomatic measures under Article 41 have been unsuccessful, then the Security Council can take action under Article 42, allowing it to take a variety of actions, including 'demonstrations, blockade, and other operations by air, sea, or land forces of Members of the United Nations'. Article 42 clearly permits acts of collective force, utilizing resources such as troops and military equipment from participating states. Examples of this may include the deployment of a multilateral UN force to resist advancing troops, a naval blockade or targeted airstrikes on the military stockpiles of the offending state.

If the Security Council determines that military force is the only viable option to maintain international peace and security, then the members of the UN are obliged to comply with this decision. Article 25 of the UN Charter indicates that states 'agree to accept and carry out the decisions of

SC Res. 748, UN SCOR, 47th sess., 3063rd mtg, UN Doc. S/RES/748 (31 March 1992), [6].

151 See, e.g., the ban on supplying military equipment, training and cooperation in 'Non-proliferation', SC Res. 1929, UN SCOR, 65th sess., 6335th mtg, UN Doc. S/RES/1929 (9 June 2010).

152 See, e.g., the no-fly zone imposed on military aircraft in Bosnian airspace in 'Bosnia and Herzegovina', SC Res. 816, UN SCOR, 48th sess., 3191st mtg, UN Doc. S/RES/816 (31 March 1993), [1] and [4].

153 ICISS Report, above note 68, [4.5].

154 'Iraq-Kuwait', SC Res. 661, UN SCOR, 45th sess., 2933rd mtg, UN Doc. S/RES/661 (6 August 1990), and 'Iraq-Kuwait', SC Res. 687, UN SCOR, 46th sess., 2981st mtg, UN Doc. S/RES/687 (3 April 1991). These sanctions were not lifted until 15 December 2010 in a series of three resolutions: 'The Situation concerning Iraq', SC Res. 1956, UN SCOR, 65th sess., 6450th mtg, UN Doc. S/RES/1956 (15 December 2010), 'The Situation concerning Iraq', SC Res. 1957, UN SCOR, 65th sess., 6450th mtg, UN Doc. S/RES/1957 (15 December 2010). 'The Situation concerning Iraq', SC Res. 1958, UN SCOR, 65th sess., 6450th mtg, UN Doc. S/RES/1958 (15 December 2010).

the Security Council', whilst Article 49 requires that states 'join in providing mutual assistance' to enforce binding decisions.

8.6.1 Responsibility to Protect

In 2000, UN Secretary-General Kofi Annan asked the following question of the UN General Assembly:

> [I]f humanitarian intervention is, indeed, an unacceptable assault on sovereignty, how should we respond to a Rwanda, to a Srebrenica – to gross and systematic violations of human rights that affect every precept of our common humanity?[155]

In response to this poignant question, the Canadian government established the Internal Commission on Intervention and State Sovereignty (ICISS), charged with the responsibility of defining the circumstances in which external military intervention can be justified to protect the citizens of a state.[156] The ICISS embarked on a wide-ranging and somewhat radical review of the concept of state sovereignty in the context of modern internal conflicts.

The result of this process was the development of the 'Responsibility to Protect' doctrine ('R2P') in December 2001. The central theme of R2P is that every sovereign state has a responsibility to protect its own citizens from avoidable catastrophes, including mass murder, rape and starvation.[157] This is because the concept of state sovereignty implies responsibility, primarily to protect the population from harm.[158] When the government of a state is unwilling or unable to protect its own citizens from these atrocities, the responsibility to protect must be borne by the international community.[159] R2P encompasses three important priorities:

1. Responsibility to Prevent – identify and seek to resolve the root causes of internal conflicts and humanitarian crises;[160]
2. Responsibility to React – respond to situations of compelling human need with measures such as economic sanctions, international prosecution and military intervention in extreme cases;[161] and

---

155 Secretary-General Kofi Annan, 'We the Peoples: The Role of the United Nations in the 21st Century', above note 86.
156 ICISS Report, above note 68, [1.7].
157 Ibid., [2.32].
158 Ibid., [2.15].
159 Ibid., Foreword.
160 Ibid., [3.18].
161 Ibid., [3.33]–[3.34].

3. Responsibility to Rebuild – provide assistance with recovery, reconstruction and reconciliation, and also address the root causes of the internal crisis.[162]

Importantly, it seeks to confine the use of force in response to humanitarian crises that require an 'exceptional and extraordinary measure'.[163] In accordance with Articles 41 and 42 of the UN Charter, military intervention can be used only as a measure of last resort, when all other peaceful avenues have been exhausted.[164] For military force to be used, 'serious and irreparable' harm to a civilian population must be imminent.[165] This is confined to a large-scale loss of life, with or without genocidal intent, or large-scale ethnic cleansing, including mass killings, forced expulsion and widespread rape.[166] An intervention should only be undertaken when there are reasonable prospects of preventing further suffering.[167]

The R2P doctrine seeks to establish broad rules of engagement for a military intervention in response to a humanitarian crisis.[168] The UN Security Council is recognized as the most appropriate body to authorize the use of military force.[169] The Permanent Five members of the Security Council should agree not to use their veto power to obstruct a resolution proposing a military intervention for human protection purposes where there is clear majority support from other states.[170] In this important way, the R2P doctrine differs from the doctrine of humanitarian intervention, which occurs outside of Security Council authorization. R2P has received significant support from the UN as an emerging international norm. Paragraph 200 of the UN's 2004 report, 'A More Secure World', explains this change as follows:

> The principle of non-intervention in internal affairs cannot be used to protect genocidal acts or other atrocities . . . which can properly be considered a threat to international security and as such provoke actions by the Security Council.[171]

---

162 Ibid., [2.29].

163 Ibid., [4.18].

164 Anne Orford, *International Authority and the Responsibility to Protect* (Cambridge: Cambridge University Press, 2011), 27.

165 ICISS Report, above note 68, [4.18].

166 Ibid., [4.18]–[4.20].

167 Ibid., [4.41]–[4.43].

168 Emma McClean, 'The Responsibility to Protect: The Role of International Human Rights Law' (2008) 13(1) *Journal of Conflict and Security Law* 123, 126.

169 ICISS Report, above note 68, [6.14].

170 Ibid., [6.20]–[6.21].

171 Secretary-General Kofi Annan, 'A More Secure World: Our Shared Responsibility', UN GAOR, 59th sess., UN Doc. A/59/565 (2 December 2004), [200].

The doctrine was also endorsed by UN Secretary-General Ban Ki-moon in his January 2009 report, 'Implementing the Responsibility to Protect'.[172] This report emphasizes that every state has the primary responsibility to protect its own population from genocide, war crimes, ethnic cleansing and crimes against humanity. Importantly, the Secretary-General explains that the next stage in the development of R2P is to 'operationalize' the doctrine in response to a situation of gross human rights abuses.[173]

The 2011 crisis in Libya is the first clear example of the R2P doctrine being invoked by the international community. International forces intervened in Libya in March 2011 in an attempt to prevent the Gaddafi regime from violently suppressing an uprising. UNSC Resolution 1970 refers to the 'Libyan authorities' responsibility to protect its population'.[174] This is a clear example of R2P terminology, and reflects the intention of international forces to prevent further atrocities being committed against the civilian population.

8.7 CONCLUSIONS

The prohibition on the use of force is an ever evolving area of international law. It is only in relatively recent history that states have been restricted in their ability to use military power as an element of diplomatic relations. Because of the inherently destructive nature of warfare, the international community has endeavoured to regulate its use of force and prohibit aggressive territorial conquests. In accordance with this stance, states are prohibited from engaging in unprovoked acts of aggression that violate the sovereignty of other states.

Despite the existence of a general prohibition on the use of force, there are several limited but important exceptions. Under Article 51 of the UN Charter, if an armed attack occurs against a state, it is an inherent right of that state to defend itself. Importantly, a state that exercises its right of self-defence must immediately report the incident to the Security Council. The exception of self-defence extends beyond an individual state responding to an imminent threat to its territorial integrity. Article 51 of the UN Charter permits collective self-defence, but the target state must explicitly request assistance and regard itself as the victim of an armed attack. However, the exception of self-defence does not extend to a pre-emptive

---

172 'Implementing the Responsibility to Protect' Report, above note 67.

173 Ibid., [71].

174 'The Situation in Libya', SC Res 1973, above note 149, Preamble.

attack on a foreign state where there is no apparent imminent threat. The widespread criticism of the 'Bush Doctrine' illustrates that self-defence cannot include nullifying potential threats that may never eventuate.

The UN Security Council is the international organ charged with the responsibility to maintain international peace and security. To achieve this broad objective, the Security Council is endowed with the authority under Chapter VII of the UN Charter to adopt both diplomatic and military measures to resolve crises that threaten international peace and security. Under Article 42 of the UN Charter, the Security Council can authorize measures of collective force, such as no-fly zones, naval blockades, targeted air strikes or the deployment of ground troops. Importantly, these measures can only be implemented if all other diplomatic avenues have been exhausted. The Security Council's authority under Chapter VII takes precedence over a state's inherent right to self-defence, as explicitly outlined in Article 51 of the UN Charter. Chapter VII allows the Security Council to perform its role as the only body which can legitimately authorize the use of force under the UN Charter. Importantly, the inclusion and use of Chapter VII indicates that the use of force is not intended to be completely removed from diplomatic relations, but instead confined to very limited circumstances.

The most dynamic and controversial area concerning the use of force is the concept of humanitarian intervention. The practice of forcibly intervening in the territory of another state without consent has been criticized as a fundamental breach of the principle of non-intervention contained in Article 2(7) of the UN Charter. However, there is a need to protect civilians of a foreign state from gross and systematic breaches of human rights, such as mass arbitrary killings and forced expulsions. As the Rwandan genocide of 1994 clearly illustrates, the consequences of international inaction in response to a widespread internal crisis can be catastrophic. As outlined by the General Assembly and Security Council, an internal humanitarian crisis can be considered a threat to international peace and security. Whilst the international community is yet to develop firm guidelines for the practice of humanitarian intervention, there is an imperative need to use appropriate measures to protect civilians of a foreign state from gross abuses of human rights.

International practice concerning the use of force will continue to adapt to ever-changing circumstances. As new international crises emerge, it is likely that the doctrines of self-defence and humanitarian intervention will be refined and applied to different situations. However, despite ongoing efforts to prohibit aggressive warfare, it is unlikely that many states will ever renounce the use of force as a tool of international diplomacy. The deterrent effect of possessing military stockpiles and armed forces is likely to remain a key aspect of national security policy for the foreseeable future. Whilst the prohibition on the use of force is likely to be further refined, it is unlikely that such efforts will ever completely satisfy the lofty objective of saving 'succeeding generations from the scourge of war'.[175]

---

[175] Charter of the United Nations, Preamble.

9. Pacific resolution of disputes

9.1 THE LEGAL FRAMEWORK

Peaceful dispute resolution at the international level has occurred more or less formally since the existence of international law itself. Long before the creation of the Permanent Court of Arbitration or, indeed, the UN Charter, states engaged in the settlement of disputes through a range of bilateral and ad hoc mechanisms. An important nineteenth-century example was the settlement of the now famous *Caroline* dispute, relating to the sinking by the British of a US ship. That event, still significant in understanding self-defence in international law, was resolved by diplomatic exchanges between the affected states.[1] More ancient examples of states resolving their disputes by peaceful means can be found at least as far back as the Roman system of *jus gentium*.[2]

Of course, disputes were not always settled peacefully and, unlike the position today under the modern UN Charter regime of collective security, there was little or no impediment under international law to states resorting to the use of force to resolve their disputes. While it is often said that prior to 1945 there was no universally accepted prohibition against the use of force by states to settle disputes, there was at least some framework in place. The Hague Peace Conferences of 1899 and 1907 were unsuccessful in preventing the Second World War, despite the creation of an arbitral framework, a Permanent Court of International Justice and a multilateral treaty rendering the use of force in large part unlawful (the Kellogg-Briand Pact[3]). Even so, these normative developments did lend greater legitimacy to the prosecution of German and Japanese leaders following the Second World War for the crime of aggression.

The United Nations Charter in 1945 gave birth to a radical new

---

1 For a detailed discussion of the *Caroline* case, see Chapter 8, section 8.5.1.

2 See Chapter 1, section 1.3.1.

3 General Treaty for the Renunciation of War as an Instrument of National Policy (opened for signature 27 August 1928, entered into force 4 September 1929) LNTS. See Chapter 8, section 8.1.5.

international framework under which states must never resort to armed force to settle disputes except in limited circumstances. Article 2(4) of the UN Charter prohibits the threat or use of force by states other than in individual or collective self-defence (Article 51). Article 2(3) provides that all members 'shall settle their international disputes by peaceful means in such a manner that international peace and security, and justice, are not endangered'. Article 33(1) further obliges parties to a dispute to seek resolution first by 'negotiation, enquiry, mediation, conciliation, arbitration, judicial settlement, resort to regional agencies or arrangements, or other peaceful means of their own choice'. Article 33(2) gives the Security Council the power to call upon parties to settle disputes by such means as those listed in Article 33(1) when it deems necessary. The Security Council also has the power under Chapter VII to take measures to maintain or restore international peace and security, which includes the creation of international criminal tribunals.[4]

9.2 NON-JUDICIAL SETTLEMENT PROCEDURES (NON-BINDING)

9.2.1 Negotiation

Negotiation involves discussions between the disputing parties seeking to understand the different positions they hold in order to resolve the dispute. There is generally no third party involvement, and the negotiations are purely consensual and informal. Therefore, for negotiations to be successful they require a measure of goodwill, flexibility and mutual understanding between the parties. Even if a negotiation fails to resolve a dispute, it will often assist the parties in clarifying the nature of the disagreement and the issues in dispute and in obtaining a clearer idea of their own and each other's positions, what they are willing to compromise on and what it might take to resolve the dispute.[5]

Many treaties provide for negotiation as a precondition to binding international dispute resolution. Examples include Article 84 of the Vienna Convention on the Representation of States in their Relations with

---

[4] United Nations Charter, Art. 39. This power was the basis of the creation of the ad hoc International Criminal Tribunal for the former Yugoslavia and the International Criminal Tribunal for Rwanda.

[5] See, e.g., the negotiation that took place between Argentina and Israel involving the capture of Nazi Adolf Eichmann: L.C. Green, 'Legal Issues of the Eichmann Trial' (1962–3) *Tulane Law Review* 641, 643, 647.

International Organizations (1975) and Article 41 of the Convention on the Succession of States in Respect of Treaties (1978).

However, neither in the UN Charter nor otherwise in international law is there any general rule that requires the exhaustion of diplomatic negotiations as a precondition for a matter to be referred to a court or tribunal.[6] Nevertheless, the court or tribunal may direct parties at the preliminary stages of the proceedings to negotiate in good faith and to indicate certain factors to be taken into account in that negotiation process.[7] Ultimately, there is no obligation on states to reach agreement, only that 'serious efforts towards that end will be made'.[8] This requires parties to 'negotiate, bargain and in good faith attempt to reach a result acceptable to both parties'.[9] Examples of a breach of good faith have included unusual delays, continued refusal to consider proposals and breaking off discussions without justification.[10] Negotiations may continue while there are other resolution processes under way, formal or informal, and a resolution may be reached at any time.[11]

9.2.2 Inquiry

Article 50 of the International Court of Justice Statute provides that the Court may 'at any time, entrust any individual, body, bureau, commission, or other organization that it may select, with the task of carrying out an enquiry or giving an expert opinion'.

The possibility of engaging a formal commission of inquiry carried out by reputable observers to ascertain facts objectively was first envisaged in the 1899 Hague Convention for the Pacific Settlement of International Disputes.[12] These provisions were revised and included in the 1907 Hague Convention following their successful application in the *Dogger Bank* case.[13] This success also led to inquiry provisions being incorporated into many treaties at the time.[14] There has been very little use of

---

6 *Cameroon v Nigeria* (Preliminary Objections) [1998] ICJ Rep 275, 303.

7 *Fisheries Jurisdiction* case (*United Kingdom v Iceland*) [1973] ICJ Rep 3, 32.

8 *German External Debts* case [1974] 47 ILR 418, 454.

9 Ibid., 453.

10 *Lac Lanoux* (1957) 24 ILR 101, 119.

11 *Aegean Sea Continental Shelf* case (*Greece v Turkey*) [1978] ICJ Rep 3, 12.

12 Convention for the Pacific Settlement of International Disputes (29 July 1899) (entered into force 4 September 1900), Arts 9 and 10.

13 *Dogger Bank* case (*Great Britain v Russia*) (1908) 2 AJIL 931–6 (ICI Report of 26 February 1905).

14 Malcolm Shaw, *International Law* (Cambridge; New York: Cambridge University Press, 2008, 6th edn), 1020.

inquiry provisions in practice over the years, though there have been some occasions in recent times, particularly in relation to arms control treaties.

9.2.3 Good Offices

Good offices is another informal means of assisting parties to resolve a dispute. This involves the attempt by an impartial third party to influence the disputing parties to enter into negotiations. The Security Council itself has engaged in this form of international diplomacy, often using a recognized and respected person to negotiate with the parties towards a settlement of the dispute. An example of this was the use by Barack Obama of former US President Bill Clinton to assist in negotiating the release of US journalists held by North Korea in 2009, and former US President Jimmy Carter to secure the release of an American citizen in 2010.[15] Another successful example was the intervention by Kofi Annan which led to an agreement between the negotiators for President Mwai Kibaki and the opposition in the Kenyan post-election turmoil, in which a dispute over an election in 2007 led to weeks of violence.[16] An unusual example was the *Beagle Channel* dispute in which the Pope was requested by both parties to provide his good offices in a dispute between Argentina and Chile, and at his suggestion both countries agreed to comply with the proposed outcome.[17]

Perhaps one of the most impressive modern examples of good offices concerns the intractable dispute relating to the *Lockerbie* incident. The problem concerned a jurisdictional dispute over who was to try two Libyan men accused of planning and executing the infamous terrorist attack on a Pan Am flight blown up over Lockerbie, Scotland, in December 1988. Both the US and the UK had initiated legal proceedings against the men, whom Libya refused to transfer in accordance with both its own extradition laws and a reading of the Montreal Convention for the Suppression of Unlawful Acts against the Safety of Civil Aviation 1971.

---

[15] Kay Seok, 'From a North Korean Hell to Home' (27 August 2010) *Human Rights First*.

[16] See, e.g., Elisabeth Lindermayer and Josie Lianna Kaye, 'A Choice for Peace? The story of 41 days of mediation in Kenya' (August 2009) *International Peace Institute* (New York) 1, 1; 'Ballots to Bullets, Organized Political Violence and Kenya's Crisis of Governance' (16 March 2008) *Human Rights Watch* (New York) (20) No.1 (A).

[17] *Beagle Channel Arbitration* (*Argentina v Chile*) [1978] 52 ILR 93.

The case went before the ICJ which, in absurd circumstances, refused to order provisional measures.[18]

UN Secretary-General Kofi Annan facilitated an agreement between a number of countries – including Libya, the UK and the US – with regard to the prosecution of the two Libyan nationals. The agreement achieved was complex, requiring the enactment of national legislation in at least two jurisdictions to enable a Scottish court to apply Scottish law in the territorial jurisdiction of the Netherlands, and for the Netherlands to facilitate this by keeping the suspects in custody and repatriating them to Scotland to serve their sentences.[19]

9.2.4 Mediation and Conciliation

Both mediation and conciliation are open to the parties in dispute as a flexible means of dispute resolution.

A mediator facilitates negotiations between the parties, and may propose solutions to the dispute. Therefore, the mediator will need to be well respected, accepted by all parties and sensitive to a range of different contextual issues.

Conciliation involves a third party investigation of the basis of the dispute and submission of a report suggesting means by which a settlement may be reached. It tends to involve elements from both inquiry and mediation. Conciliation reports are not binding, and this differentiates them from arbitration. As with inquiry, conciliation has become less popular as a method of resolving disputes.[20]

9.2.5 The General Role of the United Nations

Under Article 36 of the UN Charter, the Security Council may, at any stage of a dispute, 'recommend appropriate procedures or methods of adjustment'.[21] Article 37 requires parties who fail to resolve their differences to refer the dispute to the Security Council, and Article 38 allows for referral of disputes to the Security Council where the parties agree. Many disputes, such as that between Argentina and Israel over

---

[18] *Libyan Arab Jamahiriya v UK* [1992] ICJ Rep 3. For a good summary of the case, see Gillian Triggs, *International Law: Contemporary Principles and Practices* (Sydney: LexisNexis Butterworths, 2011) 108–9.

[19] Letter from the Secretary-General addressed to the President of the Security Council, 5 April 1999, UN Doc. S/1999/378 (1999).

[20] Shaw, above note 14, 1023.

[21] Charter of the United Nations, Art. 36.

the arrest of Adolf Eichmann,[22] have been referred to the Security Council under these provisions and this has led to a successful resolution. However, there are differing views as to the true effectiveness of the UN as a facilitator of the pacific settlement of disputes[23] with some claims that 'the line between pacific settlement and enforcement has blurred'.[24]

9.3 INTERNATIONAL ARBITRATION (BINDING)

Arbitration is a binding form of dispute resolution. Article 37 of the Hague Convention contains the accepted definition of arbitration at international law:

> International arbitration has for its object the settlement of disputes between States by Judges of their own choice and on the basis of respect for law. Recourse to arbitration implies an engagement to submit in good faith to the Award.[25]

It can be distinguished from judicial resolution as it is normally an ad hoc body, created specifically for the resolution of a particular dispute.[26] In addition, the parties have greater control over the process in that they must agree on how the case will run with regard to the issues to be decided and, although international law is applied, the parties may agree that certain principles be considered.[27] The parties must also decide on how many and who the arbitrators will be.[28] Arbitration may arise out of a treaty provision or as a result of an ad hoc agreement.

One prominent example of international arbitration is the *Rainbow Warrior* case.[29] France and New Zealand were involved in a dispute after

---

[22] See discussion above under 6.3.5.4.

[23] See, e.g., Steven R. Ratner, 'Image and Reality in the UN's Peaceful Settlement of Disputes' (1995) 6 *European Journal of International Law* 426; Saadia Touval, 'Why the UN Fails' (1994) 73(5) *Foreign Affairs* 44; Thomas M. Franck and Georg Nolte, 'The Good Offices Function of the UN Secretary-General', in Adam Roberts and Benedict Kingsbury (eds), *United Nations, Divided World: The UN's Roles in International Relations* (Oxford: Clarendon Press, 1993, 2nd edn), 143.

[24] Ratner, ibid., 426, 443.

[25] Hague Convention of 1907, Art. 37.

[26] Triggs, above note 18, 646.

[27] Shaw, above note 14, 1052.

[28] Ibid., 1050.

[29] See also, *SS 'I'm Alone'* case (*Canada v US*) (1935) III RIAA 1609.

the French military security service sank the *Rainbow Warrior* ship while in Auckland Harbour in 1985.[30] Two French secret service agents were arrested and charged in New Zealand and then convicted for manslaughter and wilful damage.[31] The French government eventually acknowledged that the agents acted under orders and argued that therefore they should not be blamed.[32] New Zealand notified France that it would be pursuing a claim for compensation.[33] Negotiations took place between the two parties over the possible repatriation of the agents on the condition that they serve the rest of their sentences.[34]

However, in 1986 France began to impede imports from New Zealand.[35] After pressure from other states to resolve the dispute, France and New Zealand agreed to refer all matters to arbitration by the Secretary-General of the UN.[36] The arbitration took place in early July 1986 and New Zealand was directed to transfer the agents into French custody on an isolated island to serve three years in a military facility; France was directed to apologize and pay compensation to New Zealand, and stop impeding New Zealand imports.[37] Both countries complied with the decision, although France allowed the agents to return to France before they completed their three-year sentences and further awarded them the highest order in France. The issue of whether this was a breach of international law was put to arbitration, and it was declared that France was indeed in breach of international law.[38]

9.3.1 Diplomatic Protection: Admissibility of State Claims

Although not limited to international arbitration,[39] the diplomatic protection of a state over its natural or juristic persons has typically taken place

---

30 Michael Pugh, 'Legal Aspects of the *Rainbow Warrior* Affair' (1987) 36 *International and Comparative Law Quarterly* 655, 656.

31 Ibid. 656.

32 Ibid. 657.

33 Ibid.

34 Ibid.

35 Ibid.

36 Ibid.

37 *Rainbow Warrior (New Zealand v France) Conciliation Proceedings* (1986) 74 ILR 241.

38 *Rainbow Warrior (New Zealand v France) Conciliation Proceedings* (1990) 82 ILR 499.

39 In theory, diplomatic protection by a state can take any form of peaceful settlement of disputes discussed in this chapter: see *Kaunda v President of South Africa* CCT 23/04, [2004] ZACC 5, [26–[27]. Key ICJ cases on the topic include

through arbitral tribunals and mixed claims commissions. As discussed in Chapter 7, a state may bring an international claim for injury to its nationals caused by an internationally wrongful act of another state. Such a claim is discretionary, as is the transfer to the national of any compensation obtained from the responsible state.[40] There exist two special procedural rules that operate as a precondition to the admissibility of claims for diplomatic protection. This is the subject of the ILC's Draft Articles on Diplomatic Protection (2006) ('Draft Articles').[41] Like the ILC Articles on the Responsibility of States for Internationally Wrongful Acts, which are without prejudice to questions of admissibility of claims,[42] the Draft Articles are only authoritative insofar as they correctly restate customary law. The first requirement is that there should be a bond of nationality between the state and the injured person,[43] or corporation.[44] The second requirement is that the national must take the case to the highest court of the responsible state before a claim for diplomatic protection is available; this is known as the 'exhaustion of local remedies' requirement.[45]

Mavromattis Palestine Concession case (*Greece v United Kingdom*) (Jurisdiction) (1924) PCIJ (Ser. A) No. 2; *Barcelona Traction, Light and Power Co. Ltd* (*Belgium v Spain*) [1970] ICJ Rep 3. Note also *Reparation for Injuries Suffered in the Service of the United Nations* (Advisory Opinion) [1949] ICJ Rep 174, which concerned the right of an international organization (the United Nations) to make a claim for diplomatic protection.

[40] See, e.g., the *Barcelona Traction* case, above note 39, [79]; 'Draft Articles on Diplomatic Protection, with Commentaries (2006)', Report of the ILC, 58th sess., UN Doc. A/61/10 (2006), 13, Art. 19; ILC Commentary to Draft Article 19, [3]. ('Draft Articles' and 'ILC Commentary to the Draft Articles').

[41] Draft Articles, above note 40, 13.

[42] Draft Articles, ibid., Art. 44; ILC Commentary to the Draft Articles, ibid., 44, [1].

[43] See *Flegenheimer Claim* (*United States v Italy*) (1958) 25 ILR 91, 150; *Nationality Decrees Issued in Tunis and Morocco* (*French Zone*) (Advisory Opinion) [1923] PCIJ (Ser. B) No. 4, 24; Draft Articles, above note 40, Art. 4; ILC Commentary to the Draft Articles, above note 40, 4, [2]. Note, however, *Nottebohm* case (*Liechtenstein v Guatemala*) (*Second Phase*) [1955] ICJ Rep 4, proposing a test of 'genuine connection', which has not been adopted in subsequent cases: *Flegenheimer Claim*, 150; *Dallal v Iran* (1983) 3 Iran-US Cl Trib Rep 157; ILC Commentary to Draft Article 4, [5].

[44] See generally the *Barcelona Traction* case, above note 39; *Elettronica Sicula SpA* case [1989] ICJ Rep 15.

[45] See, e.g., Draft Articles, above note 40, Art. 14; *Ambatelios Claim (Greece v United Kingdom)* (1956) 12 RIAA 83, 118–19; *Interhandel* case (*Switzerland v United States*) [1959] ICJ Rep 6. Note, however, in certain circumstances – where, for example, there is no undue delay or reasonable possibility of redress – this rule may be avoided: Draft Articles, above note 40, Art. 15(a)–(b); ILC Commentary to Article 15, [5]–[6]. See also the grounds in Article 15(c)–(e). But see the *Interhandel*

9.4 INTERNATIONAL TRIBUNALS (BINDING)

A growing number of disputes in international law are being resolved by formal tribunals. This trend has been brought about, at least in part, by an increasingly vast range of options available to the parties. These tribunals have enjoyed increasing success in recent years, and there is a growing willingness for states and non-state actors to have recourse to these bodies as a result of mounting recognition of the competence of these bodies in resolving disputes. Therefore, the regularity with which these dispute resolution methods are being included in modern international agreements has also increased considerably. In many instances, this increased use of specialized tribunals has given rise to more effective and efficient resolution of disputes. In particular, specialist tribunals can assist in encouraging compliance with international law through the compulsory jurisdiction they often enjoy[46] and supporting the ICJ in the ever increasing international case workload.[47] However, this trend also poses new challenges and risks, including the risk of a loss of uniformity and consistency of jurisprudence,[48] and a potential overlapping of jurisdiction which allows states and parties to 'shop' for the tribunal most likely to arrive at a favourable outcome for them.[49]

The following jurisdictions exemplify the diverse range of *sui generis* international tribunals dealing with a range of disciplines within the international legal regime.

---

case, where the ICJ stayed its proceedings when the United States Supreme Court readmitted the Swiss company's case after a delay of almost a decade.

[46] See, e.g., Jonathan Charney, 'The Impact of the International Legal System on the Growth of International Courts and Tribunals' (1999) 31 *Journal of International Law and Politics* 697, 704.

[47] Brownlie, for example, comments on the 'constraints resulting from budgetary stringencies imposed by the United Nations that the ICJ is forced to contend with': Ian Brownlie, *Principles of Public International Law* (Oxford: Oxford University Press, 2008, 7th edn), 486, 694.

[48] For example, in the decision of *Prosecutor v Tadić* (Appeals Chamber Judgment) IT-94-1-A (15 July 1999), [137], the International Criminal Tribunal for the former Yugoslavia established a test of 'overall' control in attributing the military conduct to a state, a departure from the standard of 'effective' control as established in *Military and Paramilitary Activities in and against Nicaragua* (*Nicaragua v USA*) (Merits) [1986] ICJ Rep 14, 61, 62.

[49] See, e.g., *MOX Plant Arbitration* (*Ireland v United Kingdom*) (2003) 42 ILM 1118. See also Yuval Shany, 'The First MOX Plant Award: The Need to Harmonize Competing Environmental Regimes and Dispute Settlement Procedures' (2004) 17 *Leiden Journal of International Law*, 815.

9.4.1 WTO Appellate Body

The establishment of the Appellate Body of the World Trade Organization (WTO) in 1995 is perhaps the most remarkable and effective development in international dispute resolution.[50] It has a binding and compulsory jurisdiction over its 153 members.[51] The Appellate Body is made up of seven permanent members[52] broadly representing the range of WTO membership.[53] Each appeal is heard by three members, who may then elect to uphold, modify or reverse the legal findings of the panel which was set up to resolve the particular dispute.[54] Appeals can only be initiated by parties to a dispute[55] and have to be based on points of law; there is no scope for the Appellate Body to consider new issues or to re-examine evidence.[56] Once the Appellate Body Reports are adopted by the Dispute Settlement Body (DSB), the parties are compelled to accept the findings. The ability of the Appellate Body to mandate compliance with the WTO agreement makes it one of the most powerful means of dispute resolution in the world, significantly developing the area of international trade law.[57]

9.4.2 International Tribunal for the Law of the Sea

The ITLOS is a permanent intergovernmental organization established by Annex VI of the United Nations Convention on the Law of the Sea (UNCLOS).[58] It consists of 21 independent members 'of recognized competence in the field of the law of the sea'.[59] ITLOS only has the power to resolve disputes between states, which includes the European Community.[60] Since its commencement in 1996, 15 cases have been sub-

---

[50] See also the discussion concerning international trade law in Chapter 1, section 1.5.2; Chapter 3, section 3.3.

[51] Accurate as at 16 June 2011.

[52] 'Understanding on Rules and Procedure Governing the Settlement of Disputes', 1869 UNTS 401; 33 ILM 1226 (1994), Art. 17(1).

[53] Ibid., Art. 17(3).

[54] Ibid., Art. 17(13).

[55] Ibid., Art. 17(4).

[56] Ibid., Art. 17(6).

[57] Robert Hudec, 'The New WTO Dispute Settlement Procedure: An Overview of the First Three Years' (1999) 8 *Minnesota Journal of Global Trade* 1, 27.

[58] United Nations Convention on the Law of the Sea, 1833 UNTS 3, Annex VI, ('UNCLOS'). See also discussion regarding the international law of the sea in Chapter 1, section 1.5.1.

[59] UNCLOS, Art. 2(1).

[60] The European Community is a single member of ITLOS. It is an 'international organization' within the meaning of UNCLOS, Art. 305(f) and Annex IX,

mitted to ITLOS for its review. This number is fewer than was anticipated at the time of its establishment, and is reflective of the fact that states have been hesitant in resorting to ITLOS for the more contentious issues concerning the law of the sea.[61]

9.4.3 International Criminal Court

The International Criminal Court (ICC) was created by the Rome Statute of the International Criminal Court ('Rome Statute'), which came into effect on 1 July 2002, and is the world's first permanent international criminal court.[62] It complements, and will soon supersede, a wide range of modern international and hybrid war crimes tribunals, the most important of which is the International Criminal Tribunal for the former Yugoslavia (ICTY).[63] The ICC has jurisdiction to prosecute some of the most serious crimes of international concern, including genocide, crimes against humanity and war crimes,[64] as well as the crime of aggression after 2016.[65] Its jurisdiction is complementary to that of national courts, which means that the Court will act only when states themselves are unwilling or unable to investigate or prosecute.[66] The ICC may exercise its jurisdiction on referral by a State Party or by the Security Council,[67] or through the prosecutor initiating an investigation '*proprio motu* on the basis of information' on crimes within the ICC's jurisdiction.[68] In the Court's brief history, the Prosecutor has opened investigations into six situations, including, most recently, the investigation into the alleged criminal acts in Libya.[69] Through its

---

Art. 1; it represents the states who have transferred competence to it over matters governed by the UNCLOS.

[61] Donald Rothwell and Tim Stephens, *The International Law of the Sea* (Oxford: Hart, 2010) 459.

[62] See also discussion about international criminal law in Chapter 1, section 1.5.6.

[63] See, e.g., the ICTY, ICTR, SCSL, ECCC and STL.

[64] Rome Statute of the International Criminal Court, UN Doc. A/CONF 183/9; 37 ILM 1002 (1998), Art. 5.

[65] As a result of an agreement reached by States Parties to the Rome Statute in 2010 in Kampala: for a detailed discussion, see Claus Kreβ, 'The Kampala Compromise on the Crime of Aggression' (2010) 8 *Journal of International Criminal Justice* 1179.

[66] Rome Statute, above note 64, Art. 1.

[67] Ibid., Art. 13.

[68] Ibid., Art. 15(1).

[69] The investigation into Libya was referred by the Security Council on 26 February 2011, with the investigation announced on 3 March 2011.

investigations, it has issued 14 arrest warrants and nine summonses to date.[70]

9.4.4 Human Rights Mechanisms

International mechanisms are often used for the monitoring of human rights treaties. These mechanisms can be divided into three major categories: (1) periodic reporting by governments, (2) international complaints, and (3) inquiry procedures.[71] As a general rule of international law, redress through human rights mechanisms is normally available only where domestic avenues have been exhausted. Although the establishment of such mechanisms has been an important means of developing the content of human rights, enforcing these rights and providing redress to victims, these mechanisms have not always been effective. For example, states often fail to report, or do so belatedly or inadequately, and it is also common for states to append wide reservations to treaty obligations.[72]

While most human rights mechanisms, particularly reporting mechanisms, are not binding forms of dispute resolution, there are binding human rights jurisdictions that act as powerful and effective regional regimes. The most successful of these is the European Court of Human Rights.[73] The principal reason for the success of the European Court is the compulsory jurisdiction it exercises over the 47 signatories to the European Convention on Human Rights,[74] combined with the practically binding impact of its judgments. Compliance is then ensured by the Committee of Ministers of the Council of Europe, a political body. The importance of the Court also lies in the wealth of jurisprudence it provides on international human rights norms, which are analogous to the ICCPR and other regional human rights instruments. In this way, the jurisprudence of the Court impacts globally on human rights norms and is referred

---

[70] As at 16 June 2011.

[71] Martin Scheinin, 'International Mechanisms and Procedures for Monitoring', in Catarina Krause and Martin Scheinin (eds), *International Protection of Human Rights: A Textbook* (Turku, Finland: Åbo Akademi University Institute for Human Rights, 2009).

[72] See discussion in Chapter 2, section 2.2.1.4.

[73] See Diego Rodriguez-Pinzon and Claudia Martin, 'The Inter-American Human Rights System: Selected Examples of its Supervisory Work', in S. Joseph and A. McBeth (eds), *Research Handbook in International Human Rights Law* (Cheltenham, UK; Northampton, MA: Edward Elgar Publishing, 2010), 353.

[74] Convention for the Protection of Human Rights and Fundamental Freedoms (opened for signature 4 November 1950, entered into force 3 September 1953) 213 UNTS 262 ('ECHR').

to broadly by national and other international courts and tribunals as authoritative.

9.5 INTERNATIONAL COURT OF JUSTICE

The International Court of Justice, commonly known as the 'World Court', is the principal judicial organ of the United Nations. It was created in 1945, succeeding the Permanent Court of International Justice.[75] Chapter 5 of this book examines the history of the Court, and provides an overview of its functions. This section will consider more deeply the role played by the ICJ.

9.5.1 Procedure and Practice: Admissibility and Organization

Article 92 of the UN Charter provides that the ICJ is 'the principal judicial organ of the United Nations', while Article 93(1) states that all members of the UN are parties to the Statute of the International Court of Justice.[76] The ICJ can be engaged in a dispute by the operation of Articles 35(1) and 36(1) of the UN Charter. Article 35(1) provides a means for a Member of the United Nations to bring a dispute before the General Assembly or Security Council. Article 36(1) then provides a means for the Security Council to 'recommend appropriate procedures or methods of adjustment',[77] including referral to the International Court of Justice.[78]

The Statute of the ICJ sets out the organization of the court.[79] Article 2 sets out the requirements for appointment to the Court, stating:

> The Court shall be composed of a body of independent judges, elected regardless of their nationality from among persons of high moral character, who possess the qualifications required in their respective countries for appointment to the highest judicial offices, or are jurisconsults of recognized competence in international law.[80]

---

[75] On the history of the creation of the ICJ, see Brownlie, above note 47, 677–8.

[76] Charter of the United Nations, Art. 93(1). Note also that Art. 35(2) provides a method for states which are not Members of the United Nations to bring matters to the attention of the Security Council or General Assembly.

[77] Charter of the United Nations, Art. 36(1).

[78] Ibid., Art. 36(3).

[79] Statute of the International Court of Justice, Arts 2–33.

[80] Ibid., Art. 2.

The Court consists of 15 members, with a maximum of two from any one state.[81] Judges are elected through a process whereby states nominate suitable candidates, and a simultaneous vote is held by the General Assembly and Security Council.[82] In voting, electors are asked to bear in mind that those seeking to be elected should not only be qualified, but should represent 'the main forms of civilization and . . . principal legal systems of the world'.[83] Like most of the UN courts, the ICJ system of electing judges has attracted criticism for being unduly political.[84]

Members of the Court are elected for a period of nine years, with the possibility of re-election.[85] Decisions of the court are based on a majority of judges. An interesting mechanism provided for by Article 31 of the Statute – described by Brownlie as a 'further concession to the political conditions of the Court's existence'[86] – allows states who are before the Court in a dispute each to choose a judge of their own nationality to sit on the Court.[87] While this mechanism often produces partisan voting, it can also produce important and highly regarded opinions.[88]

9.5.2 Role and Jurisdiction

9.5.2.1 Applicable law and general jurisdiction

In determining the relevant law that applies to a dispute, the chief provision to which the ICJ has recourse is Article 38(1).[89] This provides for the now universally accepted and recognized sources of international law.[90]

The general jurisdiction of the court is set out in Article 36(1):

---

81 Ibid., Art. 3.

82 Ibid., Arts 4–12.

83 Ibid., Art. 9.

84 Brownlie, above note 47, 678–80.

85 Statute of the International Court of Justice, Art. 13.

86 Brownlie, above note 47, 680. See also Hersch Lauterpacht, *The Function of Law in the International Community* (New York; London: Garland, 1973) 215 ff; Shaw, above note 14, 1060–61.

87 Statute of the International Court of Justice, Art. 31.

88 See, e.g., the Separate Opinion of the Belgian ad hoc Judge, Christine van den Wyngaert, in *Arrest Warrant of 11 April 2000* (*Democratic Republic of Congo v Belgium*) [2002] ICJ Rep 3, who produced one of the few coherent and well reasoned opinions of the Court in that case.

89 Statute of the International Court of Justice, Art. 38(1).

90 For a detailed consideration of Article 38, and the lack of a *stare decisis* principle existing at international law, see Chapter 2, sections 2.2 and 2.2.4.2.1 respectively.

> The jurisdiction of the Court comprises all cases which the parties refer to it and all matters specially provided for in the Charter of the United Nations or in treaties and conventions in force.[91]

This general jurisdiction is extended by 'transferred jurisdiction', provided under Articles 6(5) and 37, which allows for agreements made granting jurisdiction to the PCIJ to carry over automatically to the ICJ.[92]

9.5.2.2 Preliminary considerations

For a case to be brought before the ICJ, Article 36(2) of the Court's Statute requires it to be a legal dispute.[93] If there is a question in a case as to whether or not the Court has jurisdiction, two principles must be considered. The first is the *compétence de la compétence* principle, whereby Article 36(6) of the ICJ Statute provides that, in a dispute regarding the jurisdiction of the Court to hear a case, 'the matter shall be settled by the decision of the Court'. There are a number of objections a state may bring regarding jurisdiction, one of the most prominent being that local remedies have not been exhausted.[94] Other objections include that the matter is solely within the realm of domestic law, that there has been no consent to the court's jurisdiction, that there exists no concrete dispute,[95] or that the matter raises an inherently political issue. However, the fact that a matter is political will not in itself prevent the court from exercising jurisdiction, provided there is a legal issue to be determined.[96]

Provided there is a valid legal issue for consideration, the Court will not decline jurisdiction because of the presence of political factors (how could it really be otherwise?).[97] Furthermore, the mere fact that the Security Council is currently aware of, or is considering, the matter will not permit the Court to decline jurisdiction.[98] Nonetheless, the Court's

---

91 Statute of the International Court of Justice, Art. 36. Note also Art. 34(1) which provides that '[o]nly states may be parties in cases before the Court'.

92 Ibid., Arts 36(5) and 37.

93 *Nuclear Tests* cases [1974] ICJ Rep 253, 270–71.

94 See, e.g., the *Interhandel* case, above note 45, 26–9, in which this argument was successfully made. See also the *Panevezys-Saldutiskis Railway* case (*Estonia v Lithuania*) (1939) PCIJ (Ser. A/B) No. 76, 4, 19–22; *Avena and Other Mexican Nationals* (*Mexico v US*) [2004] ICJ Rep 12, [38]–[40].

95 *Northern Cameroons* (*Cameroons v UK*) [1963] ICJ Rep 15, 33–4, 37–8; *Nuclear Tests* cases, above note 93, 270–71.

96 *Tehran Hostages* case (*United States v Iran*) [1980] ICJ Rep 3, 20.

97 Ibid., although note *Legality of the Threat or Use of Nuclear Weapons* (Advisory Opinion) [1996] ICJ Rep 226.

98 Ibid., 21. See also *Military and Paramilitary Activities in and against Nicaragua* (*Nicaragua v United States*) (Jurisdiction) [1984] ICJ Rep 392, 431–4.

history suggests that, even though it is often prepared to hear matters that are inherently entangled in complex international politics, its rulings have sometimes suggested a preoccupation with the political ramifications of rendering certain rulings on strictly *legal* grounds. The *Nuclear Weapons* Advisory Opinion is a stark example.[99]

There is also a mechanism, provided by Article 62 of the ICJ Statute, to allow third parties to intervene where the party has 'an interest of a legal nature which may be affected by the decision in the case'.[100]

9.5.2.3 Contentious jurisdiction

It is one thing for all members of the UN to be made party to the ICJ. It is another thing to say that a state is subject to the jurisdiction of the court without that state's consent.[101] This would represent what states have viewed as an impermissible step into the realm of state sovereignty and, for that reason, Article 36(1) stipulates that, prior to any party being made subject to a judicial determination, the parties must refer their case to the ICJ for determination.[102] This may be achieved in a number of ways.

9.5.2.3.1 Special agreements States may refer a matter to the ICJ through a special agreement or *compromis*, consenting to its jurisdiction on an ad hoc basis. Instead of merely asking the Court to advise on the specific dispute between the two states, the special agreement allows states to ask the Court to set out the relevant principles of international law governing the conflict. This provides a degree of clarity and certainty with respect to a particular area of law, which may up to that point have been murky, and helps to reduce future conflicts premised upon similar issues. An example of this is the *North Sea Continental Shelf* cases, in which a dispute arose between Germany and the Netherlands as to where the boundary for a shared continental shelf in the North Sea should be drawn. A special agreement between Germany and the Netherlands enabled the Court to resolve the dispute, as well as declaring the broader principles applica-

---

[99] *Nuclear Weapons* (Advisory Opinion), above note 97, [20]. For a detailed discussion of this case and its implications, see Chapter 8, section 8.5.2.

[100] Statute of the International Court of Justice, Art. 62; Rules and Procedures of the International Court of Justice 1978, Arts 81 and 82. Note that Honduras and Costa Rica applied to the ICJ for permission to intervene in *Territorial and Maritime Dispute* (*Nicaragua v Columbia*) (Preliminary Objections) 13 December 2007 on 16 June 2010 and 26 June 2010 respectively.

[101] See, Brownlie, above note 47, 681–2.

[102] Statute of the International Court of Justice, Art. 36(1).

ble to the delimitation of a common continental shelf between adjacent states.[103]

Special agreements are often used in the event of territorial disputes as, for example, in the *Minquiers and Ecrehos* case,[104] which involved a dispute between France and the UK over the sovereignty of a number of islands in the English Channel, and in a dispute between Malaysia, Singapore and Indonesia relating to the island of Pedra Branca.[105]

9.5.2.3.2 Forum prorogatum Where a state makes a unilateral application to the Court, under certain circumstances the Court may determine that the respondent state has subsequently consented.[106] The consent may be given expressly or inferred from conduct, the crucial indicia being that the consent is genuine. Where jurisdiction is gained on this basis, it is known as prorogated jurisdiction (*forum prorogatum*). An early example of this can be seen in the PCIJ decision of the *Rights of Minorities in Upper Silesia* case,[107] in which Poland, whilst not having expressly consented, opted to argue the merits of the case before the Court. The act of bringing this argument was seen to accept implicitly the Court's jurisdiction to determine the case.[108]

One of the advantages of utilizing prorogated jurisdiction is that making a unilateral application to the ICJ provides an opportunity to convince the Court to adopt interim measures of protection, before more closely examining whether or not the respondent state had in fact consented to its jurisdiction.[109] In more recent times, however, the use of prorogated jurisdiction has suffered a decline, partly as a result of Rule 38(5) of the Rules of Court, which explicitly requires the consent of the respondent state before an application to the court is considered effective.

---

[103] *Corfu Channel* (*UK v Albania*) (Merits) [1949] ICJ Rep 4, was settled in a similar way.

[104] *Minquiers and Ecrehos* [1953] ICJ Rep 47.

[105] *Sovereignty over Pedra Branca/Lulau Batu Puteh* (*Malaysia v Singapore*) Special Agreement, 24 July 2003; *Sovereignty over Pulau Ligitan and Pulau Sipadan* (*Indonesia v Malaysia*) (Merits) [2002] ICJ Rep 4.

[106] See Brownlie, above note 47, 689; Hersch Lauterpacht, *The Development of International Law by the International Court* (London: Stevens and Sons, 1958) 103.

[107] *Rights of Minorities in Upper Silesia* (*Germany v Poland*) (1928) PCIJ (Ser. A) No. 15, 24–5.

[108] See also *Mavromattis Palestine Concessions* (*Greece v Great Britain*) (Merits) (1925) PCIJ (Ser. A) No. 5, 27.

[109] See, e.g., *Anglo-Iranian Oil Co.* case (*UK v Iran*) (Preliminary Objection) [1952] ICJ Rep 93.

9.5.2.3.3 Treaties providing jurisdiction Treaties will at times make reference to the ICJ, providing for its use in the event of a dispute over certain terms of the treaty.[110] Where this is the case, Article 36(1) of the ICJ Statute empowers the ICJ to assert jurisdiction, allowing for jurisdiction over 'all matters specially provided for . . . in treaties and conventions in force'.[111] A classic example of this can be seen in the *Nicaragua* decision.[112] In this instance, the Court asserted jurisdiction on the basis of the 1956 Treaty of Friendship, Commerce and Navigation between Nicaragua and the United States, notwithstanding the US's strong objections.

9.5.2.3.4 Optional clause The ICJ Statute, through Article 36(2), provides an optional method for states to recognize the jurisdiction of the ICJ:

> The states parties to the present Statute may at any time declare that they recognize as compulsory ipso facto and without special agreement, in relation to any other state accepting the same obligation, the jurisdiction of the Court in all legal disputes concerning:
> a. the interpretation of a treaty;
> b. any question of international law;
> c. the existence of any fact which, if established, would constitute a breach of an international obligation;
> d. the nature or extent of the reparation to be made for the breach of an international obligation.

This declaration may be unconditional or on 'condition of reciprocity' on the part of one or more states, for a specified time. The jurisdiction is accepted through the act of depositing the unilateral declaration with the Secretary-General. Upon doing this, the state binds itself to accept jurisdiction in relation to any other declarant, to the extent to which the declarations coincide. The result of this process was referred to by the Court in the *Nicaragua* case as creating a 'series of bilateral engagements'[113] and, in determining the 'extent to which the two Declarations coincide in conferring [jurisdiction]',[114] the ICJ will look to the substance of this bilateral relationship. The inclusion in Article 36(2) of the phrase 'in relation to

[110] Note that treaties that made reference to the PCIJ will still allow the ICJ to find jurisdiction, through the mechanism of the Statute of the International Court of Justice, Art. 37. This Article was successfully used to grant jurisdiction to the ICJ in the *South West Africa* cases, which made reference to the PCIJ.

[111] Statute of the International Court of Justice, Art. 3.

[112] *Nicaragua* case, above note 48.

[113] *Nicaragua* case, above note 48, 418. See also *Nuclear Tests* cases, above note 93, 267.

[114] *Anglo-Iranian Oil Co.* case, above note 109.

any other state accepting the same obligation' is known as the reciprocity principle. This means that where there is a commonality between two declarations, this can provide a basis for jurisdiction,[115] although on a practical level the court has experienced some difficulty in applying this principle.[116]

For Article 36(2) to be engaged there must be a 'legal dispute'. This has seldom been a substantial issue before the Court, although it did become an issue in the recent *Territorial and Maritime Dispute* in 2007.[117] This case involved a sovereignty dispute between Nicaragua and Colombia over maritime boundaries and islands in the Caribbean Sea. The Court held that, as a 1928 treaty had already resolved the question of sovereignty, there was no legal dispute for the court to rule on, and thus the attempted use of Article 36(2) failed.[118]

9.5.3 Terminating a Declaration

There are a number of reasons why a state may wish to terminate an optional clause and there are a number of judicial views as to how this can be achieved. One view expressed by the ICJ in the 1957 *Rites of Passage* case was for the Court to accept the right of states to terminate or vary their voluntary declarations of consent by simple notification, without the requirement of a notice period.[119] A termination of an optional clause was rejected in the *Nicaragua* case, where Nicaragua made an application to the Court three days after the US withdrew its application of consent. The Court found that in determining whether a termination is valid, the principle of good faith will play a significant role. Because the US had inserted, in its declaration, a six-month notice clause for termination, the Court held that the US was bound by that indication. In a recent example of the successful termination of an optional clause, Australia withdrew its open-ended acceptance of consent to the Court in anticipation of proceedings to be brought by East Timor.[120]

---

[115] See Brownlie, above note 47, 686.
[116] See, e.g., *Interhandel* case, above note 45.
[117] *Territorial and Maritime Dispute*, above note 100.
[118] Ibid.
[119] See also *Fisheries Jurisdiction* case, above note 7.
[120] See Gillian Triggs, 'Australia Withdraws Maritime Disputes from the Compulsory Jurisdiction of the International Court of Justice and the International Tribunal for the Law of the Sea' (2002) 17 *International Journal of Marine and Coastal Law* 42.

9.5.4 Provisional Measures

Article 41 of the ICJ Statute gives the Court the power to 'indicate . . . any provisional measures which ought to be taken to preserve the respective rights of either party', a procedure akin to the domestic remedy of an injunction. Article 41 also allows the court to act expeditiously so as to prevent irreparable injury to a dispute. These measures are binding upon the relevant state.[121]

The Court will grant provisional measures only where clear evidence of irreparable prejudice has been provided. An example of a case in which provisional measures were granted is in the *Genocide Convention* cases.[122] Bosnia and Herzegovina brought an action before the Court alleging breaches of the Convention on the Prevention and Punishment of the Crime of Genocide, and requested provisional measures to be provided by the court in order to prevent the crime of genocide being committed. The Court granted the request, relying upon Article 9 of the Genocide Convention for jurisdiction, and ordered Yugoslavia to 'take all measures within its power to prevent commission of the crime of genocide'. It is worth considering, however, that the ICJ's decision failed to bring any practical change, evidenced by the massacre of Srebrenica in 1995, undertaken by Yugoslavia in breach of the ICJ's directive.

On the other hand, there have been instances where the court has not found that an irreparable prejudice would result from failing to grant provisional measures.[123] In the 2009 case of *Questions Relating to the Obligation to Prosecute or Extradite* (*Belgium v Senegal*) (currently pending before the ICJ), a request was made to have the former President of Chad extradited to Belgium in light of a forthcoming war crimes trial. Pending the outcome of this extradition, Belgium requested that the President immediately be transferred to Belgium. The Court chose not to prescribe provisional measures, finding that there was no 'real and imminent risk that irreparable prejudice' would result to Belgium in its efforts to ensure the trial of the President because of Senegal's assurances that it would continue to monitor and control the President, thus ensuring his presence at trial.

---

[121] *LaGrand* (*Germany v United States of America*) (Merits) [2001] ICJ Rep 466.

[122] *Genocide Convention* cases (*Bosnia and Herzegovina v Yugoslavia (Serbia and Montenegro)*) (Provisional Measures) [1993] ICJ Rep 3.

[123] See, e.g., *Case concerning Passage through the Great Belt* (*Finland v Denmark*) (Provisional Measures) [1991] ICJ Rep 12; *Certain Criminal Proceedings in France* (*Republic of Congo v France*) (Provisional Measures) ICJ (pending).

9.5.5 Remedies and Enforcement

The most common remedy sought by states is a declaratory judgment in favour of the applicant, stating that the respondent has breached international law. This may be combined with a reparation request for the various losses suffered. This can include direct damage to the state itself, as well as to citizens and property.[124] Once a remedy has been determined, the question then turns to enforcement.

Article 59 of the ICJ provides that a decision of the court 'has no binding force except between the parties and in respect of that particular case'. This Article, therefore, indicates that the decision in a particular case is binding on the parties involved in the dispute alone, in line with the absence of *stare decisis*.[125] In practice, however, decisions and Advisory Opinions which advance the jurisprudence of international law are referenced and used in support of subsequent decisions both by the court and other international tribunals.

With regard to the parties to a specific case, Article 94 of the UN Charter provides that all Members of the UN undertake to comply with any decision of the ICJ to which they are a party and, if a state fails to comply with this decision, recourse may be had to the Security Council which may make recommendations or decide upon measures to be taken to give effect to the judgment.[126] In practice, the Security Council has refrained from enforcing ICJ decisions, and is unlikely to do so for political reasons.[127]

The record of state compliance with decisions of the ICJ has been mixed. There have been examples of states respecting and complying with the orders of the court, including the *Territorial Dispute* case where measures imposed by the court in relation to a border dispute between Libya and Chad were complied with.[128] On the other hand, there are a number of cases where states have refused to comply with the decision of the Court – for example, the *Corfu Channel* case, where an order to pay remedies was

---

[124] See, e.g., the *I'm Alone* case, above note 29, 1609, and *Rainbow Warrior* case (*France v New Zealand*) 74 ILR 241, 274; 82 ILR 499, 575. Brownlie, 'Remedies in the International Court of Justice', in Vaughan Lowe and Malgosia Fitzmaurice (eds), *Fifty Years of the International Court of Justice* (Cambridge: Cambridge University Press, 1996) 557.

[125] See Chapter 2, section 2.2.4.1.1.

[126] Charter of the United Nations, Art. 94.

[127] Triggs, above note 18, 720.

[128] *Territorial Dispute* (*Libya v Chad*) [1994] ICJ Rep 6.

ignored by Albania,[129] and the *Tehran Hostages* case, where Iran ignored the Court's order to free the hostages.[130]

The compliance rate is substantially lower with regard to provisional measures.[131]As Advisory Opinions merely provide clarity to an area of law, they are not binding on any one state, although obviously if a state does not comply with clear statements of law made – such as those made in the *Israeli Wall* case to remove the wall and compensate the affected Palestinians[132] – this can result in a breach of international law giving rise to a subsequent application by another state.

9.5.6 Advisory Opinions

Under Article 65(1) the ICJ is granted the power to give an Advisory Opinion on 'any legal question at the request of whatever body may be authorized or in accordance with the Charter of the United Nations to make such a request'. Under Article 96 of the UN Charter, the General Assembly and Security Council may request an Advisory Opinion. The General Assembly also has the power to authorize other organs and specialized agencies to do so. The purpose of an Advisory Opinion is to provide guidance on the legal principles governing a particular area of law. They have proved to be a powerful method for the ICJ to articulate and develop various areas of international law, with 24 opinions being given since 1946. In more recent times, the ICJ has reaffirmed its willingness to provide Advisory Opinions.[133]

An Advisory Opinion is, as the name suggests, not binding upon any of the parties, but its importance cannot be denied. Advisory Opinions are available or have been requested, amongst other things, in relation to the legality of the threat or use of nuclear weapons,[134] self-determination[135]

---

129 See, e.g., the *Corfu Channel* case, above note 103.

130 *Tehran Hostages* case (*US v Iran*) [1980] ICJ Rep 3. See also *Fisheries Jurisdiction* case, above note 7; *Nicaragua v USA*, above note 48, where the orders made by the Court were ignored.

131 See, e.g., *LaGrand* (*Germany v US)* (Provisional Measures) [1999] ICJ Rep 9.

132 *Legal Consequences of the Construction of a Wall in the Occupied Palestinian Territory* (Advisory Opinion) [2004] ICJ Rep 136.

133 *Accordance with International Law of the Unilateral Declaration of Independence in respect of Kosovo* (Advisory Opinion) 22 July 2010, ICJ General List No. 141.

134 *Nuclear Weapons* (Advisory Opinion), above note 97.

135 *Namibia* (*Legal Consequences*) (Advisory Opinion) [1971] ICJ Rep 31.

and self-defence.[136] The ICJ and the PCIJ before it have shown a willingness to grant requests for an Advisory Opinion – with a substantive exception being the *Eastern Carelia* case.[137] The Court has noted that it would require 'compelling reasons' to convince it not to provide an Advisory Opinion.[138] It may decline to give an opinion unless 'the questions put to it are relevant and have a practical and contemporary effect and, consequently, are not devoid of object or purpose'.[139]

One common argument made for the ICJ to reject a request to provide an Advisory Opinion is that the issue has significant political implications. However, Article 65 of the ICJ statute clearly provides that the Court can deal with 'any legal question' in an Advisory Opinion. Therefore, even if the request is political, so long as it involves a legal question or component, a contentious political context will not act as a bar to the Court's willingness to consider the case, a recent example being the *Israeli Wall* case.[140] Whilst political grounds are not sufficient to decline a request to provide an Advisory Opinion, it was noted in the *Western Sahara* case that the court still retained discretion to decline to provide an Advisory Opinion, based on the 'permissive character of Article 65'.[141]

9.6 CONCLUSIONS

The resolution of disputes by international bodies has seen immense growth in recent times. With the docket of the ICJ consistently full, and the growing role that *sui generis* international tribunals are playing within the international system, a number of observations can be made.

It is clear that the ICJ increasingly shares space with a range of specialized tribunals, regulating a range of behaviour and interests within international law. Some of these tribunals are more binding, and have a more general reach and significance, than others. Perhaps the most striking example is the International Criminal Court, which clearly enjoys global relevance and support; another example is the European Court of Human Rights. While this fragmentation of the international dispute

---

[136] *Nuclear Weapons* (Advisory Opinion), above note 97; *Legal Consequences of the Construction of a Wall in the Occupied Palestinian Territory*, above note 132.

[137] *Status of Eastern Carelia* (Advisory Opinion) (1923) PCIJ (Ser. B) No. 5.

[138] *Western Sahara* (Advisory Opinion) [1975] ICJ Rep 2.

[139] Ibid., 37.

[140] *Legal Consequences of the Construction of a Wall in the Occupied Palestine Territory*, above note 132.

[141] *Western Sahara* case, above note 138, 21.

resolution system has the potential to dilute or confuse decision-making in international law, it also indicates a greater acceptance by states and other subjects that the resolution of disputes by peaceful means is both available, and appropriate. Furthermore, fears as to substantial inconsistent standards of law arising from the fragmentation of the international dispute resolution system have so far been confined to a handful of cases.

Regardless of the enhanced role of *sui generis* tribunals, it is clear that the ICJ has been and will remain the benchmark for a juridical international law. The key issues in international law continue to be determined by the ICJ, and the advancement of international law is equally in the hands of the court. This status may, however, be called into question if the Court is not careful to maintain the highest standards of decision-making, and to strike a balance between legal conservatism and the progression of international law in, and a keen understanding of, its delicate political context.

Index